VISUAL EXPLORER GUIDE

NEW YORK

City

VISUAL EXPLORER GUIDE

NEW YORK *City*

PETER MAVRIKIS

amber BOOKS

First published in 2022

Published by
Amber Books Ltd
United House
North Road
London
N7 9DP
United Kingdom
www.amberbooks.co.uk
Instagram: amberbooksltd
Facebook: amberbooks
Twitter: @amberbooks
Pinterest: amberbooksltd

Project Editor: Michael Spilling
Designer: Rick Fawcett
Picture Research: Terry Forshaw

ISBN: 978-1-83886-051-6

Printed in China

Contents

Introduction

Welcome to the Big Apple! Saying that there is lots to see and do in New York City is a true understatement. You can be a resident of Manhattan, the nearby boroughs and the surrounding counties, and still find somewhere new to visit and sights to see every time you step outside your door. That's why New York City is one of the most frequently visited places in the world. There's simply too much to do!

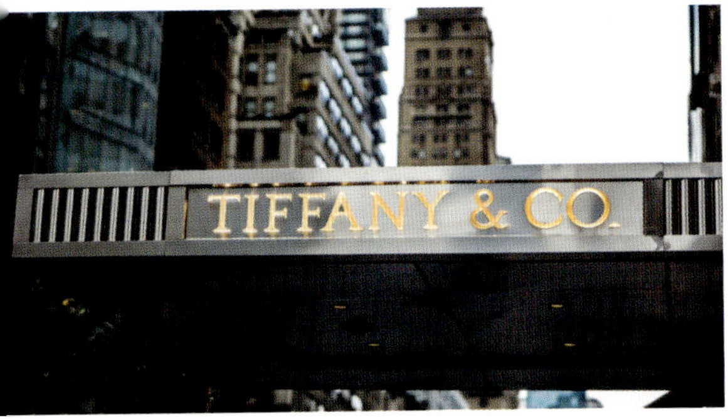

The goal of this visual guide is to offer both visitors and people who call New York City home a taste of what this city has to offer. The list of places to go and things to do is long and growing, whether it's must-see sights such as historic buildings, museums and bridges, or the neighbourhoods of Little Italy, Chinatown, Greenwich Village and Coney Island.

If one thing is true, it's that New York City has something to offer everyone from everywhere – so enjoy your time here, whether it's for a weekend or for a lifetime.

ABOVE:
Luxury retail store Tiffany & Co. on Fifth Avenue.

OPPOSITE:
Aerial view of Central Park, Manhattan.

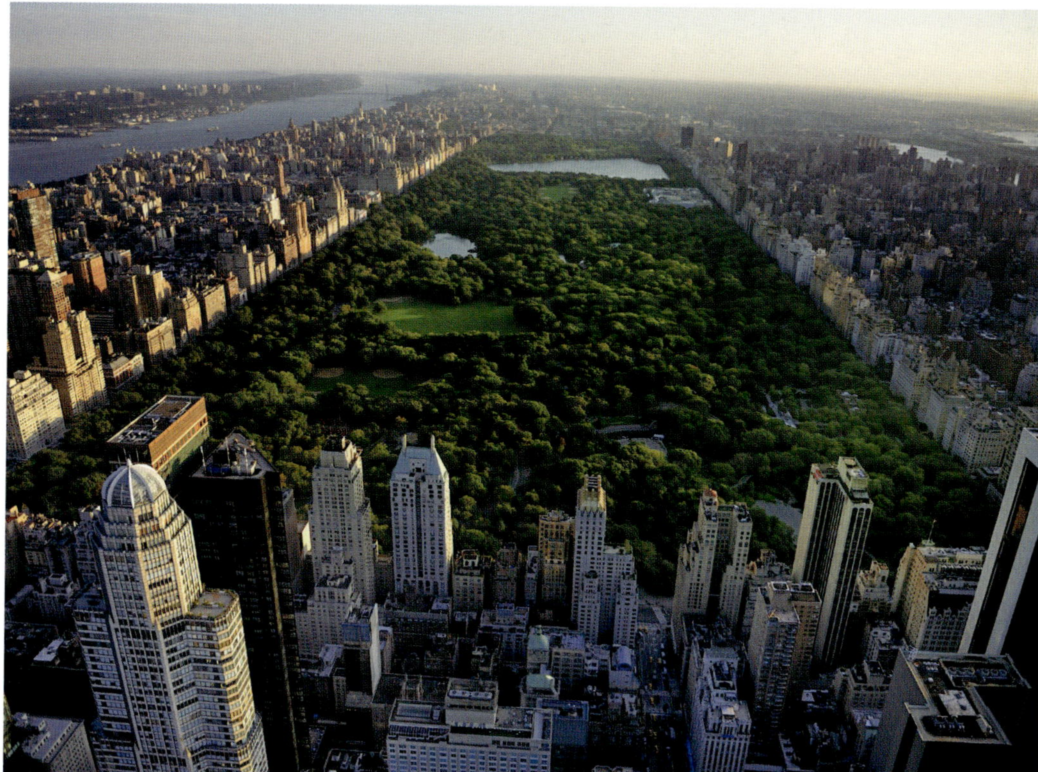

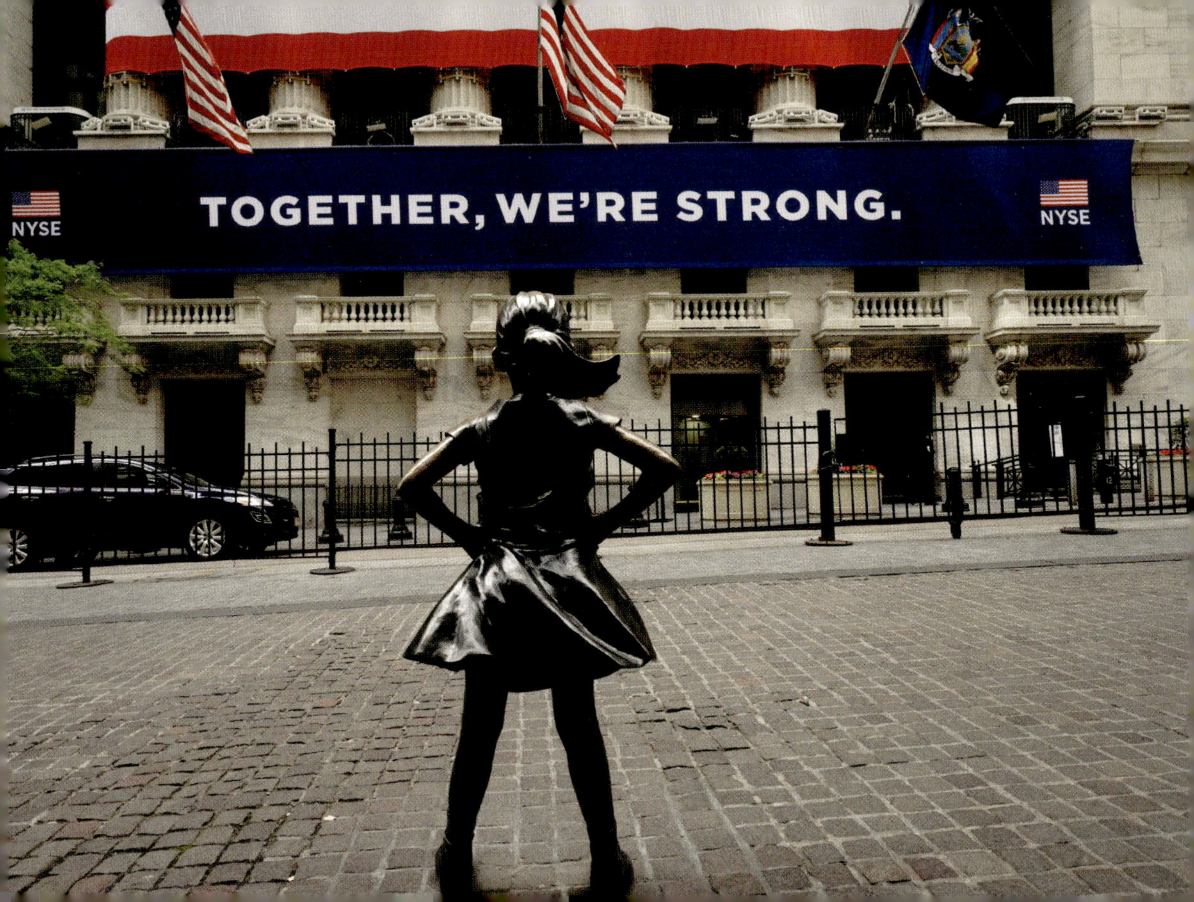
NYSE
TOGETHER, WE'RE STRONG.
NYSE

Parks and Spaces

For most, New York City is a fast-paced, busy and crowded metropolis with people always on the move. After all, in addition to being the 'Big Apple', it is also known as the 'city that never sleeps'. But life in New York is more than just rush, rush, rush. Many residents and visitors also discover its parks, recreation facilities and green trails lined with thousands of tall trees and vibrant flora.

For those who want to relax, enjoy a leisurely day basking in the sun, play a sport or attend one of the many art fairs and free concerts, there are over 1,700 parks throughout the five boroughs. In addition to iconic Central Park, known for its open green meadows, ornate bridges and cherry-blossom trees, there are around 7,700 hectares (19,000 acres) of natural parkland and recreational areas nestled in hundreds of neighbourhoods throughout the city.

Combined, New York City provides the public with access to playgrounds and sports fields, miles of beaches, nature reserves, historic houses, botanical gardens, and the well-known statues and sculptures that beautify these spaces. The parks and open green areas not only offer a quiet place in the midst of the traffic and street bustle, but also an opportunity to slow the pace down and enjoy the city's calmer side.

OPPOSITE:

'The Fearless Girl'

Created by the American sculptor Kristen Visbal, this bronze statue of a 1.2m (4ft) tall girl can be found facing The New York Stock Exchange Building.

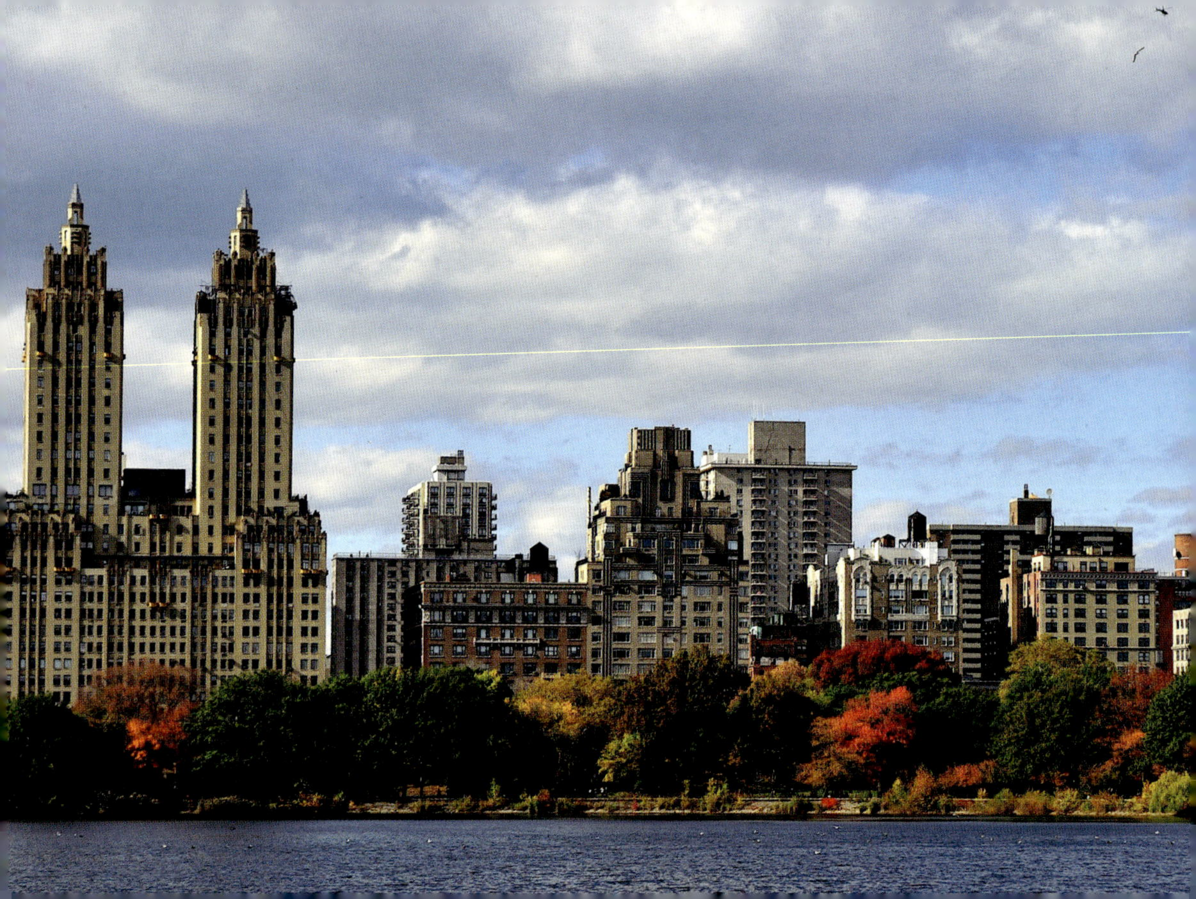

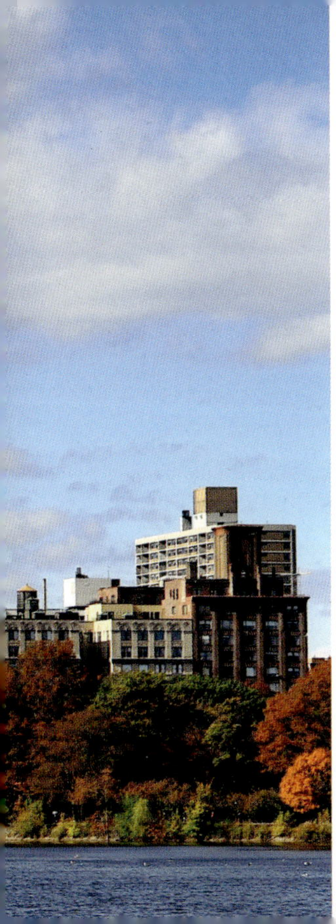

LEFT:

Central Park

Covering 341 hectares (843 acres), Central Park is located between the Upper East Side and Upper West Side of Manhattan, and has ample water features in it.

RIGHT:

Central Park carriages

One of New York City's oldest traditions, horse-drawn carriage rides around Central Park first started in the early 1850s. Carriage rides offer a unique opportunity to see what was once called The Great Park.

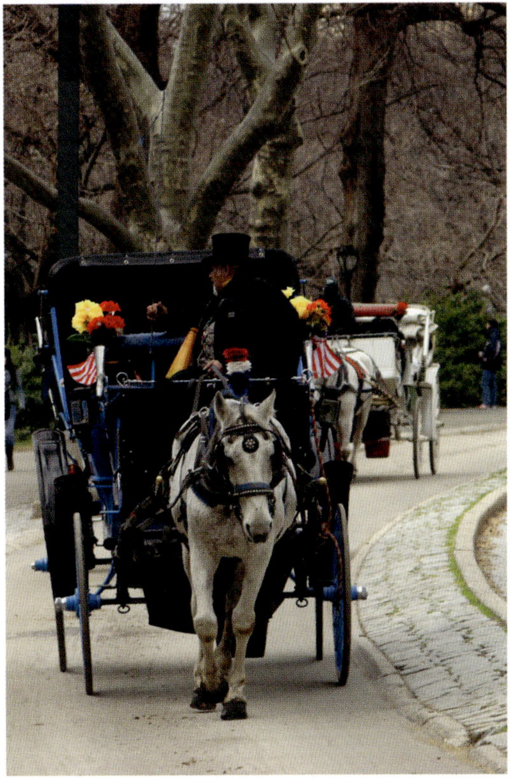

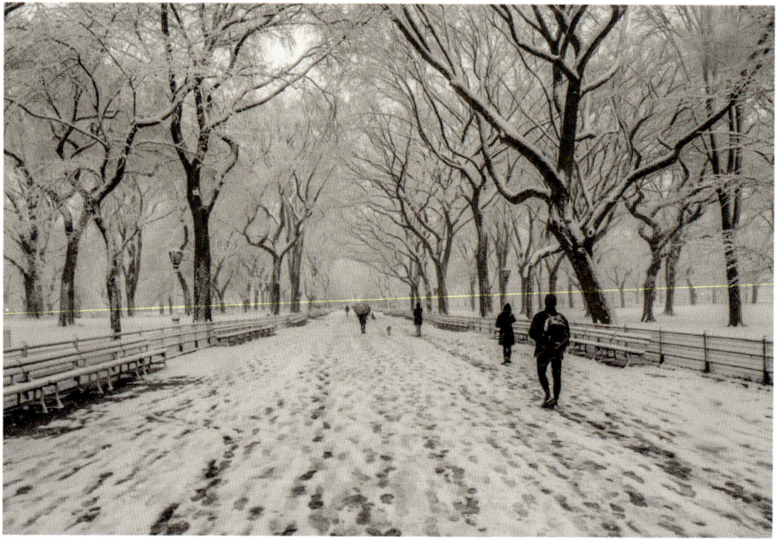

ABOVE:

Mall, Central Park

Originally built to accommodate horse-drawn carriages, the Mall is now a walkway that runs through the middle of Central Park from 66th to 72nd Street. Large American elm trees and park benches border the walkway leading to Bethesda Terrace.

RIGHT:

Bow Bridge, Central Park

Built in 1862, this 18m (60ft) bridge spans the Central Park Lake. The cast-iron archway leads from Cherry Hill to the Ramble.

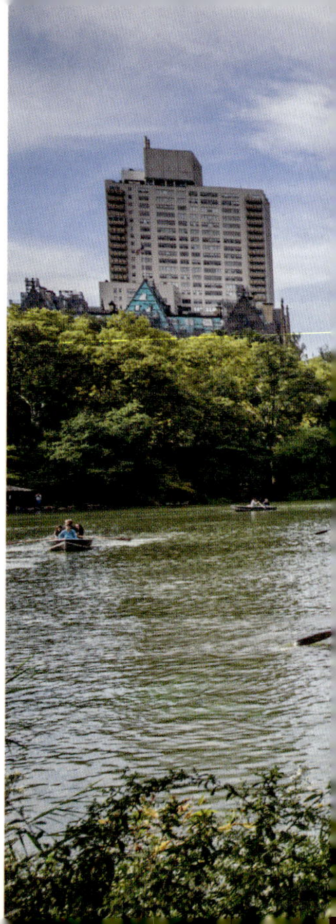

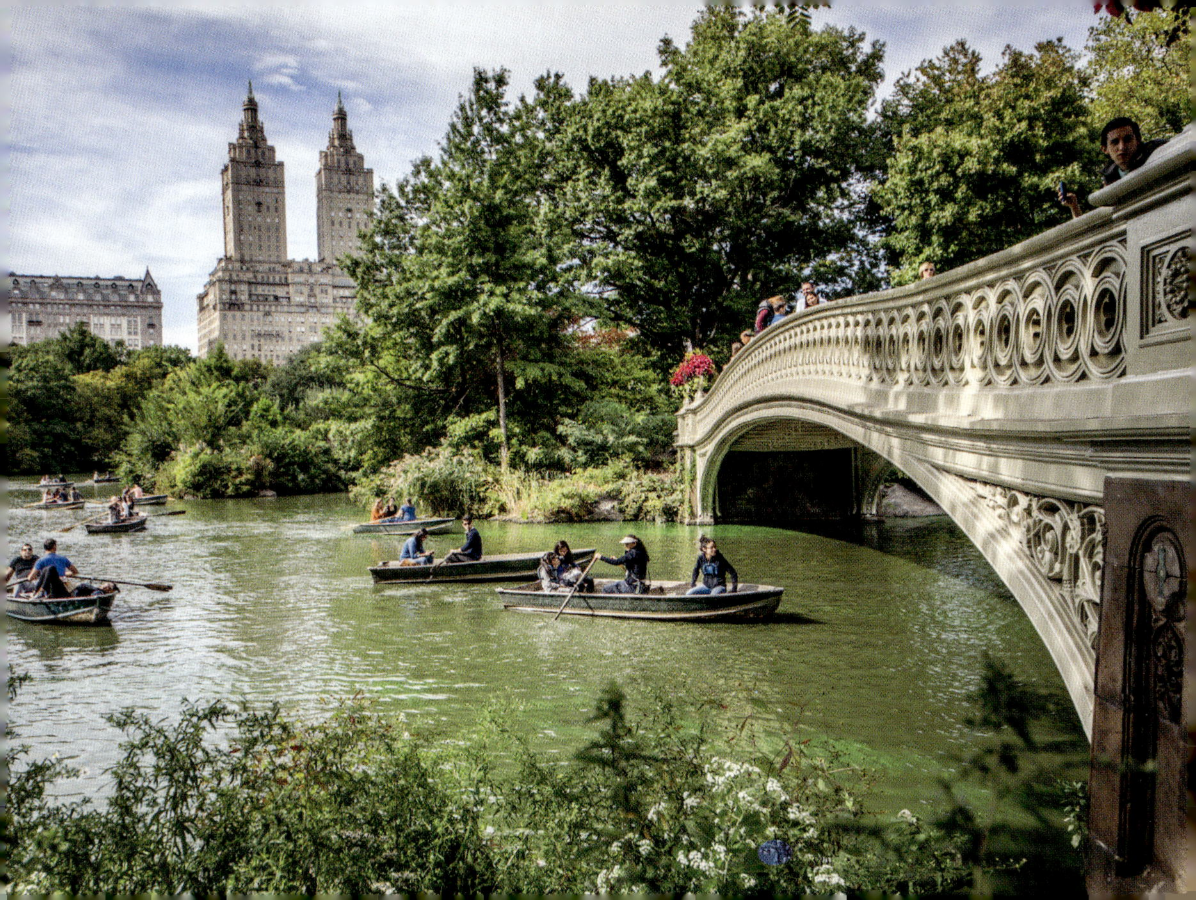

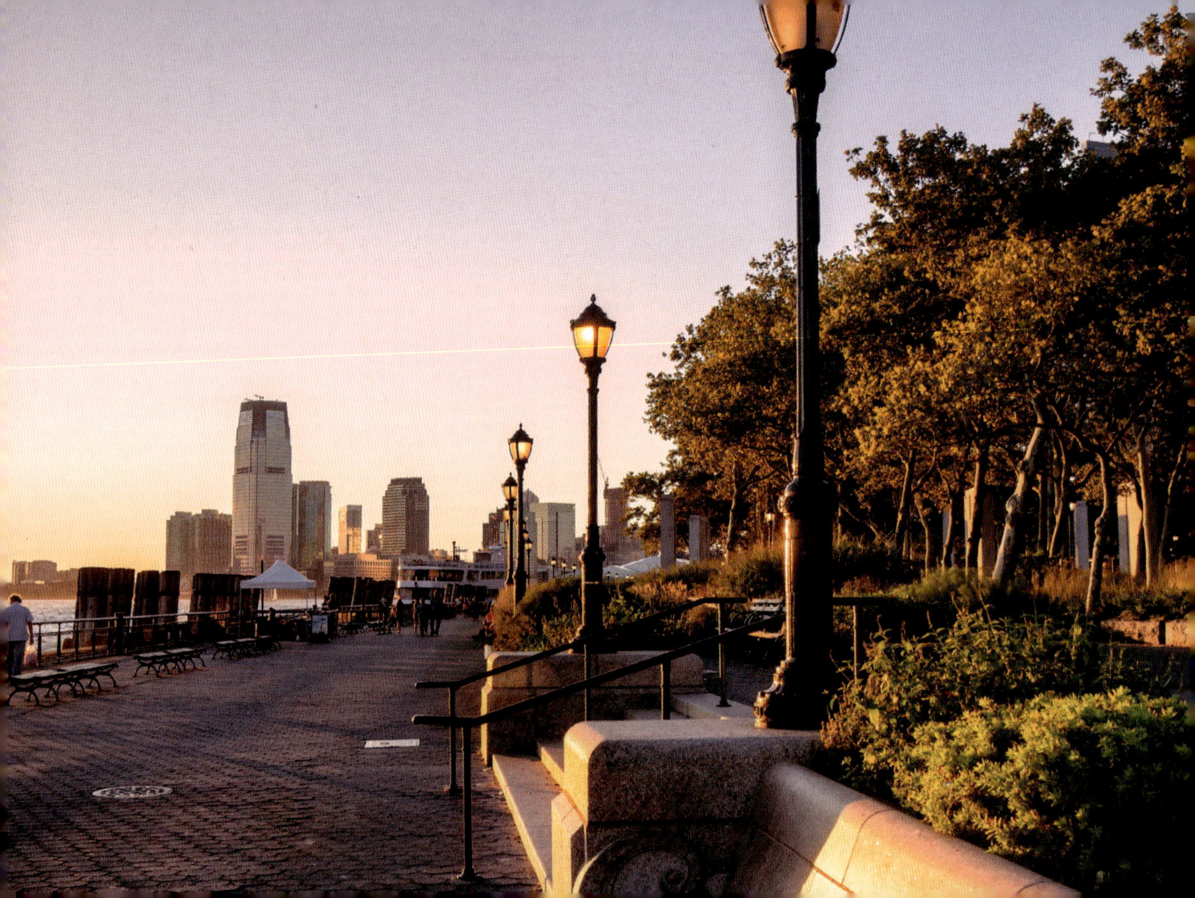

OPPOSITE:

The Battery

Named for the artillery batteries placed to defend New Amsterdam from attack, The Battery, once known as Battery Park, remains a popular destination for residents and tourists for its bike paths, watery views and opulent gardens.

RIGHT:

The Battery memorial

Located on the southern tip of The Battery and facing the Statue of Liberty across the harbour, the East Coast Memorial was erected in 1963 and stands as a monument in honour of the servicemen lost at sea during World War II.

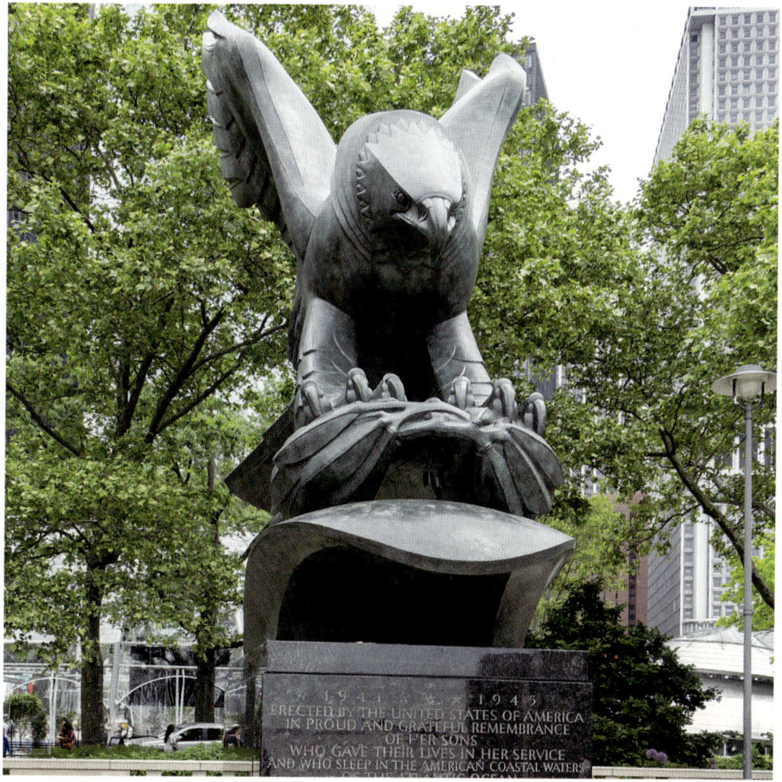

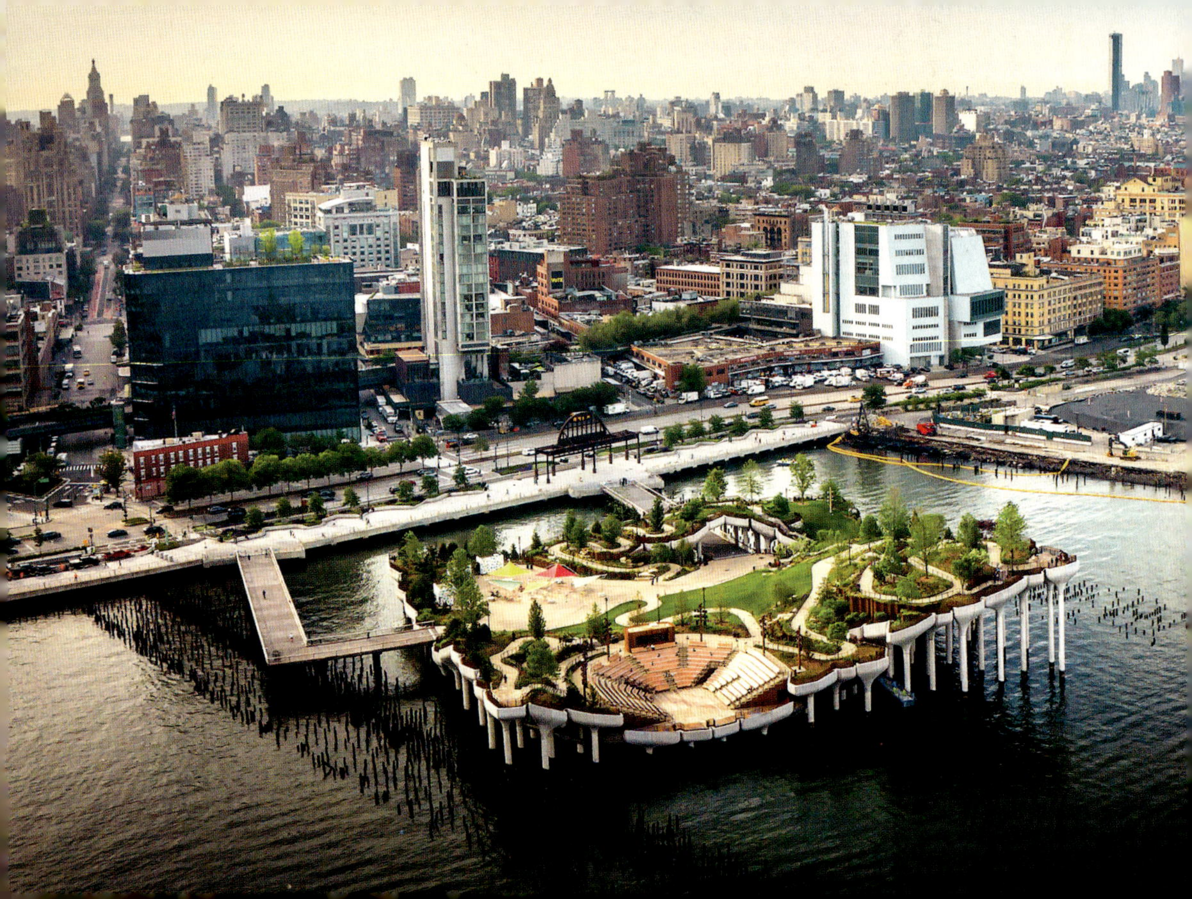

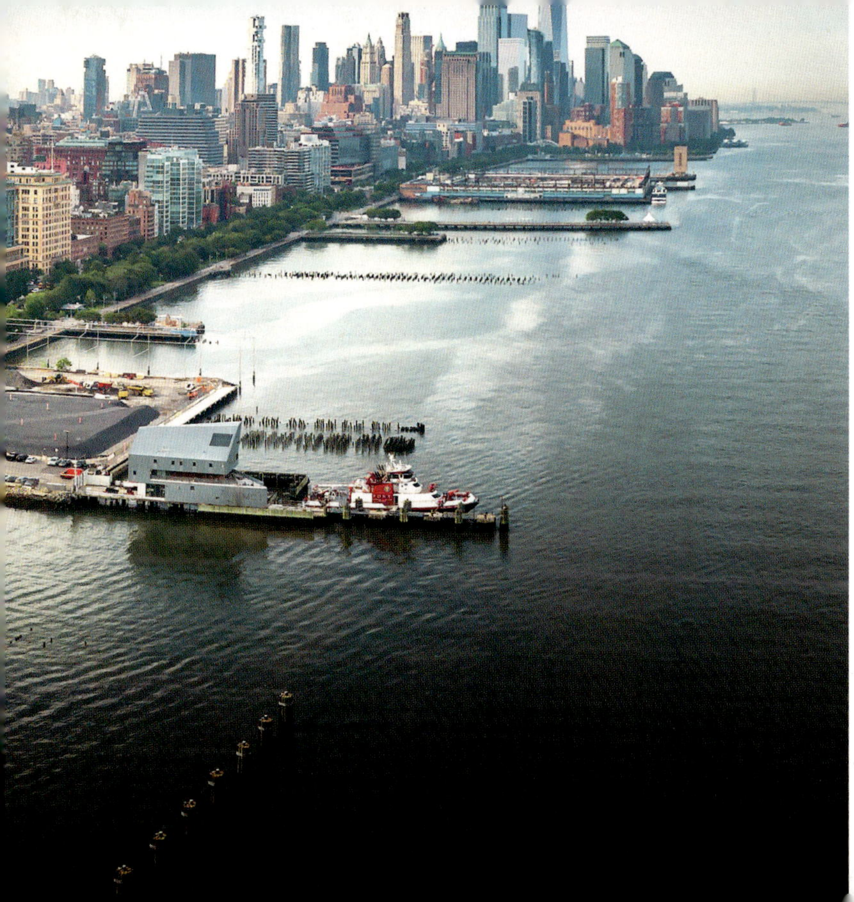

Little Island
Opened to the public in May 2021, Little Island is located within the Hudson River Park at Pier 55 and covers a hectare (2.4 acres). It boasts a lawn space, a 687-seat outdoor venue, and hundreds of species of vibrant flowers and trees. Visitors of the island also enjoy spectacular views of New York City and the river.

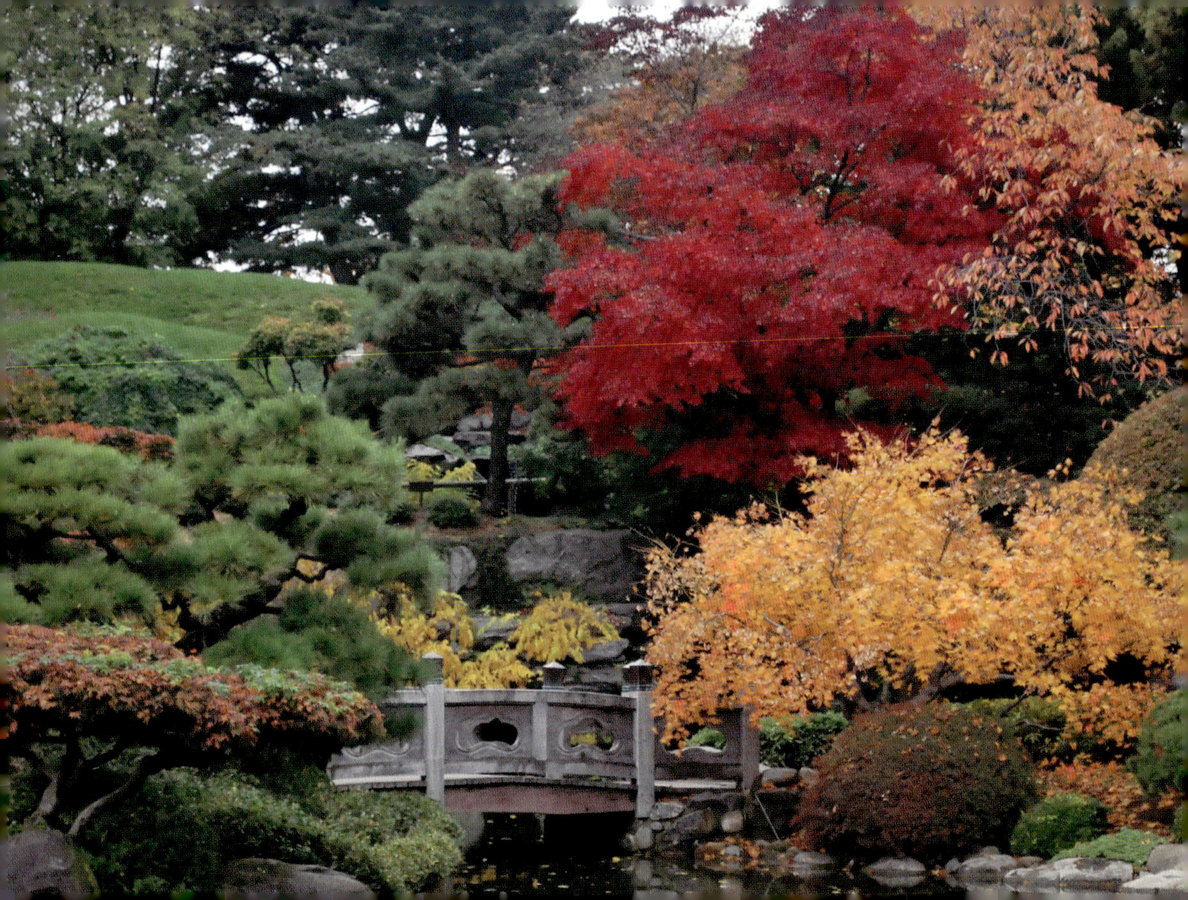

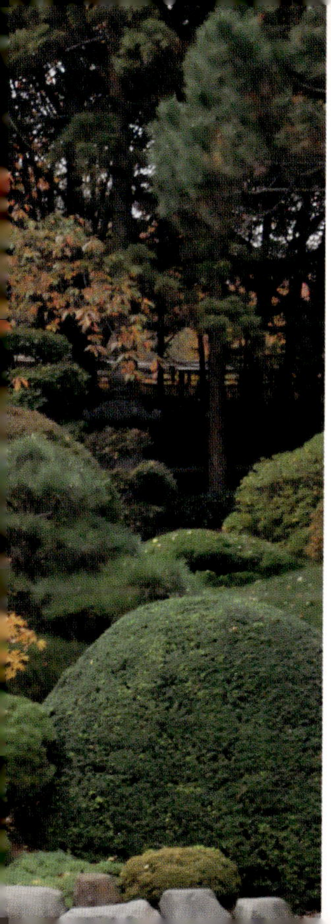

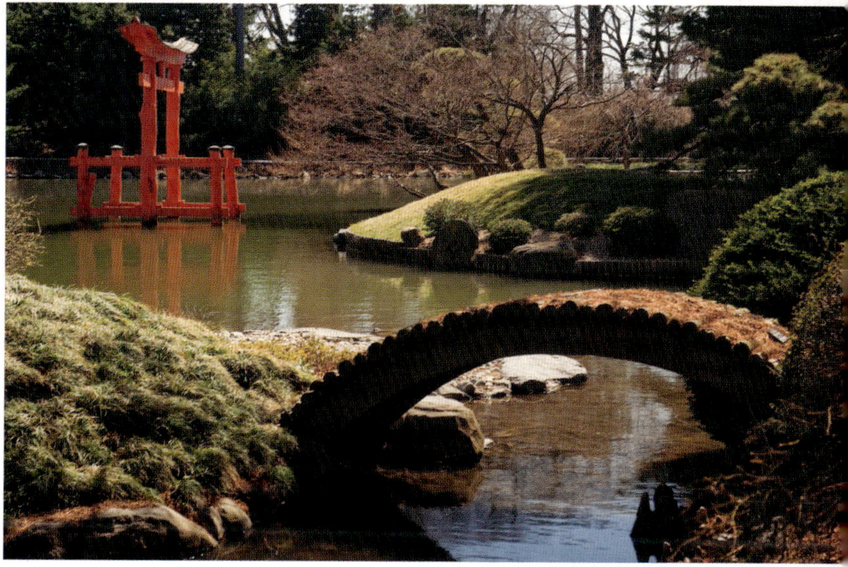

ALL PHOTOGRAPHS:
Brooklyn Botanical Garden
Located in the borough of Brooklyn, this botanical garden covers 21 hectares (52 acres) and first opened to the public in 1910. One of the key attractions is the Japanese Hill-and-Pond Garden, which includes arched wooden bridges, winding paths, and a viewing pavilion where visitors can enjoy picturesque vistas of the garden. A vivid red *torii* gateway and a Shinto shrine can be seen emerging from the middle of the pond.

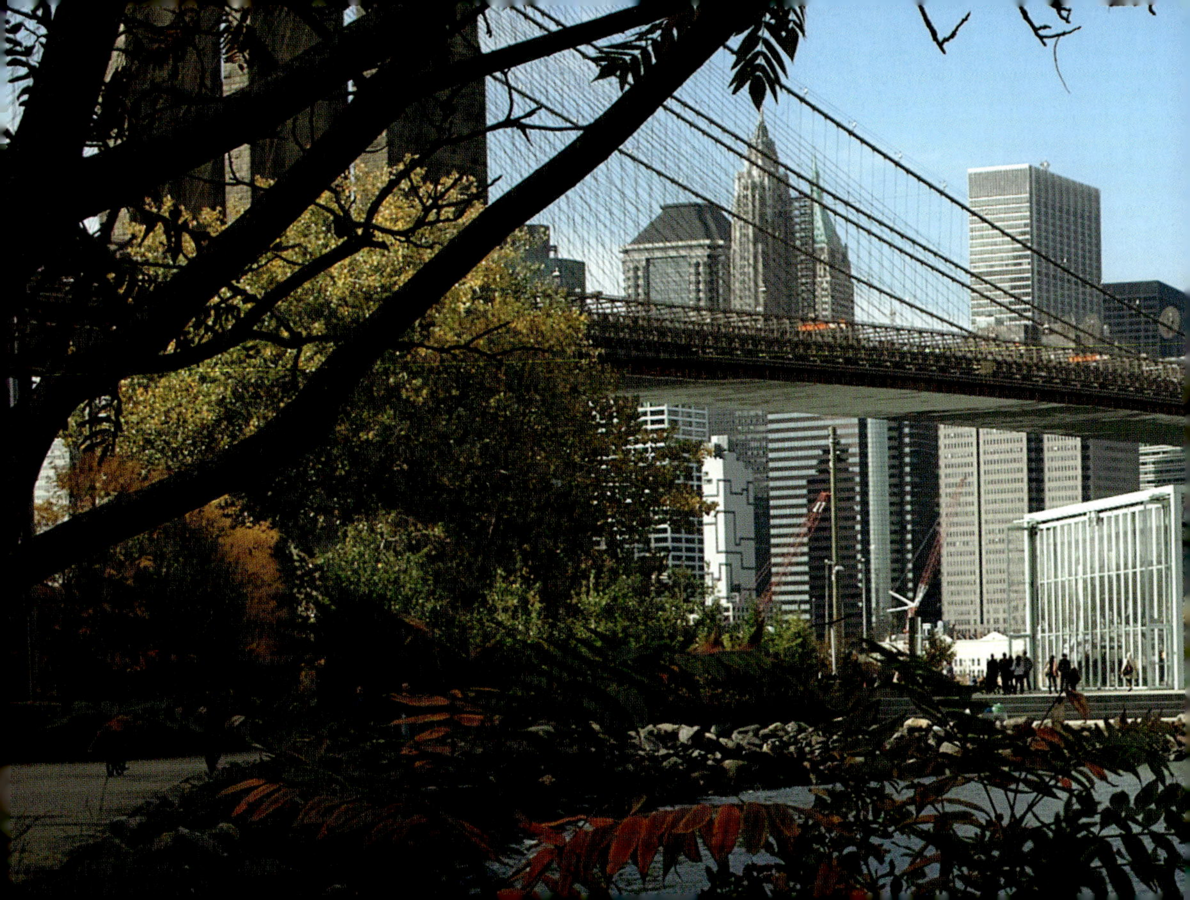

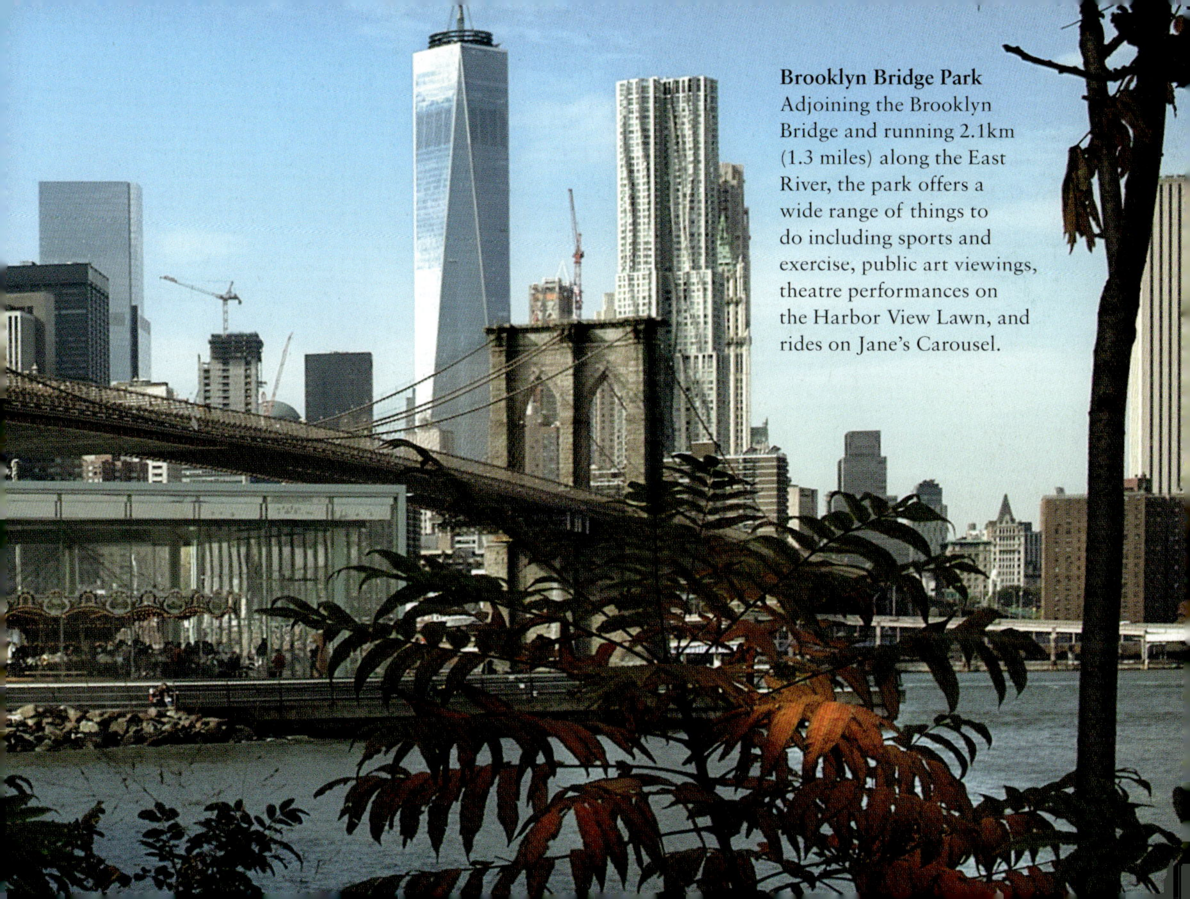

Brooklyn Bridge Park
Adjoining the Brooklyn Bridge and running 2.1km (1.3 miles) along the East River, the park offers a wide range of things to do including sports and exercise, public art viewings, theatre performances on the Harbor View Lawn, and rides on Jane's Carousel.

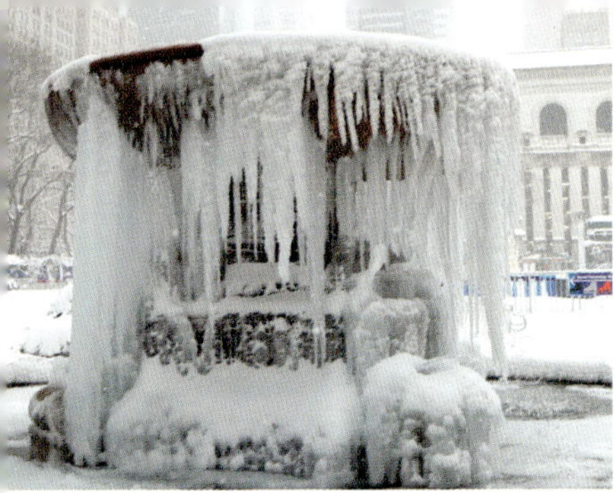

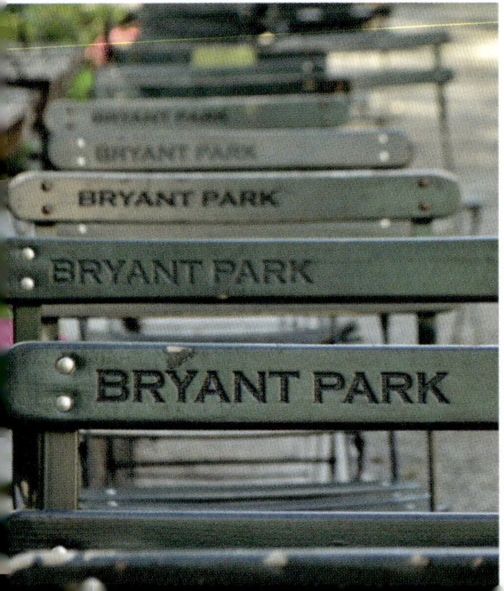
BRYANT PARK
BRYANT PARK
BRYANT PARK
BRYANT PARK
BRYANT PARK

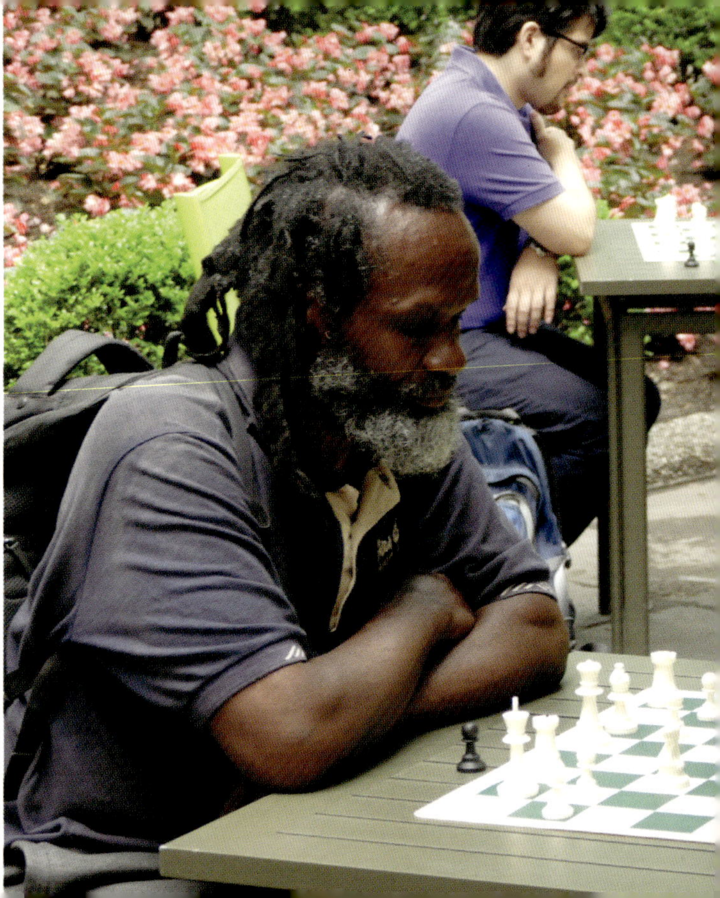

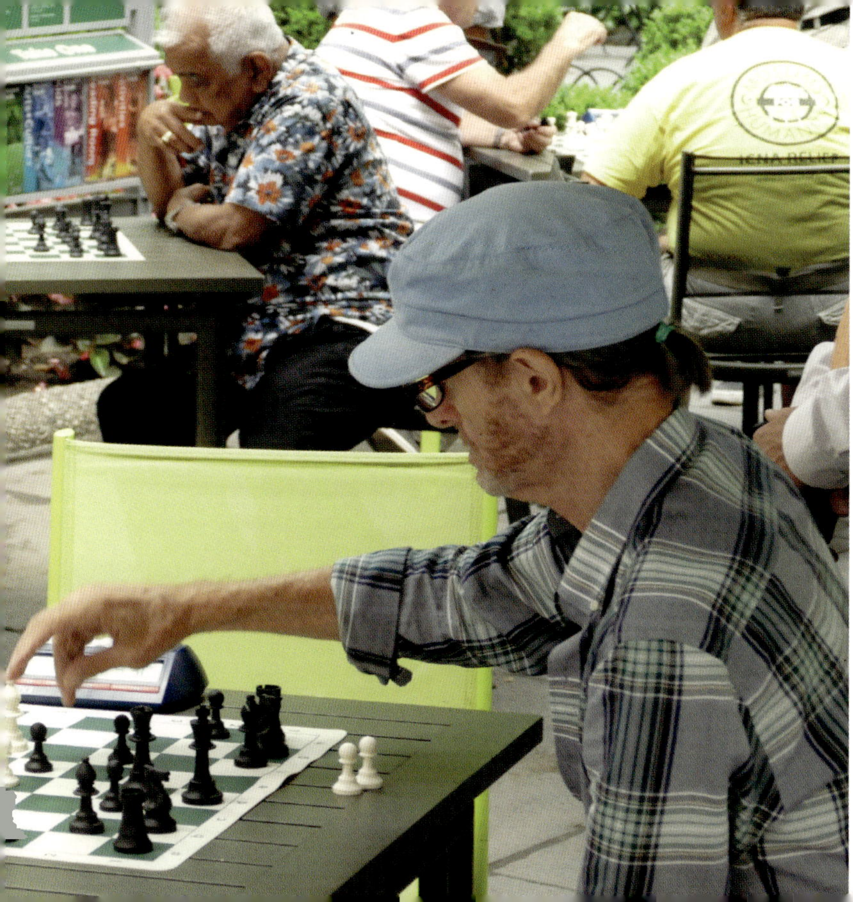

OPPOSITE TOP:

Josephine Shaw Lowell Memorial Fountain

This granite and bronze fountain in Bryant Park, dedicated to the 19th-century social worker Josephine Shaw Lowell, runs all year round thanks to an internal heating system. But that doesn't stop it from forming icicles on very cold days.

OPPOSITE BOTTOM AND LEFT:

Bryant Park

A popular location for a quick game of chess, Bryant Park is located in Midtown Manhattan between Fifth and Sixth Avenue and 40th and 42nd Street. It's also a wonderful spot for local office workers who want to spend some time outdoors.

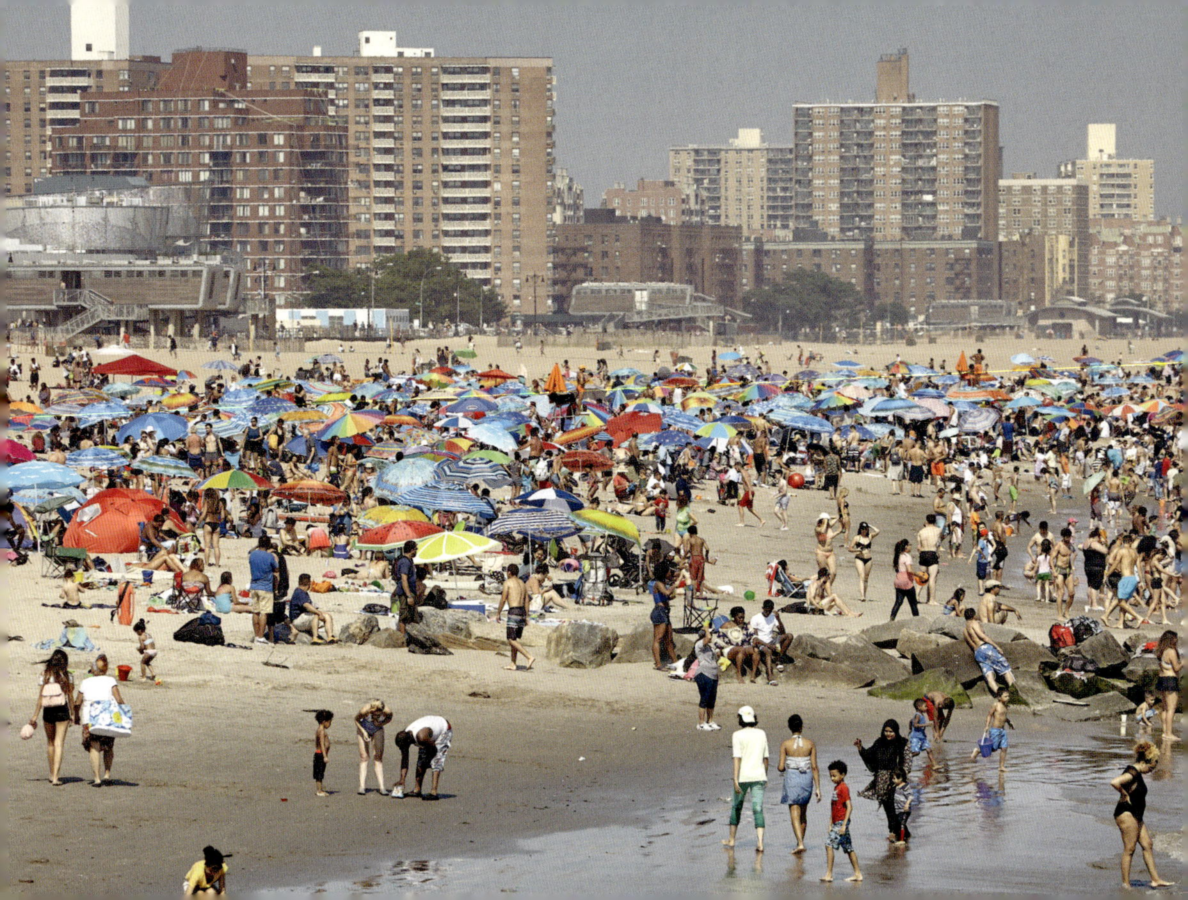

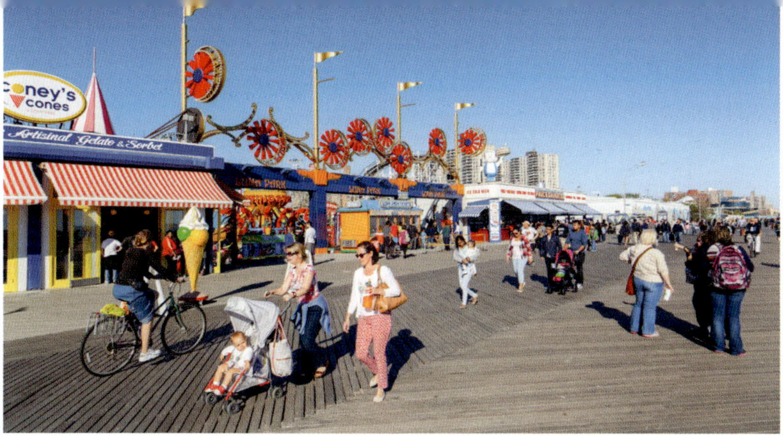

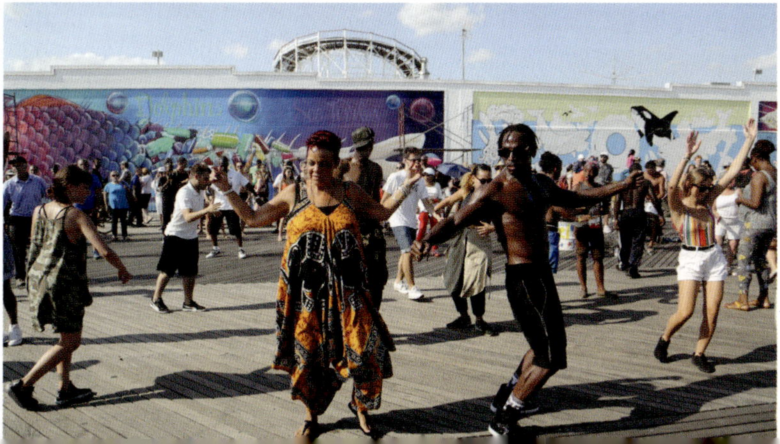

ALL PHOTOGRAPHS:

Coney Island

Located in the borough of Brooklyn, Coney Island has a long history as a popular destination for New Yorkers and tourists alike. Starting as a seaside resort in the mid-19th century, it soon became known for its amusement parks. Today, not much has changed since those early years, as people still come to spend the day on the beach, stroll along the boardwalk, and enjoy the rides at Luna Park and Deno's Wonder Wheel Amusement Park.

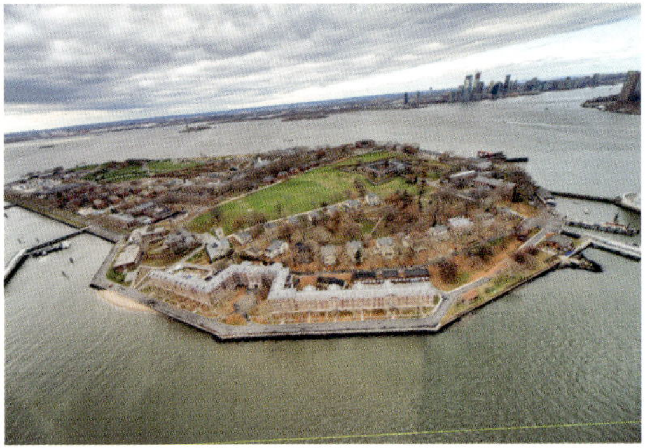

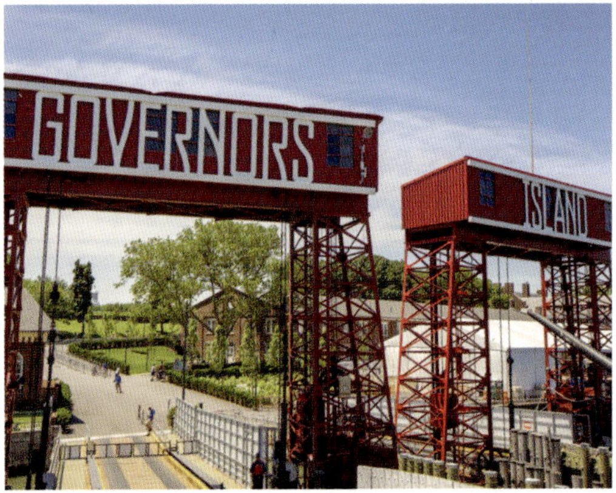

LEFT AND BELOW:
Governors Island
Once used as a fortification to defend New York Harbour, this island park between Lower Manhattan and Brooklyn sees close to one million visitors per year looking to enjoy recreational activities, art programmes, and cultural events.

RIGHT:
Fort Tryon Park
Situated on a ridge in Upper Manhattan along the Hudson River, this public park is a popular destination for runners and walkers looking to explore the 13km (8 miles) of paths within the city's largest garden. It's also the location of Manhattan's longest dog run.

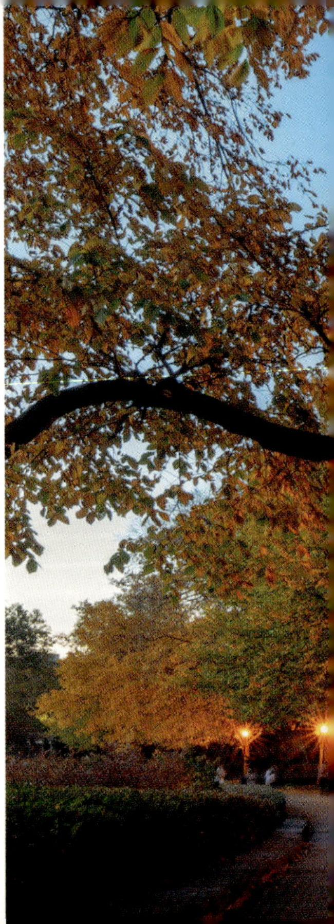

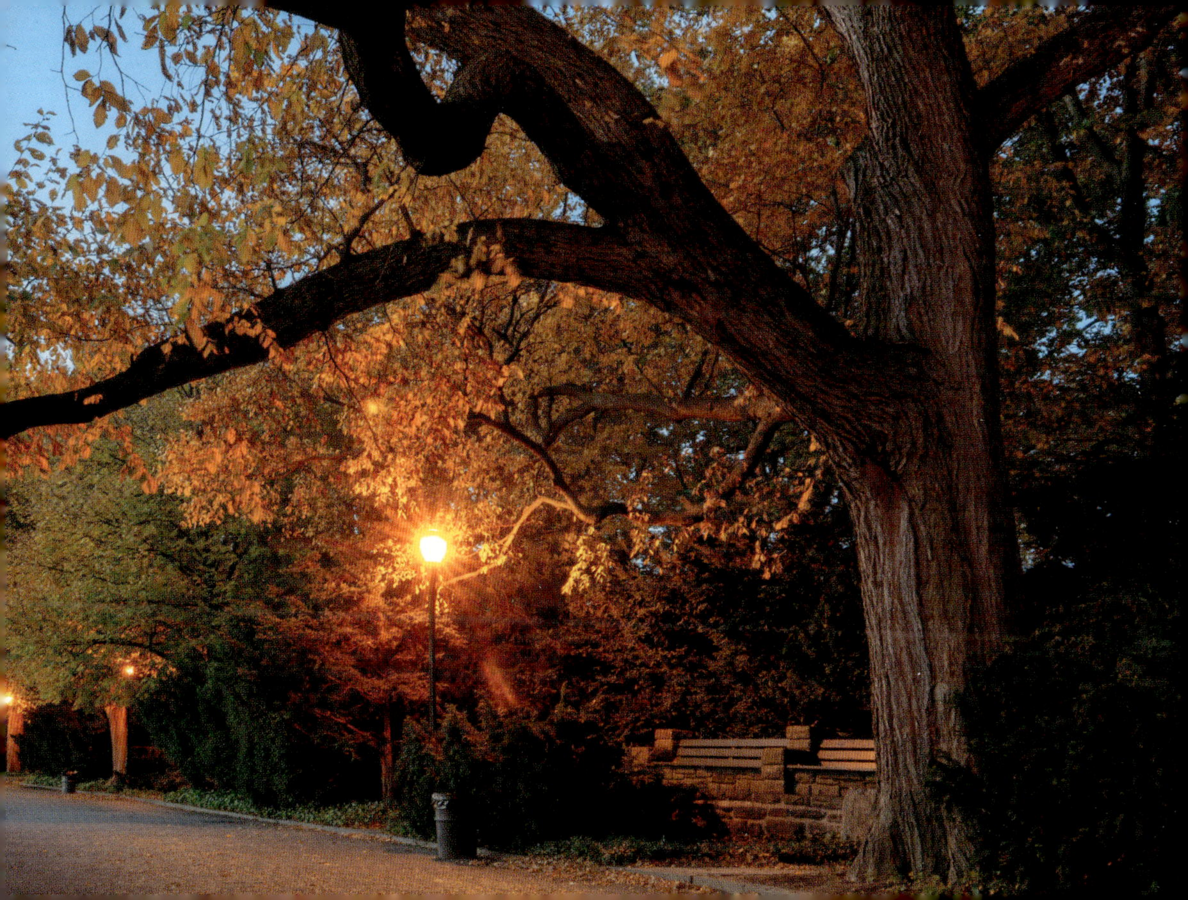

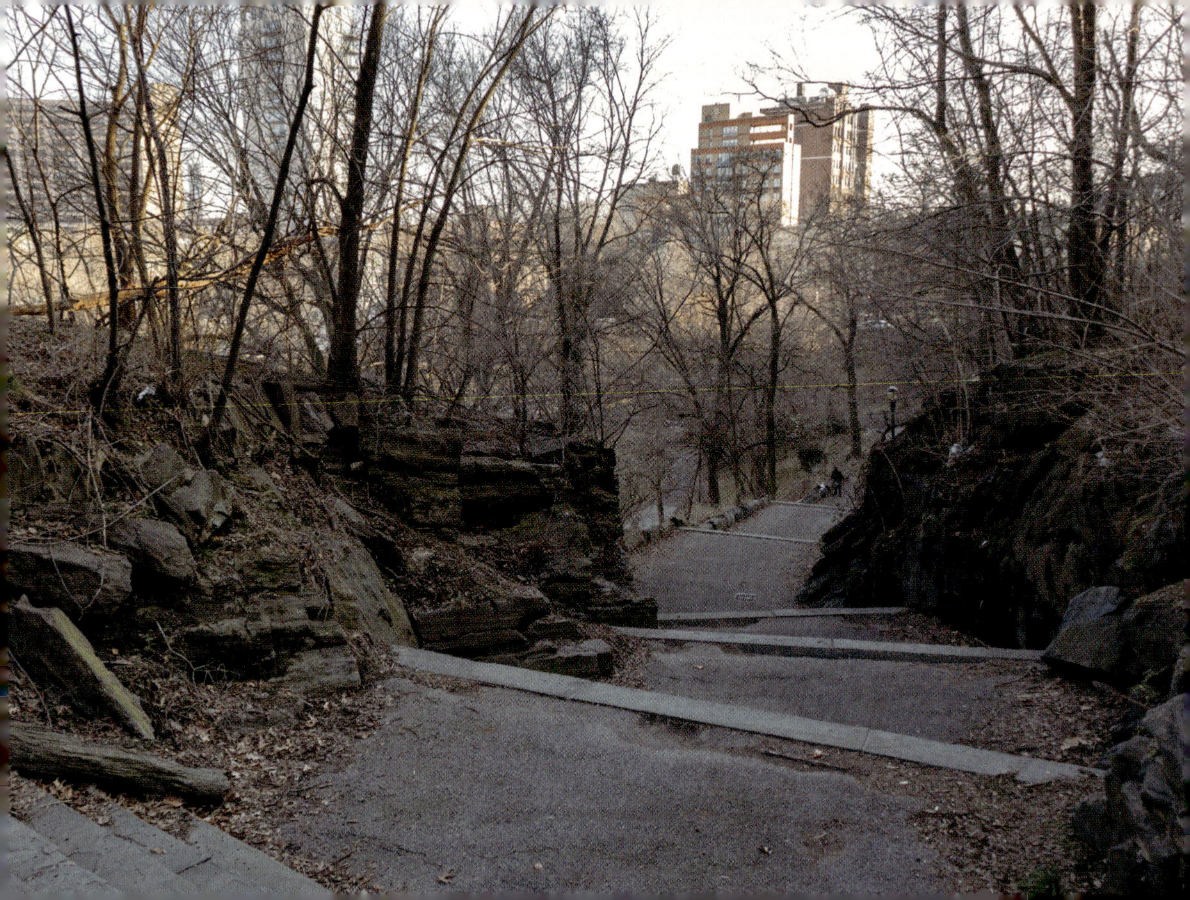

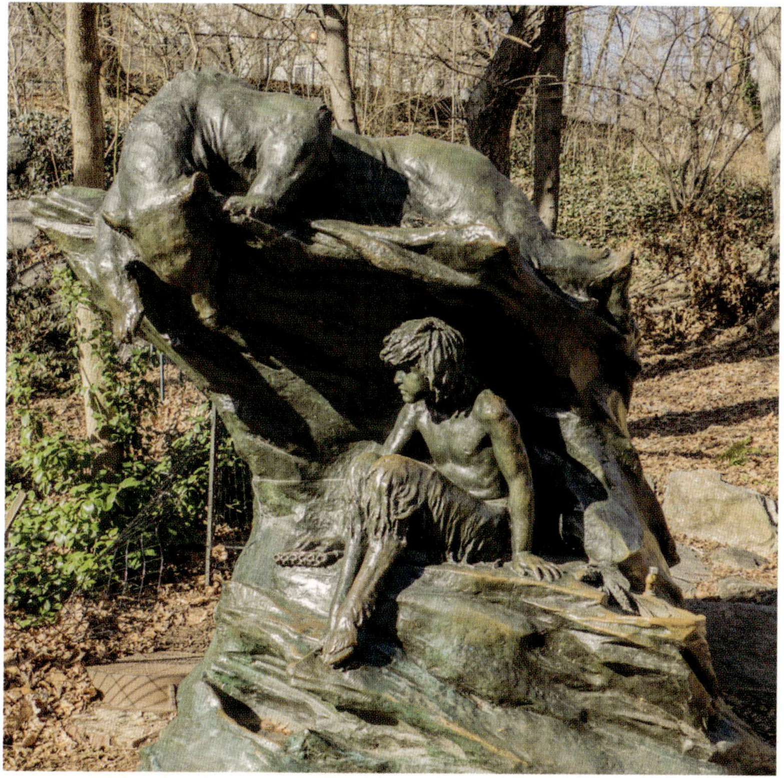

ALL PHOTOGRAPHS:
Morningside Park
Commissioned in the late 19th century, this unique park stretches for thirteen blocks from 110th to 123rd Street. Running through the park's natural geography is a cliff separating Morningside Heights from Harlem. An arboretum, artificial pond and waterfall, gardens, athletic fields and three sculptures are also here. Made of bronze, the 2m (7ft) tall 'The Bear and The Faun' sculpture can be found near the 114th Street entrance.

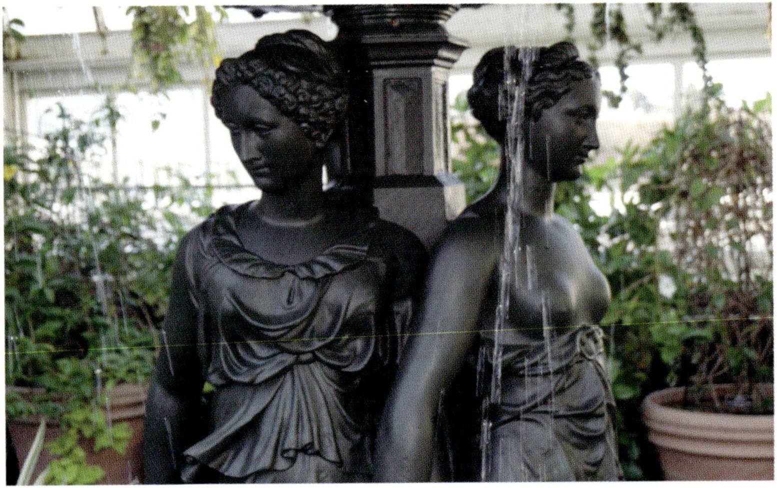

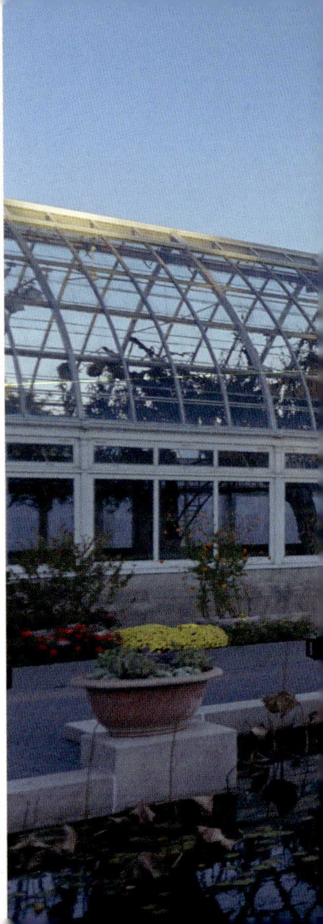

ALL PHOTOGRAPHS:

Enid A. Haupt Conservatory

Completed in 1902, this landmark glass conservatory is located in New York City's northernmost borough, the Bronx. Beneath the palm dome pavilion and behind the glass walls of 11 adjoining houses, collections of living plants are on display from several habitats found around the world. During the warmer months of the year, two pools next to the conservatory contain water plants including water lilies and lotuses. The conservatory has undergone several renovations in its 120-year history, with the latest completed in 2020 at a price tag of $18 million (about £13.5 million).

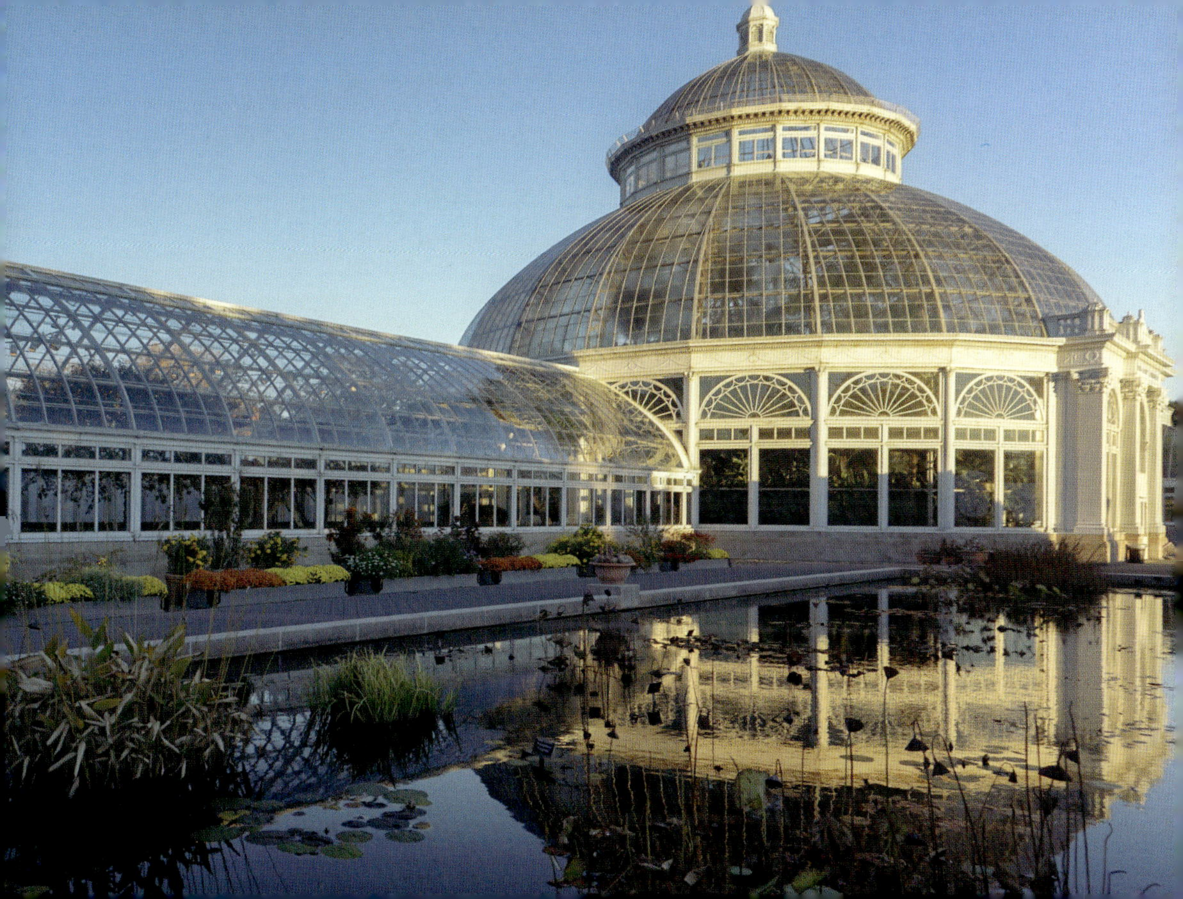

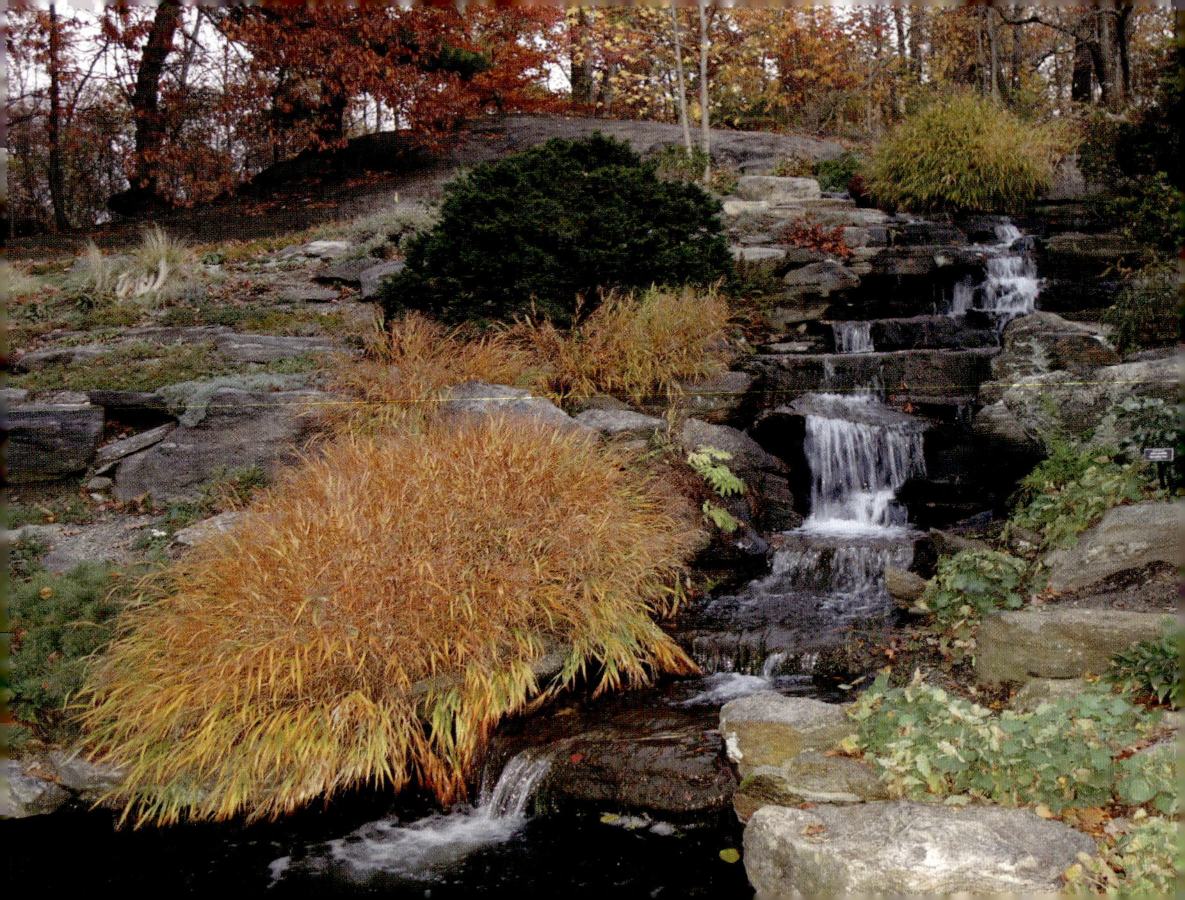

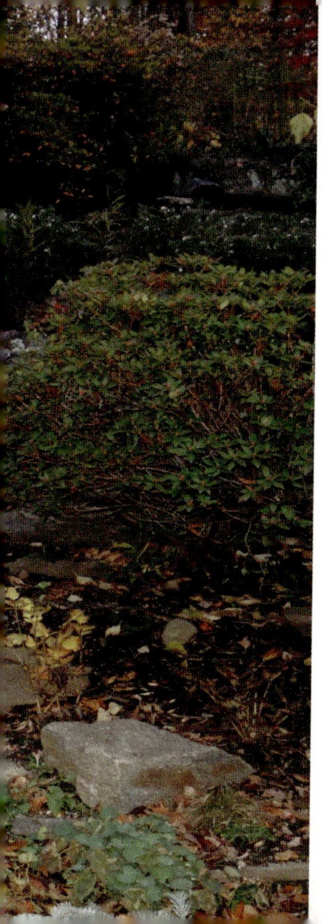

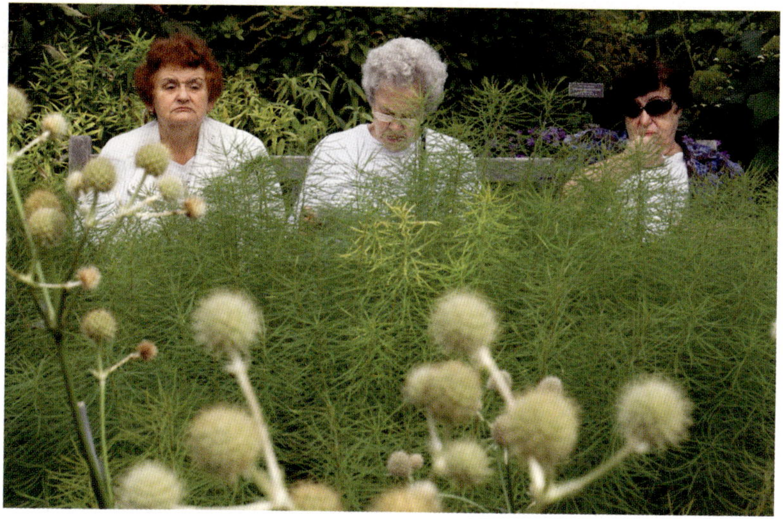

ALL PHOTOGRAPHS:

New York Botanical Garden

Declared a National Historical Landmark in 1967 and the site of the Enid A. Haupt Conservatory, the botanical garden is home to over one million plants including endangered orchids and prehistoric cycads. Set on 10 hectares (250 acres), the garden provides visitors with a picturesque setting that includes a 20-hectare (50-acre) forest, a cascading waterfall, 50 distinct gardens, and an herbarium with over seven million botanical specimens from around the world.

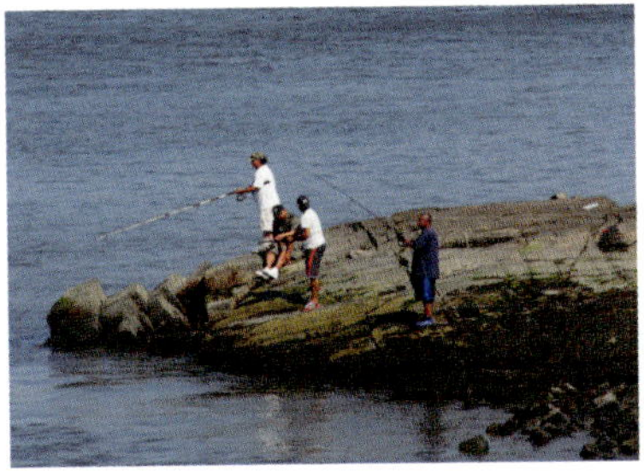

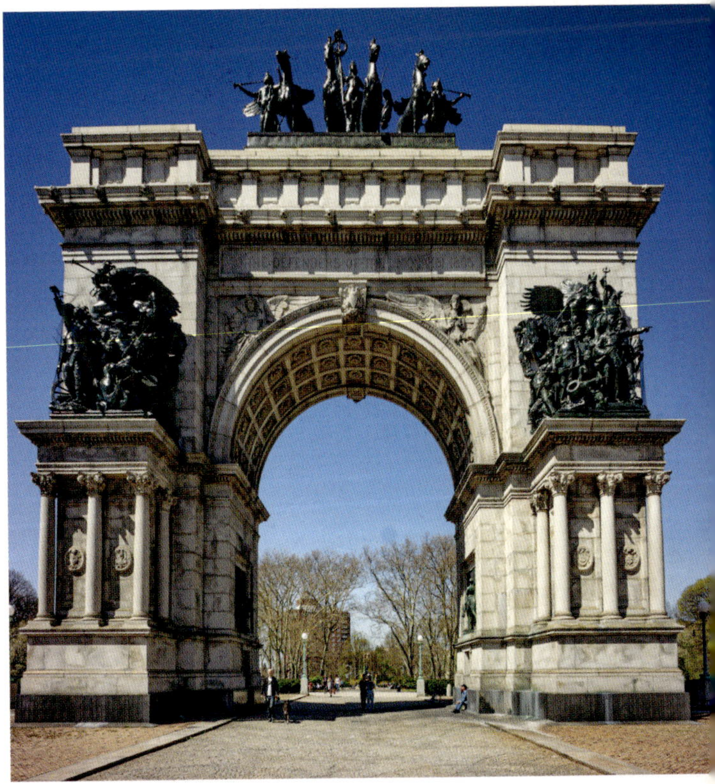

ABOVE:

Pelham Bay Park

Three times the size of Manhattan's Central Park, Pelham Bay Park is in the northeast corner of the Bronx and is the largest public park in New York City. Fishing for striped bass and summer flounder is a favourite activity.

RIGHT AND OPPOSITE:

Prospect Park

A triumphal arch dedicated to those who fought defending the Union during the American Civil War stands at 24m (80ft) at the main entrance of the park. Within its 213 hectares (526 acres), visitors can explore the park's open spaces, woodland, and water and bridges.

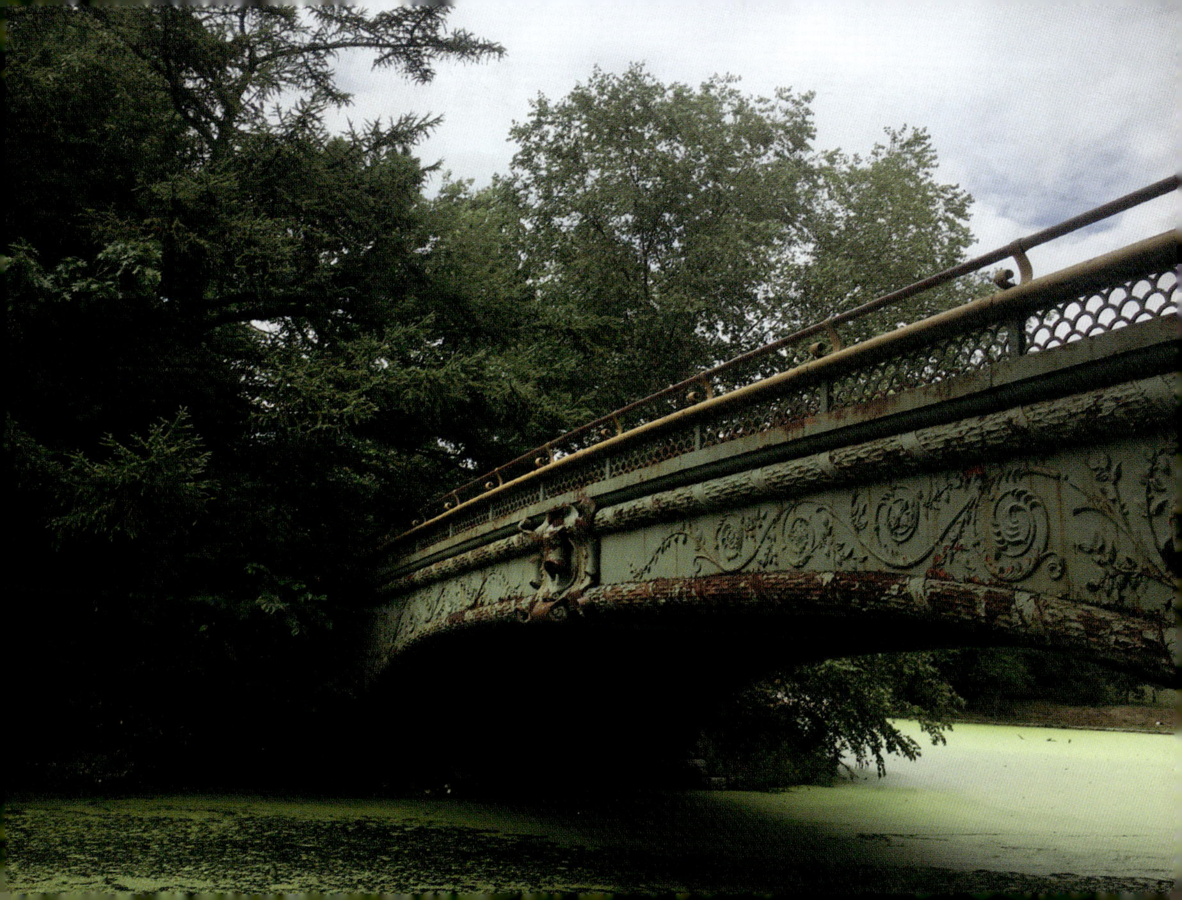

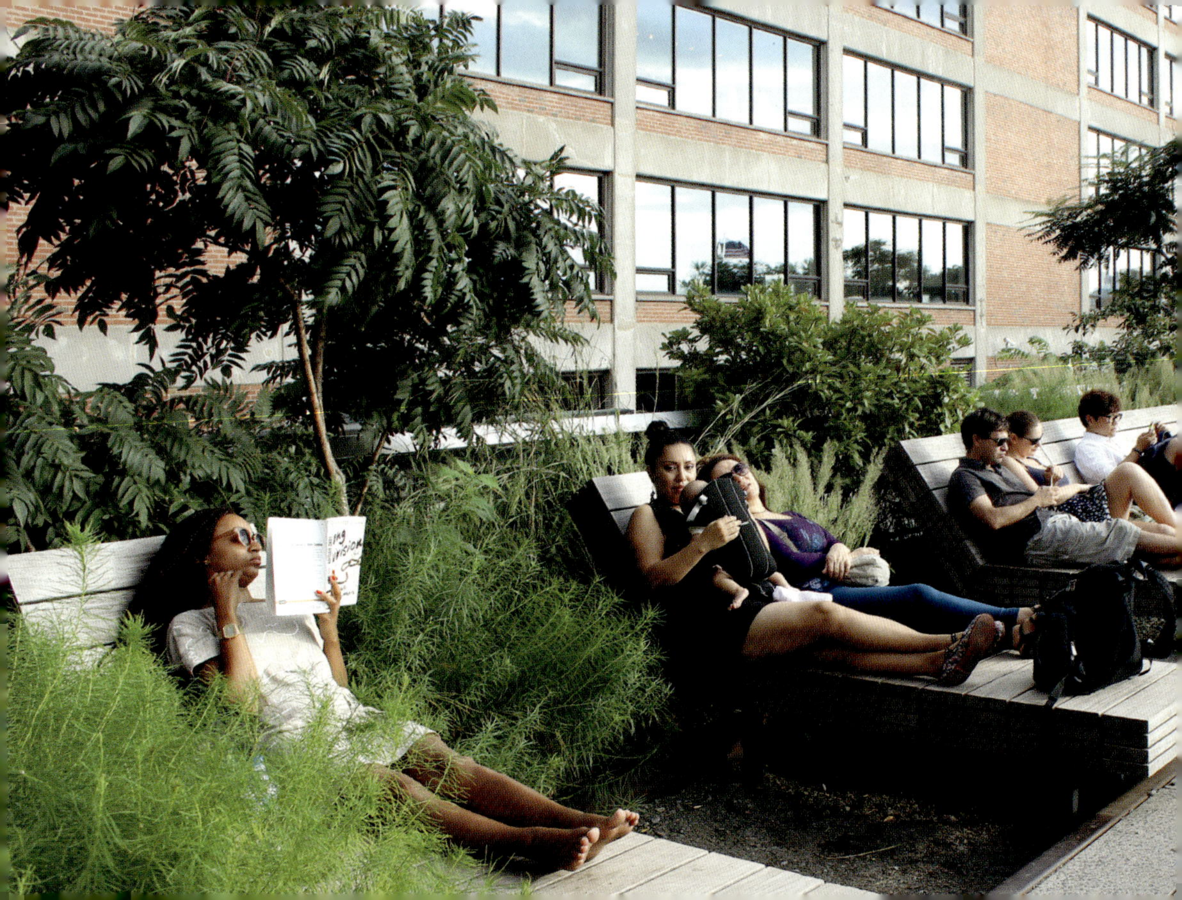

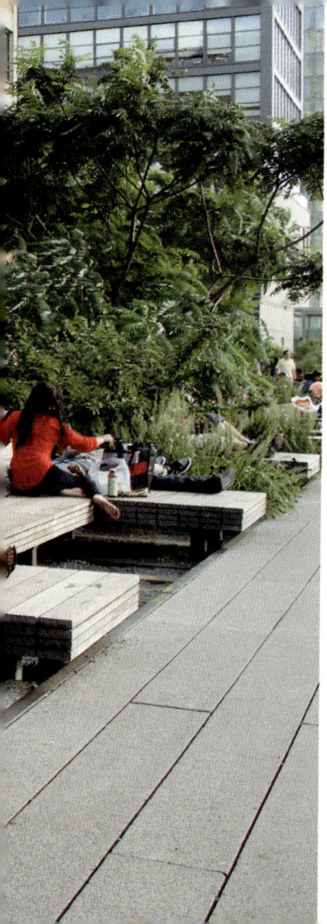

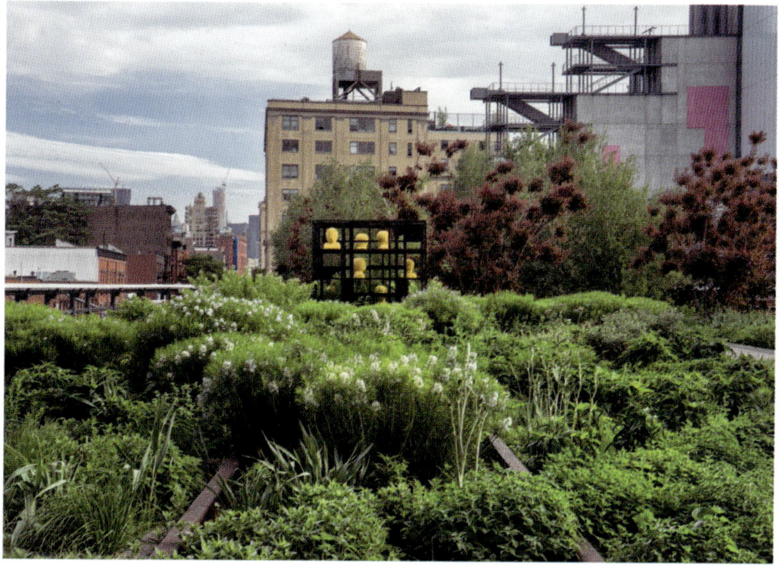

ALL PHOTOGRAPHS:
The High Line
Whether it's soaking up the sun, going for a stroll, or simply enjoying the elevated views, the High Line offers a different perspective of life in the city. Built on an old New York City railway line, the High Line is a raised walkway and urban park that spans 2.4km (1.5 miles) and runs along the west side of Manhattan. Resilient meadow plants, native shrubs, and lush gardens that change with each season can be found along the entire stretch of the park.

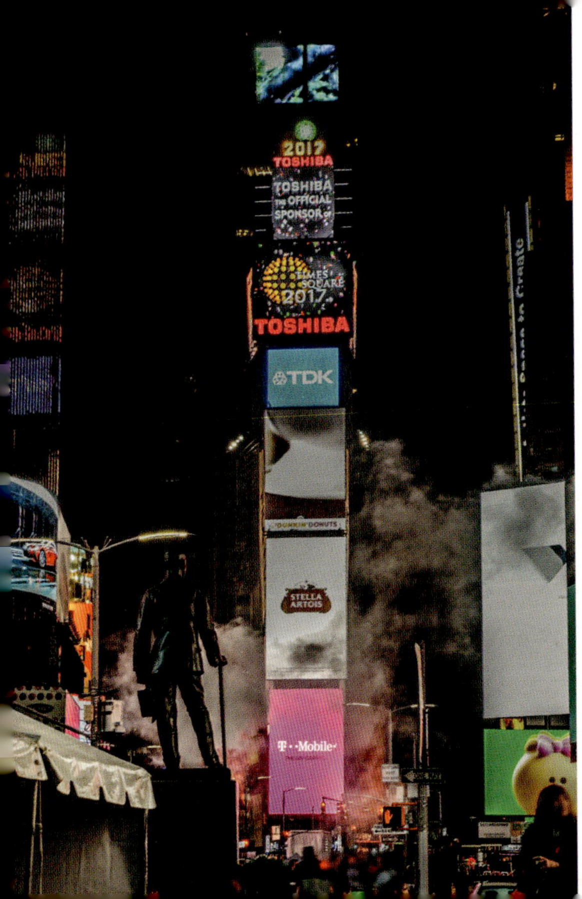
2017
TOSHIBA
TOSHIBA THE OFFICIAL SPONSOR OF
TIMES SQUARE 2017
TOSHIBA
TDK
DUNKIN' DONUTS
STELLA ARTOIS
T··Mobile
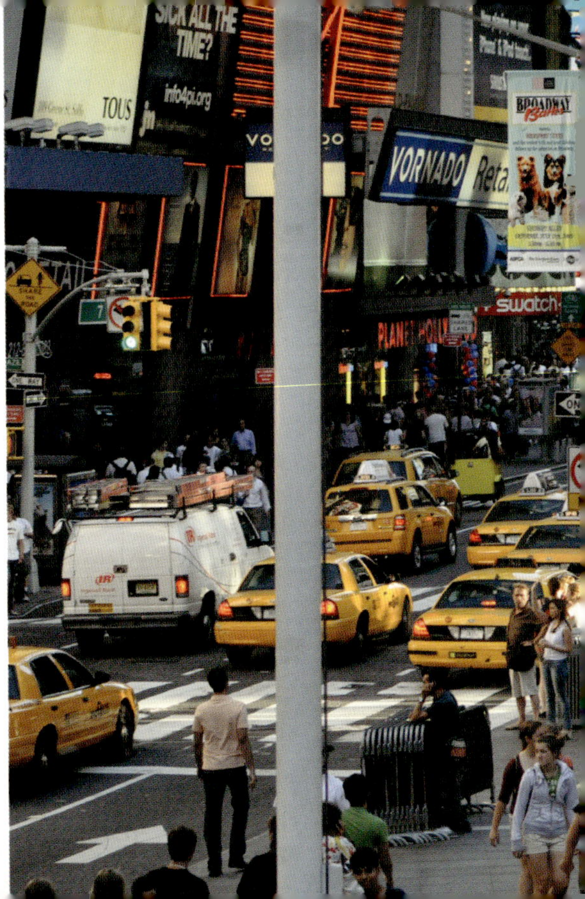
SICK ALL THE TIME?
info4pi.org
TOUS
VORNADO
BROADWAY Barks
swatch
SHARE THE ROAD

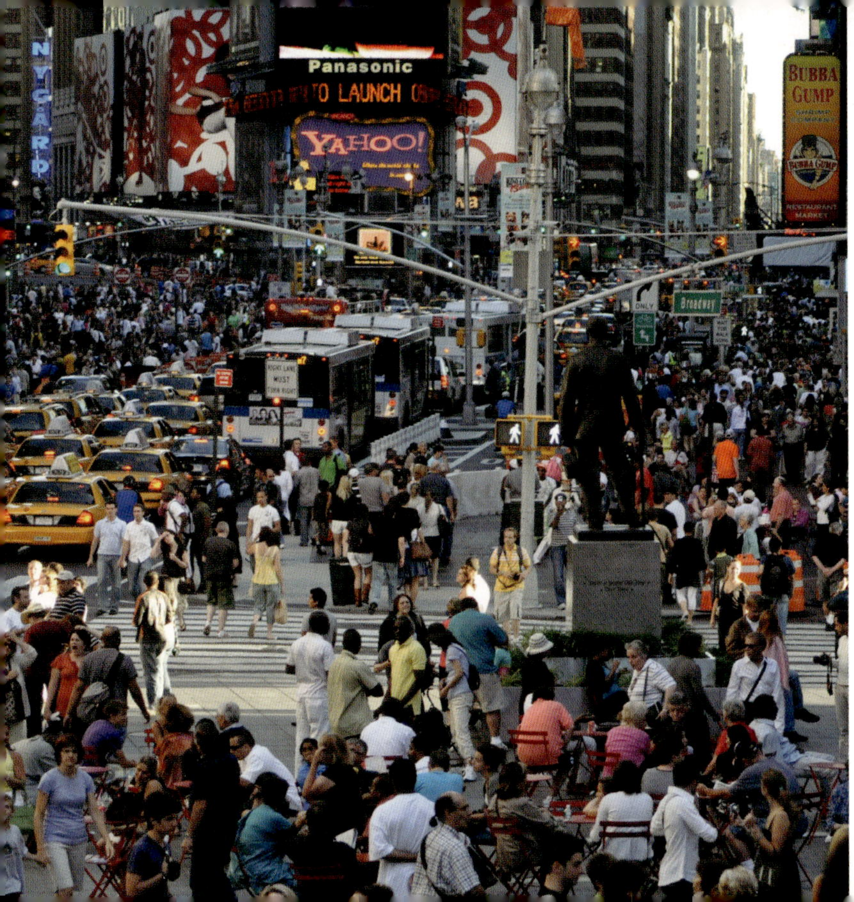

ALL PHOTOGRAPHS:

Times Square

One of the busiest parts of New York City – if not the world! – Times Square is located in Midtown Manhattan, by Broadway and Seventh Avenue. Lined with busy shops, tourist-filled restaurants and museums, and home to dozens of theatres, Time Square attracts an estimated 50 million people annually. This central location in the heart of the city also hosts the annual New Year's Eve celebration and 'ball drop' attended by over one million spectators and viewed by countless more around the world.

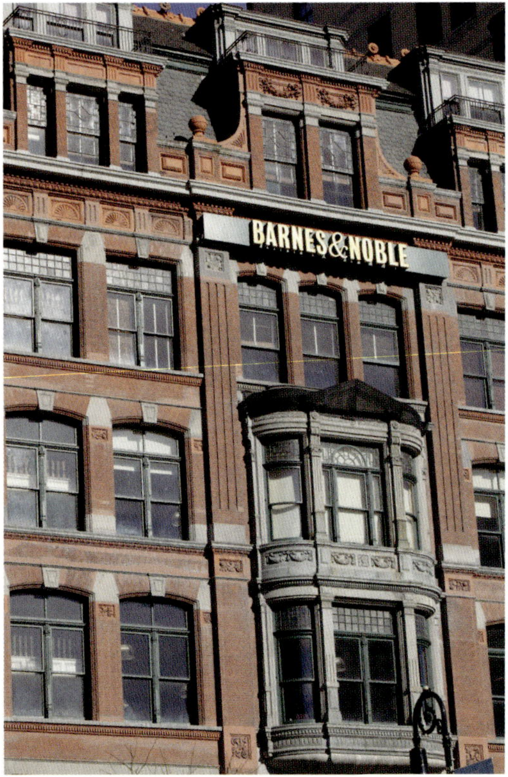

LEFT:

Barnes & Noble Store

Across Union Square and on 17th Street, visitors in the area can visit Manhattan's largest Barnes & Noble bookstore, which features an indoor café, author readings and four floors of books.

RIGHT:

Union Square

Opened in 1839, Union Square is a popular destination for New Yorkers, thanks to its central location and access to multiple subway lines. Throughout its history, the park has been used as a destination for rallies and speeches, and as a platform to raise awareness about social and economic issues. But you can also just have a stroll, too.

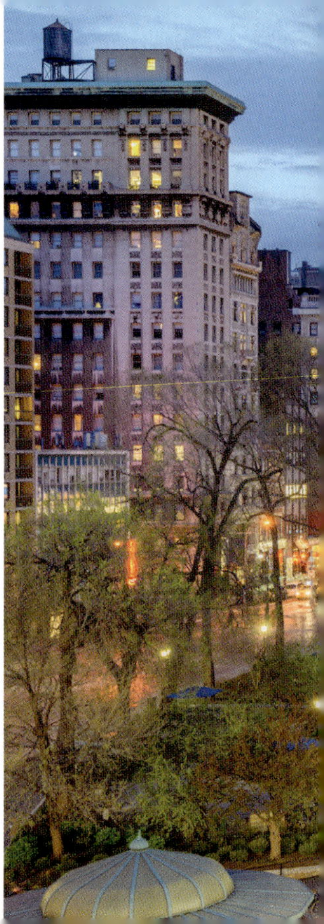

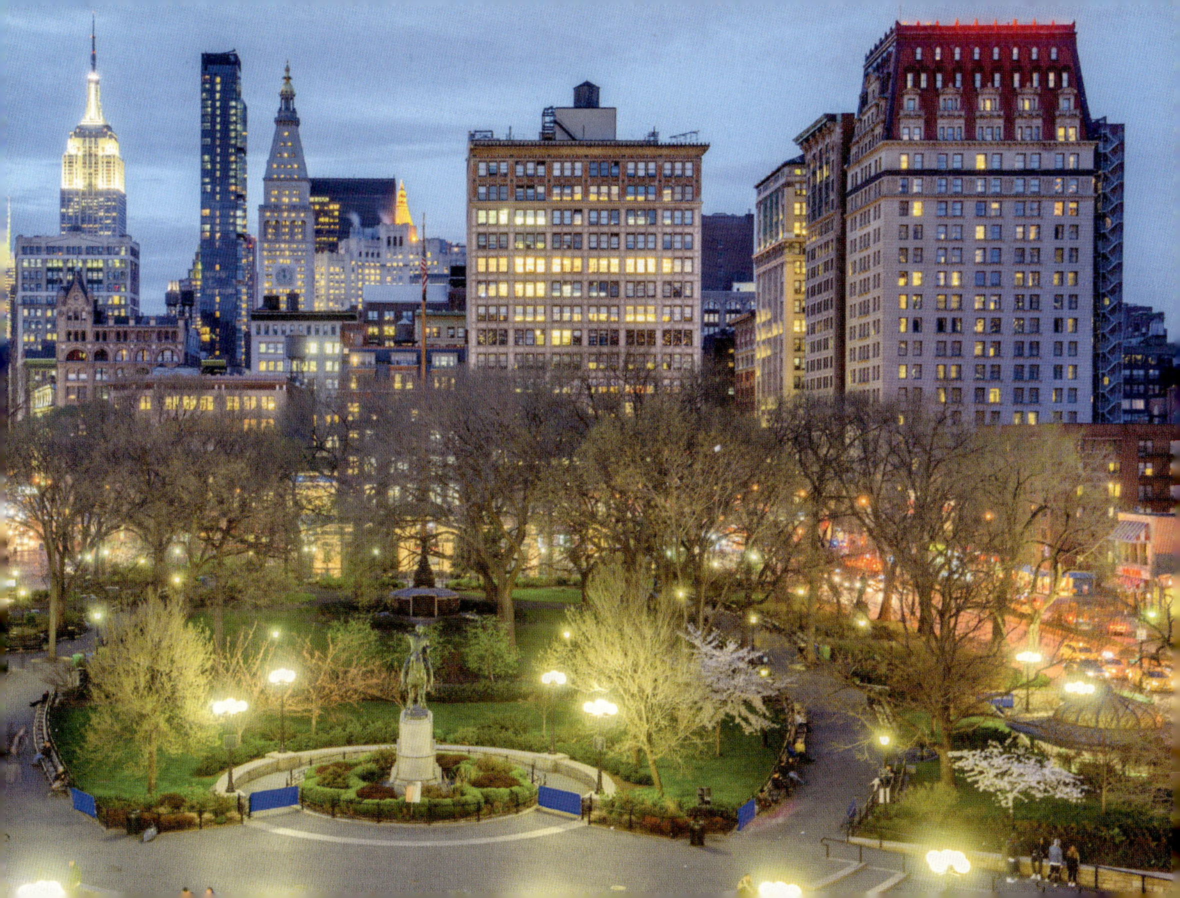

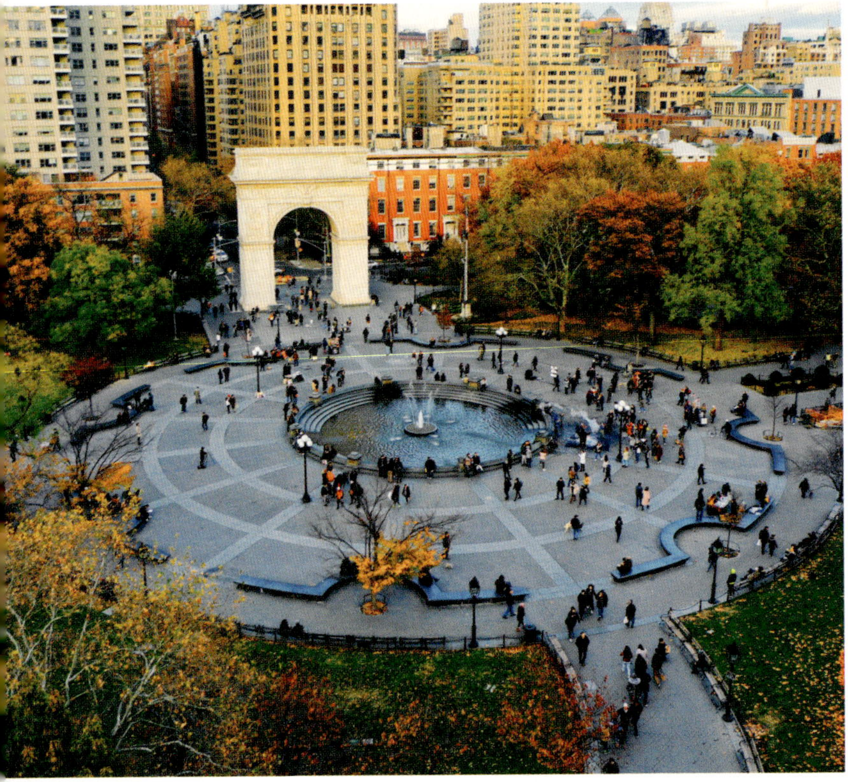

ALL PHOTOGRAPHS:

Washington Square Park

Named after the first president of the United States, Washington Square Park is located in Lower Manhattan in Greenwich Village. To the north of the park is the Washington Square Arch monument, which stands at a height of 23m (77ft). Another popular attraction is the circular fountain which runs from April or May until mid-October. Though the cold winter months bring fewer visitors, the park looks beautiful in the snow.

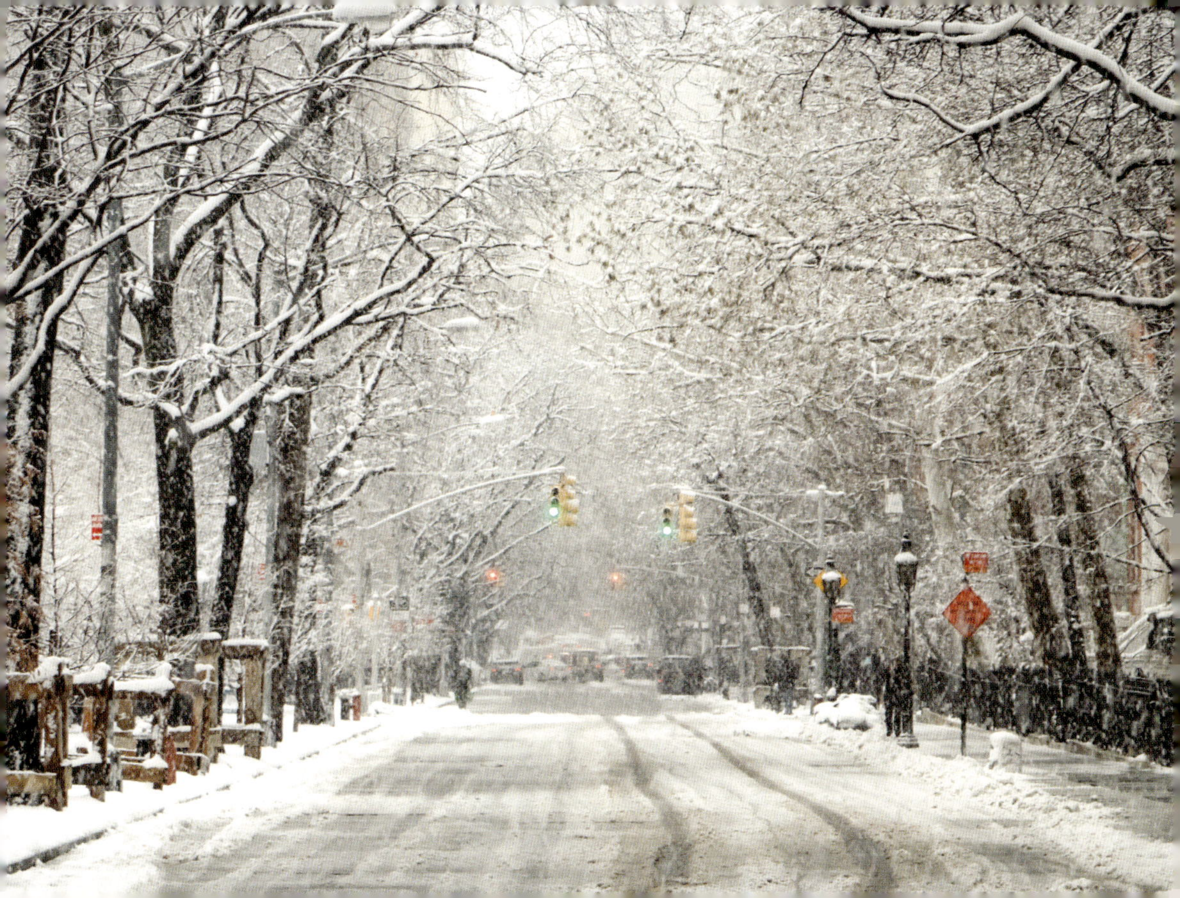

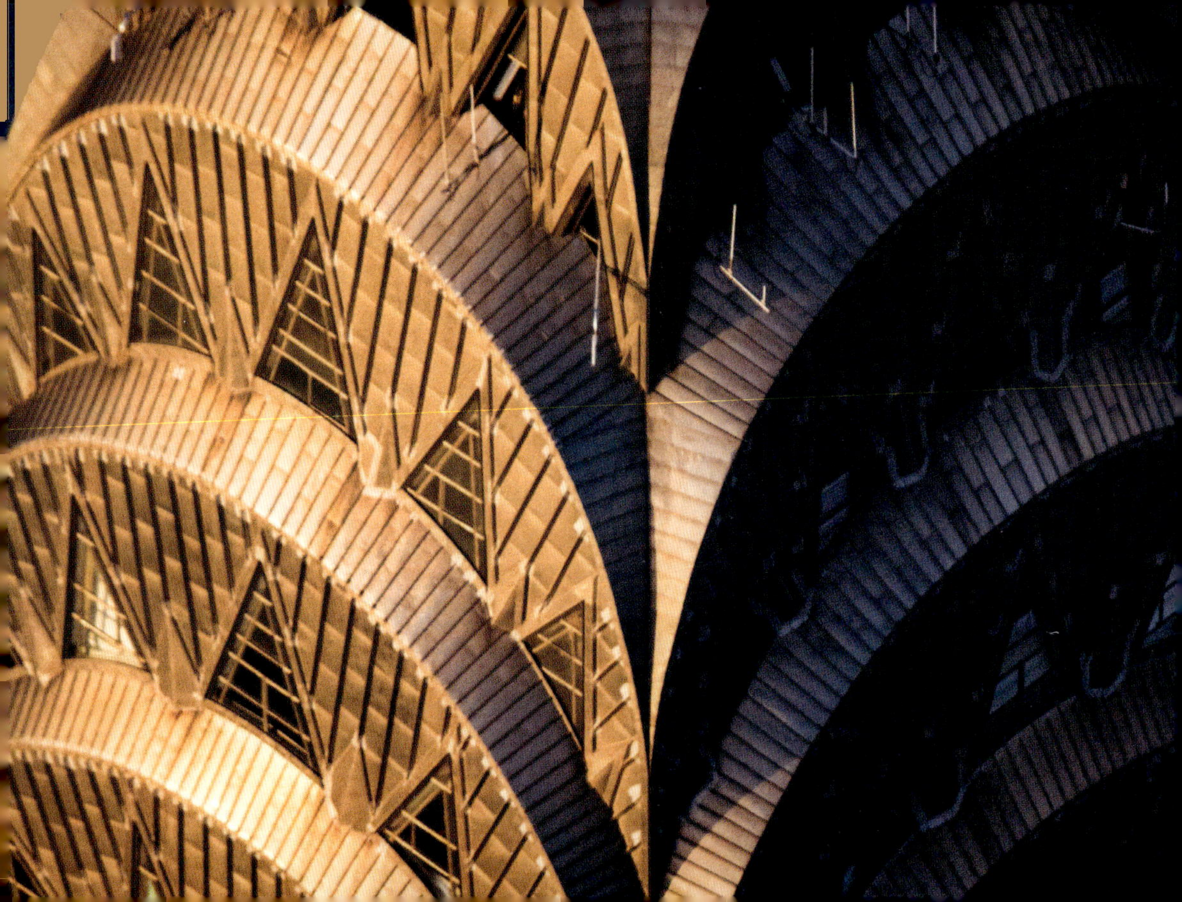

Landmarks

If you are looking for impressive and imposing human-made structures that reach for the sky, New York City is home to many of the world's most iconic buildings and skyscrapers. Designed by architects and engineers, erected with the sweat and blood of generations of builders, and dressed by master craftsman and artists of world-renown, hundreds of tall buildings and structures adorn the Manhattan skyline.

Outside, the buildings display a wide range of exterior architecture. Whether built of granite and limestone or shiny towers of steel and glass, each skyscraper and structure in the city is an easily recognisable landmark rich in history and personality. Inside, these megastructures display the latest in mechanical and electrical systems, and offer each visitor an aesthetic experience unique to each building.

Must-see attractions can be found throughout the city's five boroughs. Whether it's on Wall Street – the heart of the financial market – or taking a boat ride across the harbour and climbing the stairs to the top of the Statue of Liberty, tourists quickly learn that sightseeing in New York takes more than one trip. It's also a good excuse to make this city a return destination.

OPPOSITE:

Chrysler Building

The bold geometric Art Deco style was popular among architects when the first skyscrapers started appearing in US cities in the early decades of the 20th century.

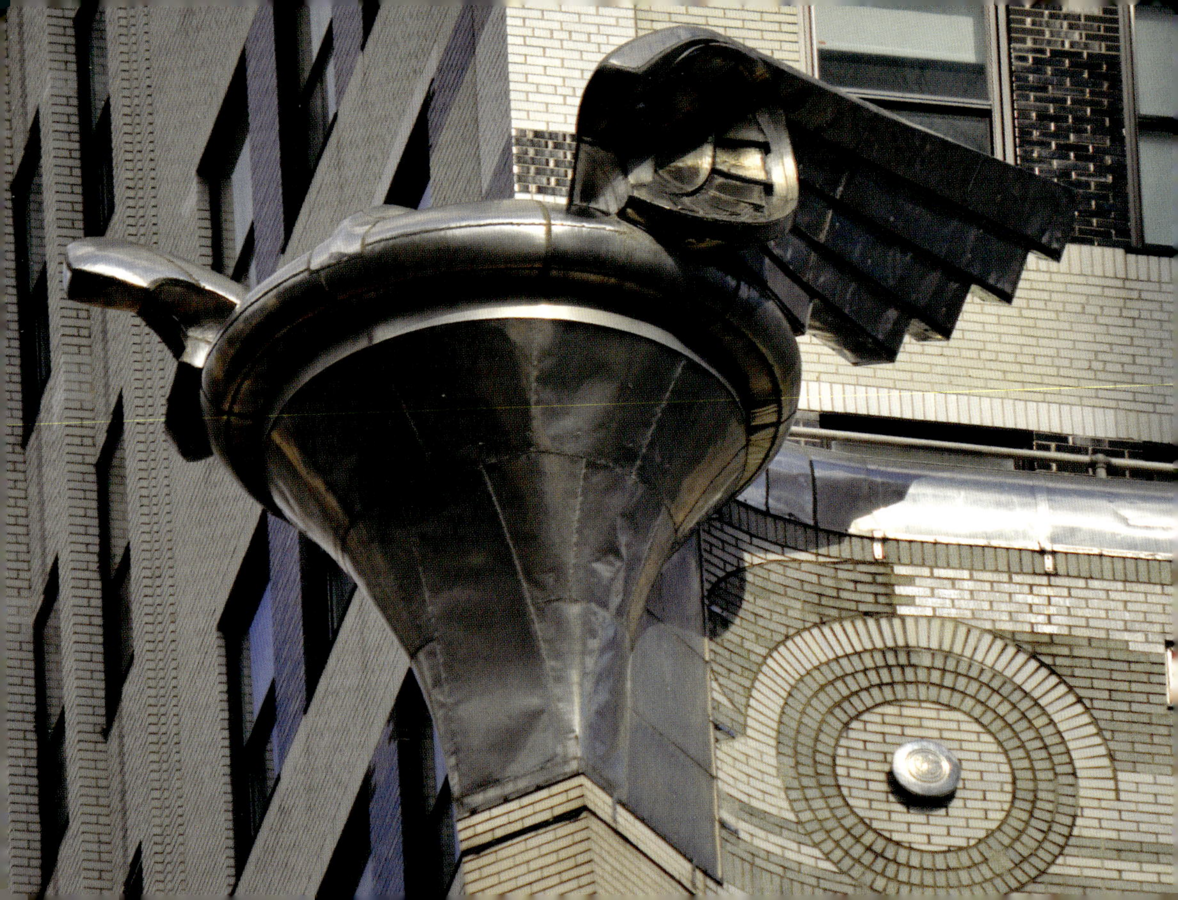

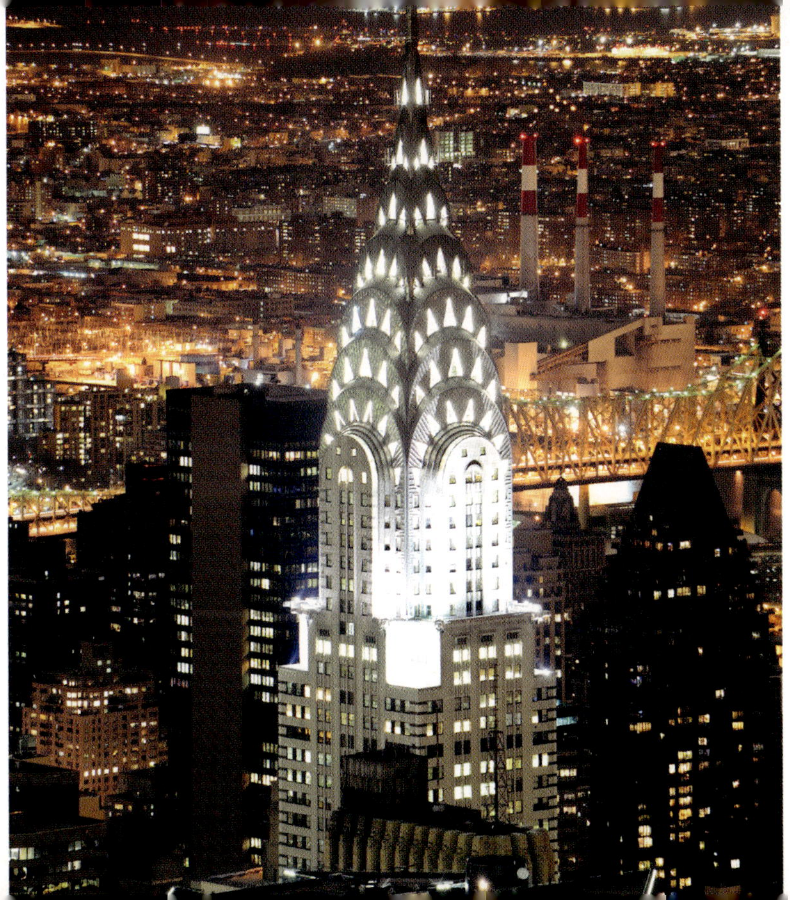

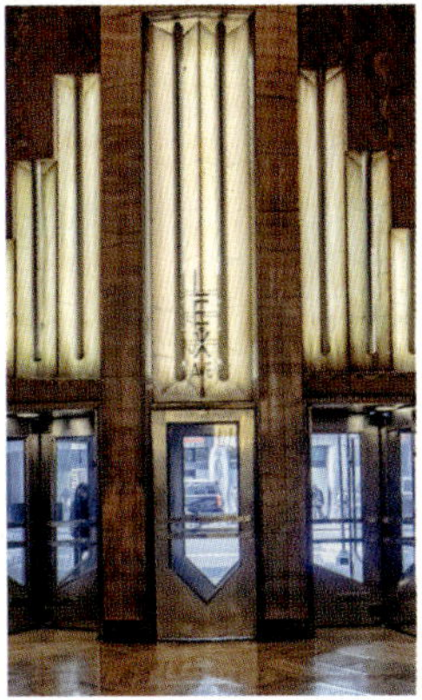

ALL PHOTOGRAPHS:

Chrysler Building architecture

Outcroppings featuring eagles' heads and wings located hundreds of feet above ground can be viewed on the building's exterior. Inside, the walls and floors display patterns and shapes highlighting the building's Art Deco influences.

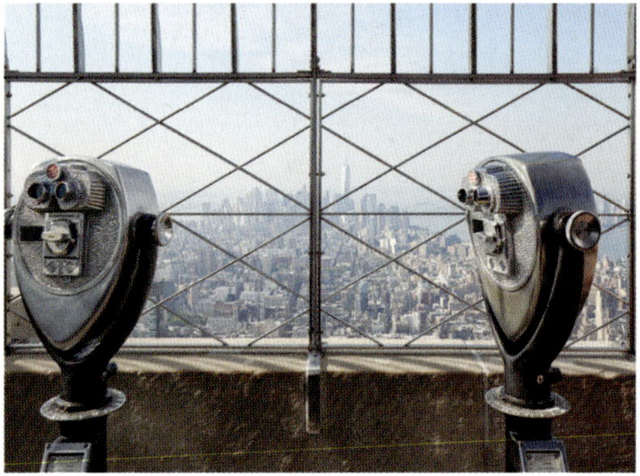

ALL PHOTOGRAPHS:

Empire State Building, observation deck

Located on the highest floor of the building – the 102nd floor – the observation deck is 381m (1,250ft) above ground. Renovated in 2019, the deck offers a panoramic, unobstructed view of the city and the surrounding area, including the Hudson River, East River, New Jersey, and even Pennsylvania. On a clear day, lucky visitors can see as far as 130km (80 miles) out. Around four million people visit the Empire State Building annually.

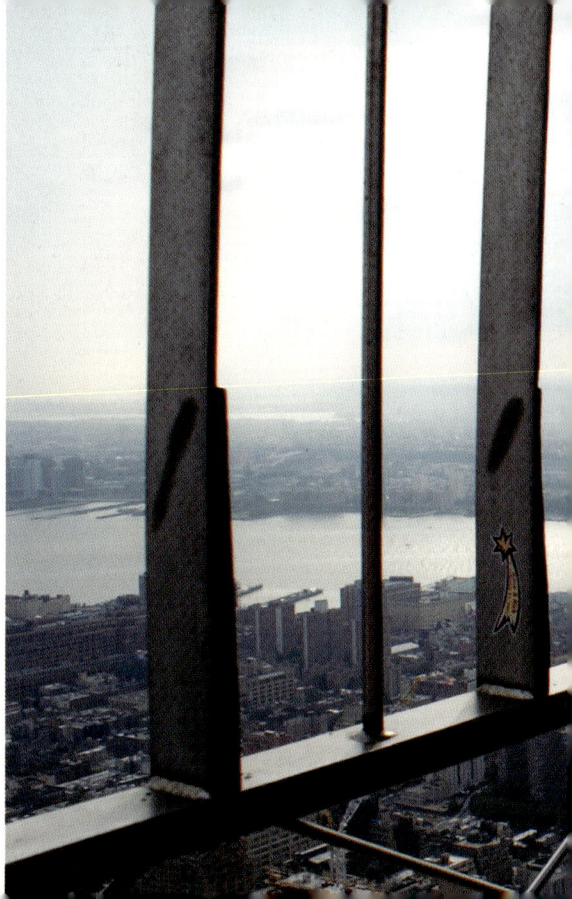

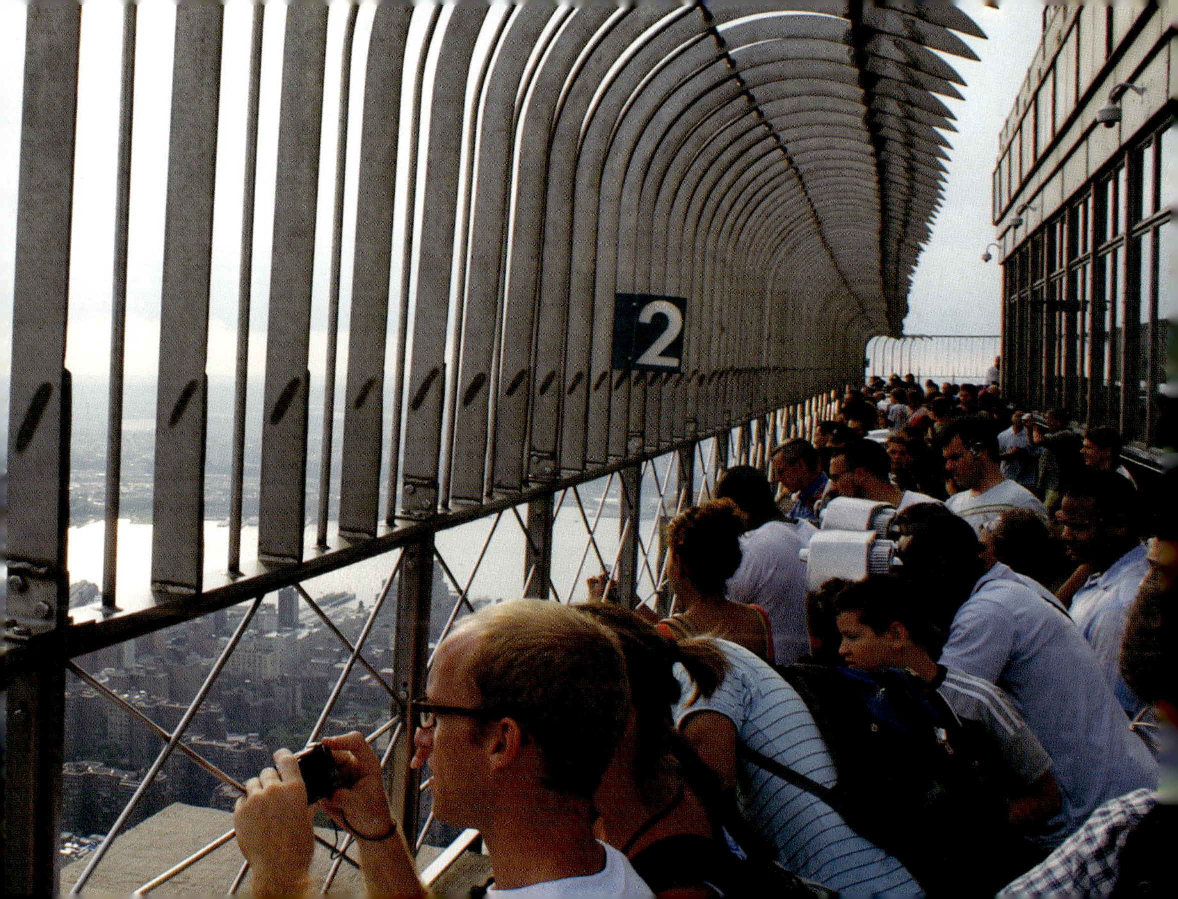
2

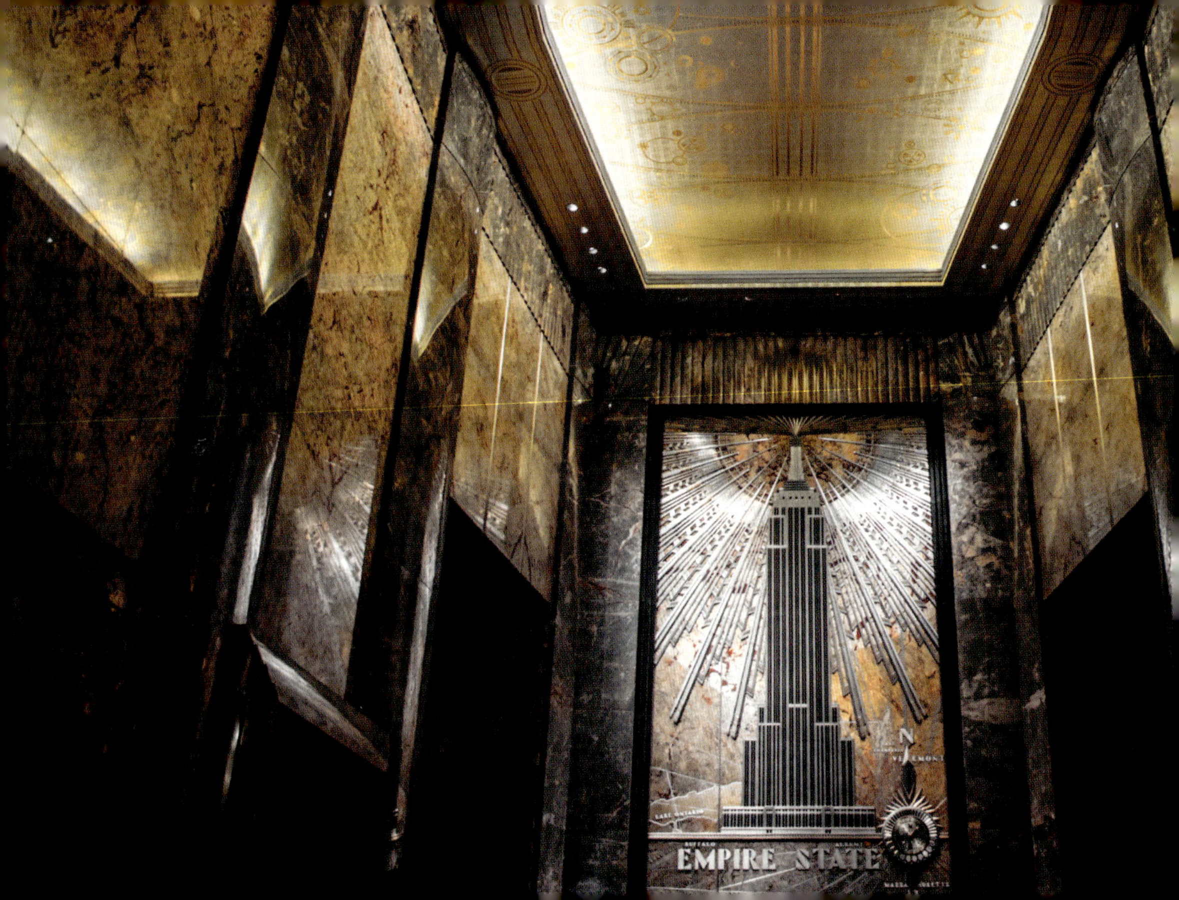
EMPIRE STATE

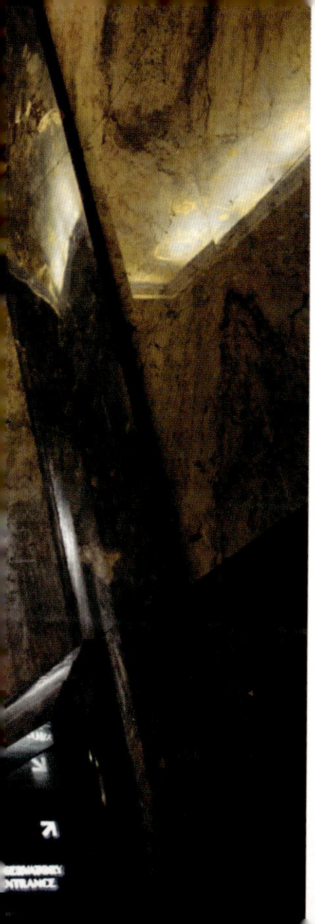

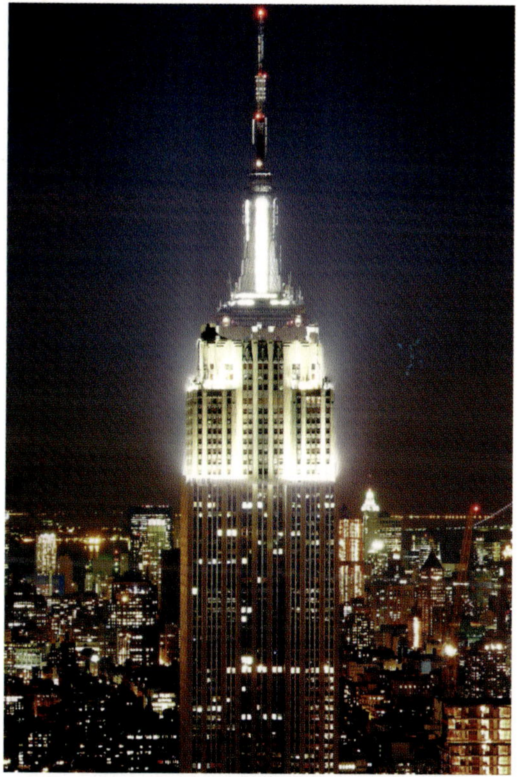

ALL PHOTOGRAPHS:

Empire State Building architecture

Also influenced by the Art Deco style popular during its time of construction, the building was completed in 1931 and took the title of the world's tallest structure from the Chrysler Building, which had been completed just a year earlier. At a height of 449m (1,473ft) the Empire State Building remained the tallest building in the world until 1971.

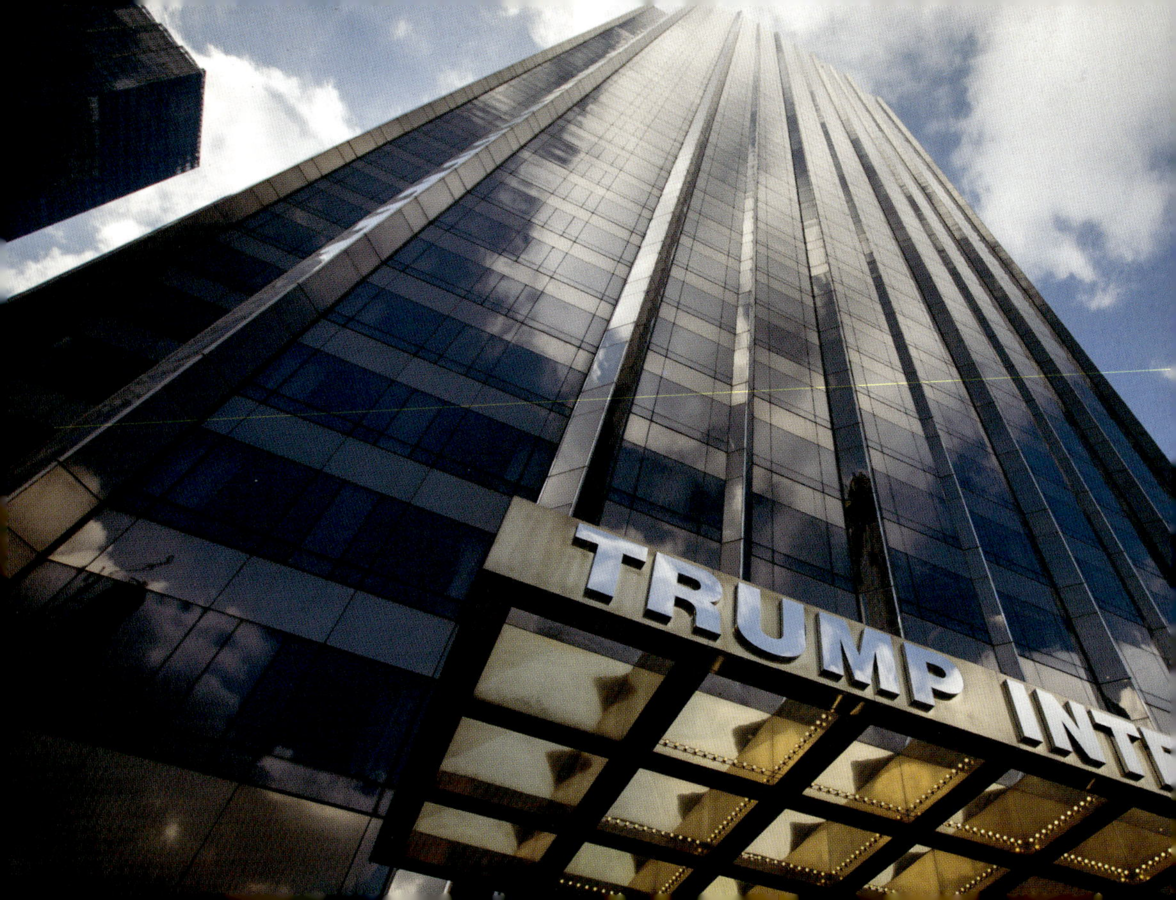
TRUMP INTE

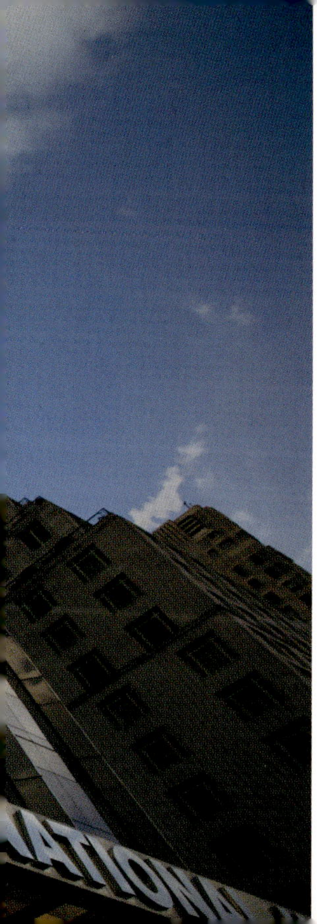

LEFT:

Trump Tower

This 202m (663ft) skyscraper is a mixed-use building housing business offices and personal residences, including the penthouse condominium of former US president, Donald Trump.

RIGHT:

Wall Street

Named after a wall built by early Dutch settlers to defend against English attack, this eight-block stretch of land is one of the oldest parts of Manhattan. It is also the heart of the financial district of New York City – if not the world.

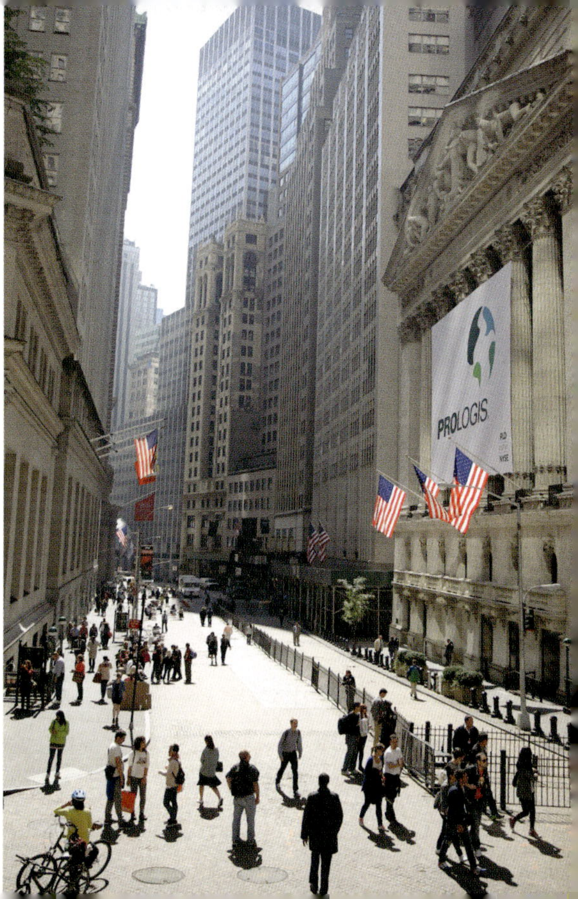

New York skyline

Whether viewed from a plane, helicopter, the top floors of a skyscraper or even a postcard, the breathtaking view of the Manhattan skyline is a testament to the progress and innovation that involves thousands of architects, engineers, masons, welders and builders of all types.

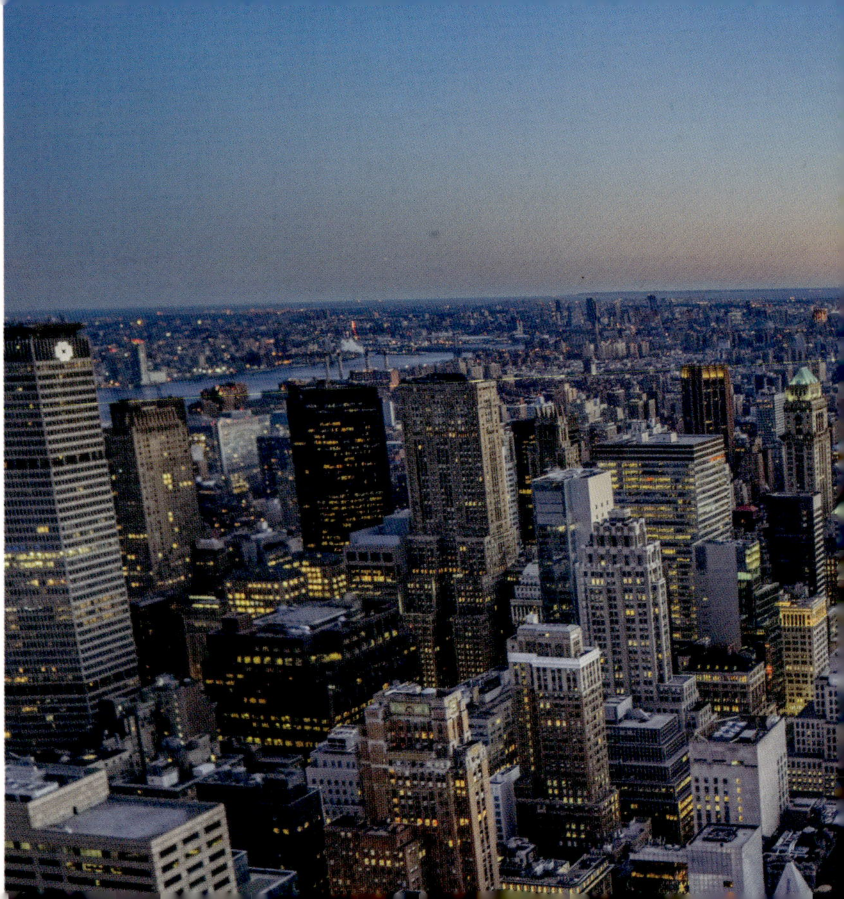

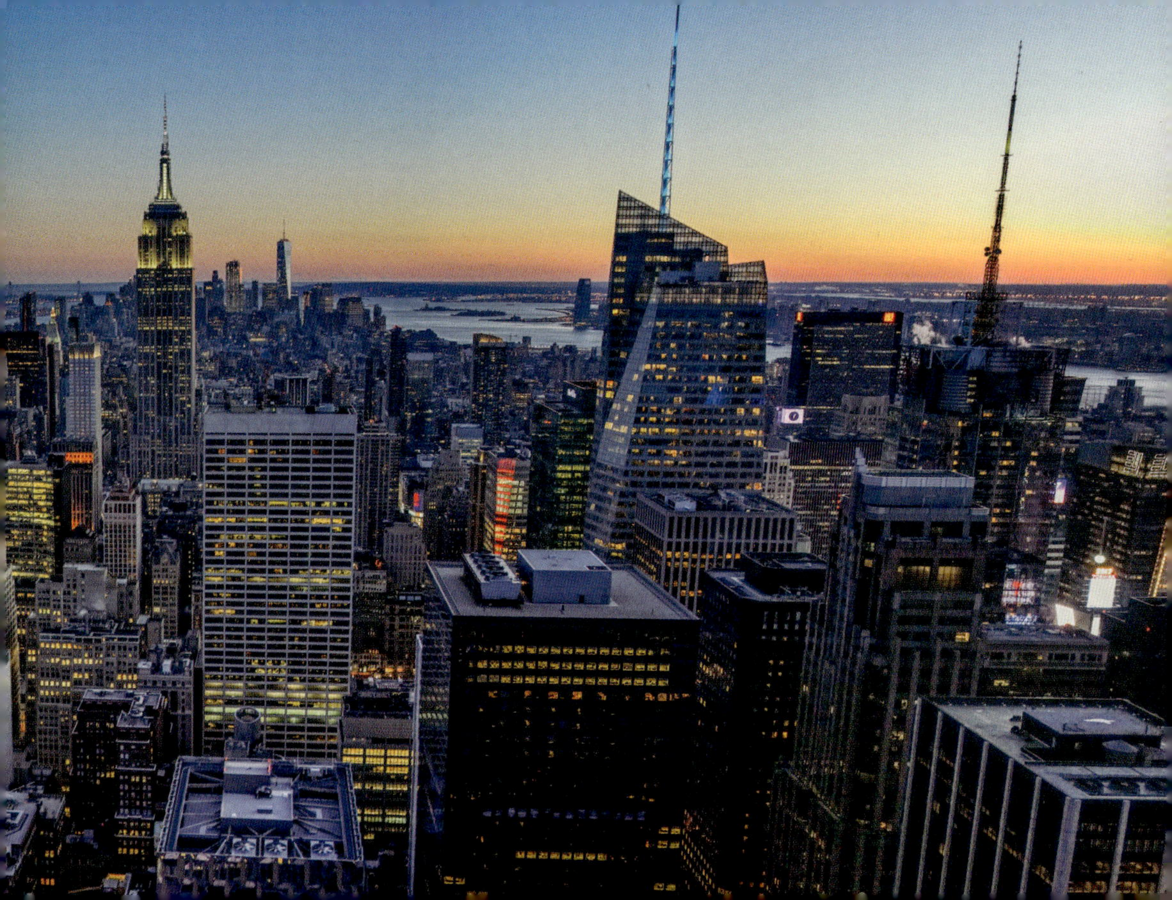

ALL PHOTOGRAPHS:

Flatiron Building

Originally called the Fuller Building, this early high-rise was built in 1902 and was constructed in a triangular patch of land between Broadway and Fifth Avenue and 22nd and 23rd Streets. The steel-framed building displays an intricately carved facade constructed of limestone and terra-cotta. Most New Yorkers believe that the building's name originates from its shape and resemblance to a laundry iron used to press clothes in the early 20th century. The truth is that the site was called 'Flat Iron' before the building was ever constructed.

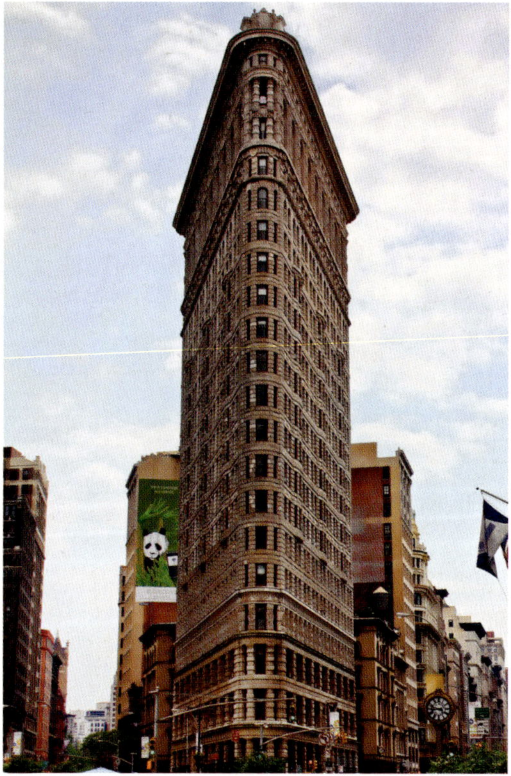

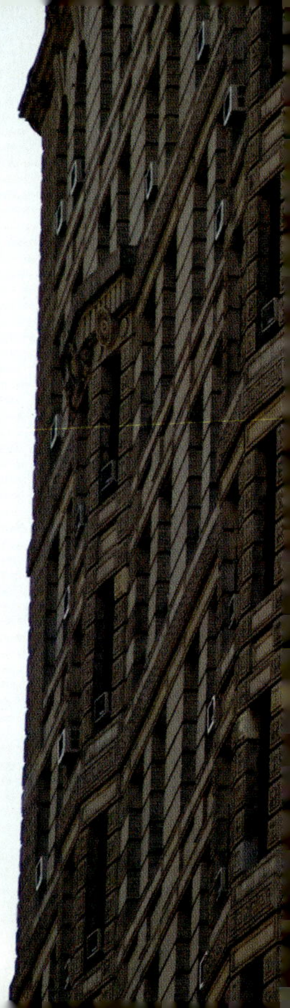

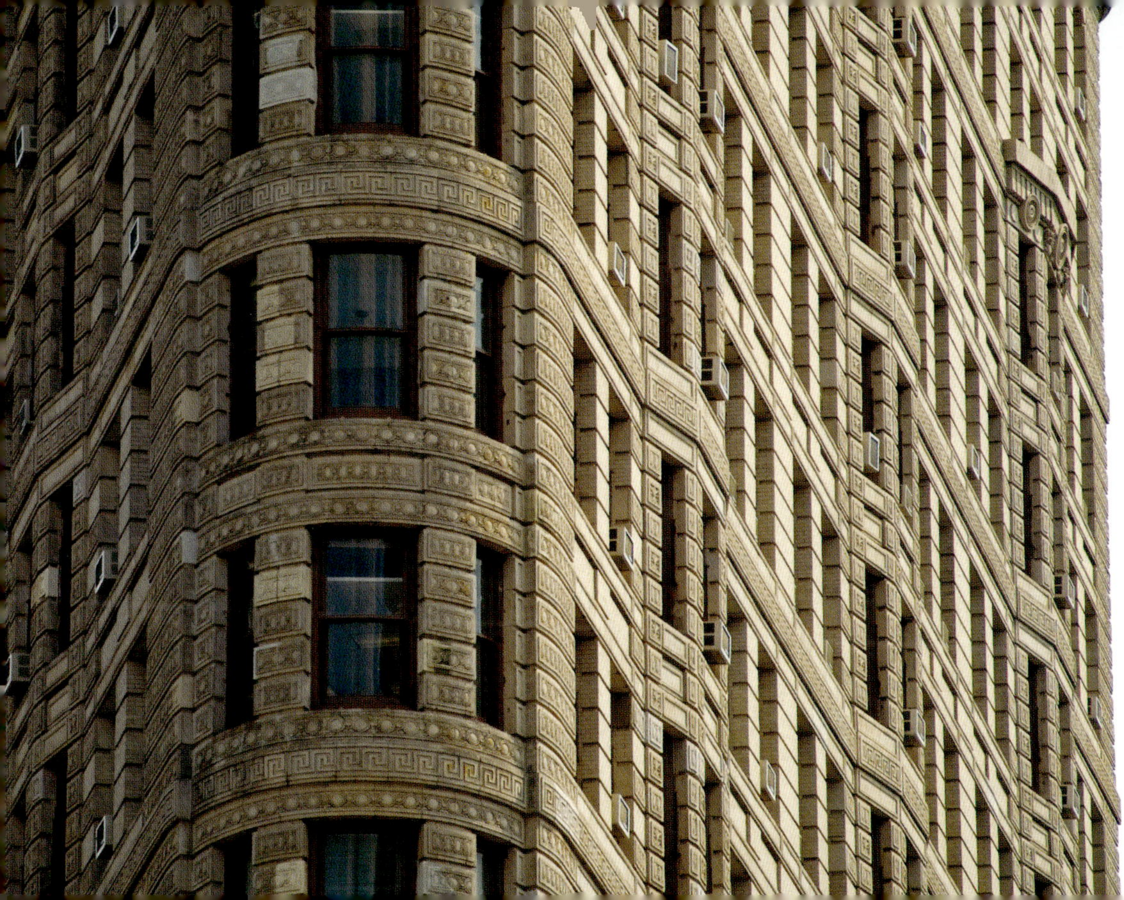

9/11 Memorial and Museum

The 9/11 Memorial pays tribute to the 2,977 people killed as a result of the terrorist attacks on 11 September 2001. The memorial is built at the World Trade Center site where the Twin Towers once stood.

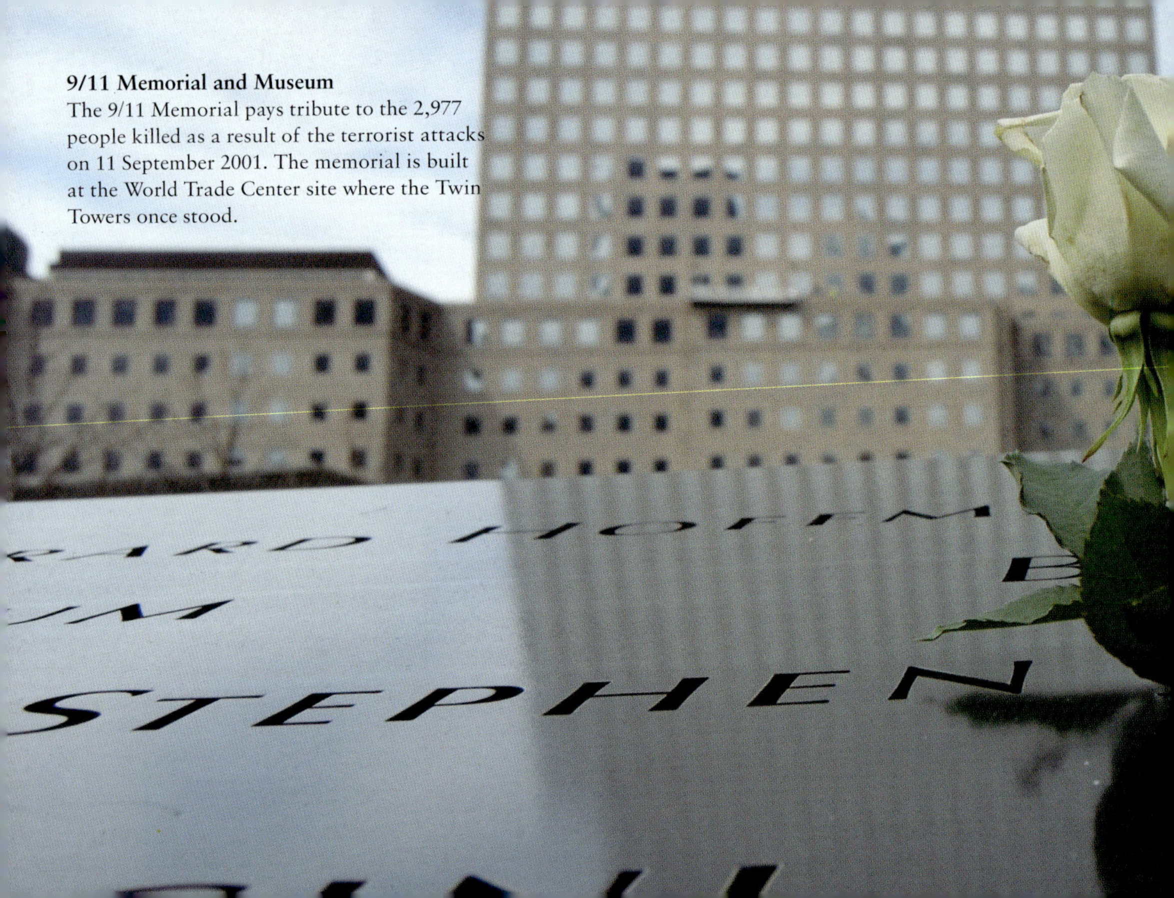

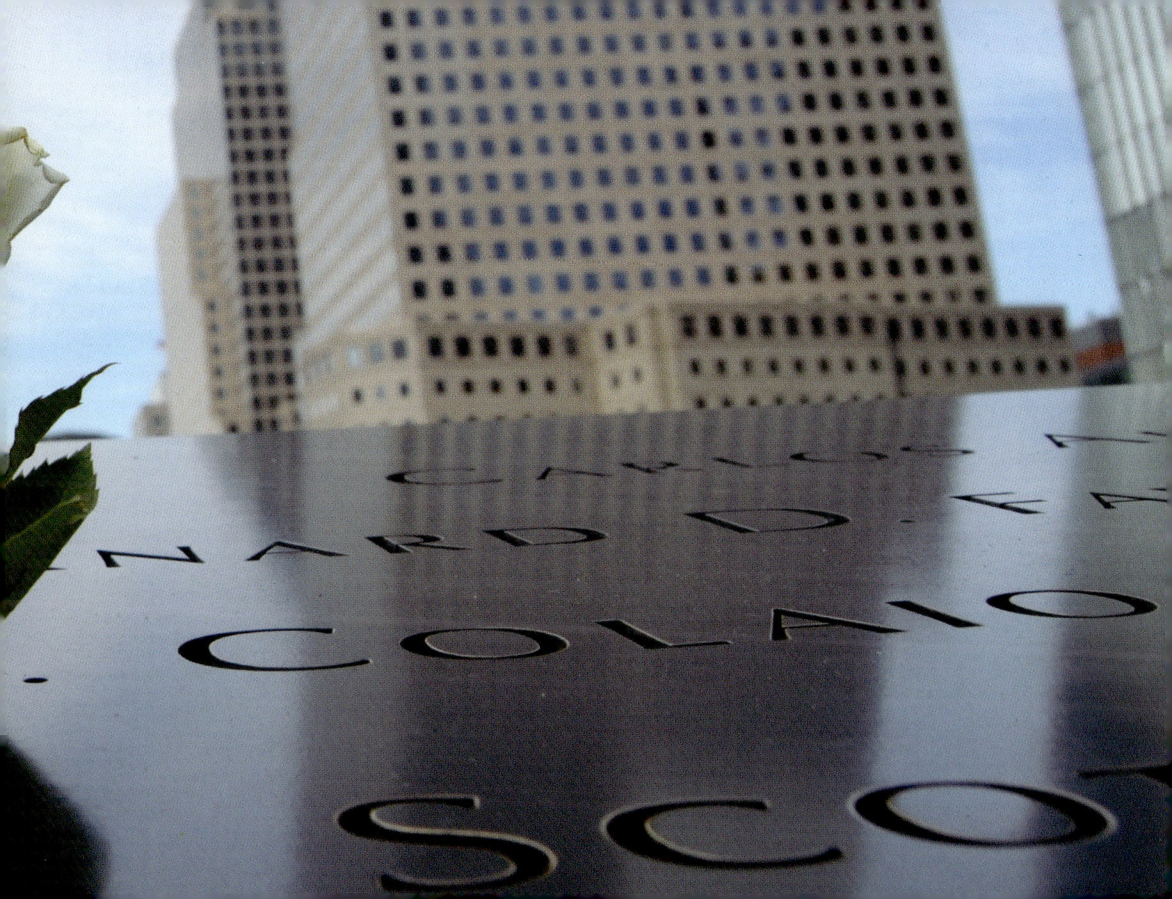
COLAIO

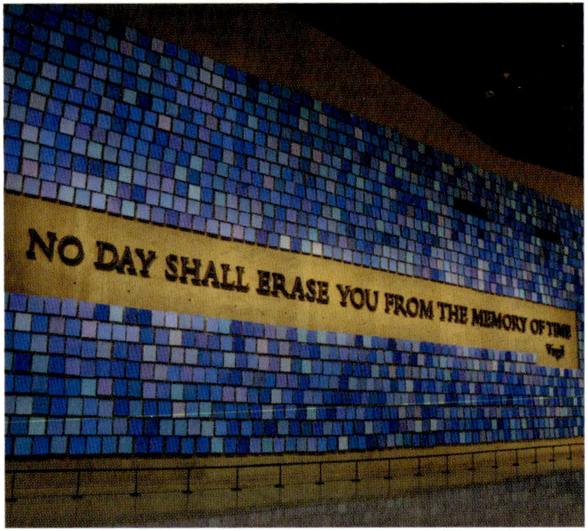

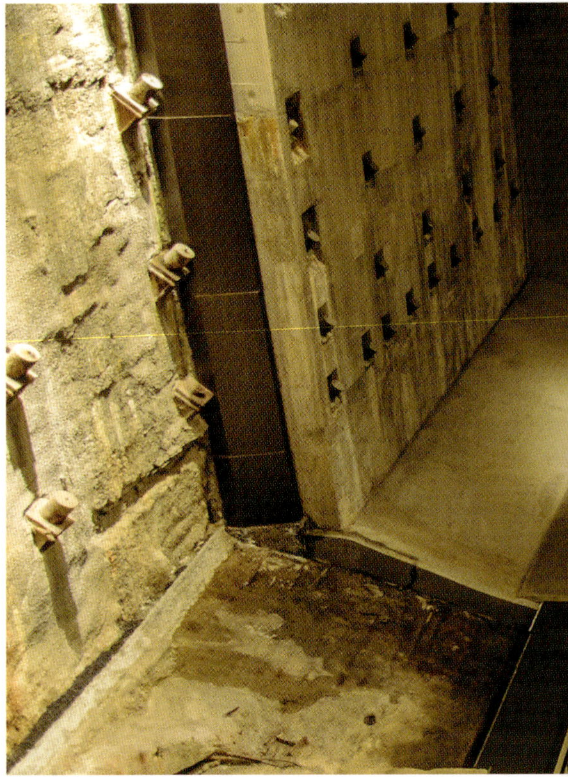

ALL PHOTOGRAPHS:

9/11 Memorial and Museum artefacts

Built on 6.5 hectares (16 acres) in Lower Manhattan, it includes twin-reflecting pools, each 0.4 hectares (1 acre) in size, and the largest human-made waterfall in North America. The museum offers a historical exhibit of the events of 11 September 2001 through artefacts, imagery, and audio and video recordings.

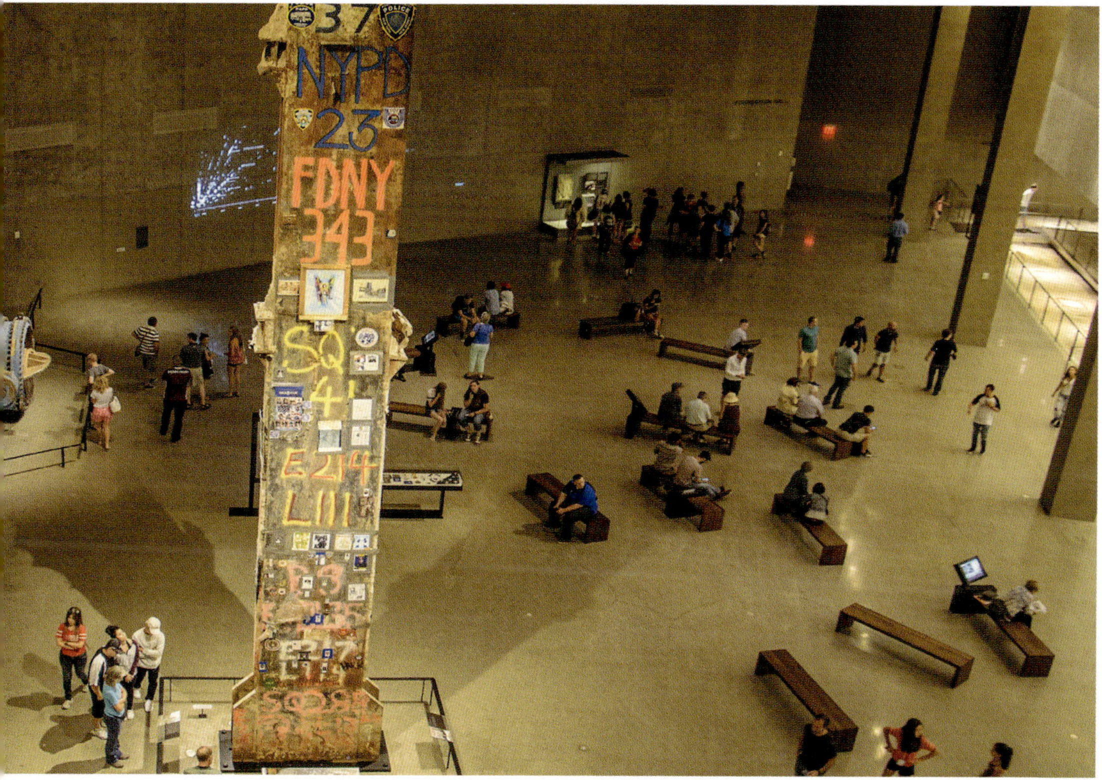
37
POLICE
NYPD
23
FDNY
343
SQ 41
E214
L111

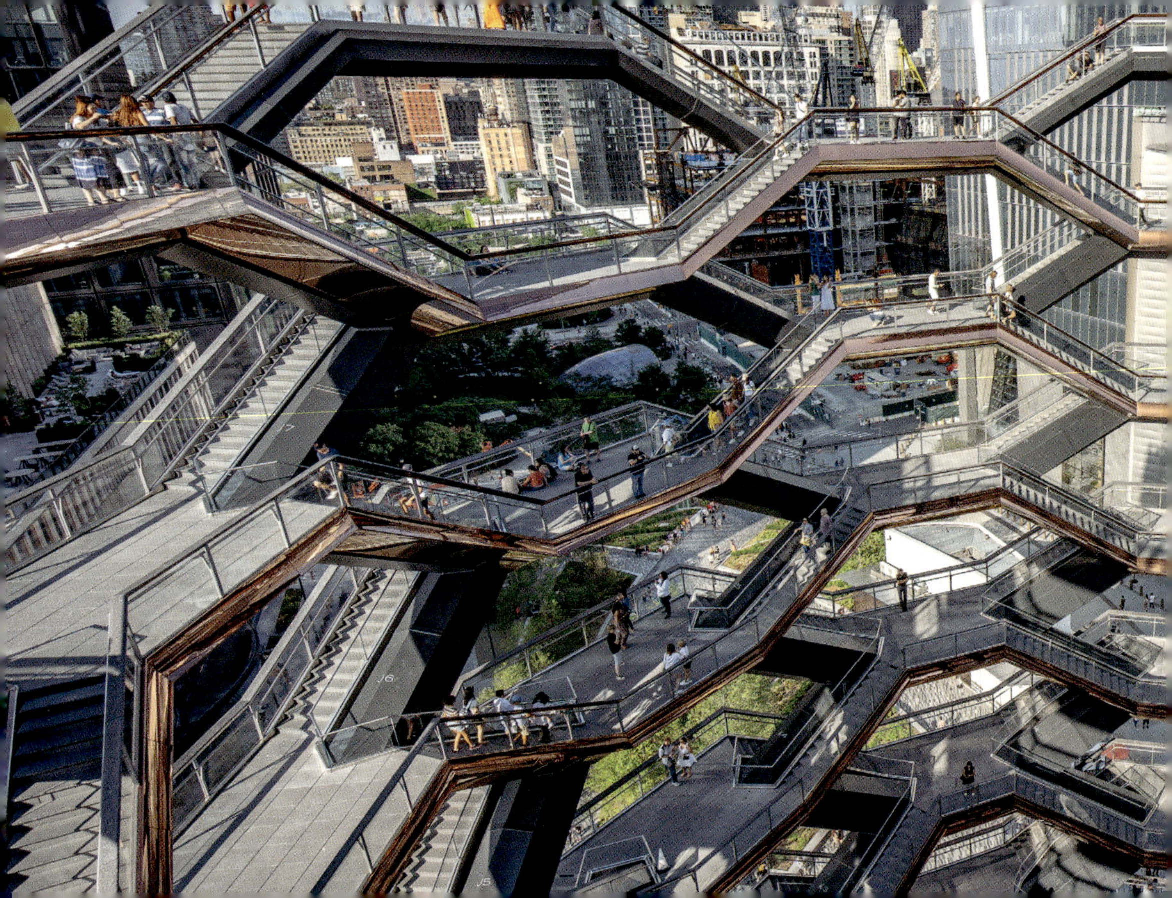

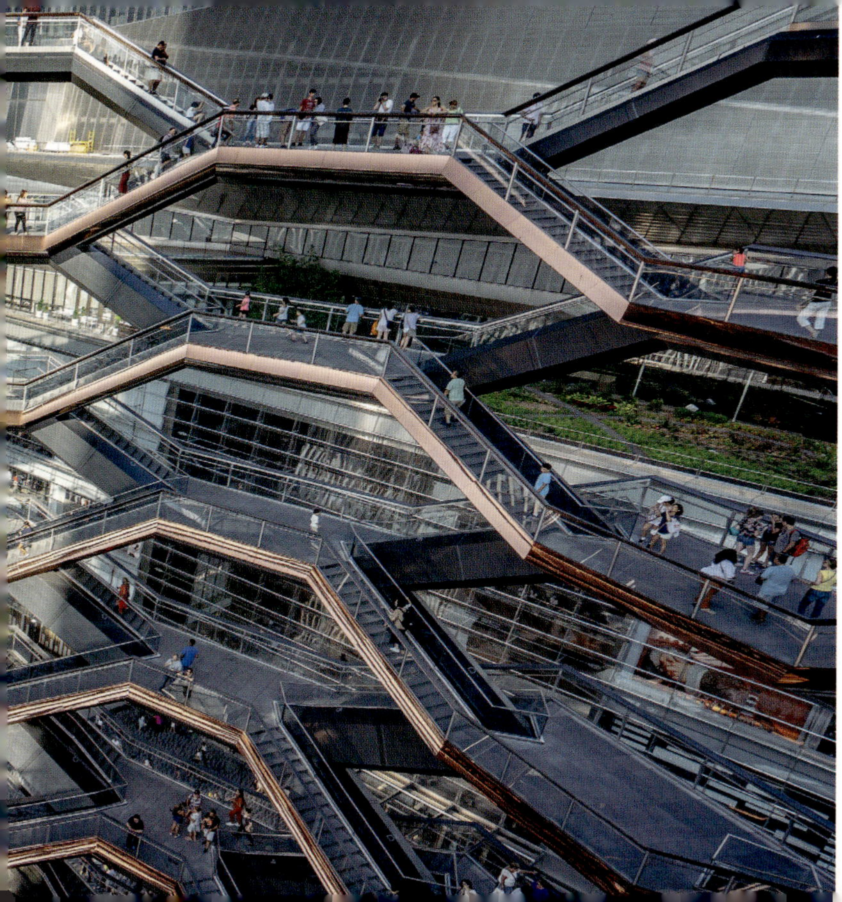

Hudson Yards

Once occupied by rail yards, this mixed-use development is planned to be completed in 2024. About a dozen high-rise buildings are slated for residents, businesses, shops and restaurants. Development plans include a 2.4 hectare (6 acre) public plaza, a seven-story mall, and visitor attractions like the Vessel (pictured left). This 16-storey, honeycomb, open-air building and public square opened on 15 March 2019.

New York Public Library
After the Library of Congress in Washington DC, the New York Public Library is the second-largest library system in the United States. The main branch of the library is in the Stephen A. Schwarzman Building and contains over 2.5 million volumes.

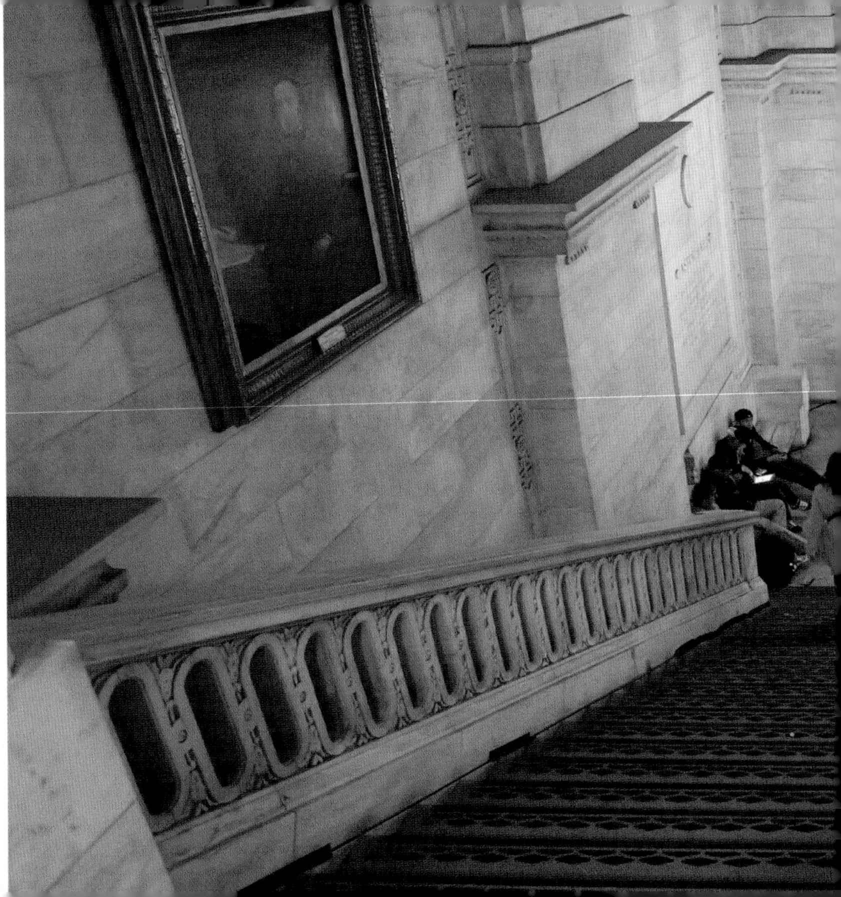

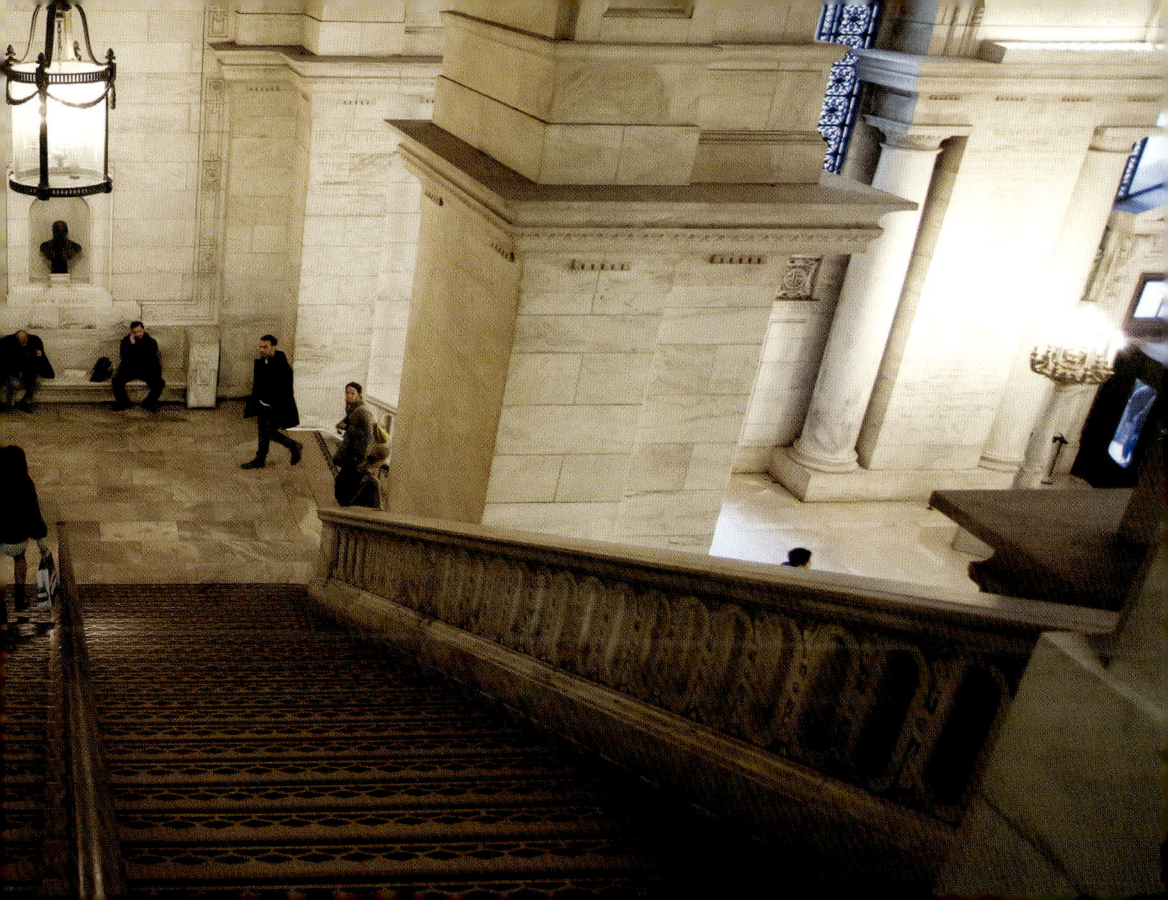

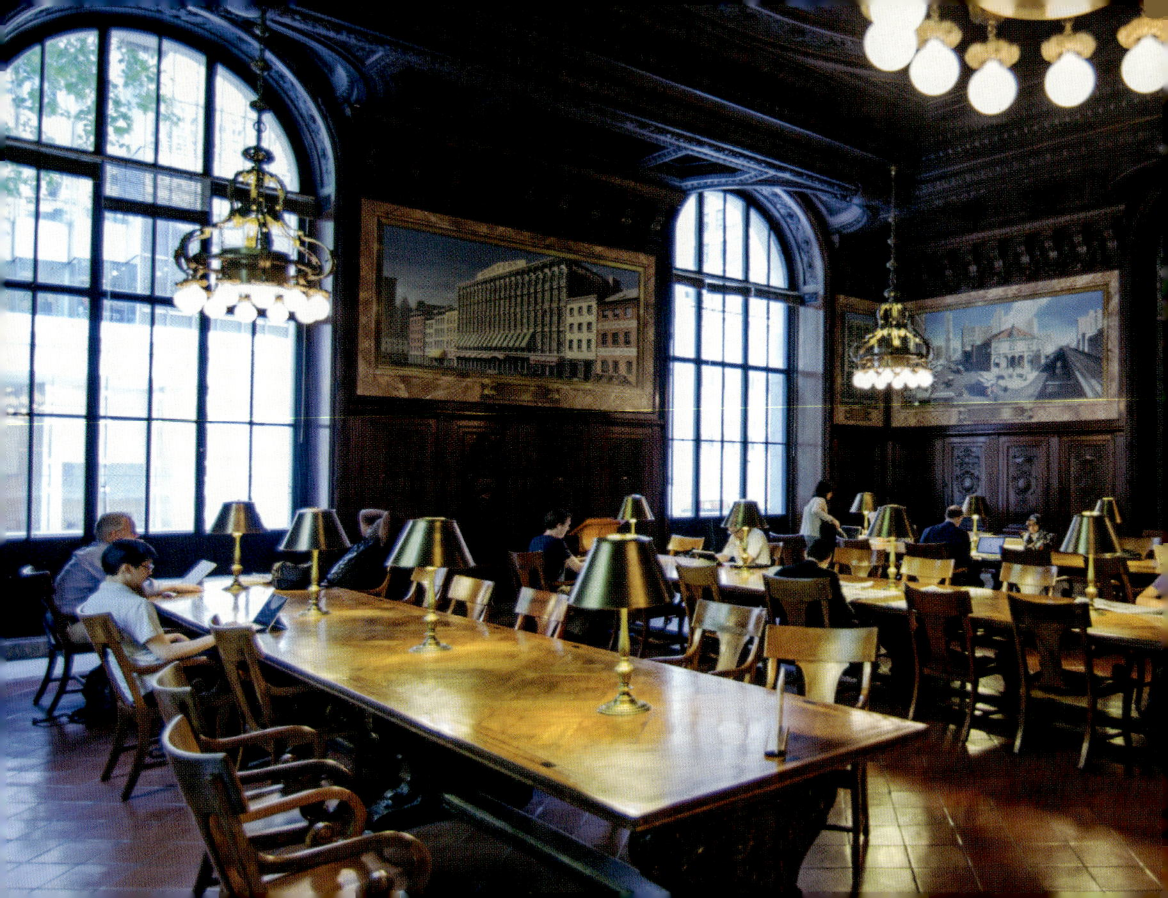

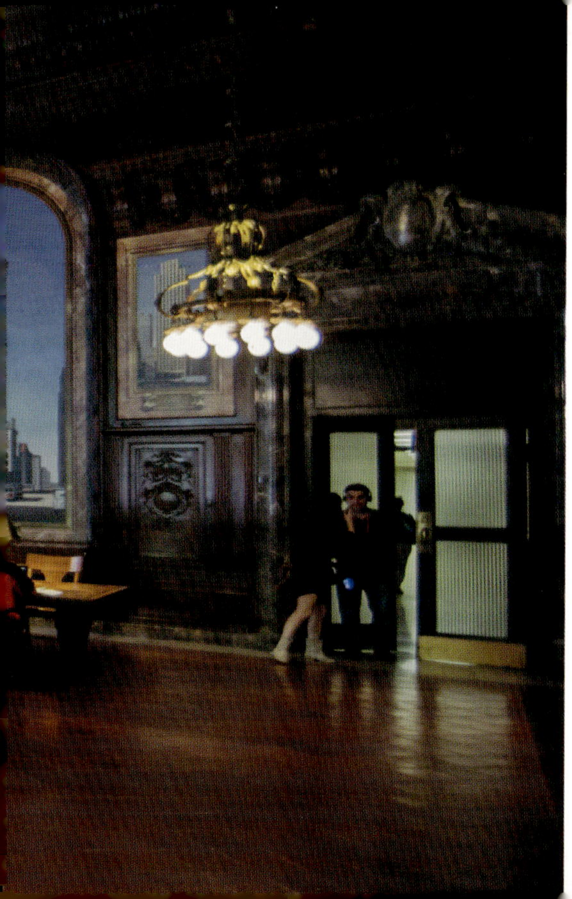

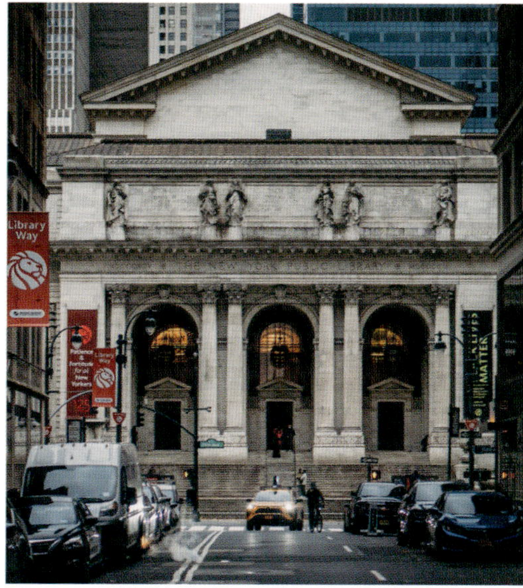

ALL PHOTOGRAPHS:

New York Public Library architecture and interior
East of Bryant Park, the main branch of the library opened on 23 May 1911 and was declared a National Historic Landmark in 1967. Visitors looking for a quiet place to read or study can do so in the Rose Main Reading Room.

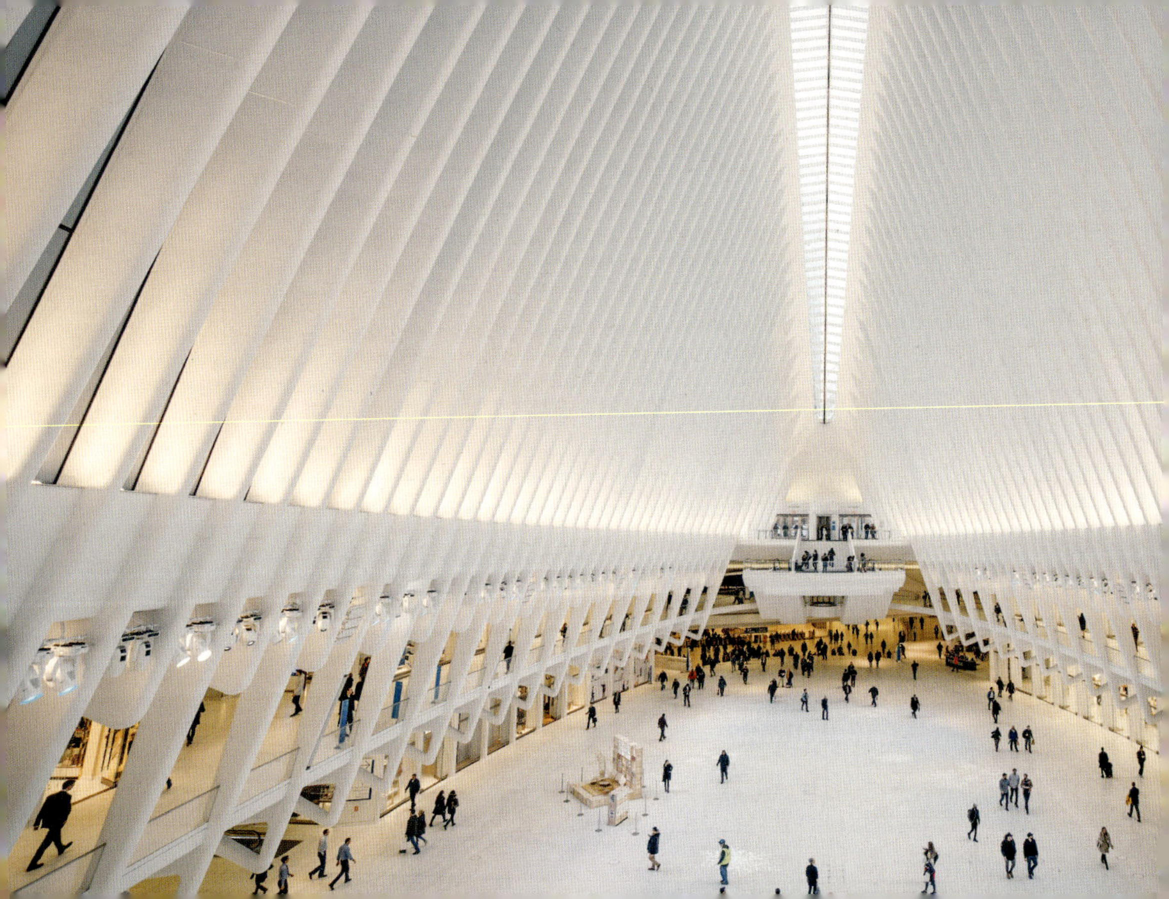

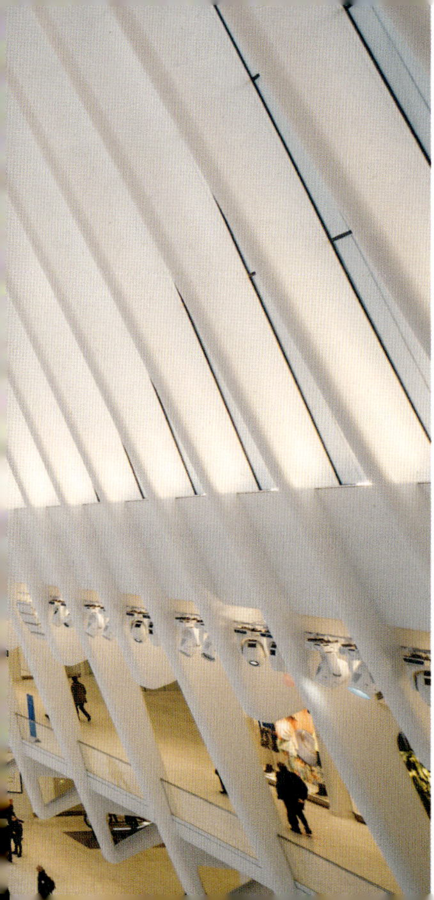

ALL PHOTOGRAPHS:

One World Trade Center

Opened in October 2014 and standing at a height of 541m (1,776ft), this landmark building is the tallest structure in the Western Hemisphere. At night, a concentrated beam of light emanates from the top of the building, rising up into the dark sky.

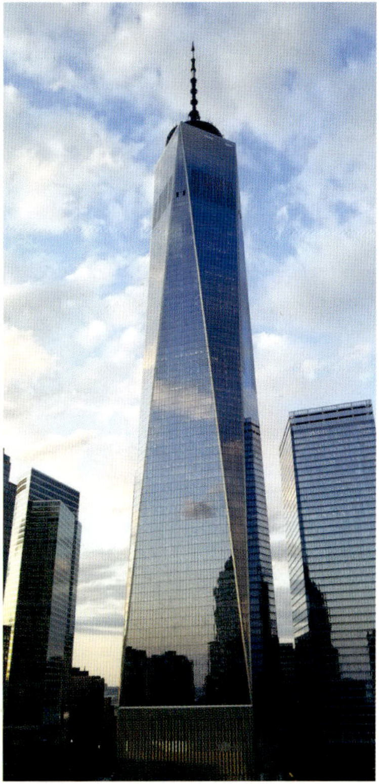

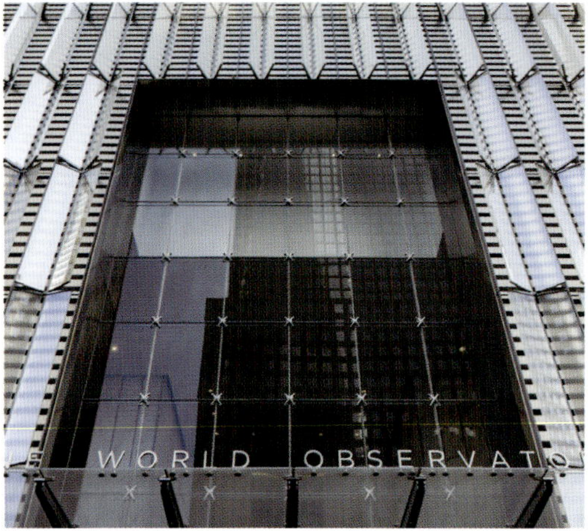

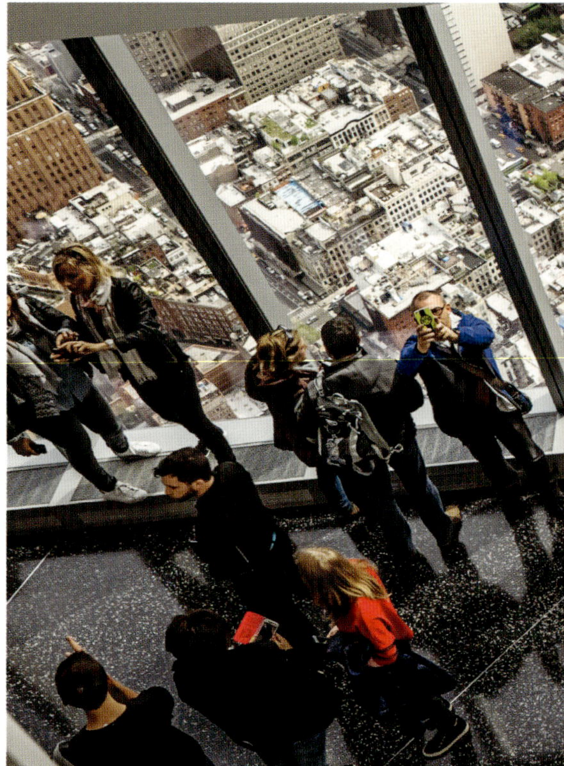

ALL PHOTOGRAPHS:

One World Observatory

High-speed elevators take visitors up 102 stories in 47 seconds, offering an audio-visual experience unique to this building and a breathtaking experience of New York City. And this is even before they step onto the observatory, located 541m (1,250ft) above ground level.

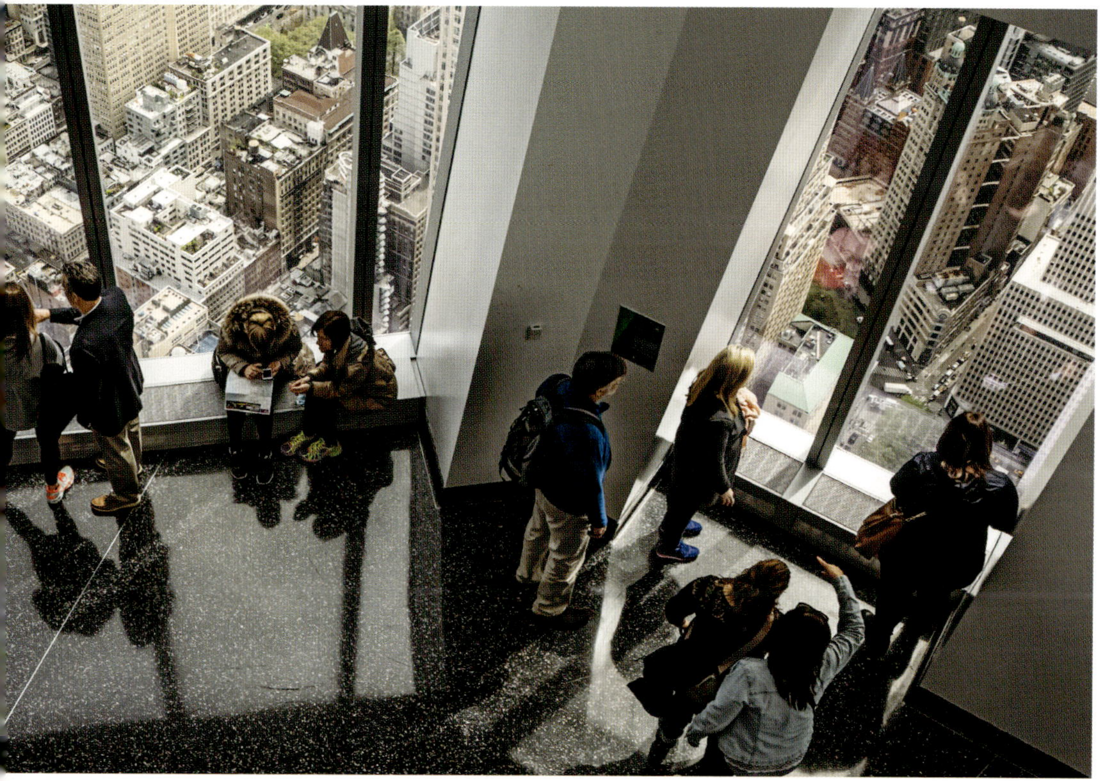

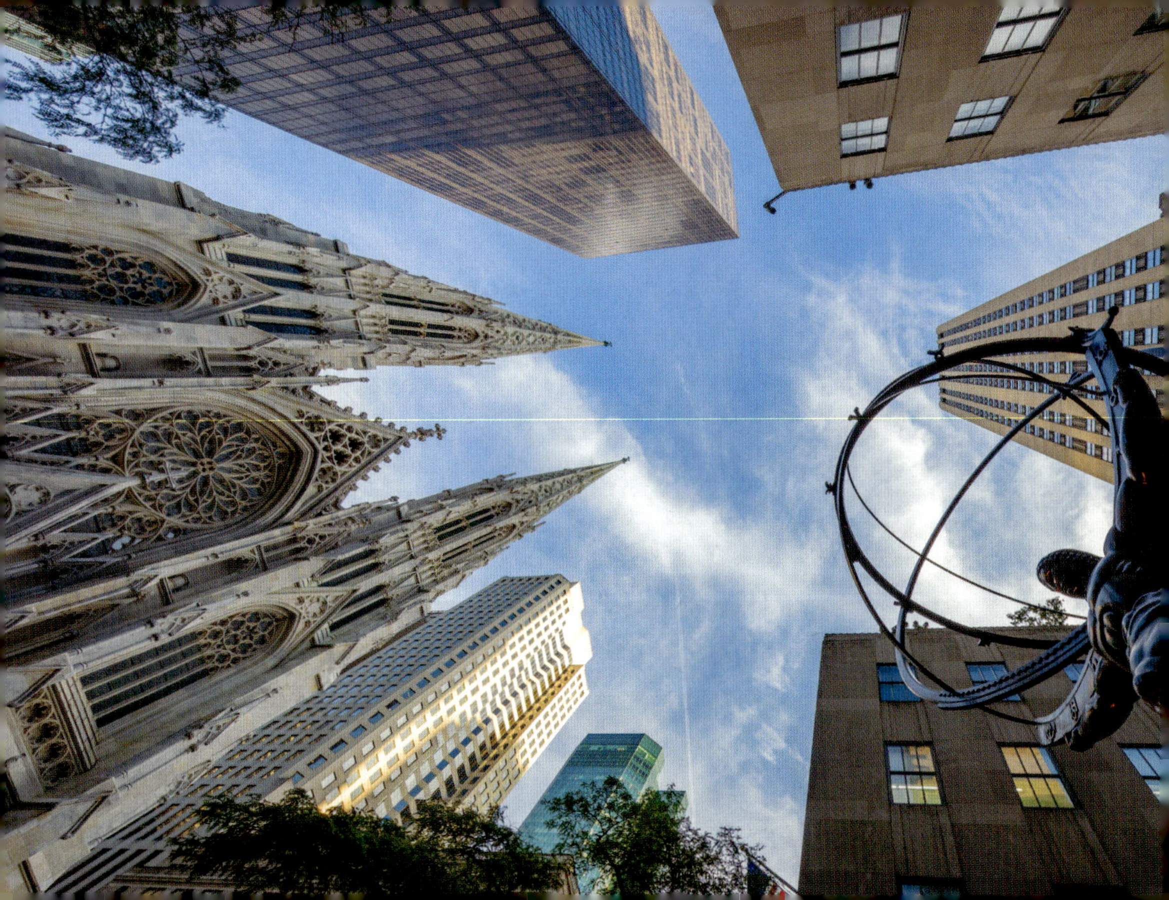

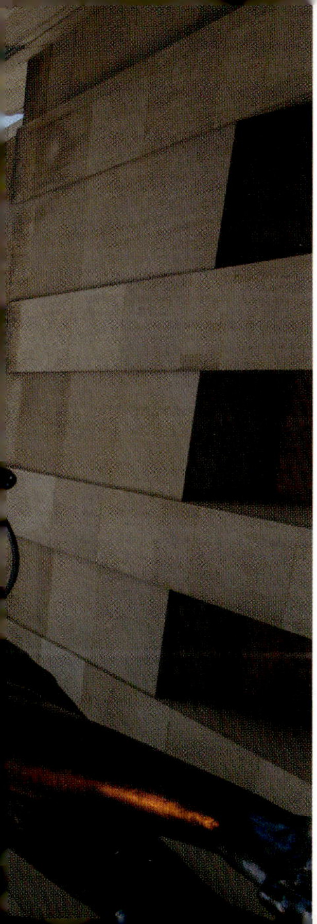

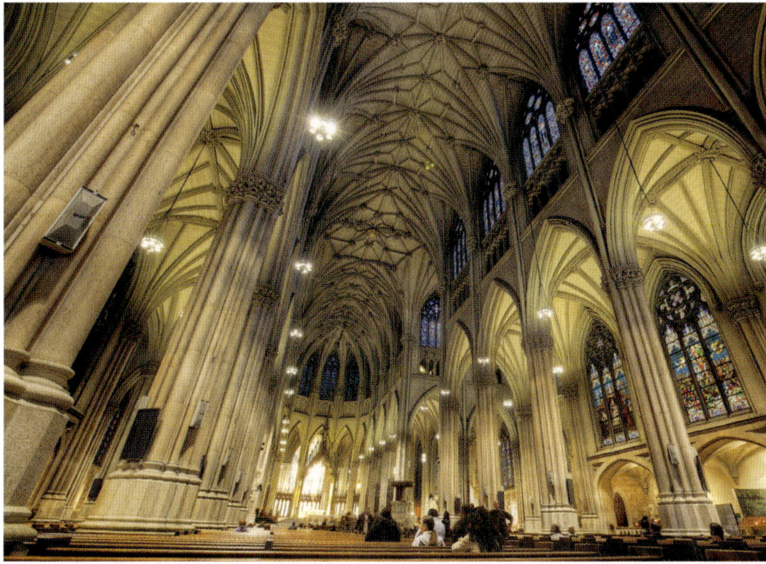

ALL PHOTOGRAPHS:

St Patrick's Cathedral

Known as 'America's Parish Church', the cathedral occupies one city block in Midtown Manhattan. Two giant bronze doors invite an estimated 5 million annual visitors into an intricately designed interior of Italian marble and stone.

ALL PHOTOGRAPHS:

Rockefeller Center

Erum Radio City Music Hall, 30 Rockefeller Plaza (aka 30 Rock), and The Rink – accompanied by the annual Christmas tree – are just a few of the popular features of this Midtown Manhattan landmark. Usually a Norway spruce, The Rockefeller Christmas tree goes up in mid-November with an annual lighting broadcast live to millions of people each year.

OVERLEAF:

FDNY Memorial Wall

Dedicated to the 343 firefighters who lost their lives on 11 September 2001, the bronze bas-relief sculpture is 17m (57ft) long and 3.3m (6ft) high.

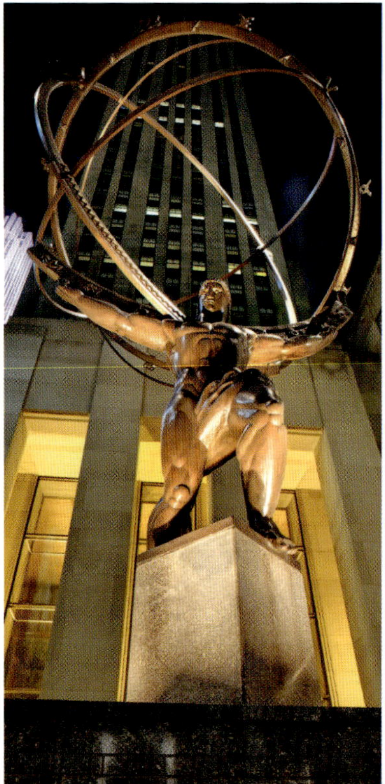

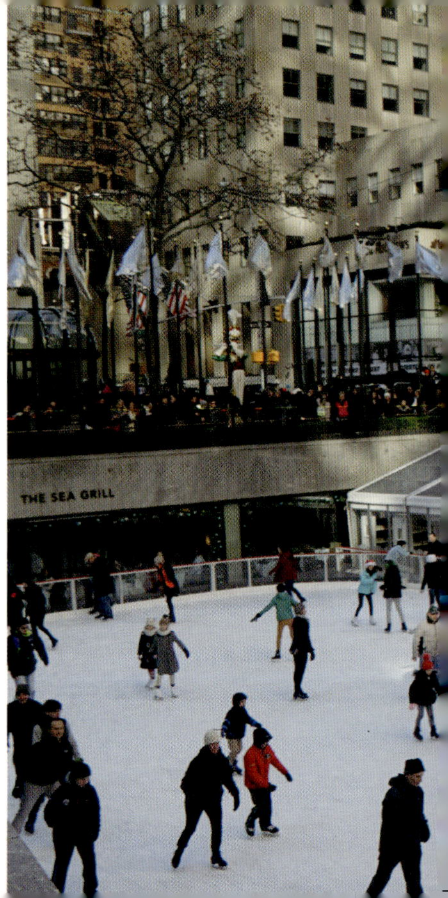

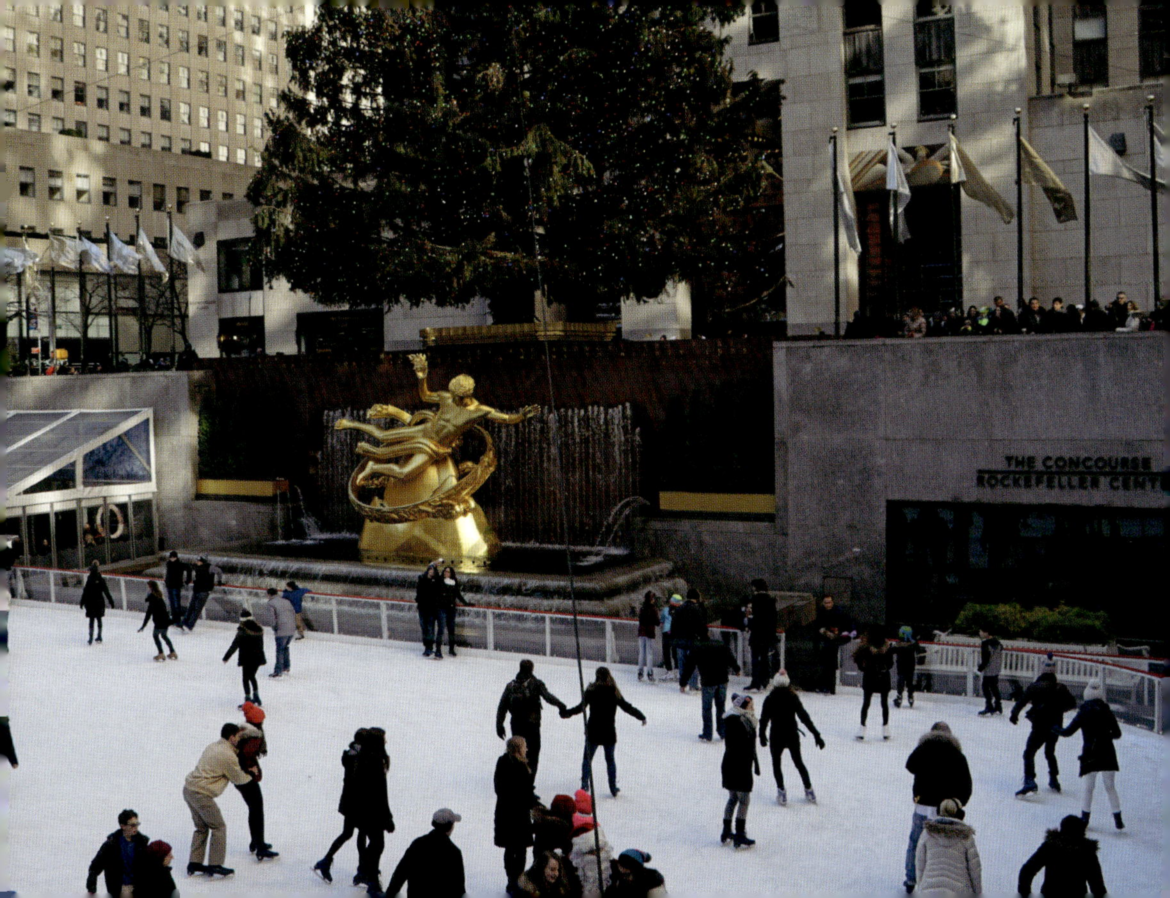
THE CONCOURSE
ROCKEFELLER CENT

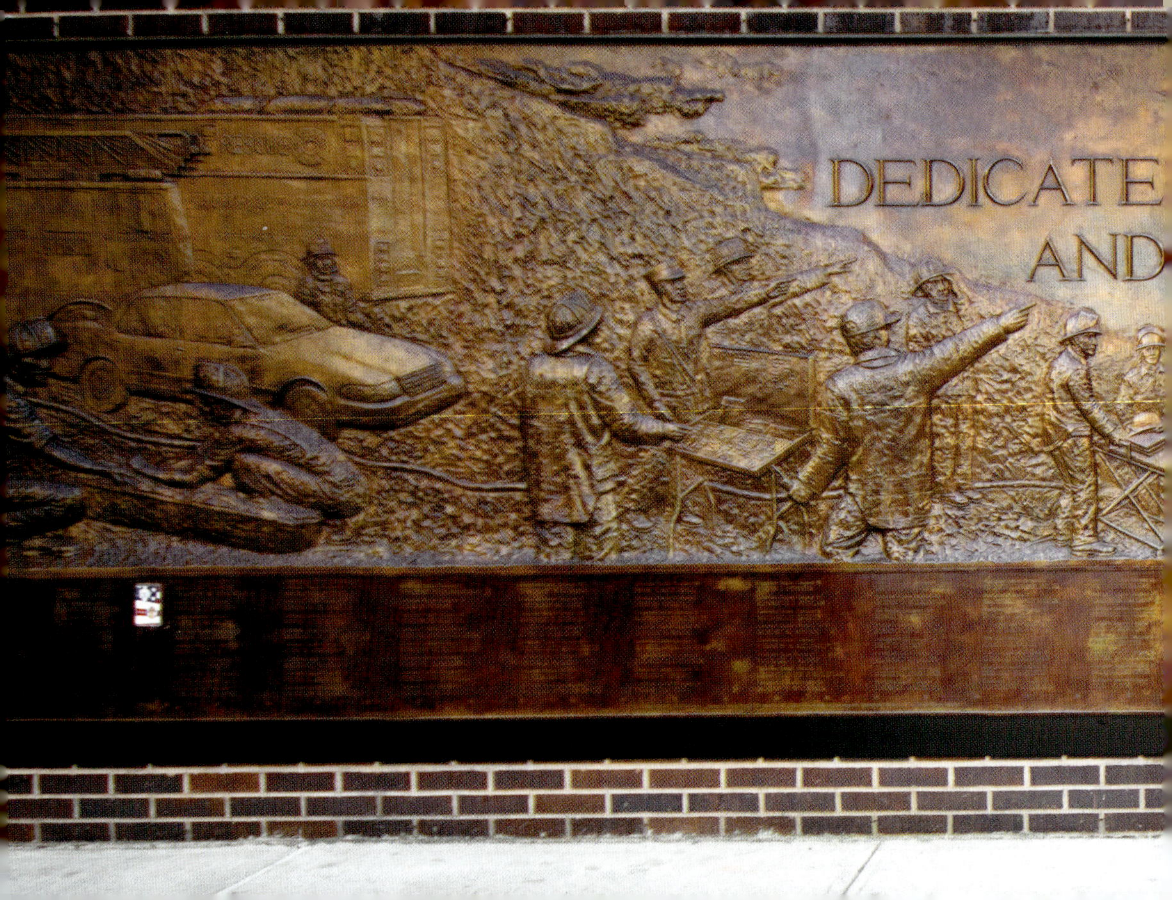
DEDICATE
AND

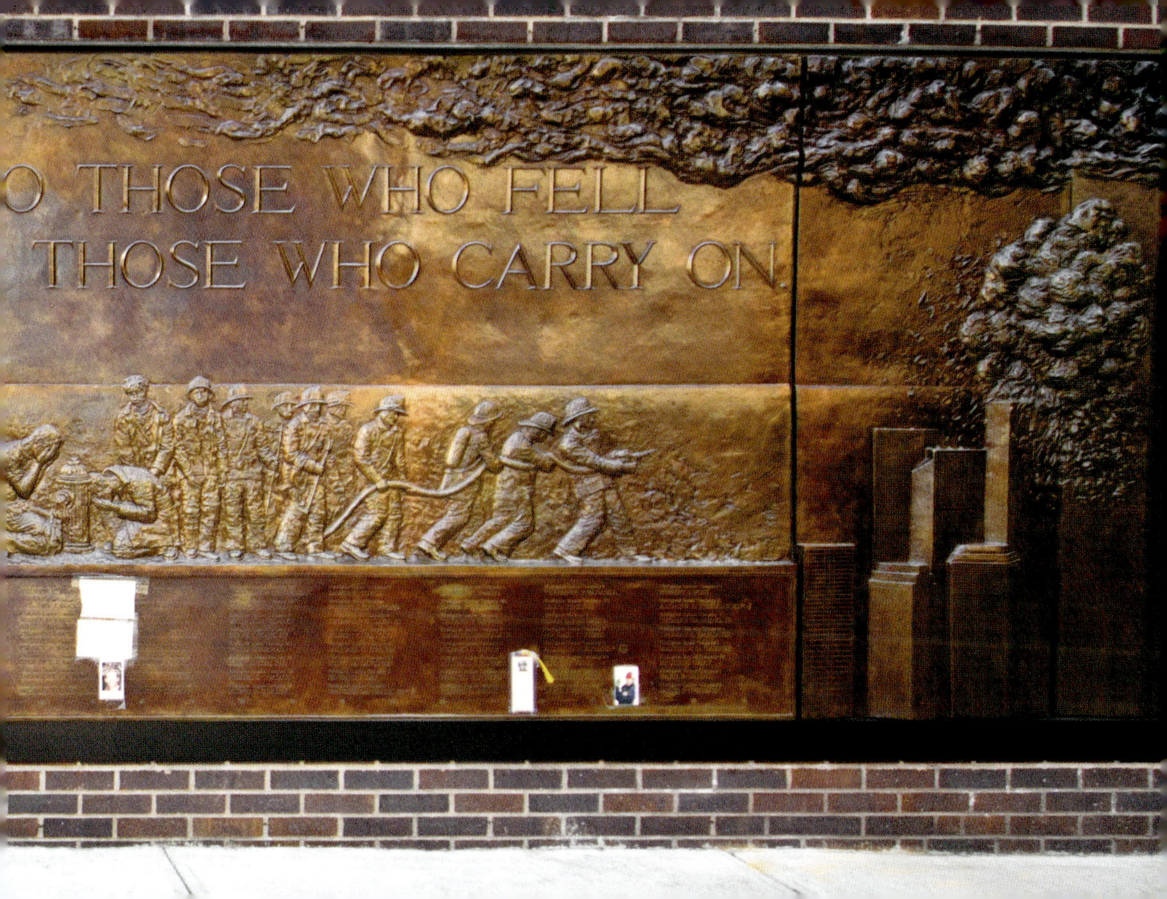
O THOSE WHO FELL
THOSE WHO CARRY ON.

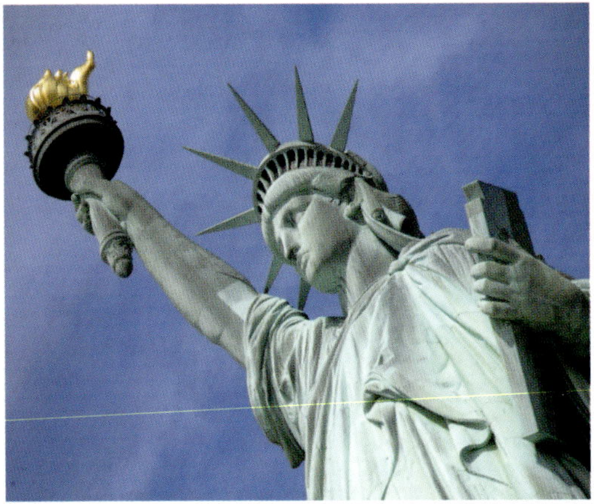

ALL PHOTOGRAPHS:
Statue of Liberty
Gifted by France and dedicated on 28 October 1886, this statue was one of the first structures to be seen by immigrants entering the United States in the late 19th and 20th centuries. At the time it was built, the statue cost $250,000 – about $5.4 million (£4 million) today. The tablet she holds displays the date of the Declaration of Independence in Roman numerals: 4 July 1776.

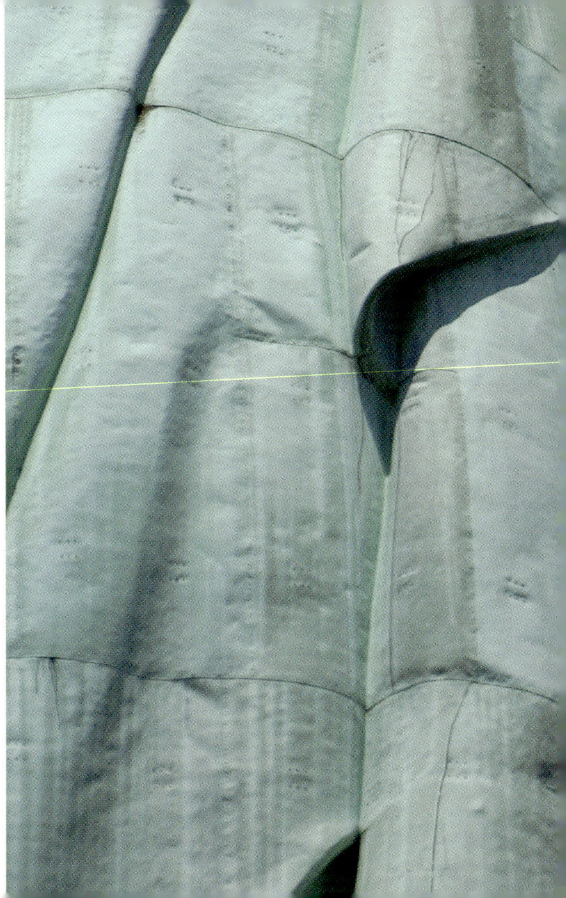

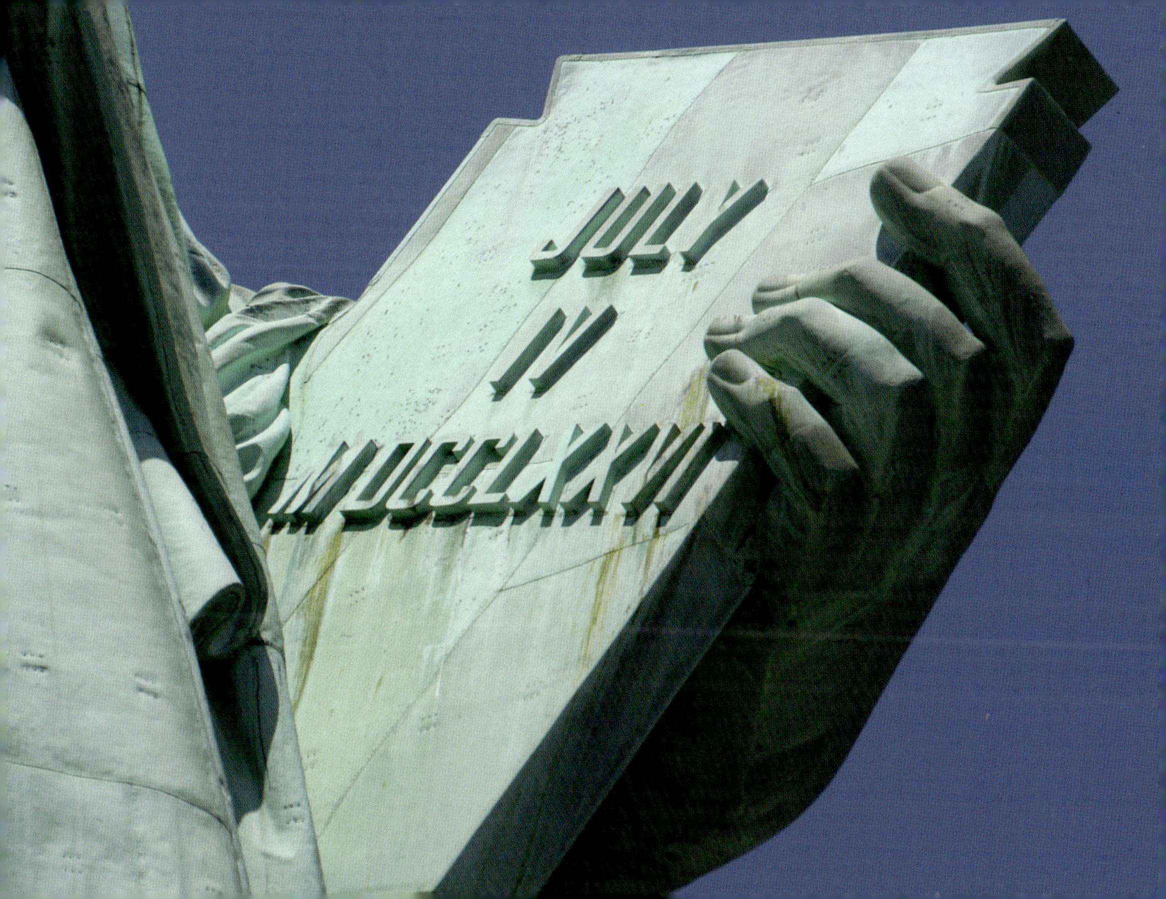
JULY
IV

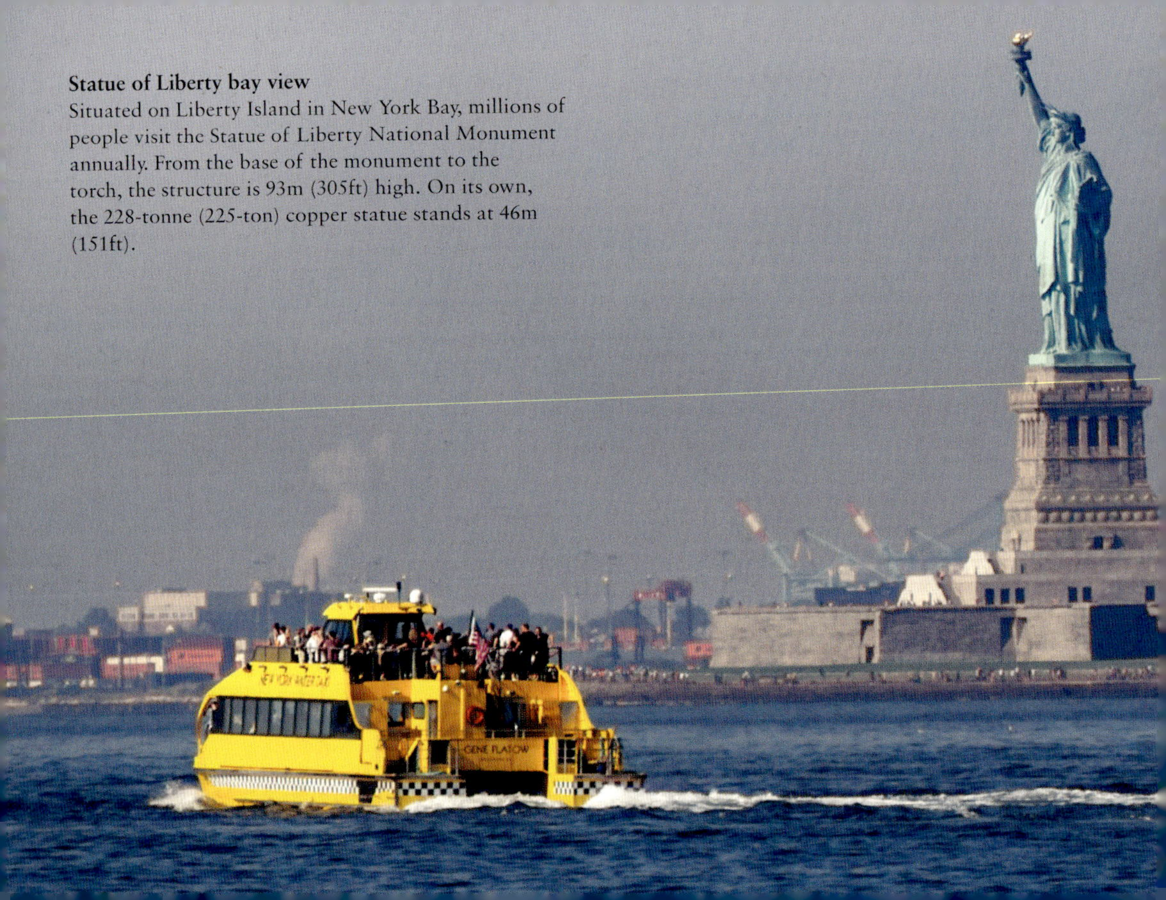

Statue of Liberty bay view

Situated on Liberty Island in New York Bay, millions of people visit the Statue of Liberty National Monument annually. From the base of the monument to the torch, the structure is 93m (305ft) high. On its own, the 228-tonne (225-ton) copper statue stands at 46m (151ft).

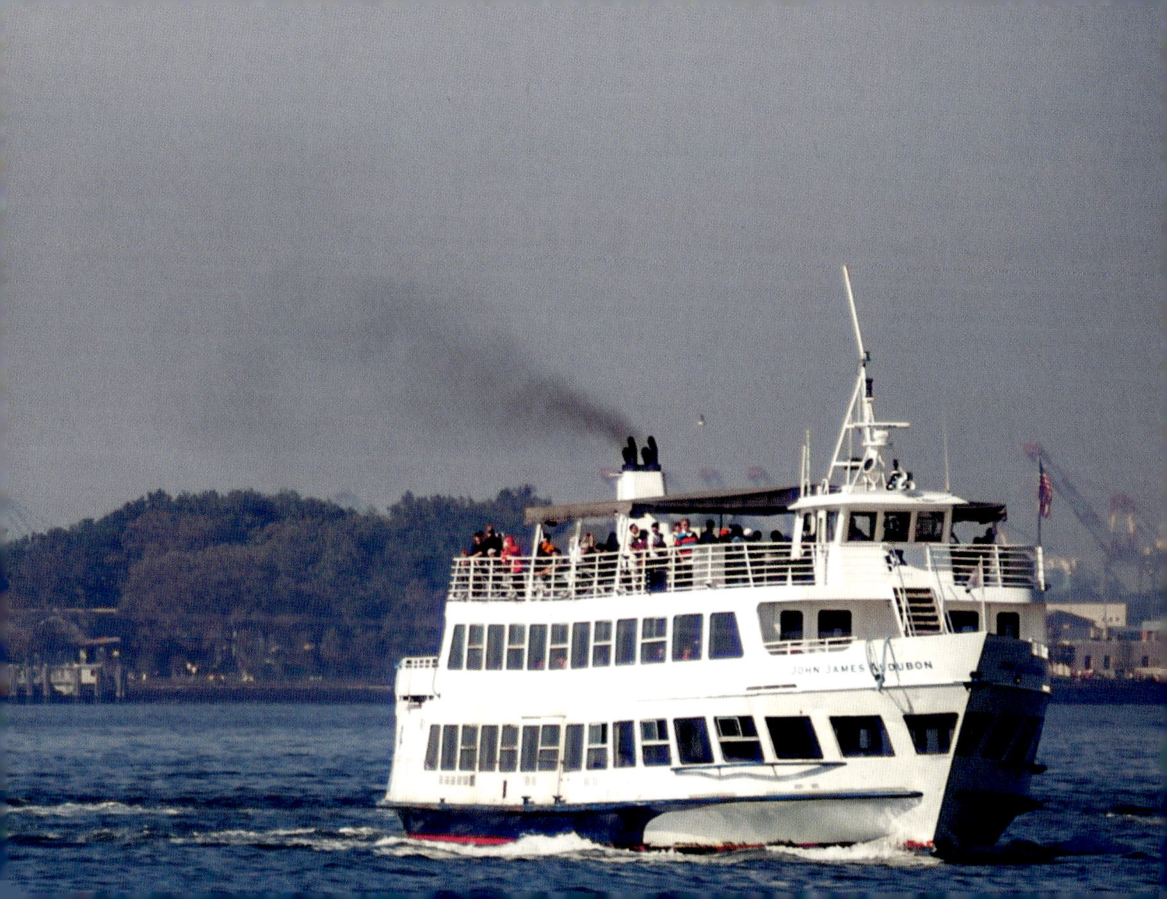
JOHN JAMES AUDUBON

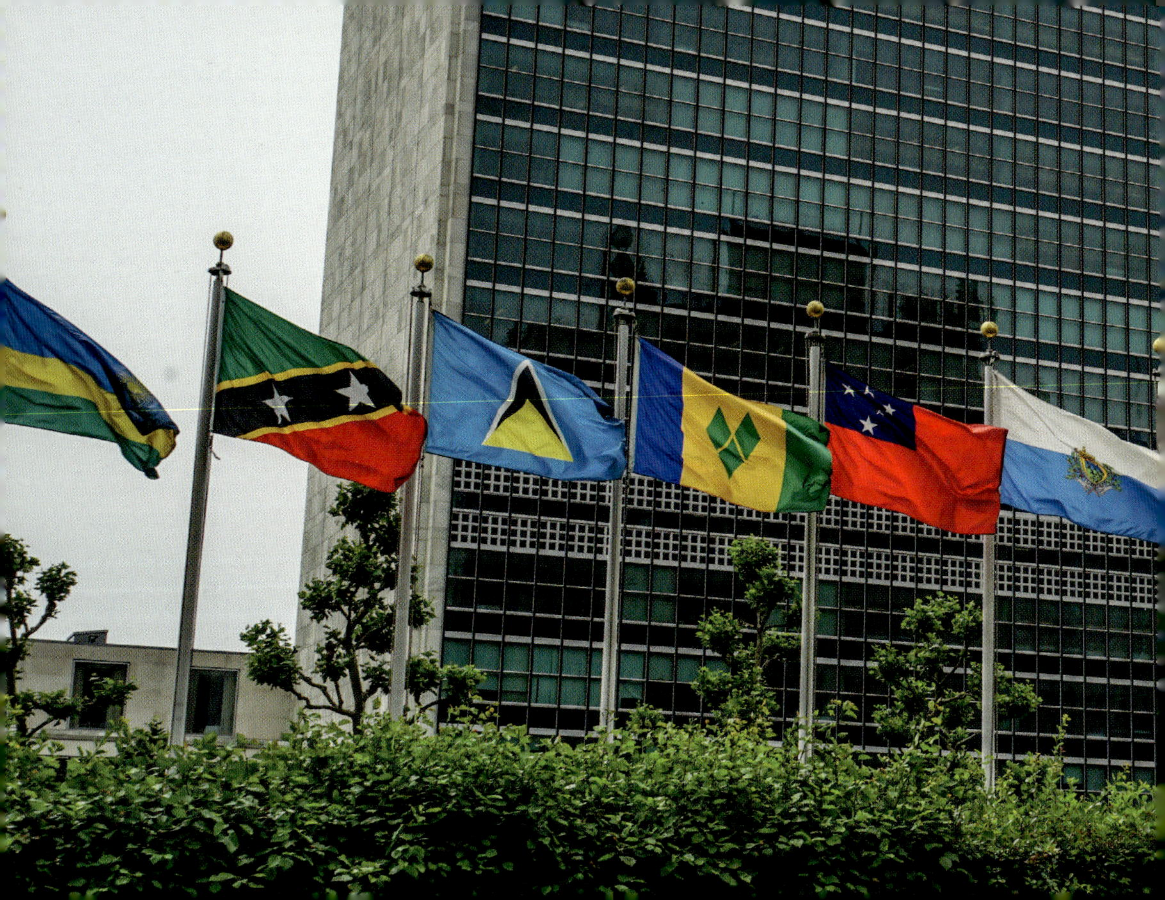

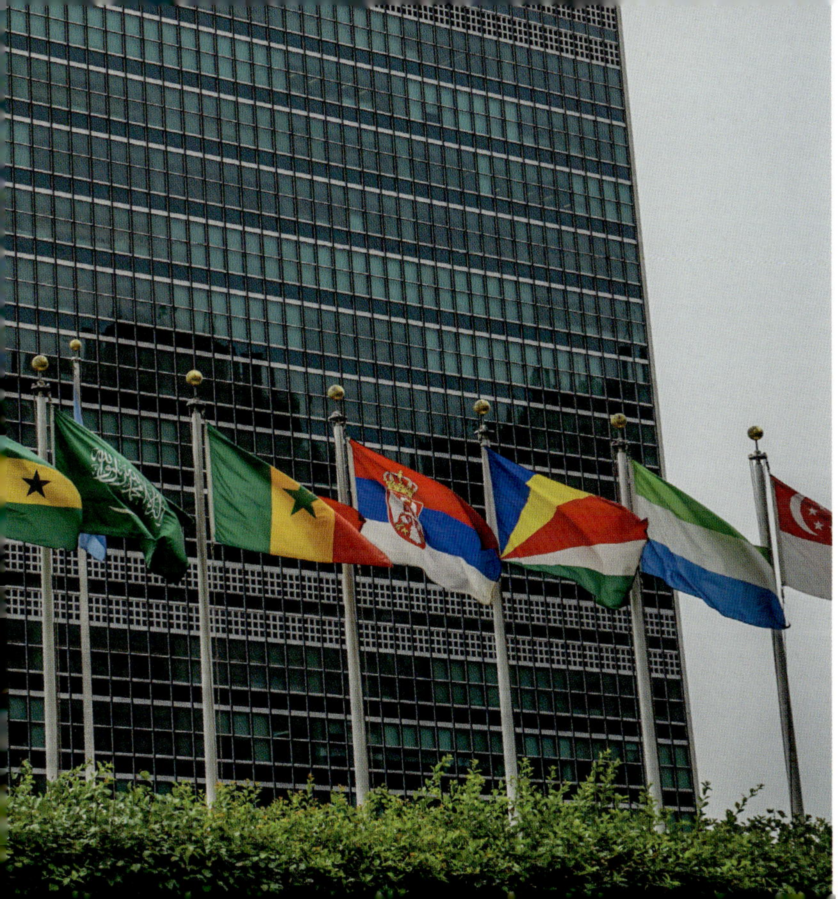

United Nations HQ
Located at 760 United Nations Plaza, the UN is an international organisation established in 1945, after the end of World War II. Originally composed of 51 countries, this intergovernmental body was founded to promote and maintain world peace, protect human rights, uphold international law, and deliver aid and support to countries in need. Currently made up of 193 countries, representatives from around the world meet annually from September to December.

ALL PHOTOGRAPHS:

United Nations sculpture
Signed on 26 June 1945, one of the key mandates in the UN Charter is that all member states work to promote universal respect for human rights and fundamental freedoms. The Knotted Gun, a bronze sculpture located outside the UN Headquarters, represents the UN's commitment to non-violence.

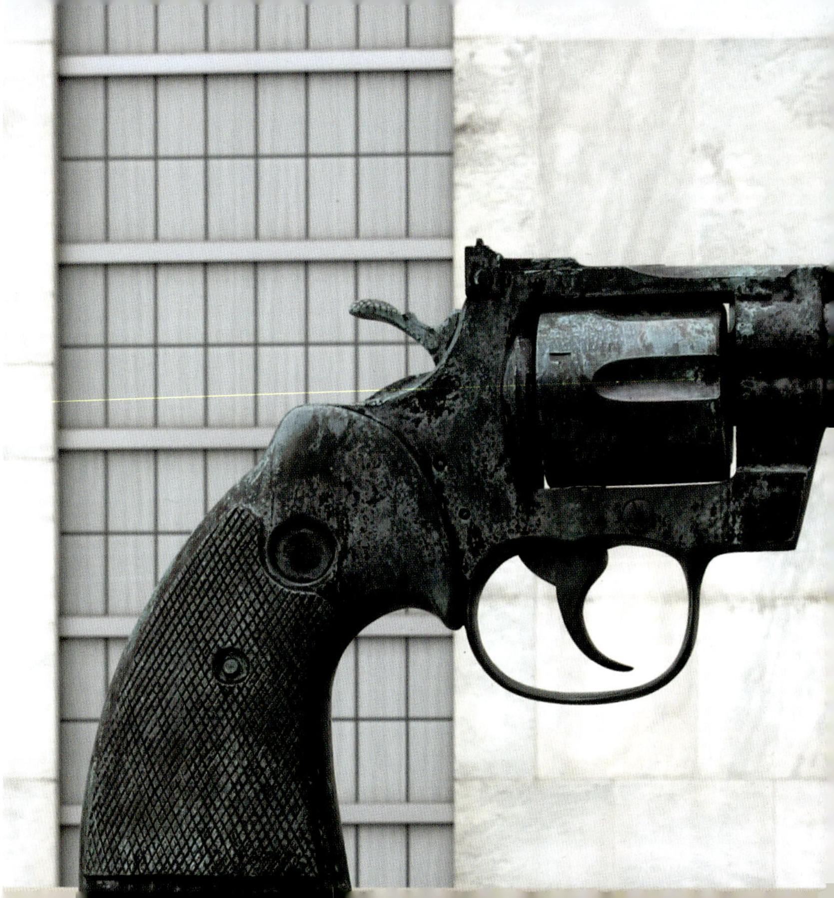

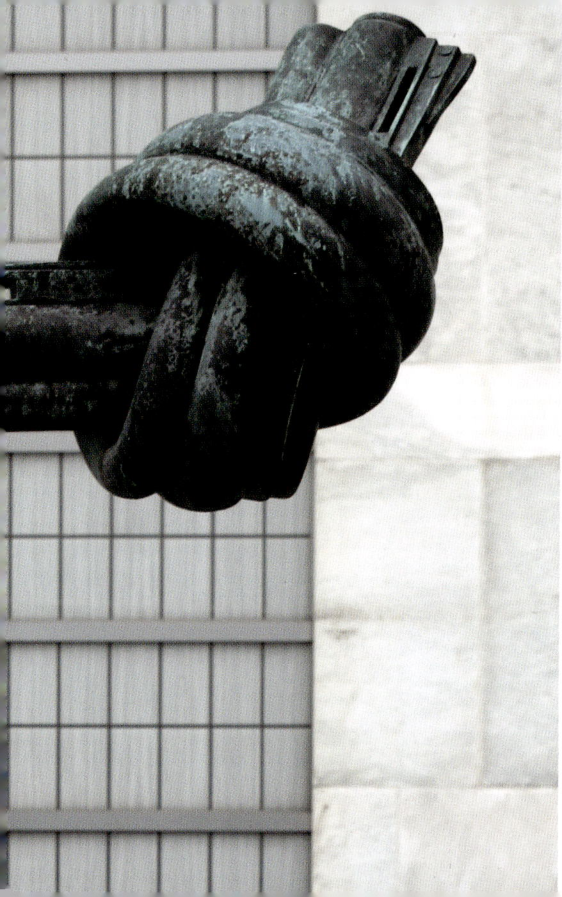

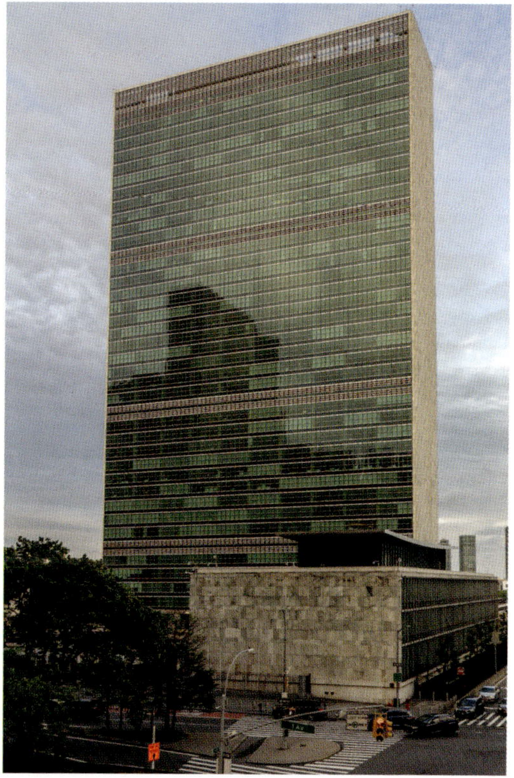

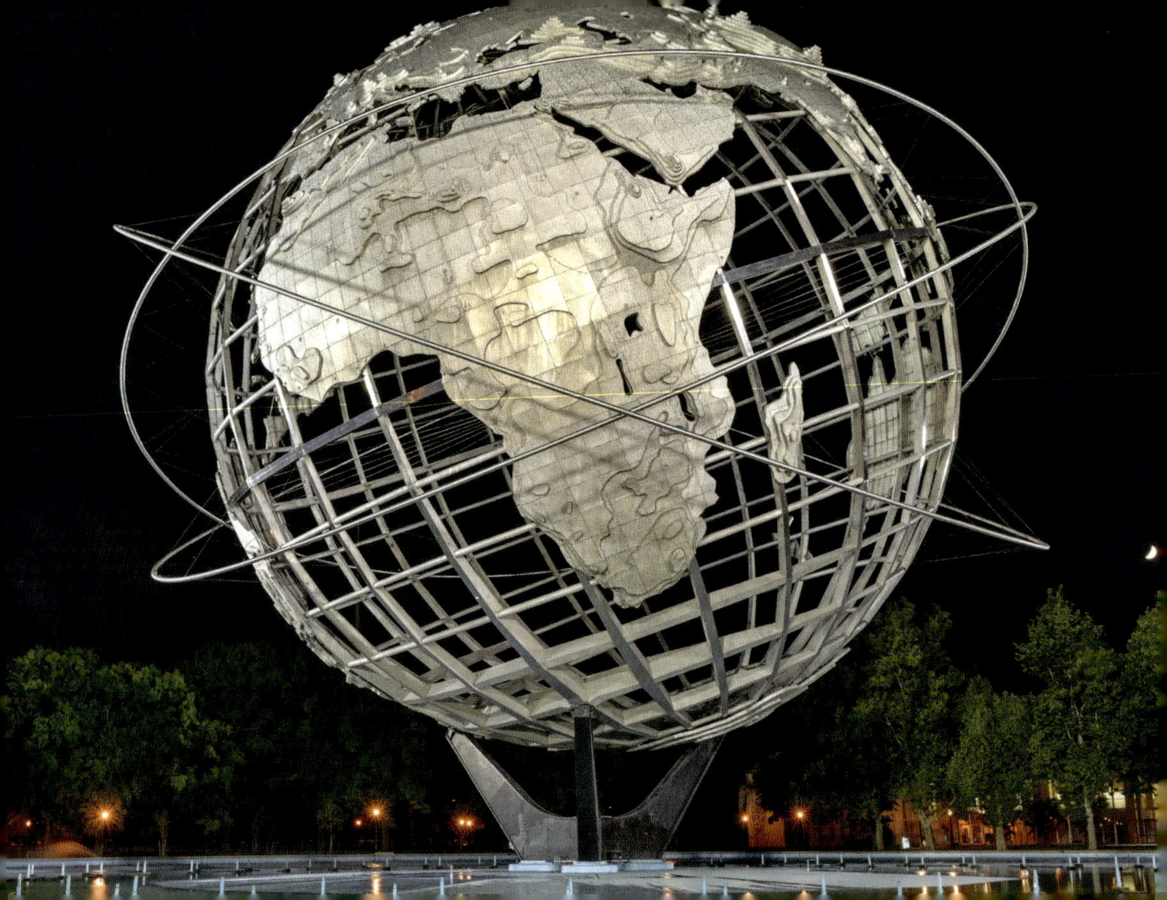

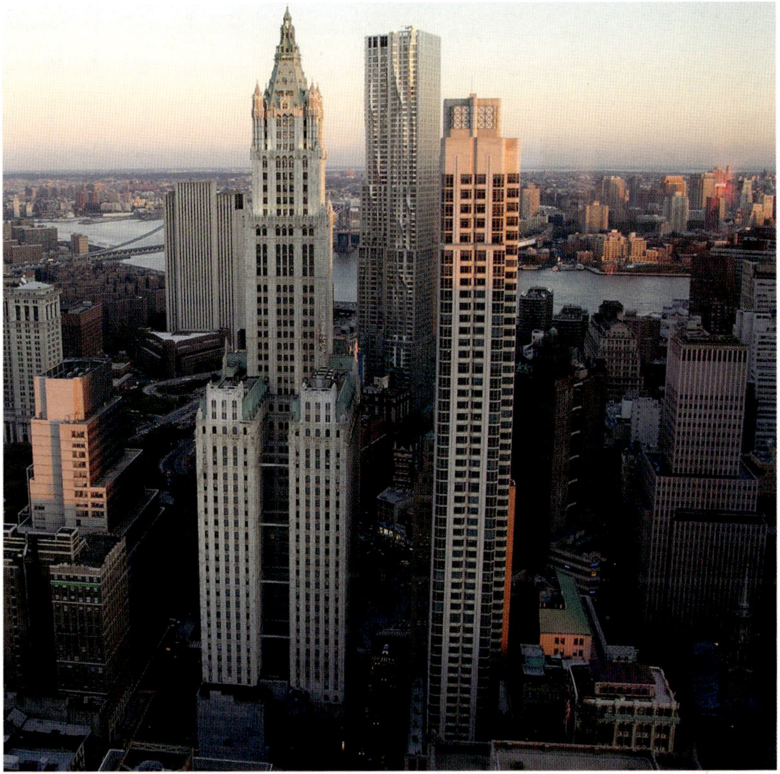

OPPOSITE:
Unisphere
Found in Queens, in Flushing Meadow Corona Park, this aluminum globe of the world's continents was commissioned for the 1965 World's Fair, which had a theme of 'Peace Through Understanding'.

LEFT:
Woolworth Building
Completed in 1913, this was the tallest building in the world until 1930. Named a National Historic Landmark in 1966, the 241m (792ft) building is in the Tribeca district in Lower Manhattan.

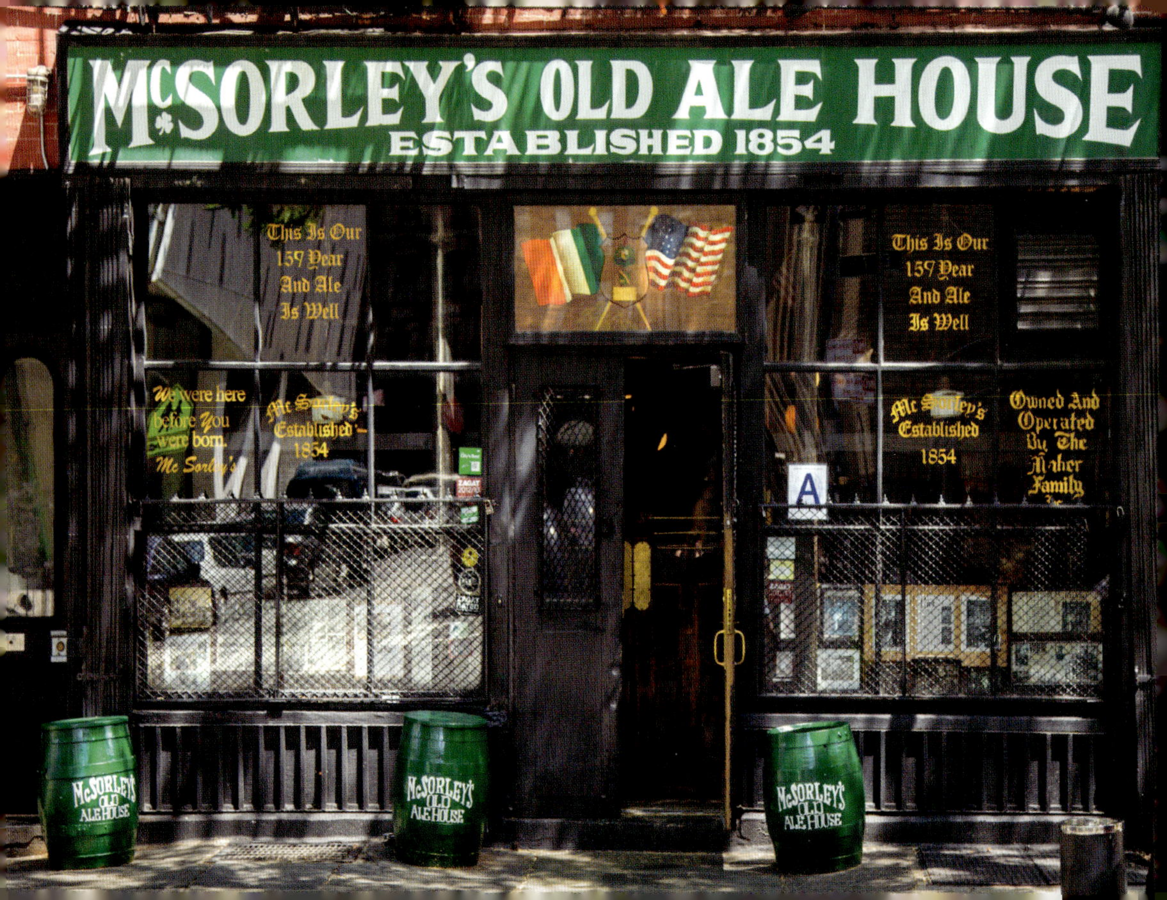

McSORLEY'S OLD ALE HOUSE
ESTABLISHED 1854
This Is Our
159 Year
And Ale
Is Well
We were here
before You
were born.
Mc Sorley's
Mc Sorley's
Established
1854
Owned And
Operated
By The
Maher
Family
A
McSORLEY'S
OLD
ALE HOUSE

Eating and Drinking

Though many cities around the world are known for their great restaurants and food, none can boast the same level of variety that New York City has to offer. Thanks to its large immigrant population, dishes and delicacies from all corners of the globe have found representation across all five boroughs and in all districts of the city. Whether it's Thai, Italian, Greek, Mexican, Moroccan or the American fare of burgers, chicken wings and hot dogs, there is something for every taste and palate.

Any resident or visitor would agree that it's practically impossible to walk a city block without passing a restaurant, bakery, diner or food truck. Whether it's a slice of New York pizza, deli sandwiches stacked high with meat, or $5 street-side lunch specials, New York is a city for foodies.

For many, exploring the city's sights and landmarks also includes discovering the culinary delights it has to offer. From bagels for breakfast and dumplings in Chinatown for lunch, to an evening enjoying tapas and drinks in one of the many city rooftop bars, the options are plentiful. Dining in New York is more than just eating. It's an activity that will engage the senses. Sight, smell, touch and taste easily intermingle and complement each other in this city of over 24,000 restaurants, 1,700 cafes, and 20,000 bars and clubs.

OPPOSITE:

McSorley's Old Ale House

The oldest Irish bar in New York City, McSorley's opened in 1854 and has been a fixture in the East Village of Lower Manhattan ever since.

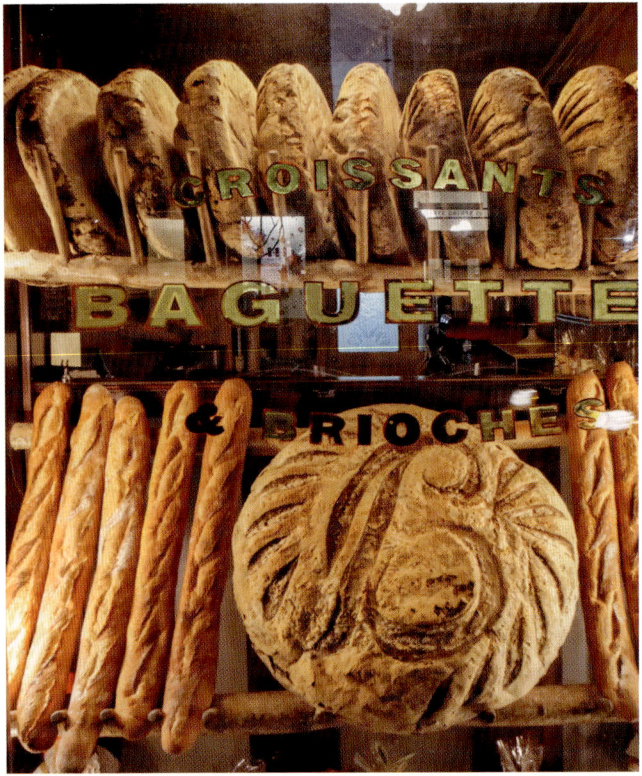
CROISSANTS
BAGUETTE
& BRIOCHES

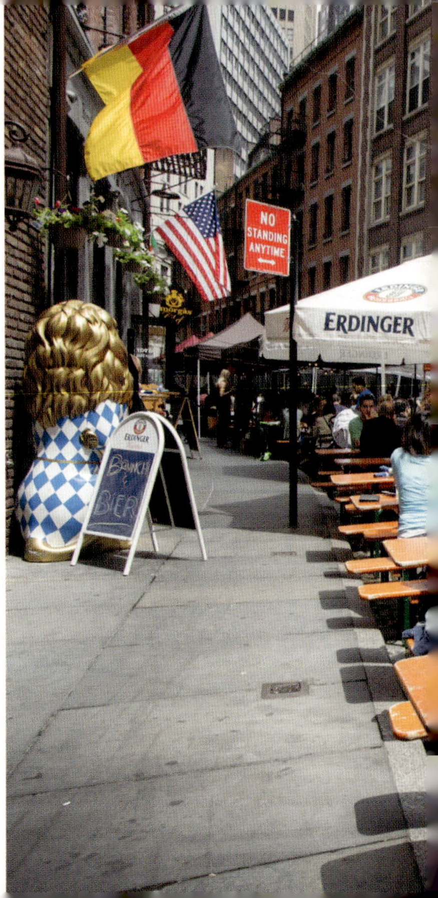
NO STANDING ANYTIME
ERDINGER

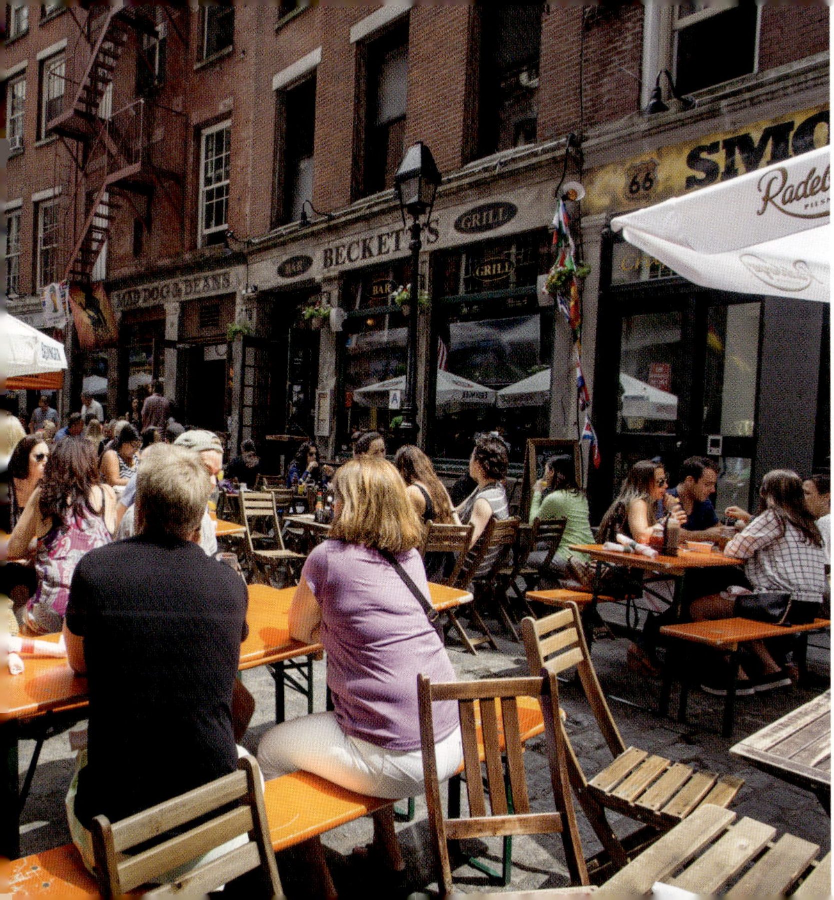

OPPOSITE:

Balthazar Bakery

The window display at Balthazar Bakery offers an easy distraction and enticement for tourists and locals looking to enjoy signature breads, pastries, and a wide selection of other delectable offerings.

LEFT:

Stone Street

This cobblestone street in Lower Manhattan is closed to vehicle traffic allowing diners to enjoy outdoor eating options and a variety of foods offered by the surrounding restaurants and bars.

Zabar's Deli

This specialty deli is located in the Upper West Side of Manhattan on Broadway and 80th Street. Open since 1934, the family-run business founded by Louis Zabar has been providing New Yorkers and visitors with bagels, a variety of cheeses and deli meats, smoked fish and caviar, gourmet sweets, and blends of coffees and teas.

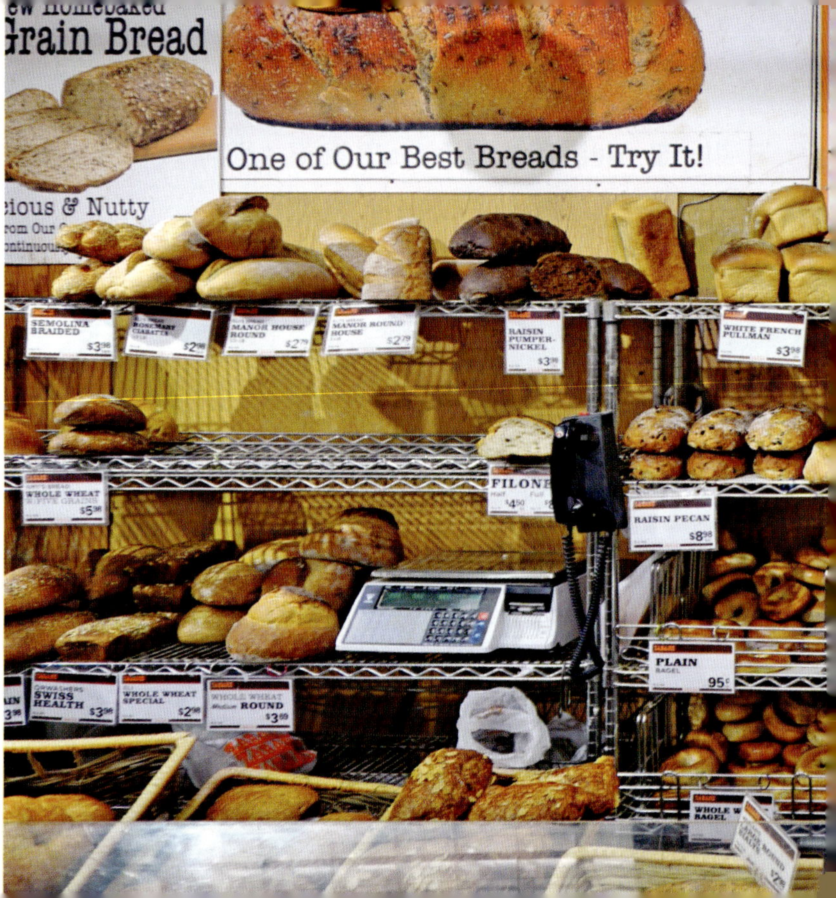

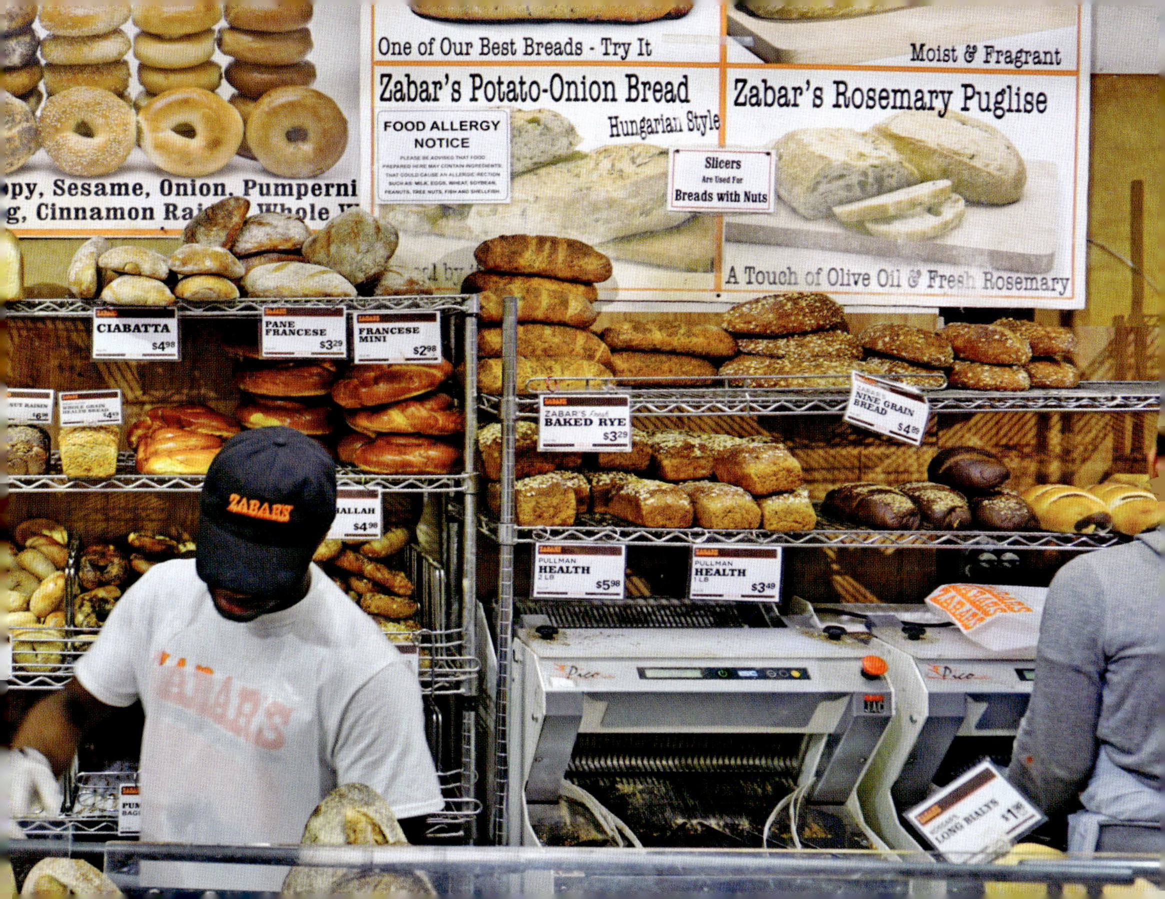
One of Our Best Breads - Try It
Zabar's Potato-Onion Bread
Hungarian Style
FOOD ALLERGY NOTICE
Moist & Fragrant
Zabar's Rosemary Puglise
Slicers
Are Used For
Breads with Nuts
A Touch of Olive Oil & Fresh Rosemary
CIABATTA
$4.98
PANE FRANCESE
$3.29
FRANCESE MINI
$2.98
ZABAR'S Fresh BAKED RYE
$3.29
ZABAR'S NINE GRAIN BREAD
$4.95
PULLMAN HEALTH
2 LB
$5.98
PULLMAN HEALTH
1 LB
$3.49
ZABARS

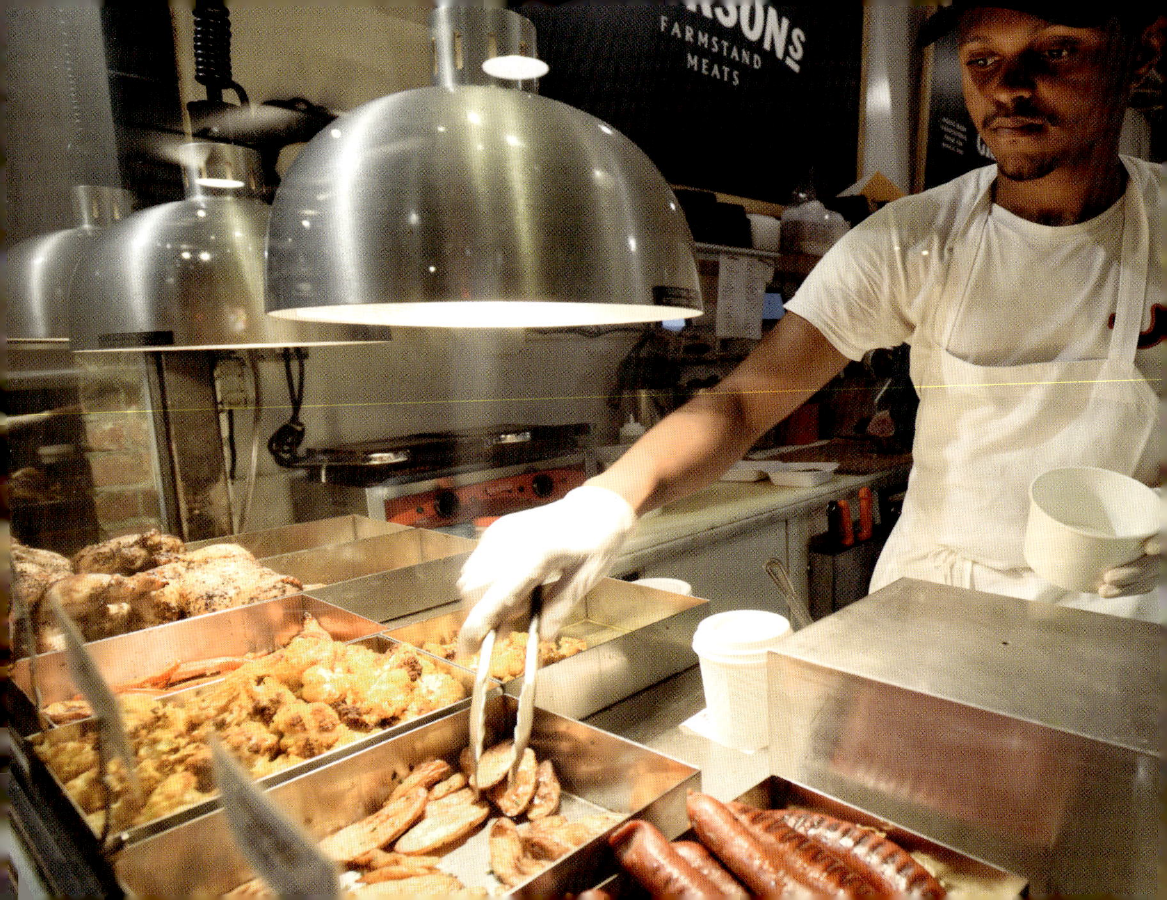
FARMSTAND
MEATS

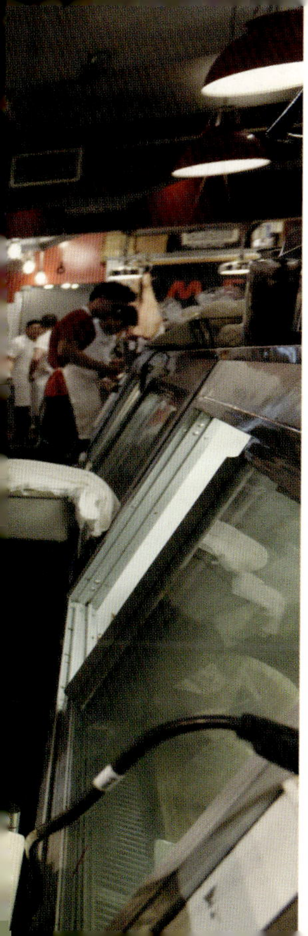

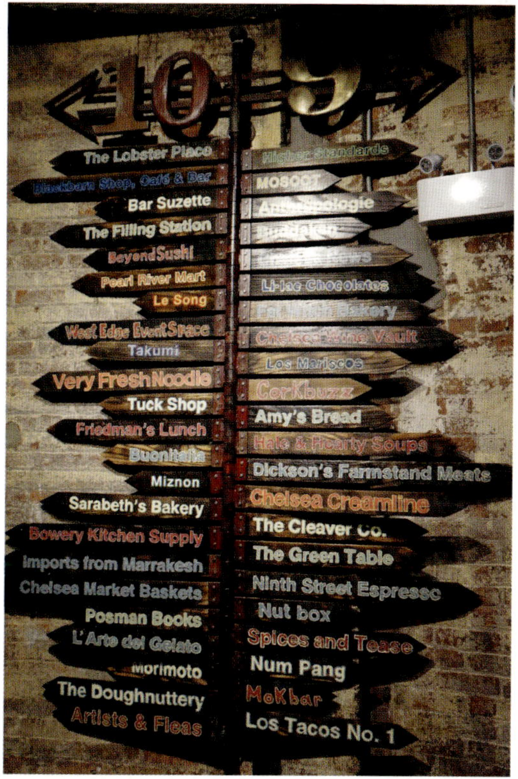

ALL PHOTOGRAPHS:

Chelsea Market food

Occupying an entire city block in the far Westside of Manhattan between 15th and 16th Streets, the market is considered to be the largest indoor food market in the world. Built in the heart of the Meatpacking District, the market has a long history of catering to the needs of visitors and tourists and has seen a resurgence in the late 1990s that continues today.

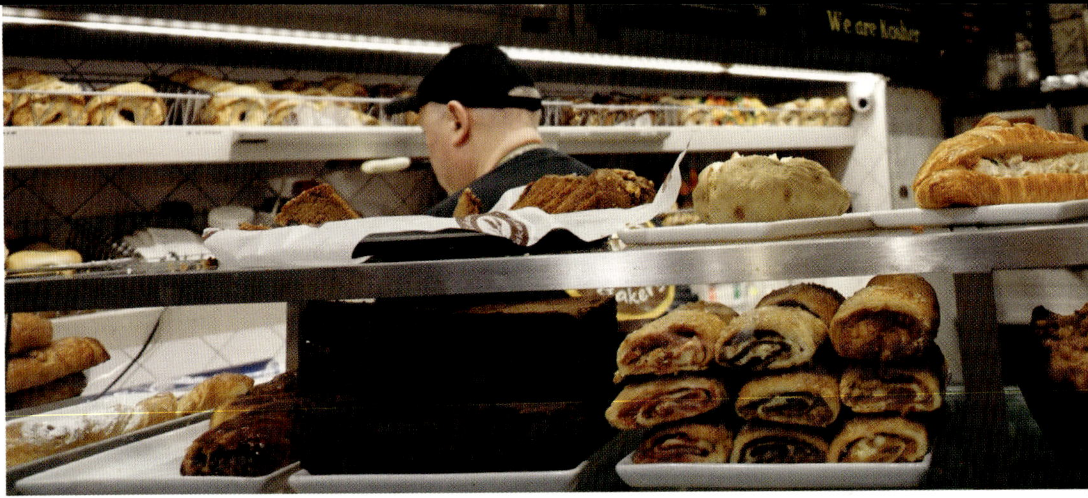

ABOVE:

Davidovich Bakery

Breads, pastries and breakfast foods are a familiar display at this artisan bakery in Chelsea Market, but what the shop is particularly popular for is its handmade bagels.

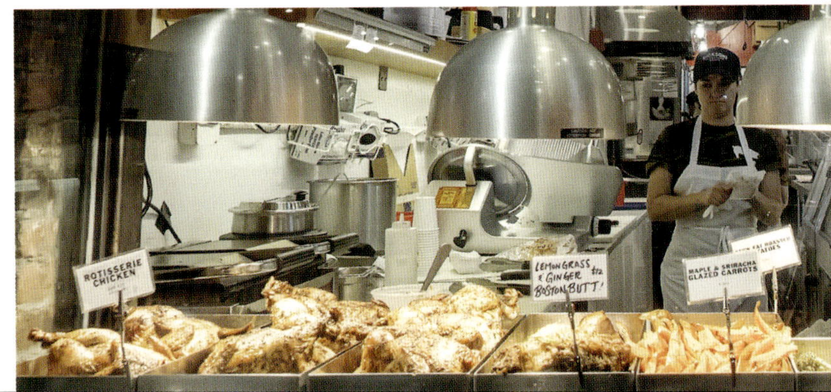

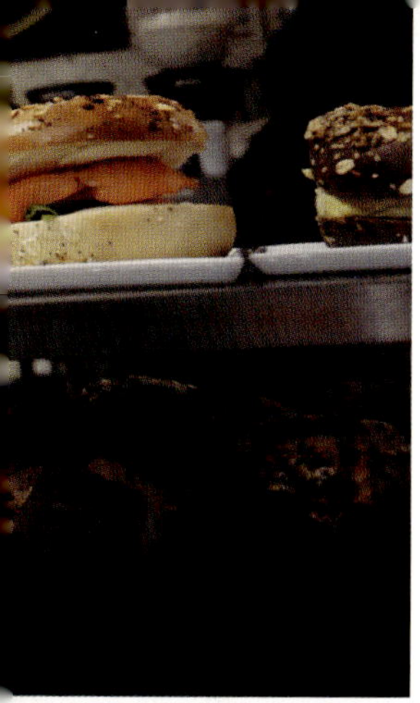

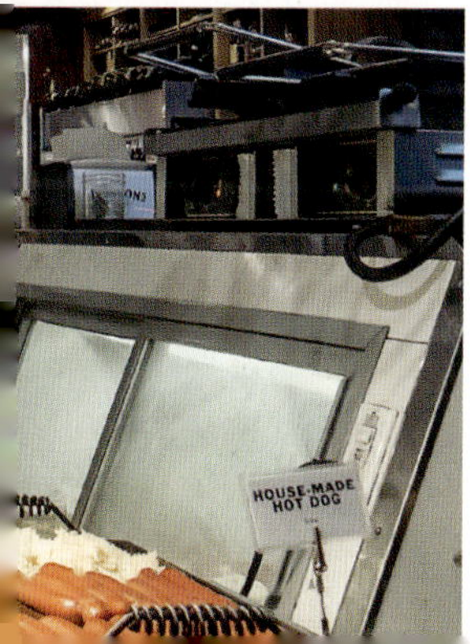

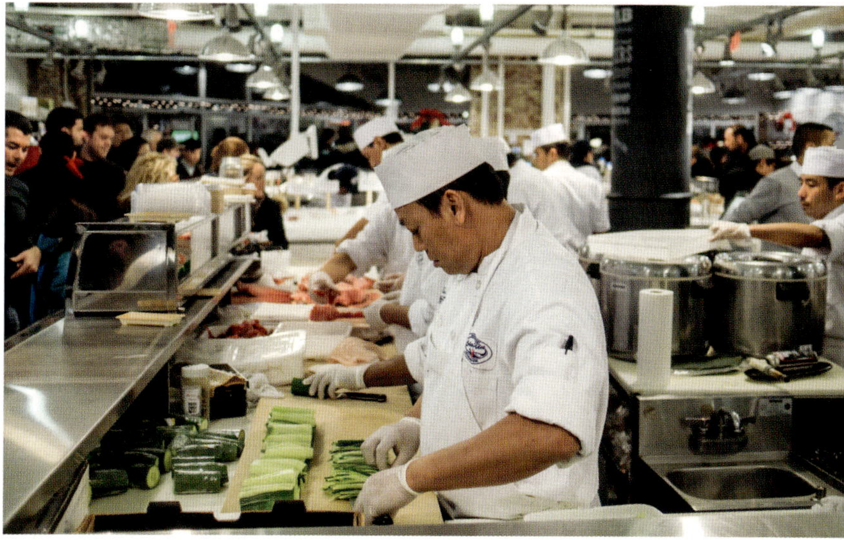

BELOW LEFT AND ABOVE:

Chelsea Market vendors

Shoppers at the market get a first-hand view of cooks, bakers and other store employees hard at work preparing a wide variety of meals and treats. There are around 30 food vendors in the city's most popular food court.

Chelsea Market architecture
Whether it's shopping for prime cuts of meat, seafood, fresh produce or pastries, the market has a wide variety of stores that are sure to meet any visitor's tastes. Six million people visit the market annually to shop and enjoy the unique and diverse experience.

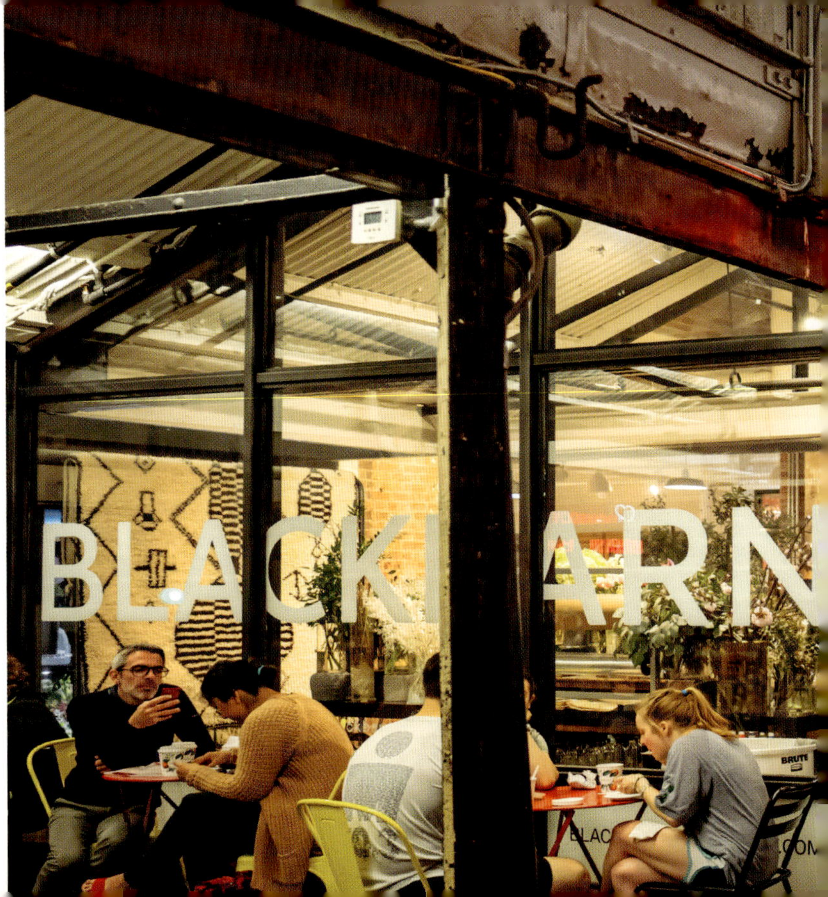

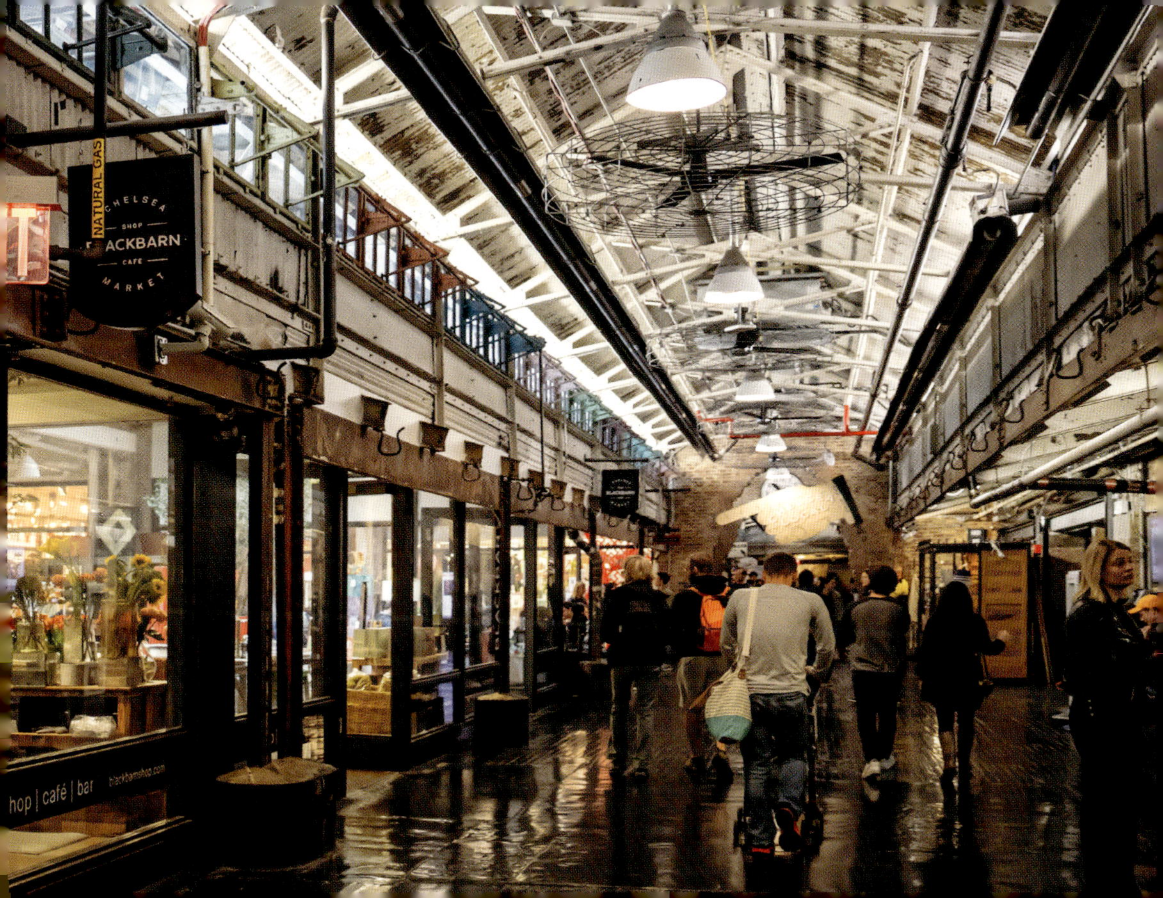
NATURAL GAS
CHELSEA
SHOP
ACKBARN
CAFE
MARKET
hop | café | bar
blackbarnshop.com

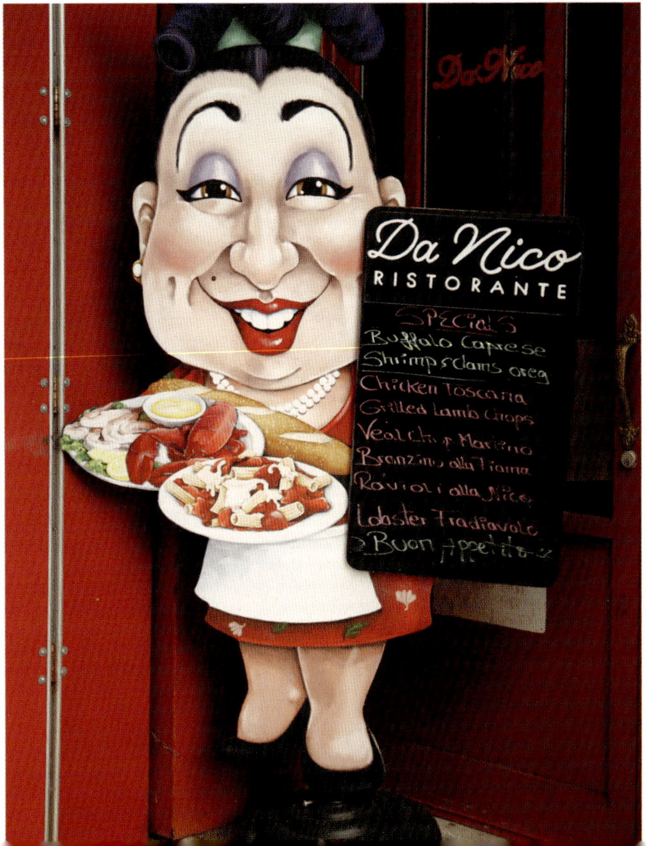
Da Nico
Da Nico
RISTORANTE
SPECIALS
Buffalo Caprese
Shrimp & clams oreg
Chicken Toscana
Grilled Lamb Chops
Ravioli alla Nico
Lobster Fradiavolo
Buon Appetito

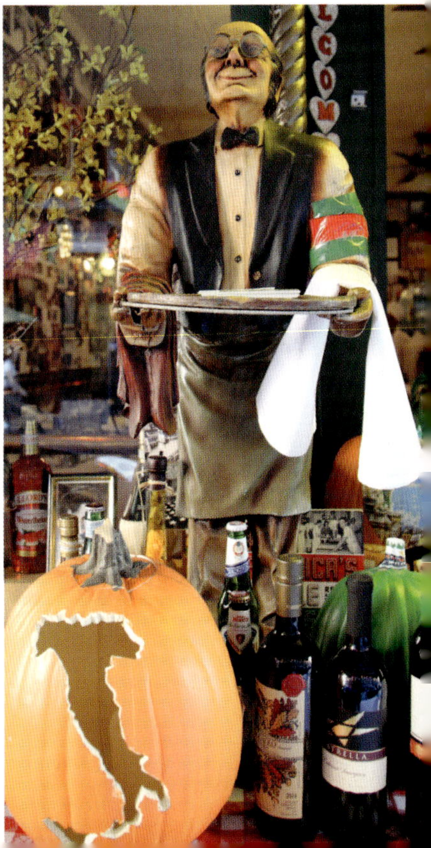

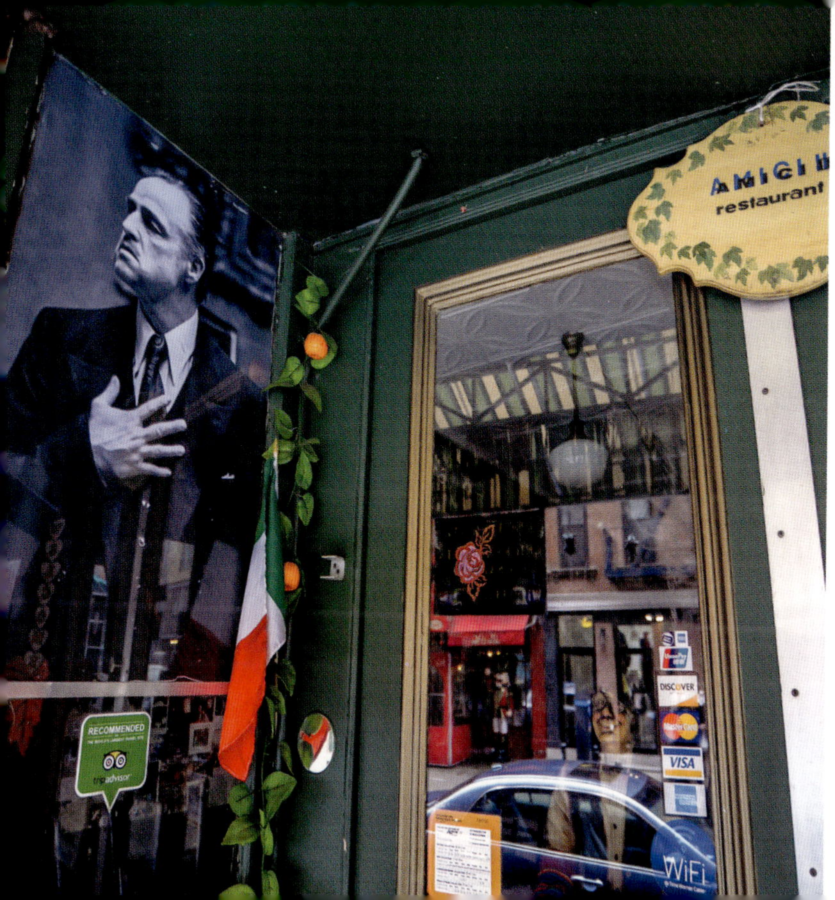

ALL PHOTOGRAPHS:

Little Italy

This neighbourhood in Lower Manhattan was once home to tens of thousands of immigrants arriving from Italy from the late 19th century. Today, it still shows signs of its rich Italian heritage in its shops, restaurants, cafes and bars. Now concentrated within three blocks on Mulberry Street, Little Italy once ran from Broadway to the Bowery, and East Houston to Worth Street.

Russian Tea Room

Founded in 1927 by members of the Russian Imperial Ballet, the tea room provides visitors with an elegant experience and the opportunity to enjoy world-class food and Russian delicacies. Located on 57th Street between Sixth and Seventh Avenue, the Art-Deco designed restaurant is popular with actors and audiences and is especially known for its afternoon tea, a tradition dating back to the 18th century.

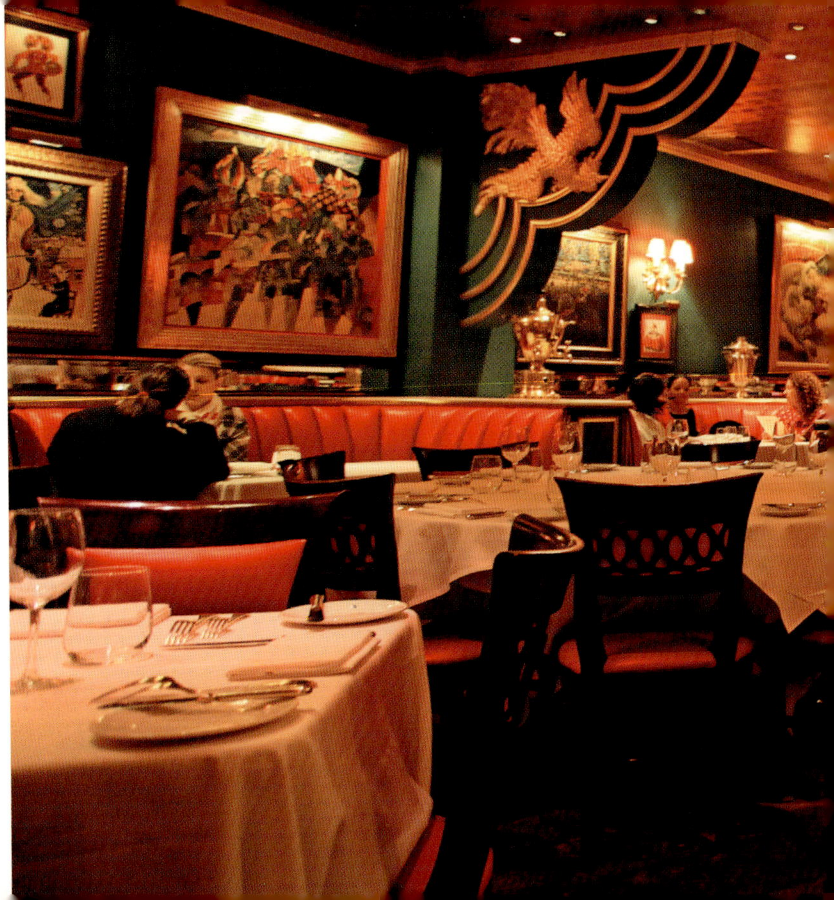

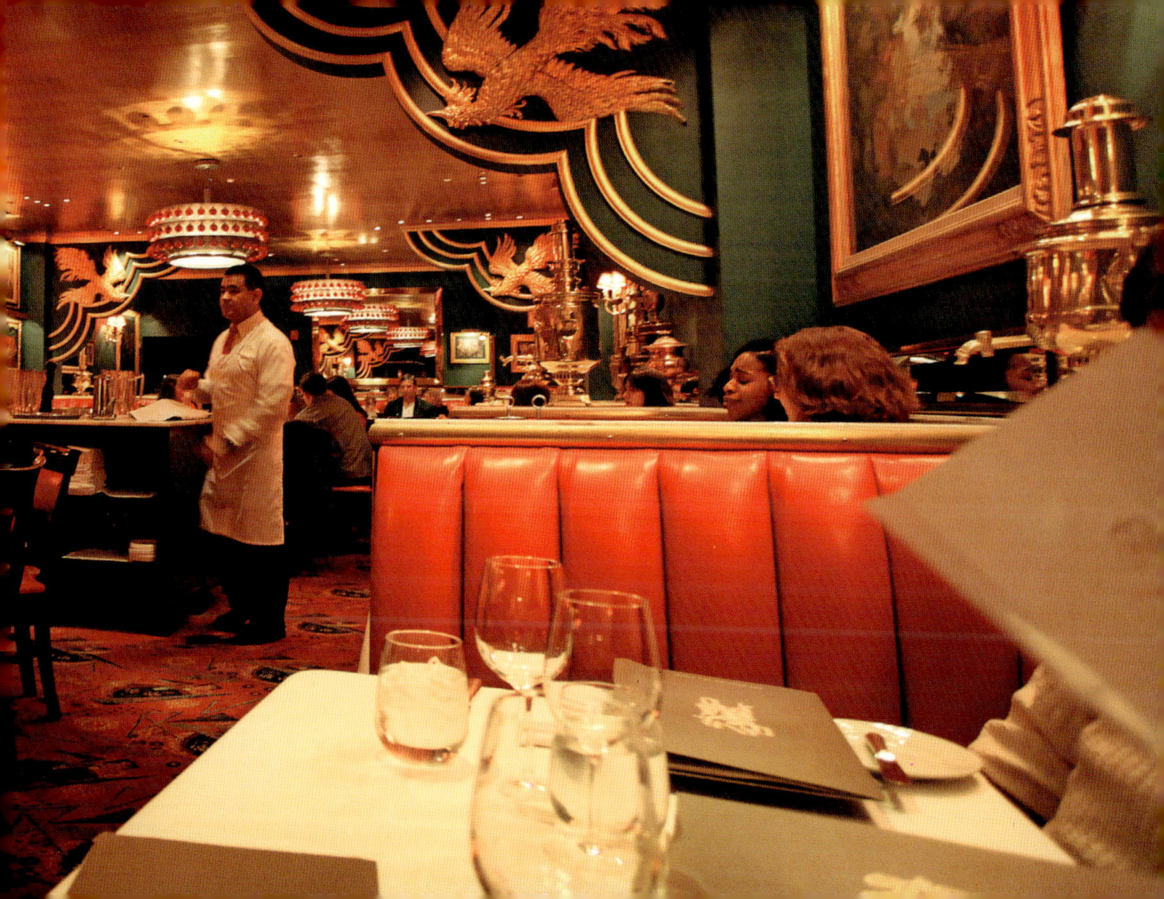

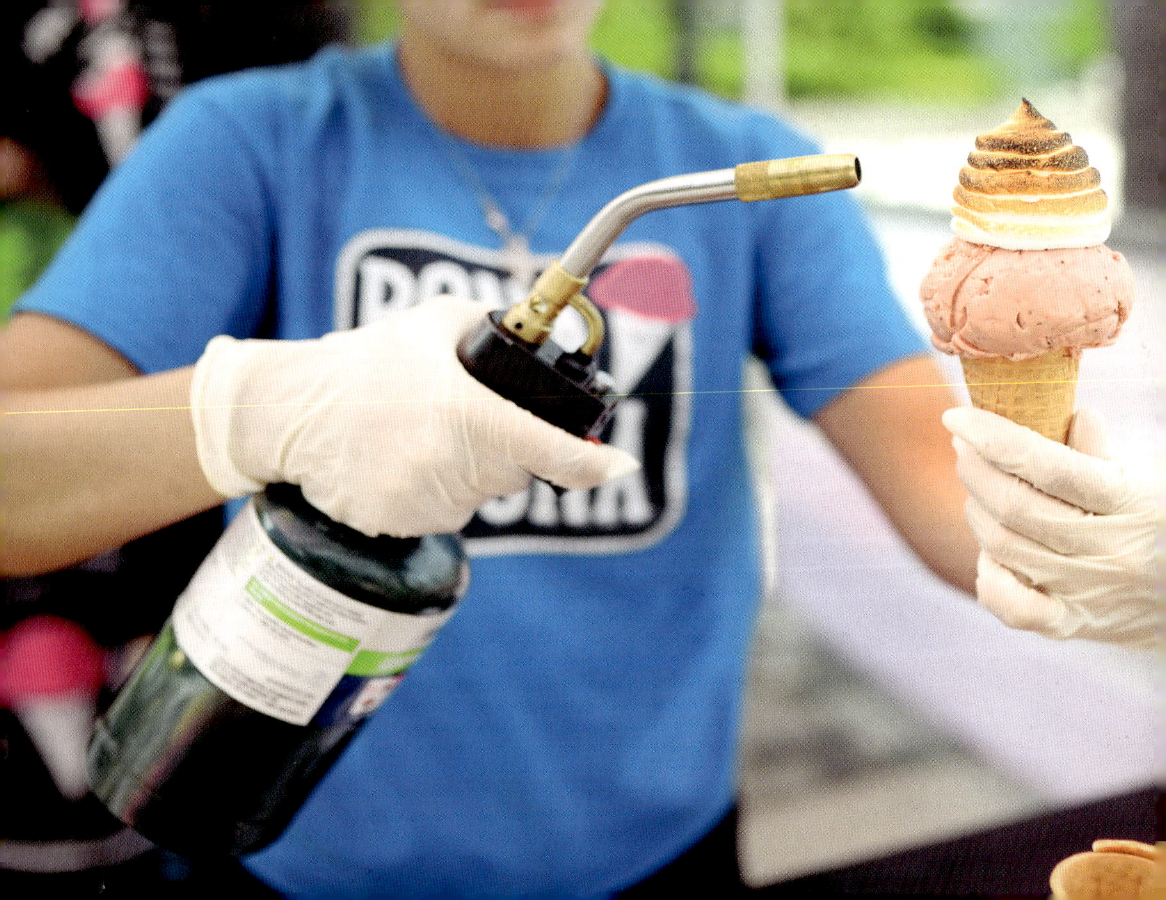

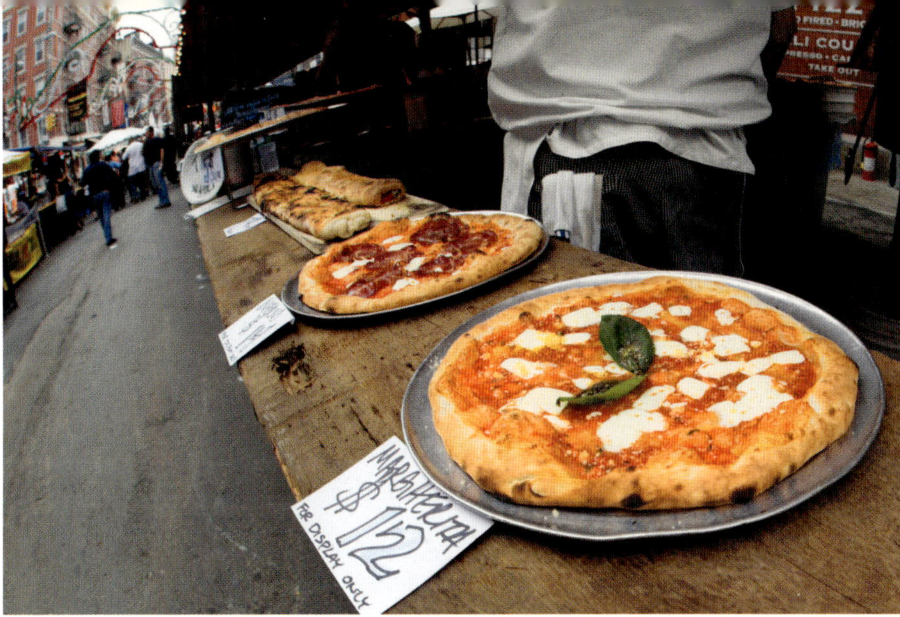

LEFT:

Street vendors

Visitors and New Yorkers looking for a quick treat can find street vendors throughout the city selling hot dogs, burgers, pretzels and ice creams with a wide range of toppings, including this one, the flame-toasted twisted marshmallow.

ABOVE:

Pizza

The pizza was introduced to New Yorkers in 1905 and was sold out of a grocery store on Spring Street. Neapolitan-American pizza has grown to become one of the most popular foods sold throughout the city and across the country.

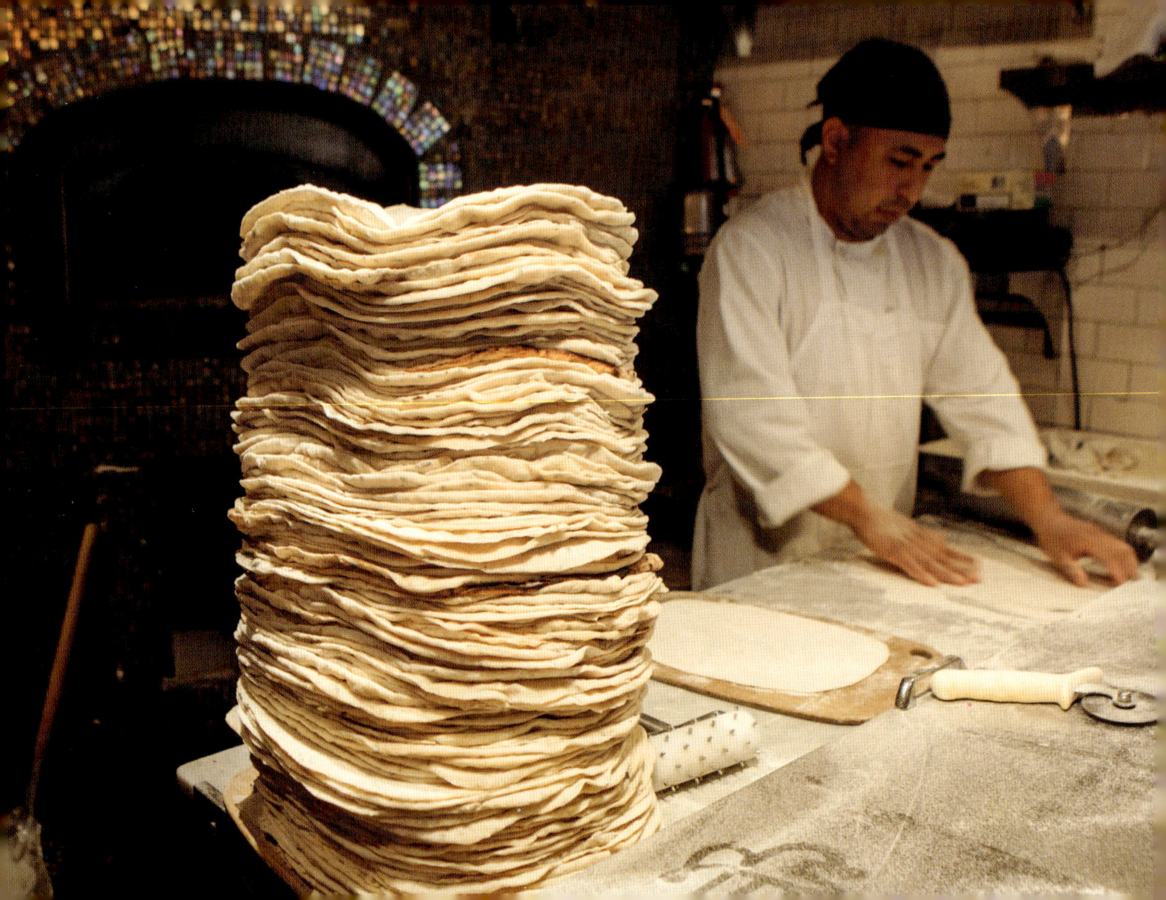

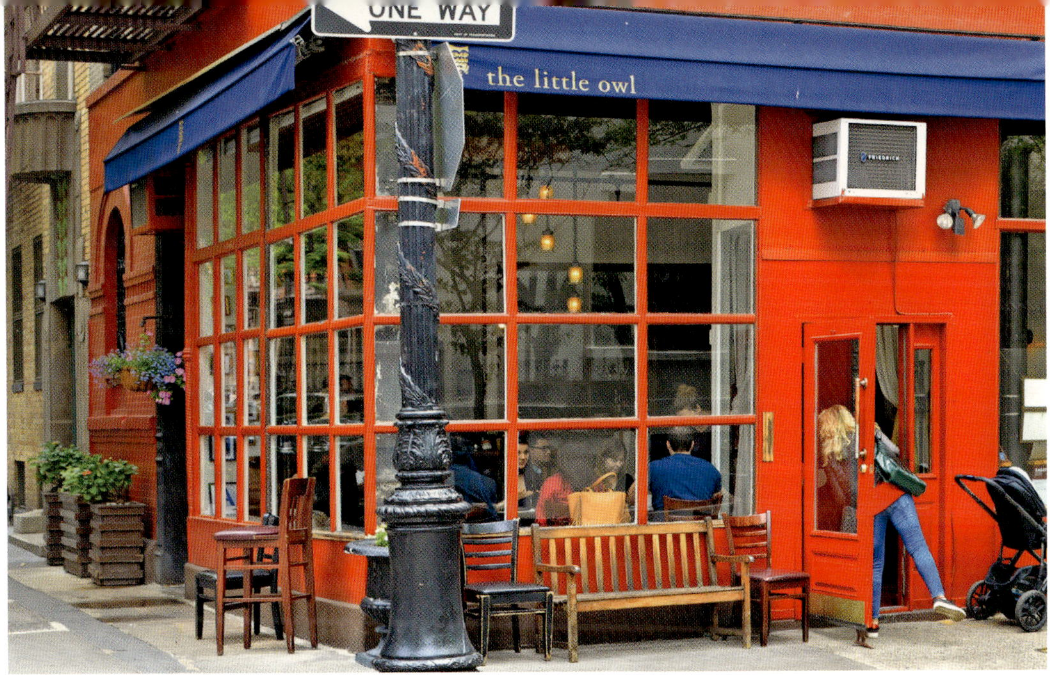

OPPOSITE:

Pizza chefs

Busy pizzerias can sell hundreds of pizzas a day. To prepare, pizza chefs need to start making dough early in anticipation of lunch, dinner and late-night orders.

ABOVE:

Greenwich Village

A window seat at any of the cafes and eateries in the Village allows for a popular New York activity – people-watching.

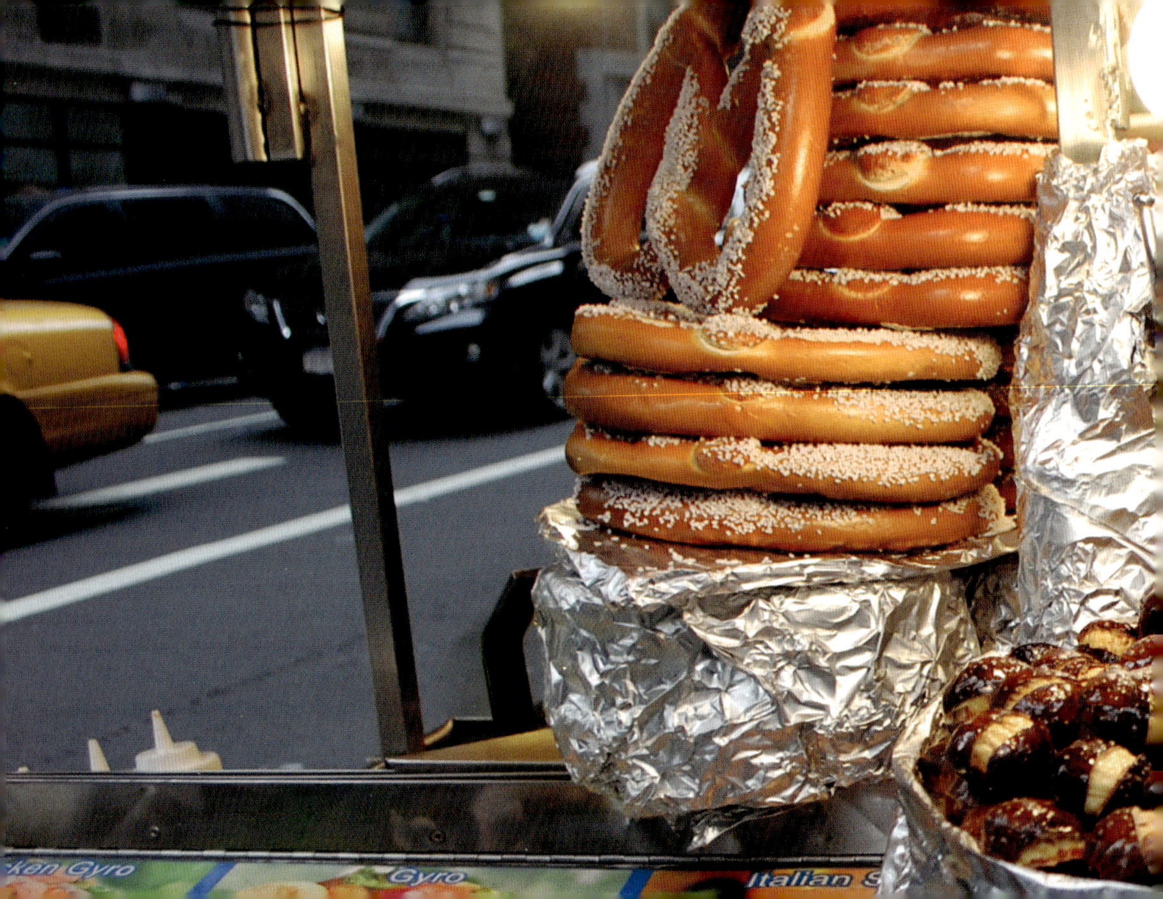
Gyro
Italian

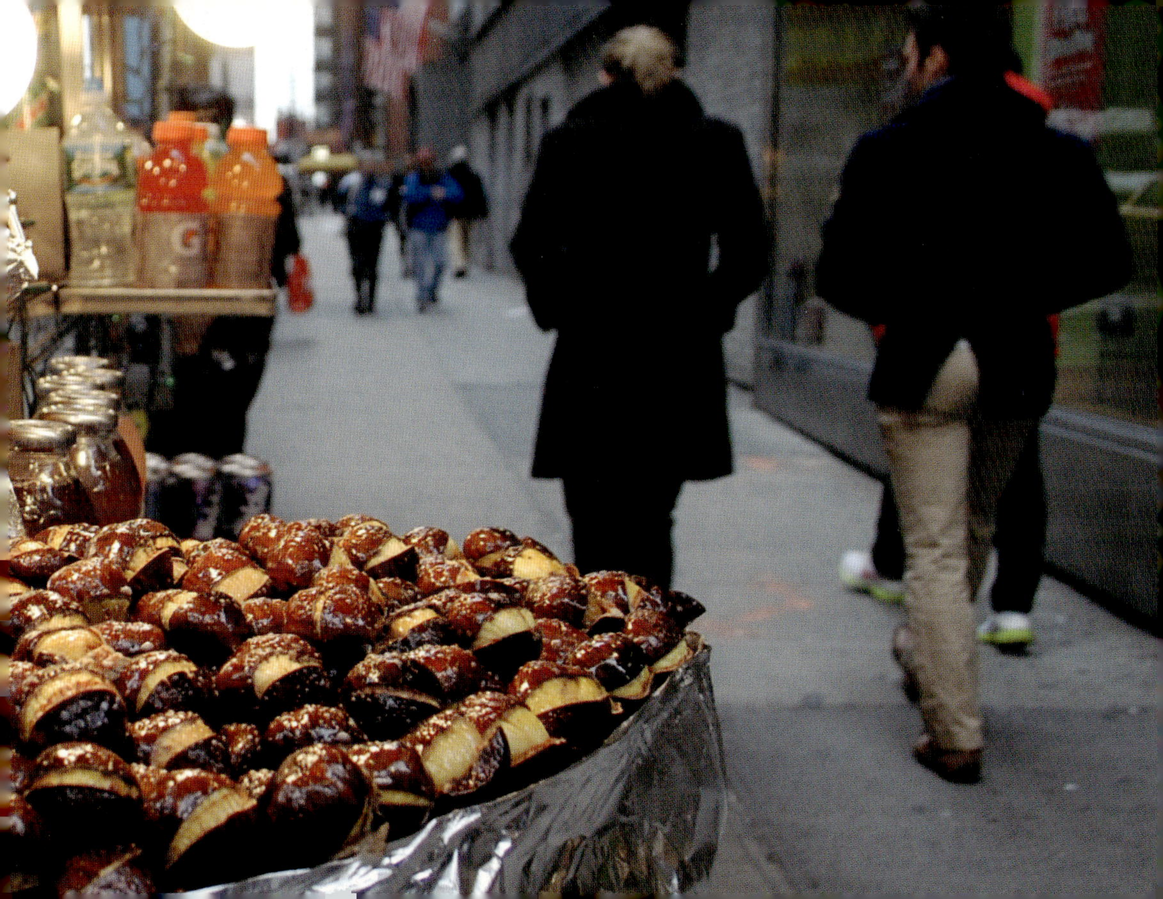

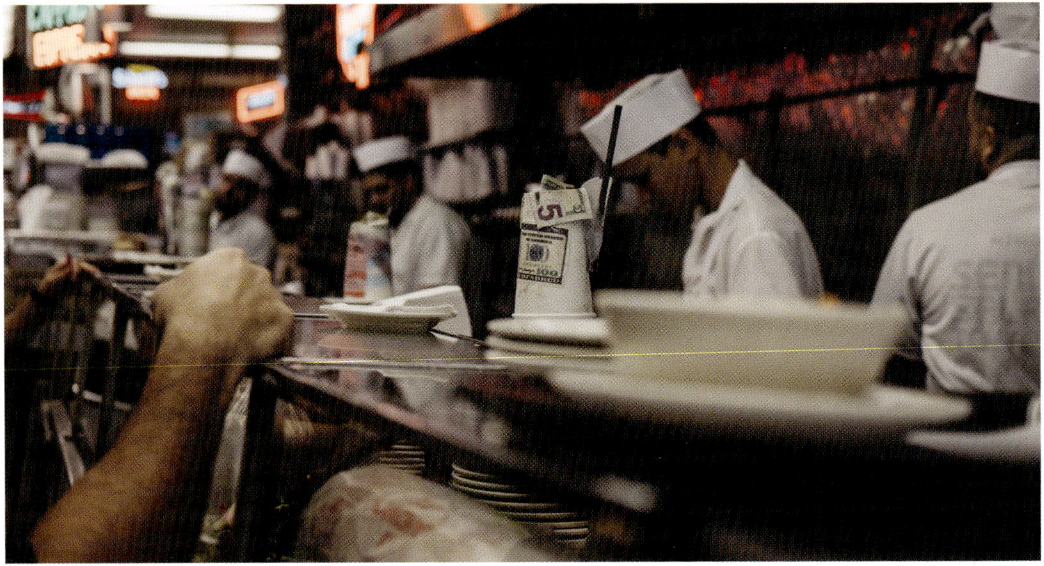

PREVIOUS PAGES:

Street food

Food trucks and carts are a common sight throughout the year. Rain or shine, you'll find them on street corners everywhere. As well as the standard hot dogs, pretzels, bagels and doughnuts visitors can find sushi, vegan food and barbeques.

ABOVE AND OPPOSITE:

Katz's deli

Don't be surprised if there's a line of people waiting to get in. Located in the Lower East Side of Manhattan, this popular kosher deli has been in business for over 100 years. Today, Katz's continues to serve corn beef, salami and pastrami.

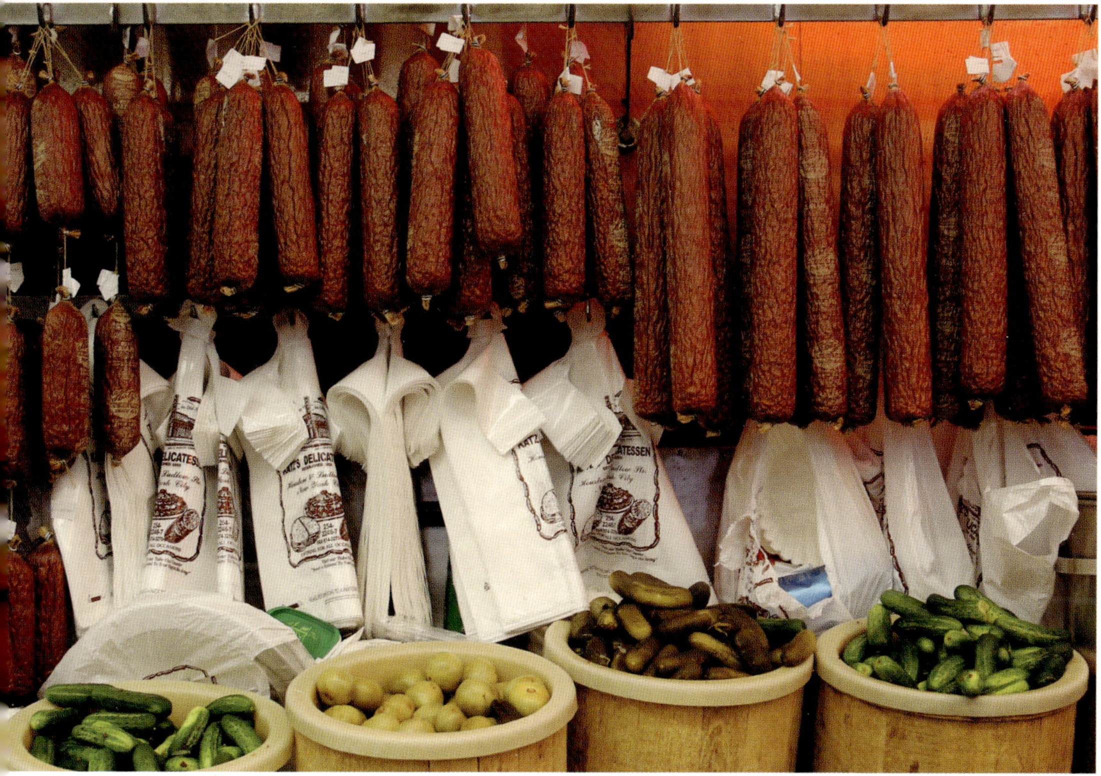

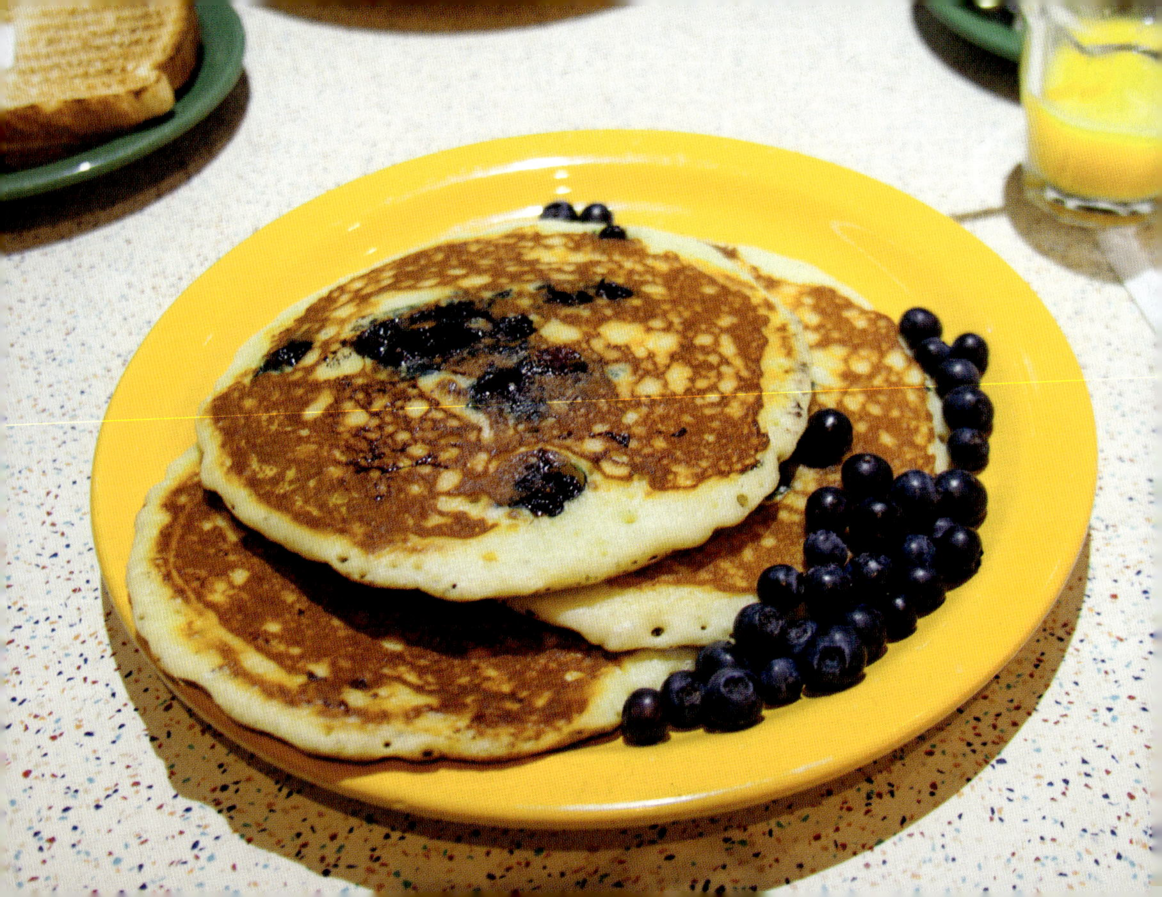

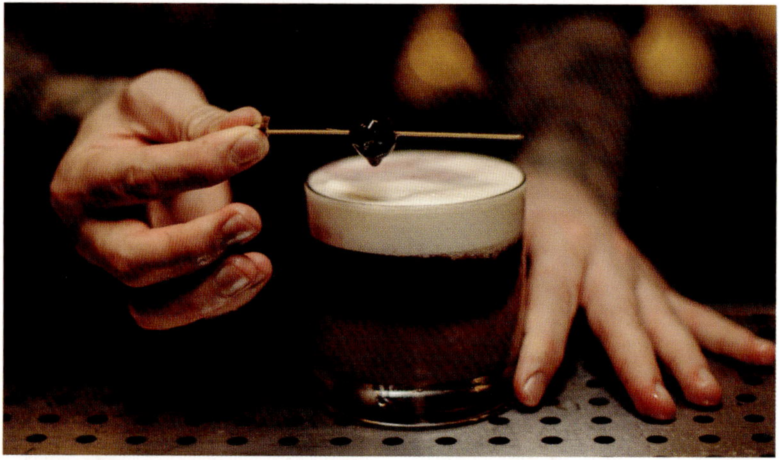

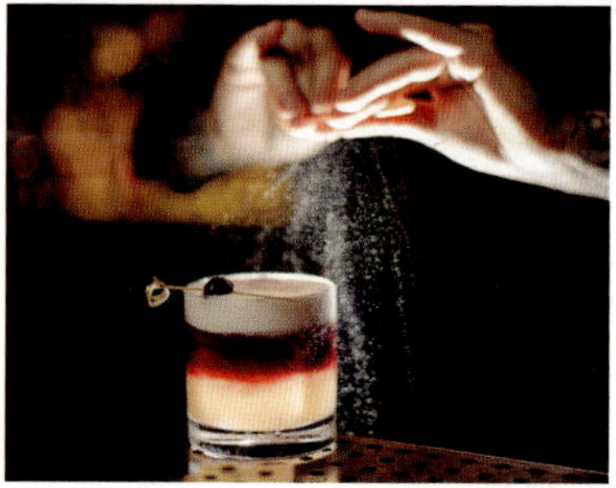

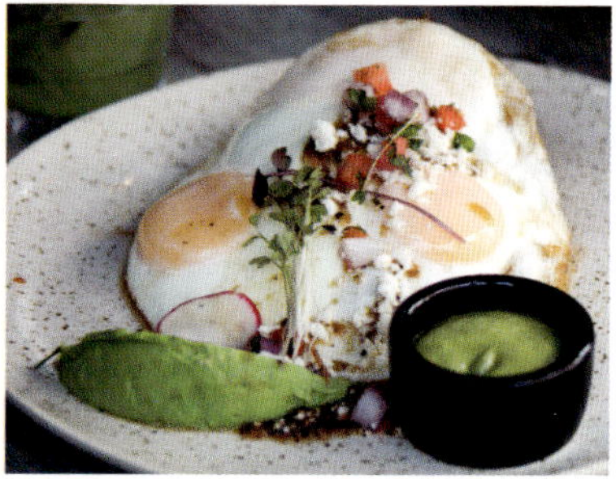

ALL PHOTOGRAPHS:

Pancake heaven

This international city of 8.5 million residents with 66.6 million annual visitors caters to everyone's tastes and fancies, whether it is blueberry pancakes, a popular cocktail or local specialty, or a gourmet meal, the city does not leave anyone disappointed as far as food and drink options go.

OVERLEAF:

Pastrami sandwich

A classic sandwich made popular in Jewish delis in the late 19th century consists of pastrami meat stuffed between two slices of rye bread and topped with spicy brown mustard.

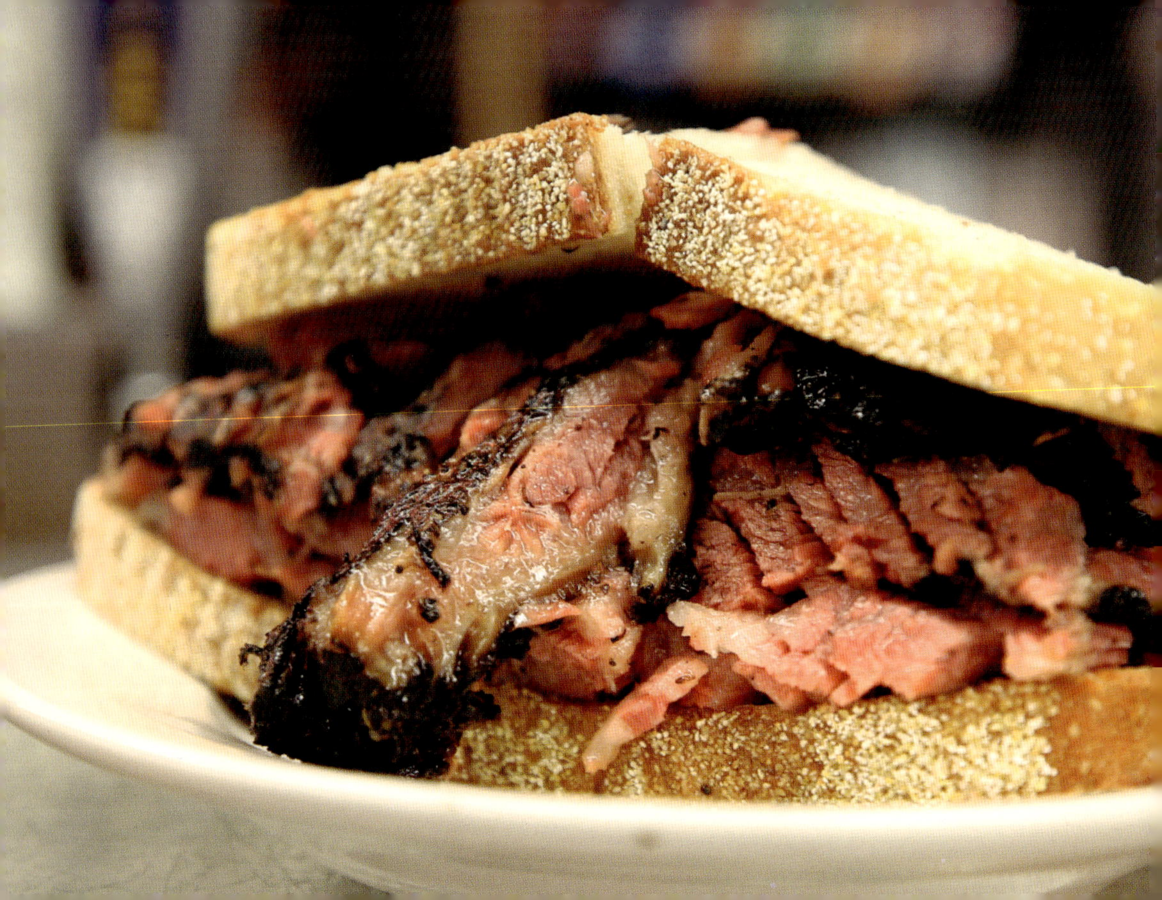

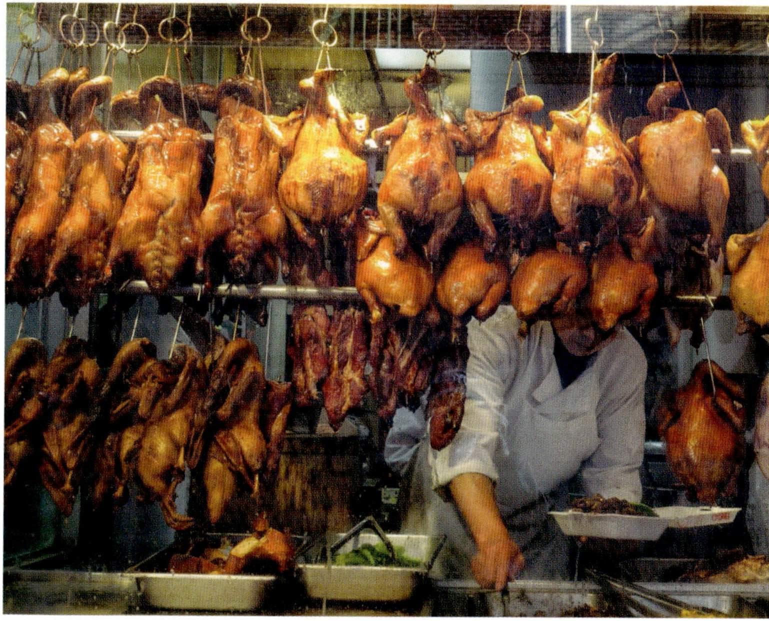

ABOVE:

Peking duck

Named after the city from which it originated, this imported dish can be found on the menu of most Chinese restaurants and can be seen on display in the windows of Chinatown's eateries.

Rooftop bars

Whether it's for a date or for meeting friends, nothing beats the view and vibe of a New York rooftop bar. The many rooftop bars found throughout the five boroughs offer bright city lights from different locations across town.

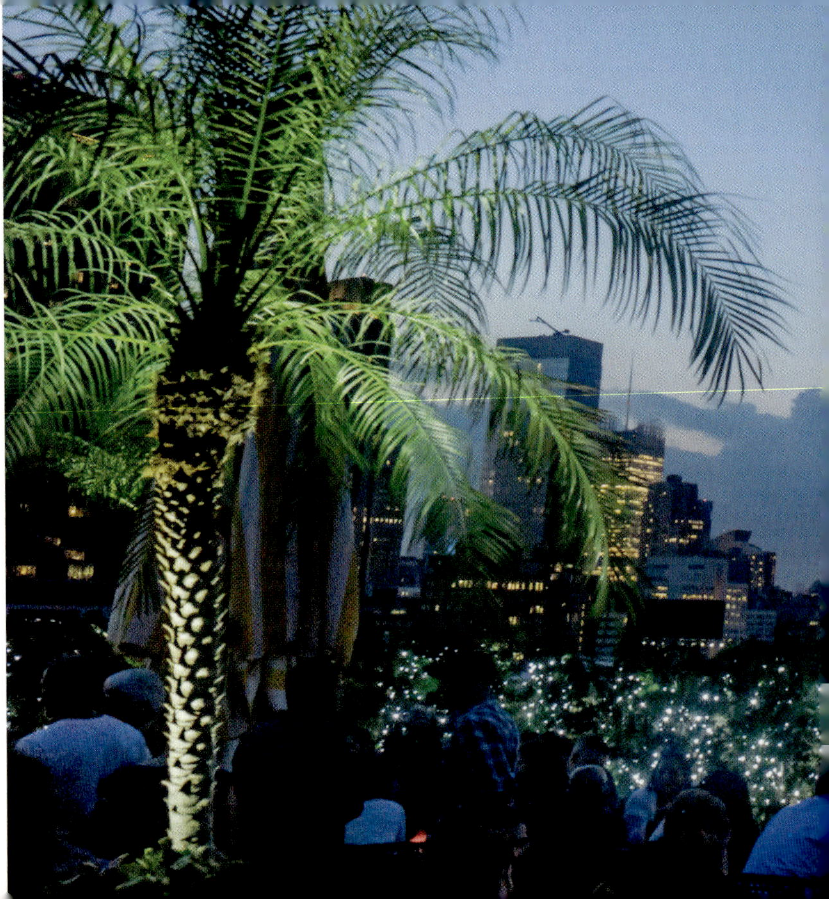

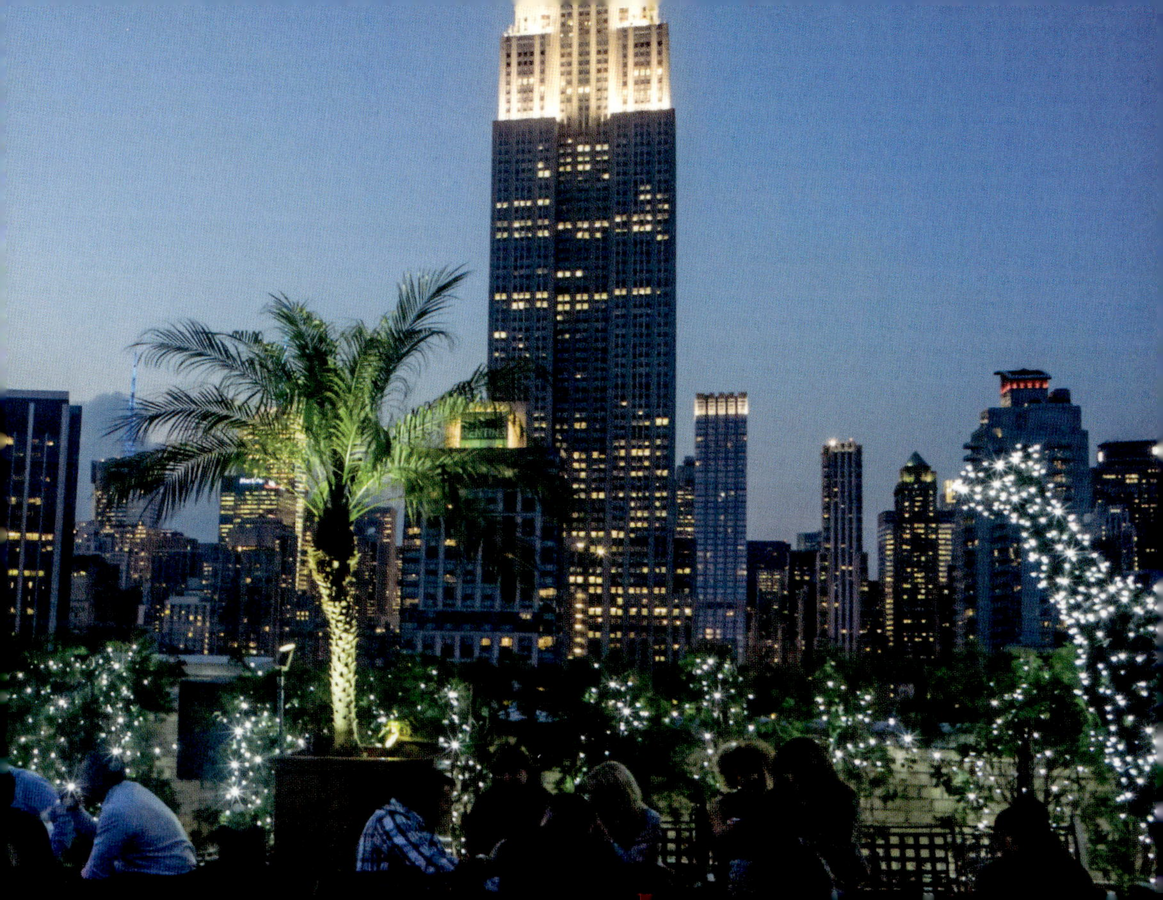

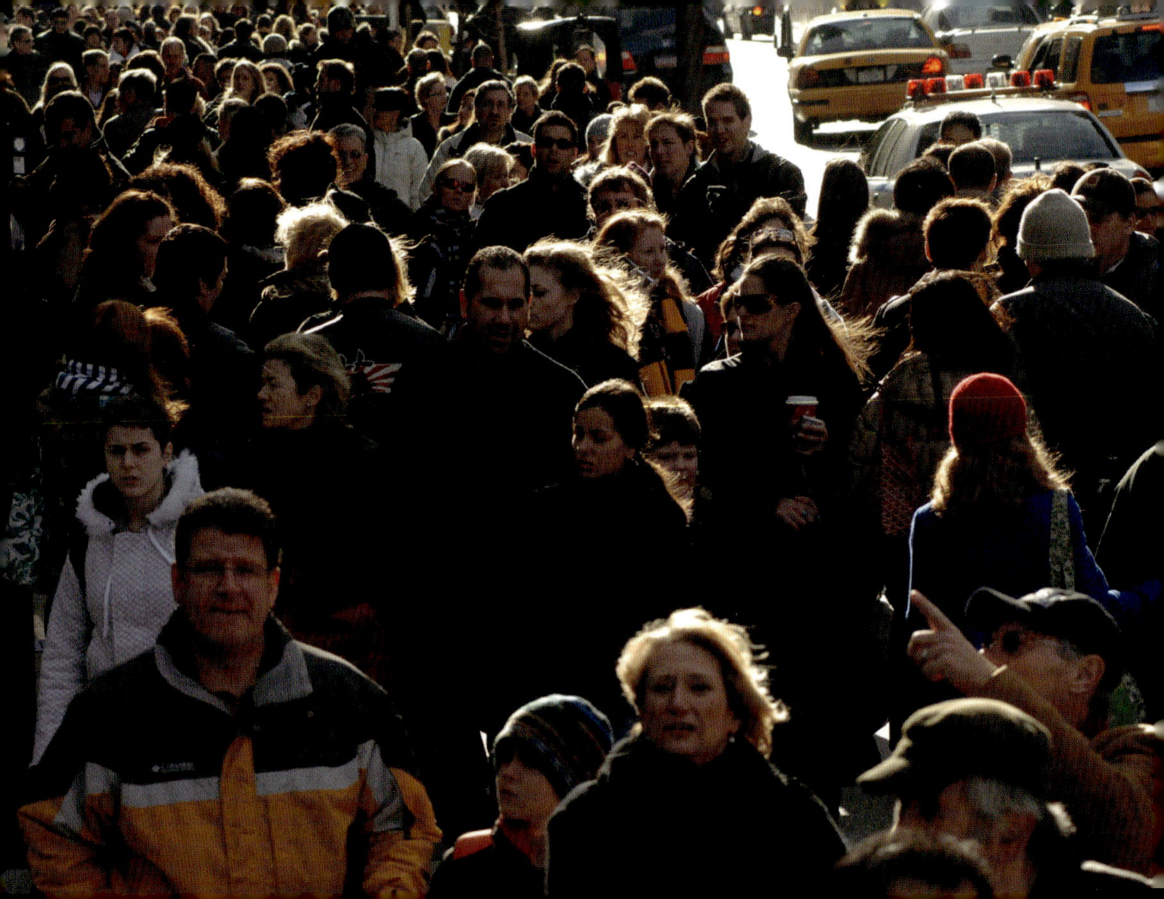

Shopping

Few places in the world compare when it comes to shopping in New York City. Whether it's strolling past the expensive shops of Fifth Avenue, vintage stores on Bleecker Street, food markets in Chelsea, or looking for a bargain in a local flea market in Queens, the options are very wide. New York City is home to thousands of businesses, from small shops and retailers to flagship stores. And for window shopping, look no further than the giant department stores like Macy's and Bloomingdale's, and the mega-malls, such as Westfield, located underground in the World Trade Center.

A stroll through Greenwich Village or the Rockefeller Center, or down Madison Avenue or Canal Street, will showcase everything from high-end fashion and jewellery to cheap knock-offs of the same brands. And for visitors looking to take home a souvenir or two from the Big Apple, Broadway is lined with stores offering 'I Love New York' T-shirts, mugs, and just about anything else stamped with the sentiment so many who visit the city share.

OPPOSITE:

Fifth Avenue shoppers

Nicknamed 'Millionaires' Row', this 12-block stretch of Manhattan is one of the most expensive shopping avenues in the world. It is also used as the main route for many of New York City's major parades.

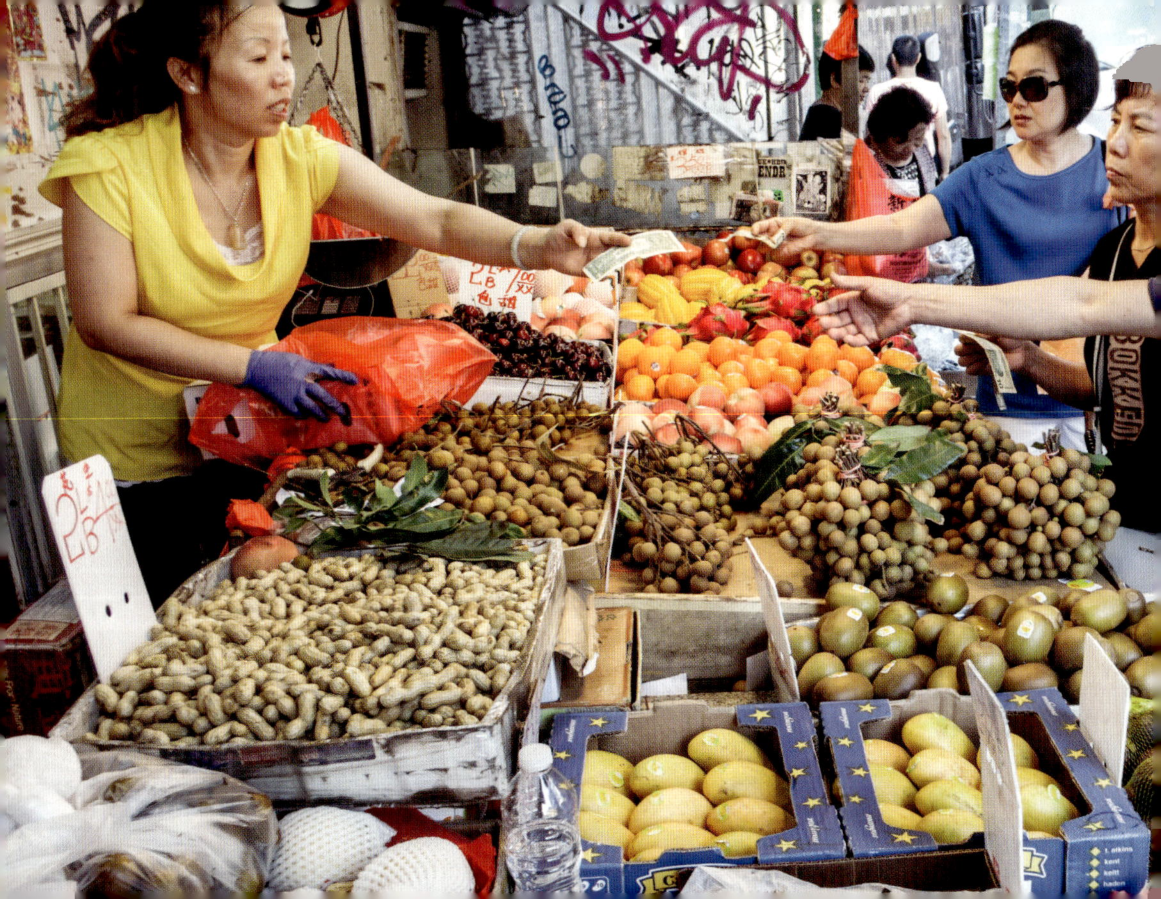
kent
keitt
haden

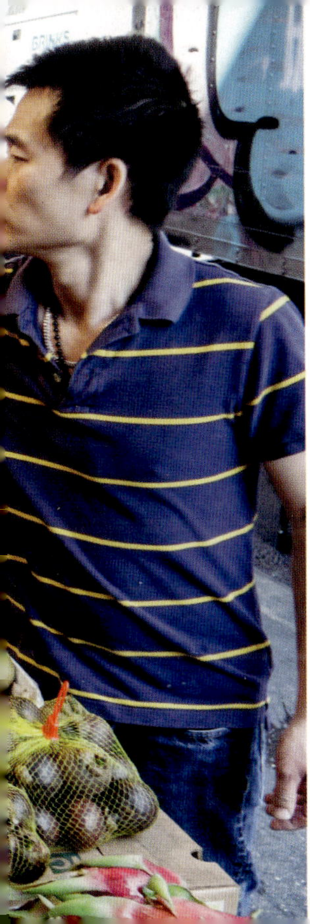

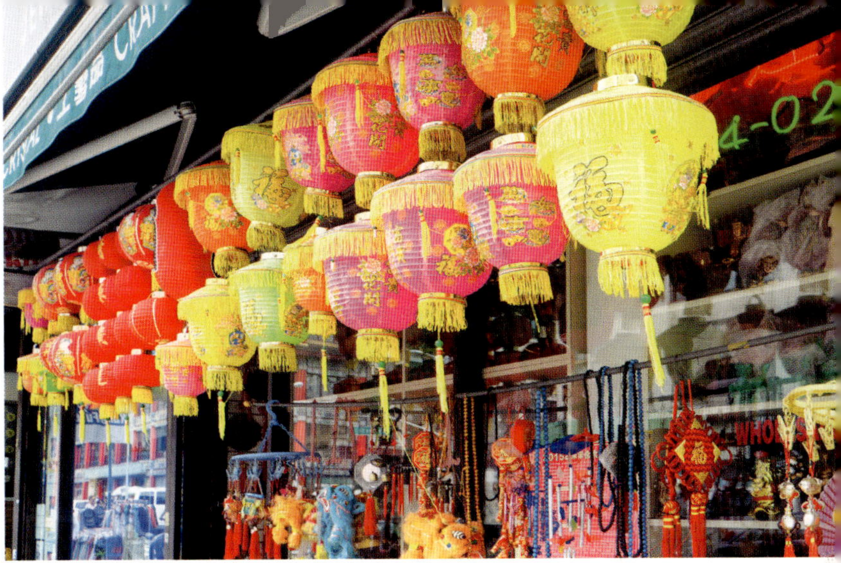

ALL PHOTOGRAPHS:

Chinatown

This unique area of Lower Manhattan blends both the traditional and the modern. Many locals visit for familiar foods, spices and ingredients native to China, while others seek out exotic fruits and delicacies. More recently, high-end restaurants and bars are finding a home in this historic district, alongside traditional tea houses and street vendors.

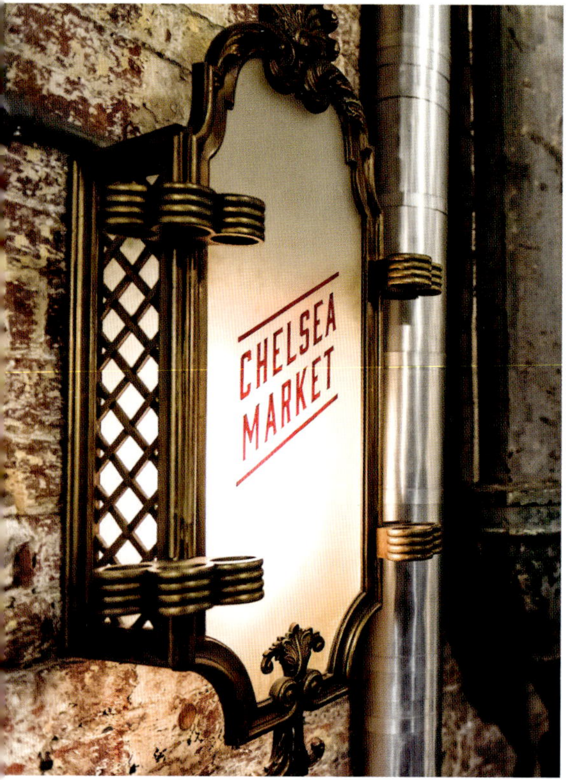
CHELSEA
MARKET

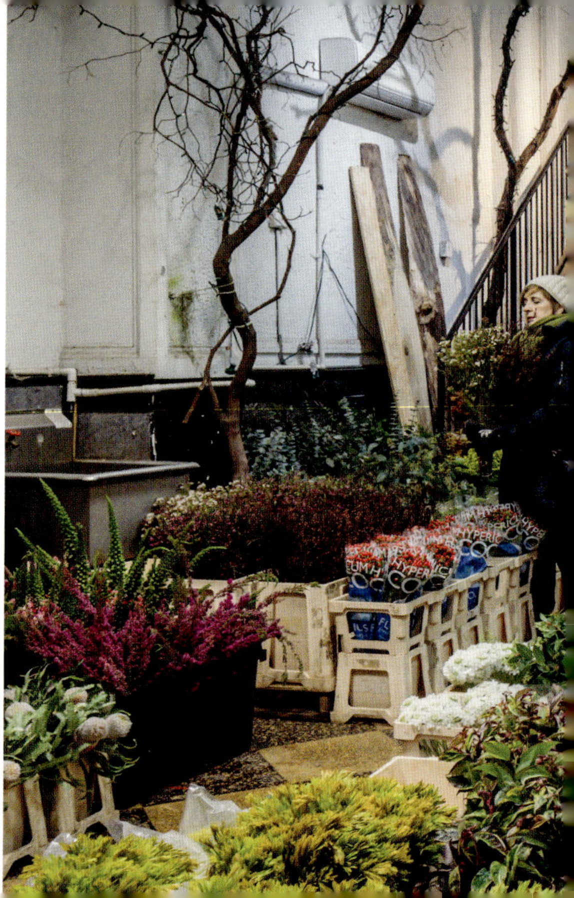

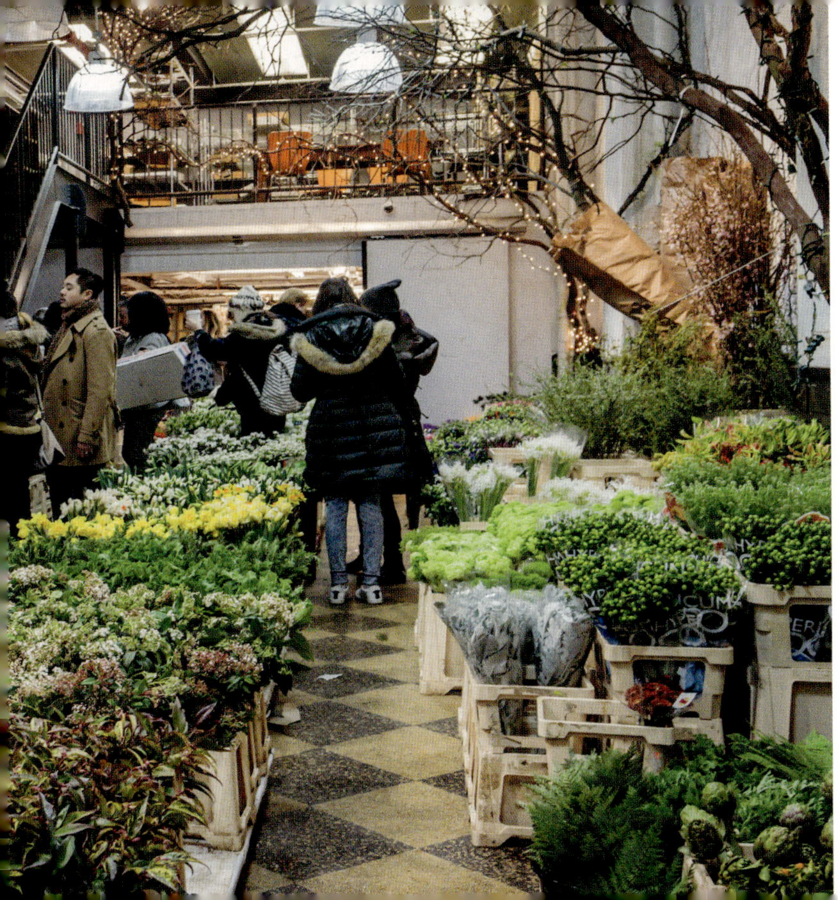

ALL PHOTOGRAPHS:

Chelsea Market shopping
More than just a place to eat lunch or grab a drink, this popular indoor market place is also a one-stop shopping site that can meet most New Yorker's needs. Opened in 1997, it covers 111,484 sq m (1.2 million sq ft), providing more than enough room to accommodate the heavy traffic of shoppers.

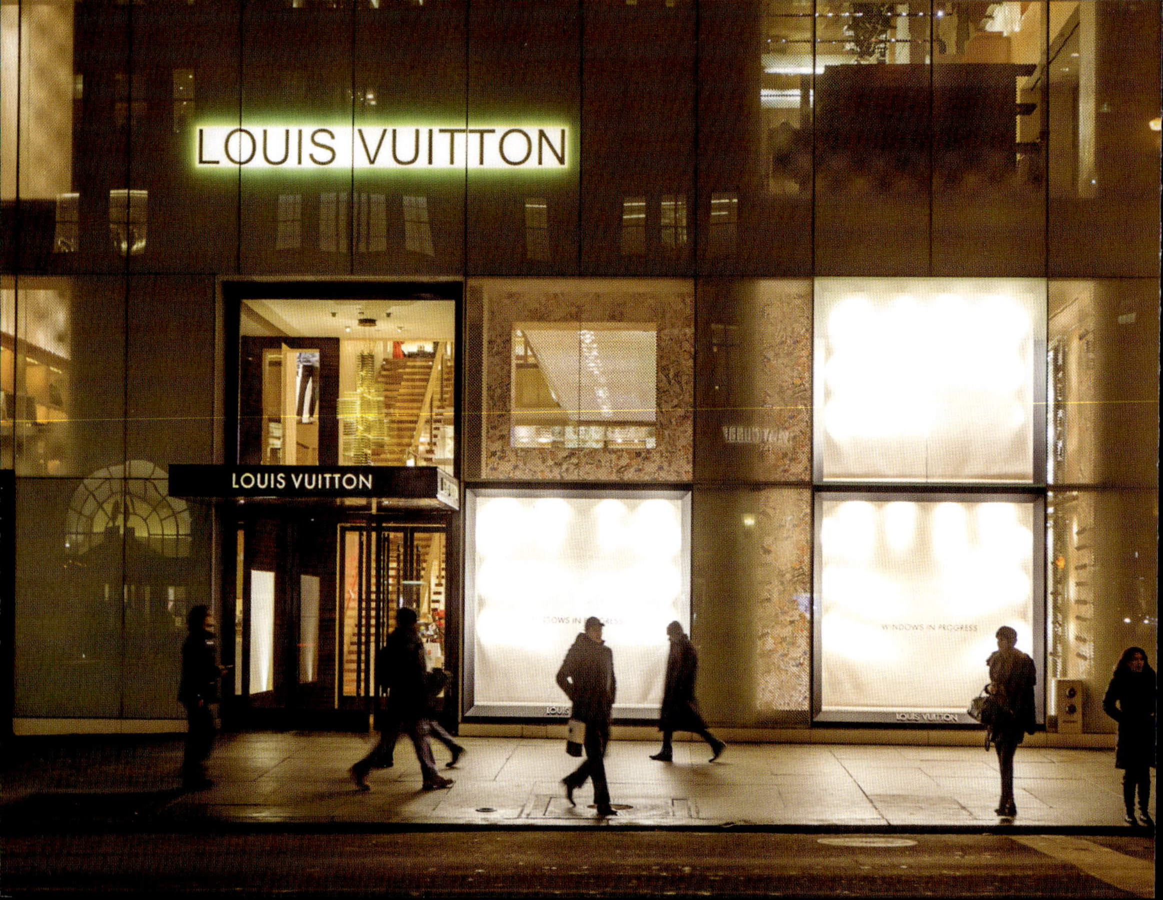
LOUIS VUITTON
LOUIS VUITTON
WINDOWS IN PROGRESS
LOUIS VUITTON

OPPOSITE:

Louis Vuitton

Founded in Paris, France, in 1854, this world-famous luxury retailer has its flagship store on Fifth Avenue and 57th Street. Its 'LV' monogram is one of the most recognisable – and faked – logos in the world.

RIGHT:

Chelsea Flower Market

Also known as the Flower District, shoppers looking for the right bouquet will not be disappointed with the vibrant and fragrant varieties on display in storefronts along 28th Street, between Sixth and Seventh Avenues.

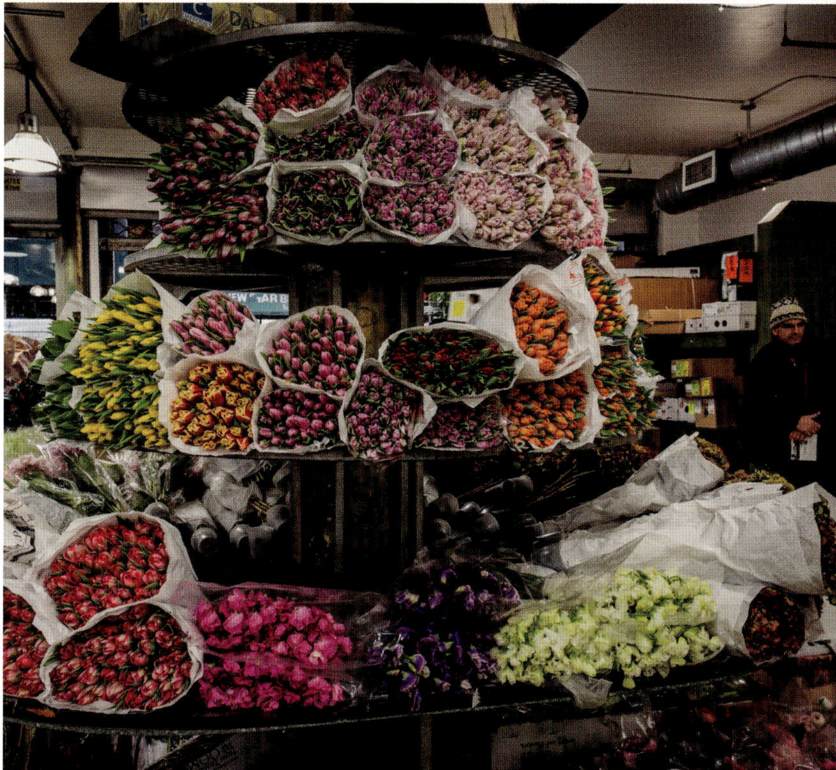

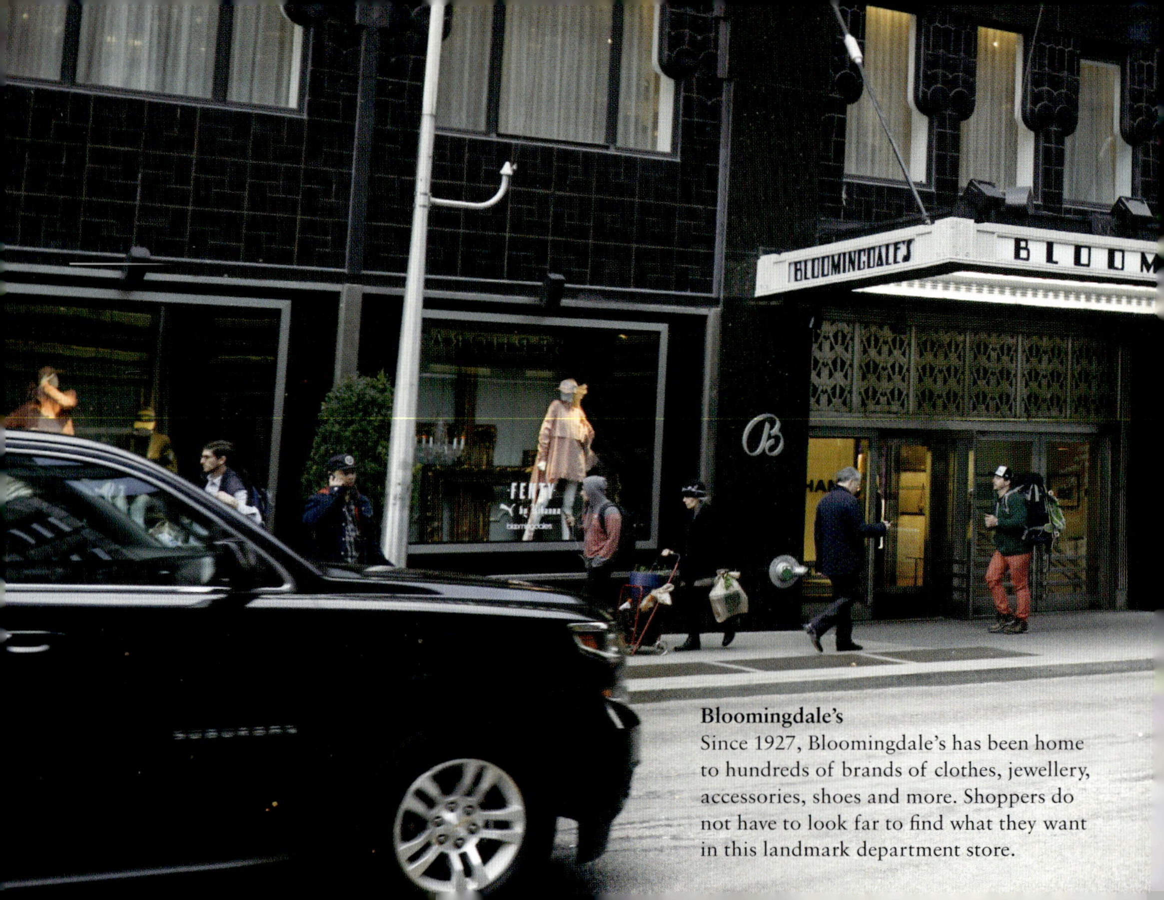

Bloomingdale's

Since 1927, Bloomingdale's has been home to hundreds of brands of clothes, jewellery, accessories, shoes and more. Shoppers do not have to look far to find what they want in this landmark department store.

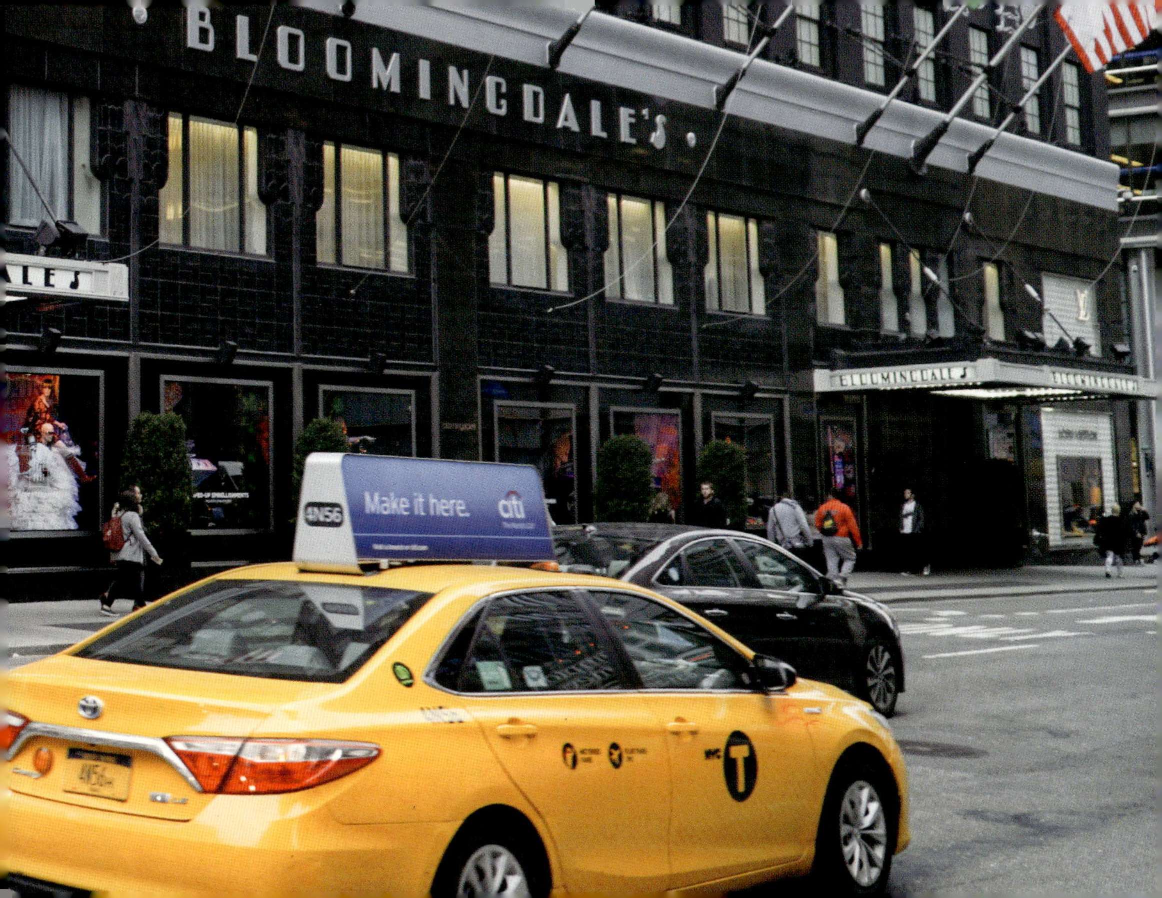
BLOOMINGDALE'S
4N56
Make it here.
citi

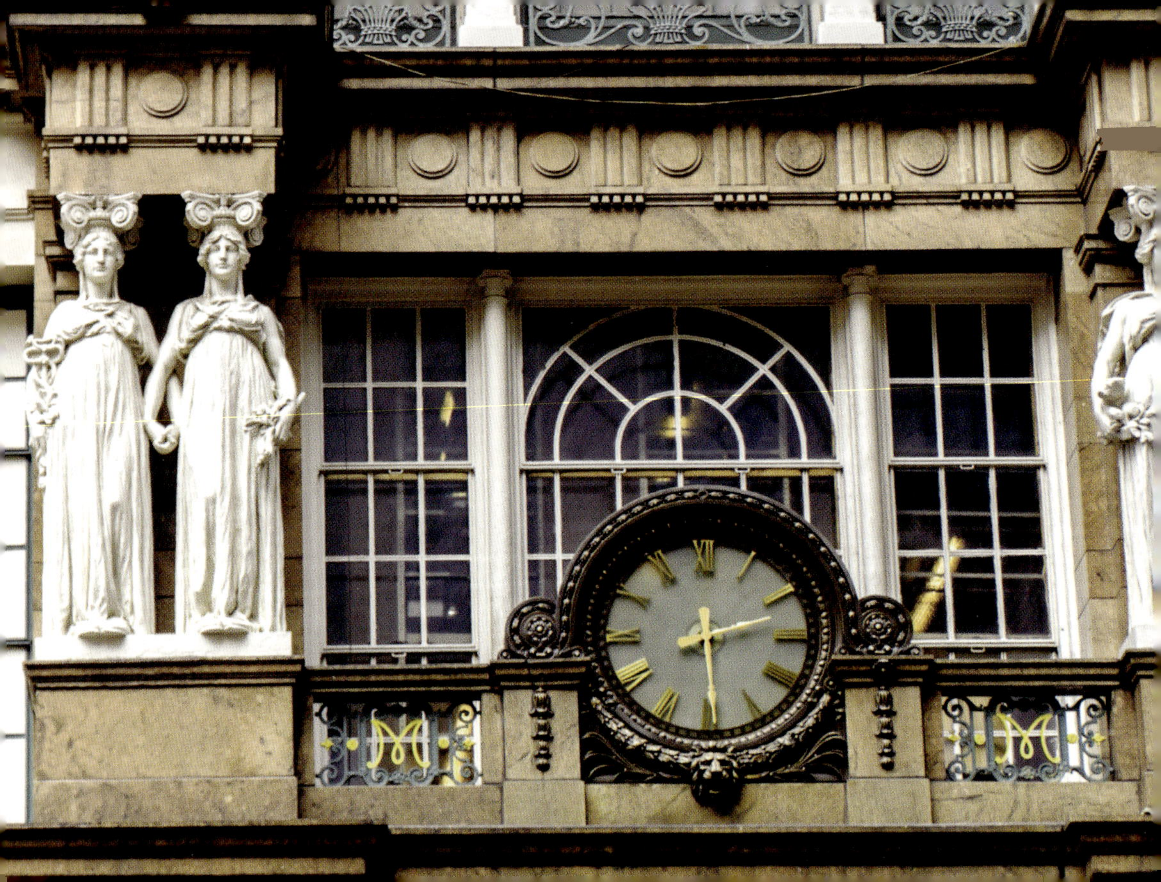

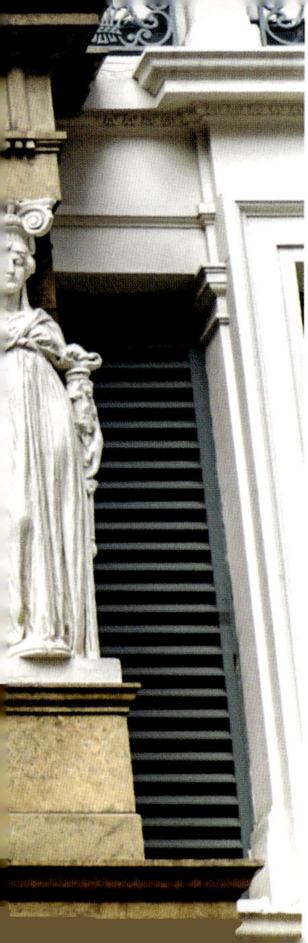

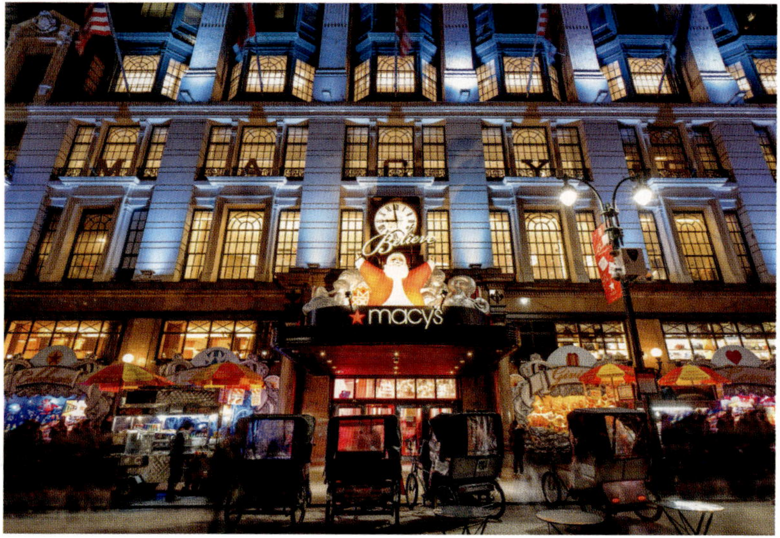

ALL PHOTOGRAPHS:

Macy's

Established in 1858, Macy's is known as the 'Great American Department Store'. Although there are hundreds of stores across the country, none match the history and size of the Harold Square location in Midtown Manhattan. Ranked as the largest department store in the world, the building takes up one entire city block. Whether on a shopping trip, or just walking by, Macy's is sure to catch peoples' attention with its elaborate window displays and seasonal decorations.

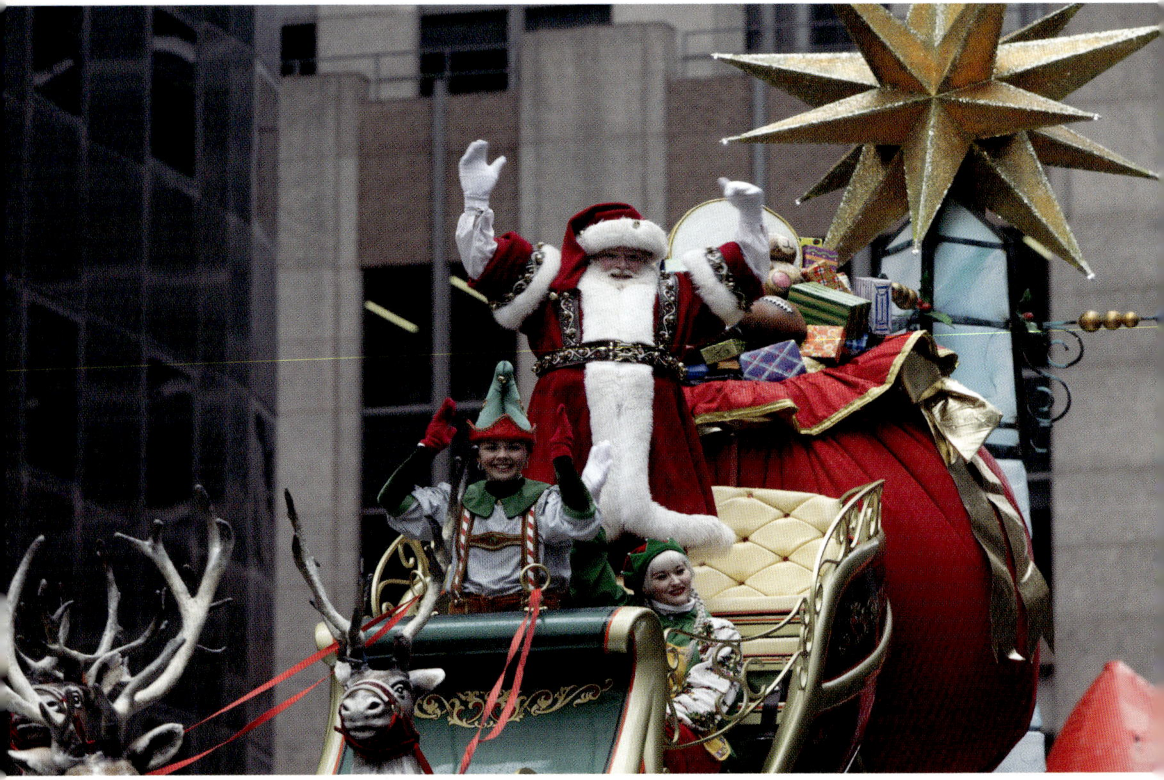

OPPOSITE:

Macy's Thanksgiving Day Parade

This annual parade started in 1924 and is one of the oldest Thanksgiving parades in the United States. The three-hour event, filled with floats, giant balloons, bands and musical performances, is televised nationally and always ends with the arrival of Santa Claus to mark the start of the Christmas season.

RIGHT:

Madison Avenue

Located between Park and Fifth Avenue, Madison Avenue was synonymous with advertising, especially between the 1930s and 1980s. Today, it is better known for its high-end shopping.

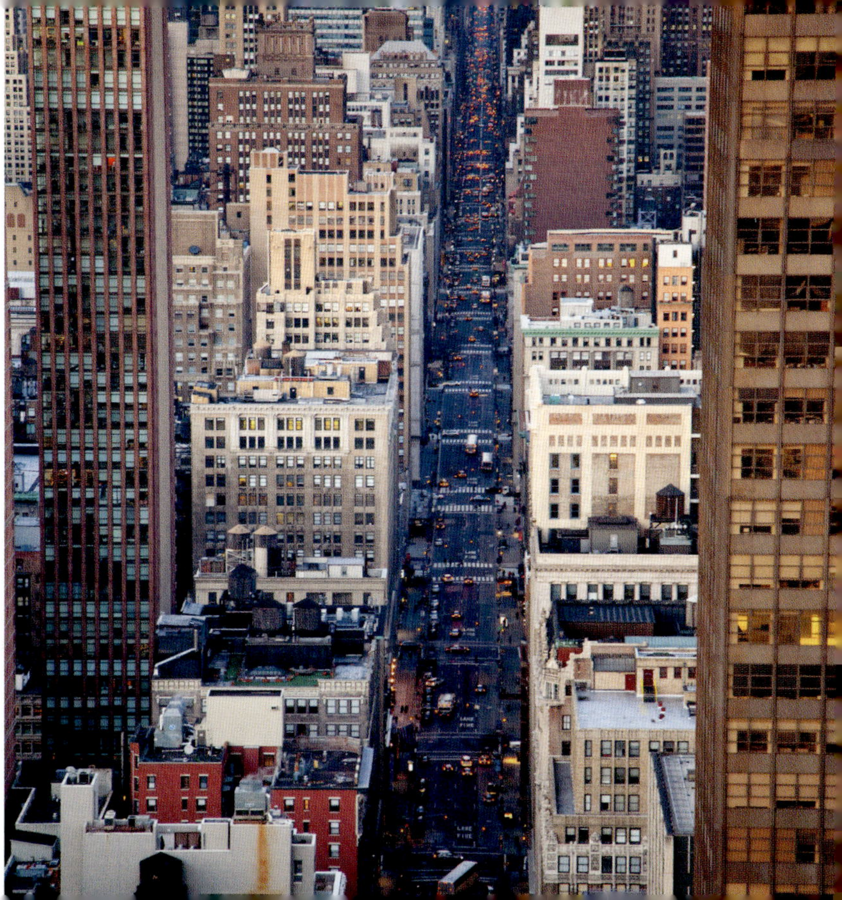

ALL PHOTOGRAPHS:

Tiffany & Co.

Known by many simply as Tiffany's, this iconic luxury jewellery shop is headquartered on Fifth Avenue and 57th Street. Since 1940, Tiffany's has been selling diamond, pearl, and sterling silver jewellery. A gift from this shop is difficult to hide thanks to its easily recognisable light blue box and white ribbon.

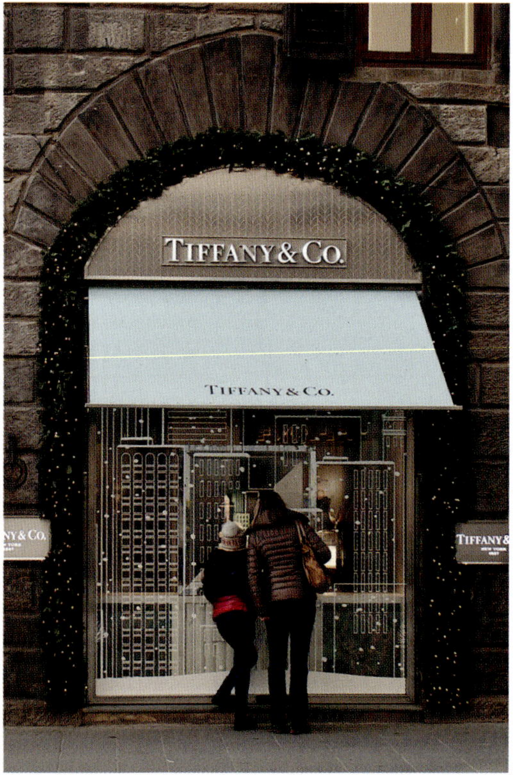

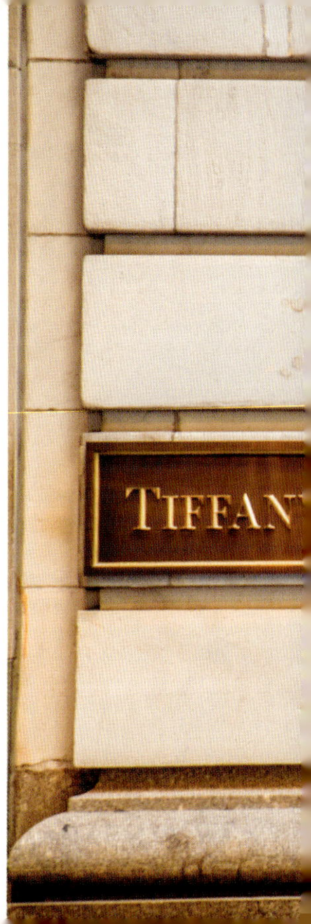

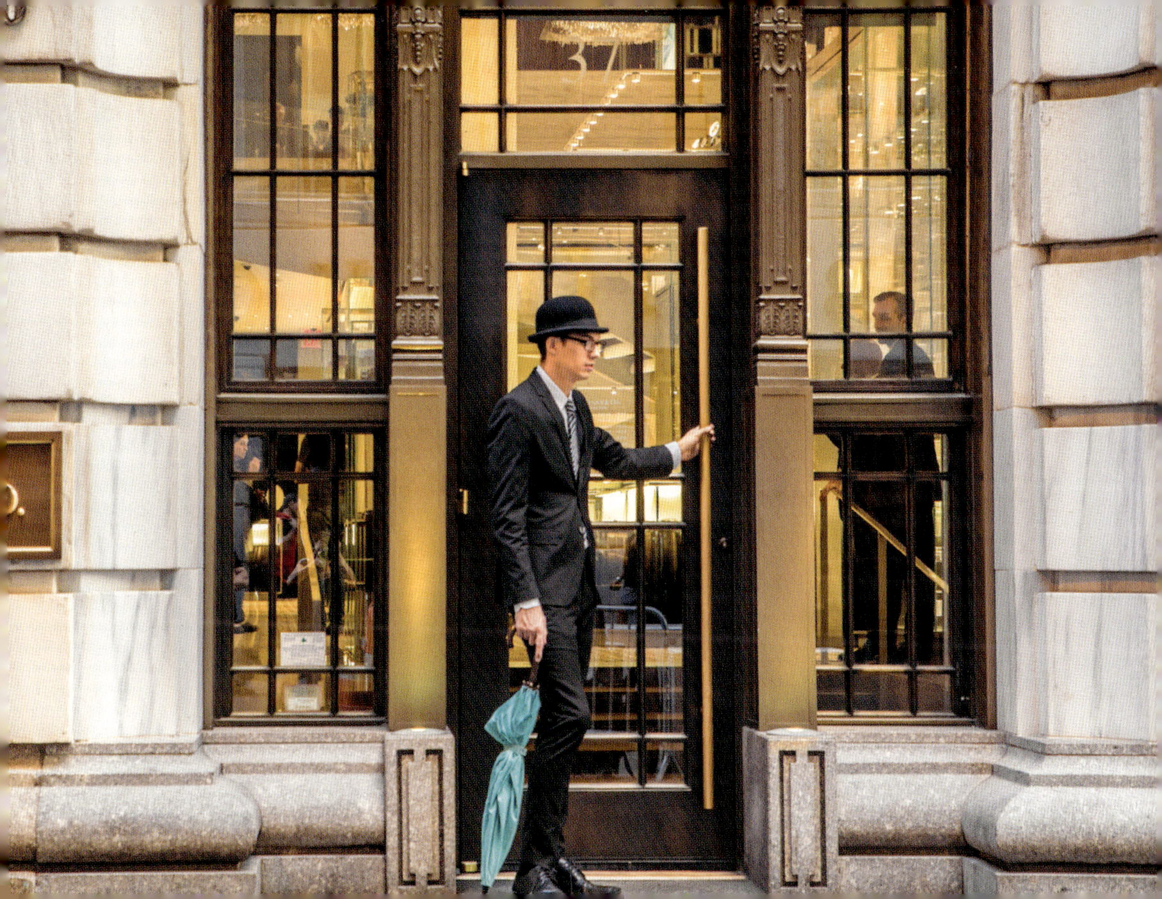

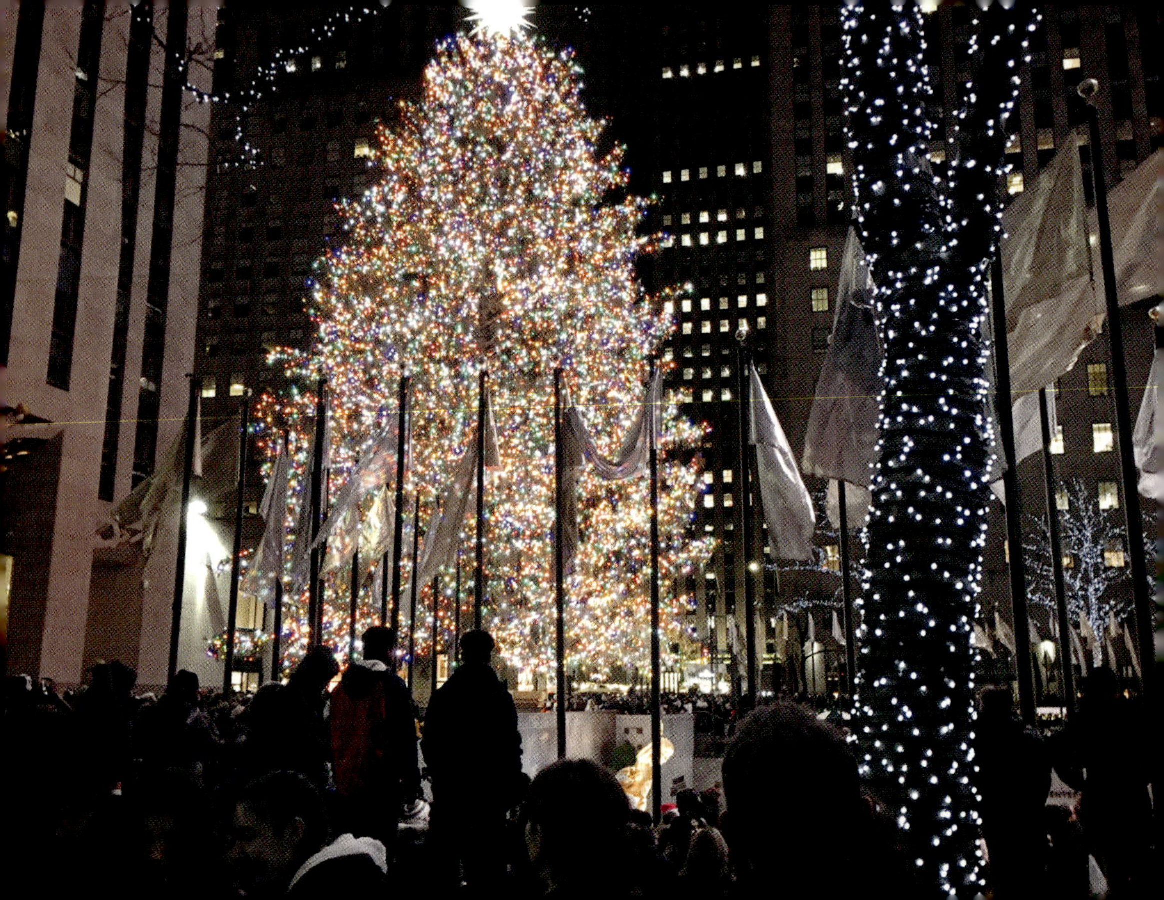

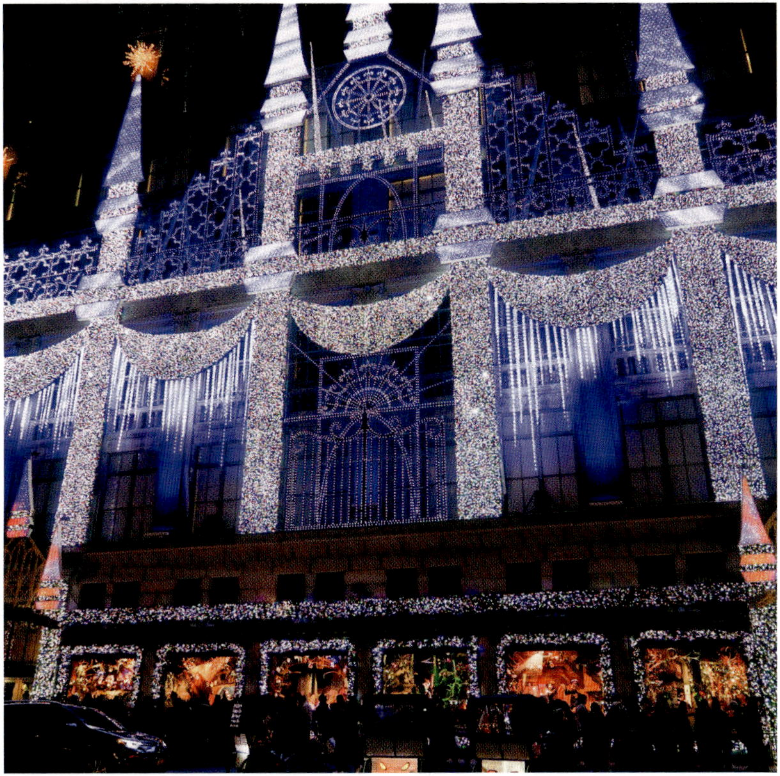

OPPOSITE:

Rockefeller Center

The lighting of the Rockefeller Christmas Tree has been an annual event since 1933. The ceremony takes place on the Wednesday following Thanksgiving. Since 1951, millions of people have watched the televised lighting, which more recently has included musical guests and live performances.

LEFT:

Saks Fifth Avenue

Built in 1924, Saks is one of the oldest luxury retailers in Manhattan. The 10-story structure is draped with elaborate lighting throughout the holiday months.

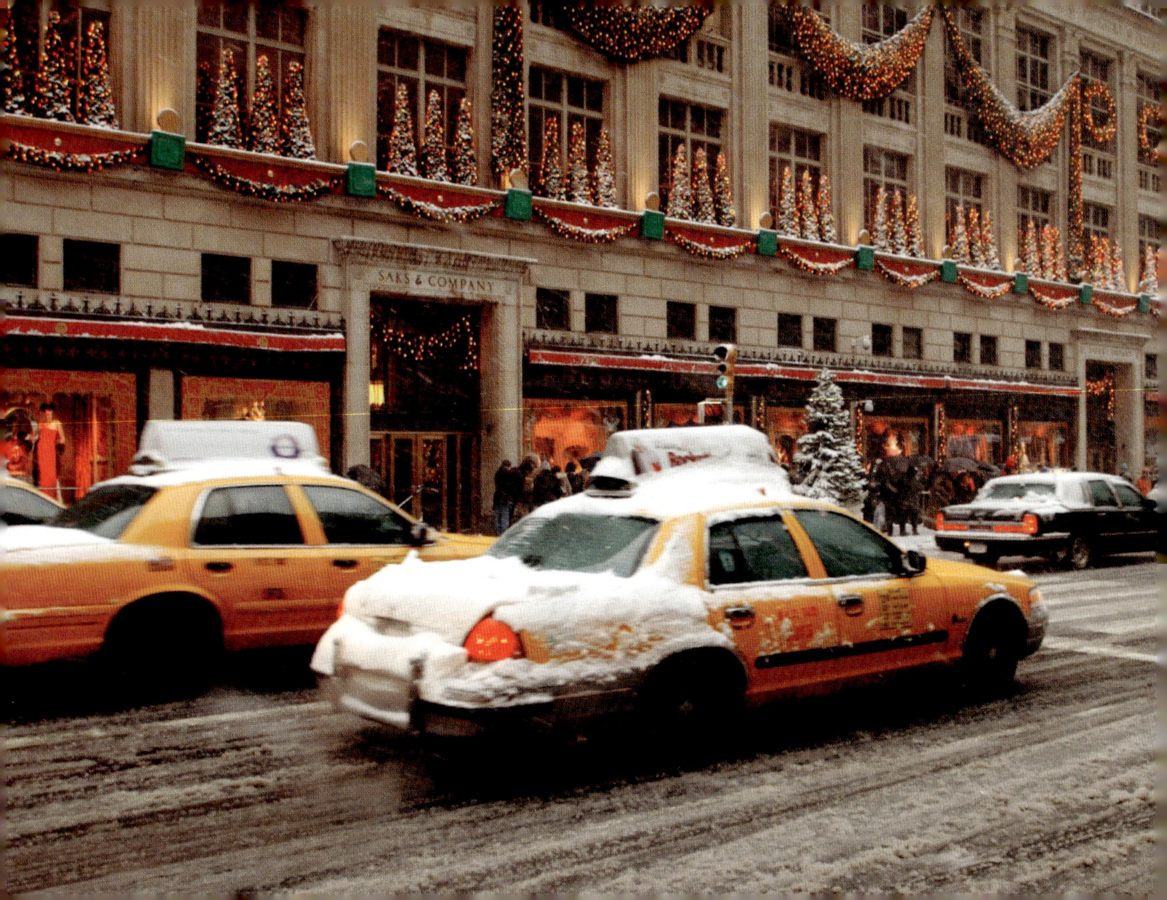
SAKS & COMPANY

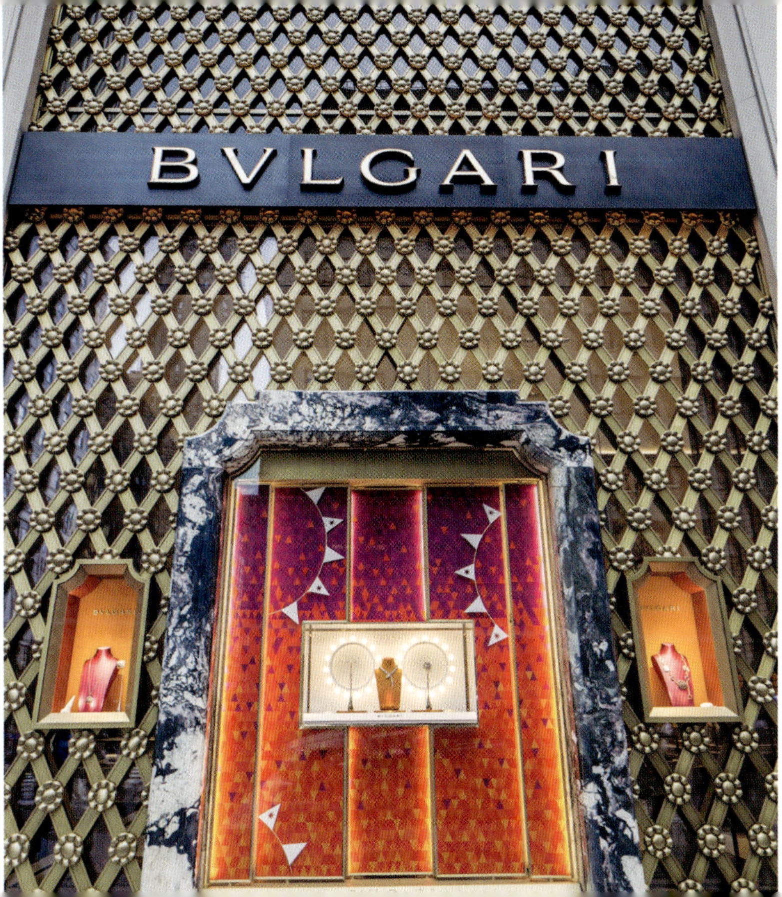

OPPOSITE:

Saks Fifth Avenue

At ground level, and running alongside Fifth Avenue, pedestrians can view the many large window panels displaying the latest winter fashions.

LEFT:

Bulgari

Located on the corner of 57th Street and Fifth Avenue, this Italian luxury goods company brings the vibe and style of Rome to the Big Apple with an ornamental bronze exterior screen and an interior of marble flooring, columns and ornate chandeliers.

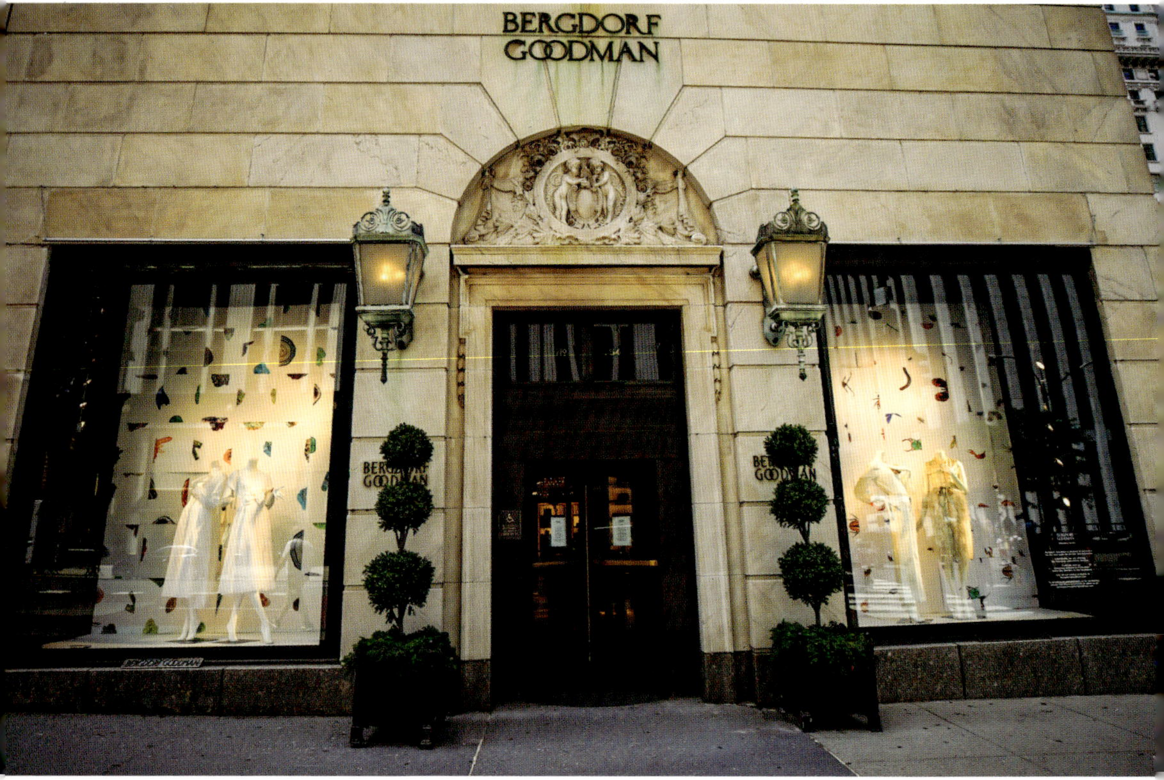
BERGDORF
GOODMAN

ALL PHOTOGRAPHS:

Bergdorf Goodman

Founded in 1899, this department store has a long history of bringing French fashion to the American market and introducing ready-to-wear clothing to a larger audience. Unlike other retail department stores, there are only two Bergdorf Goodman stores and both are located across the street from each other on Fifth Avenue, between 57th and 58th Streets.

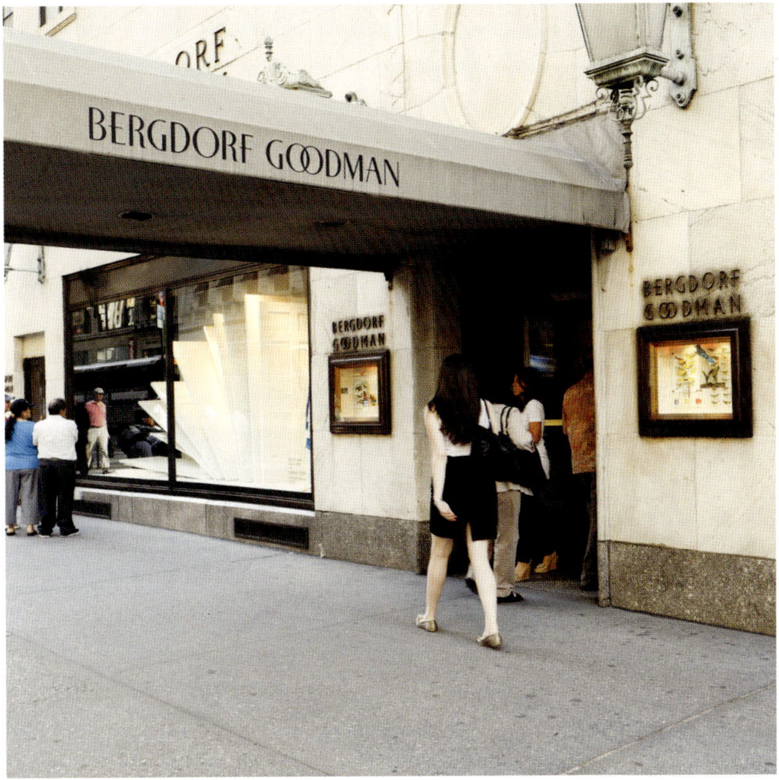

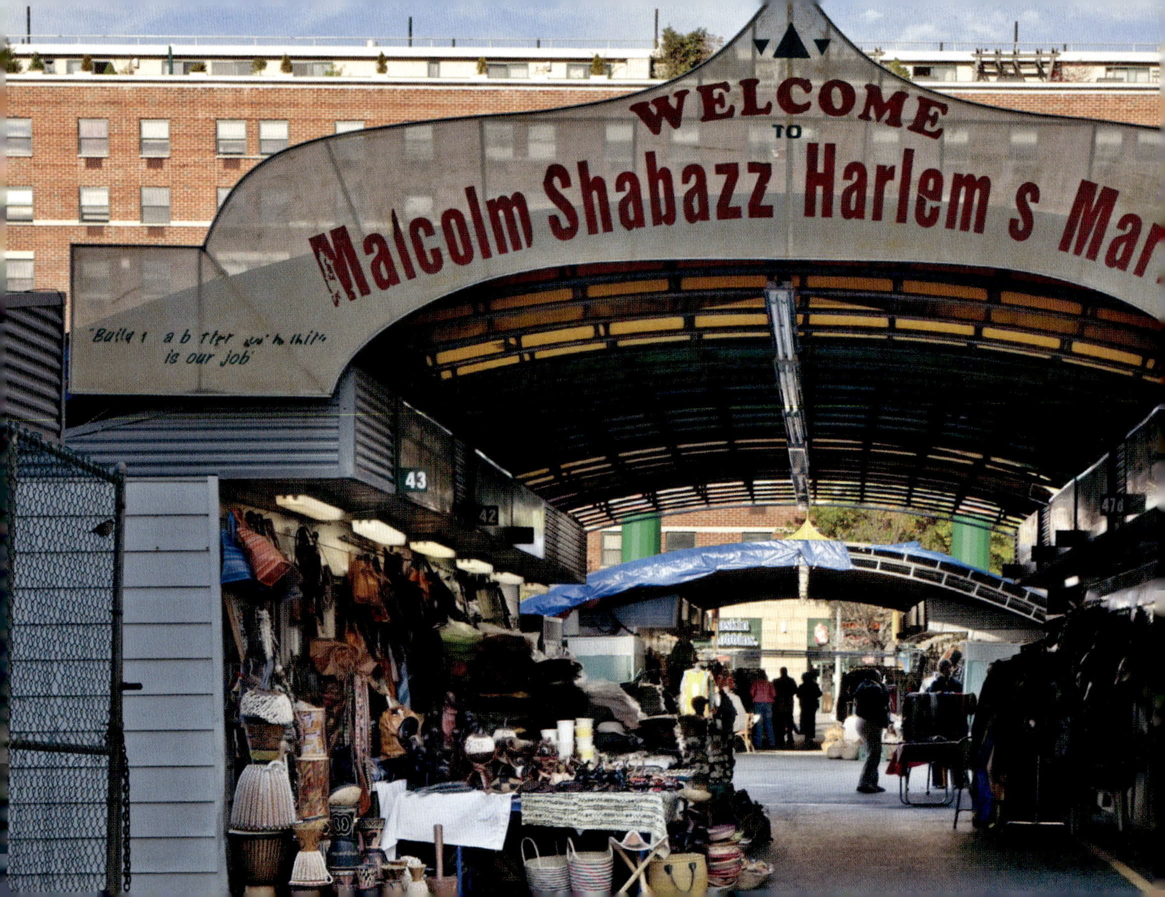
WELCOME
TO
Malcolm Shabazz Harlem s Mar
43
42

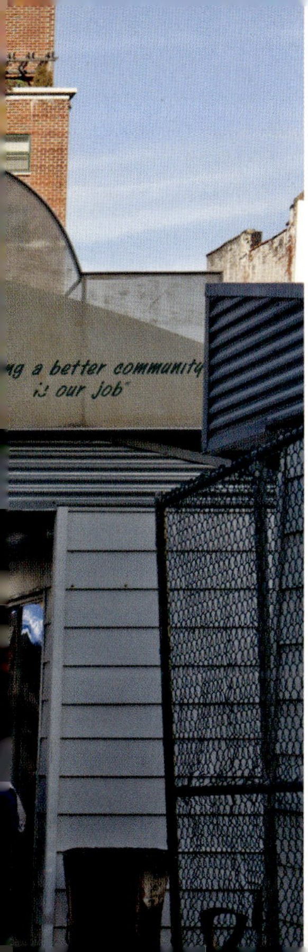

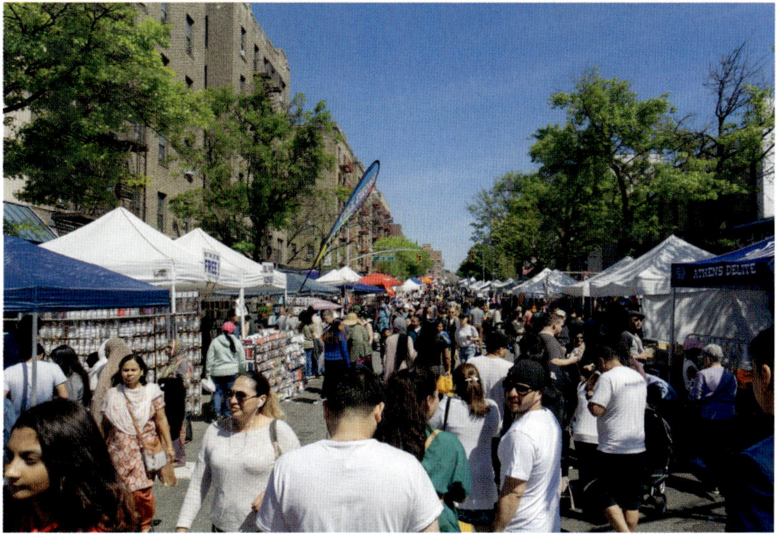

LEFT:

Malcolm Shabazz Harlem Market

This outdoor market concentrates on African goods and products including textiles and clothing, carved wooden crafts, and jewellery. Visitors can also sample traditional foods from countries like Kenya, Senegal and Ghana.

ABOVE:

Weekend market, Woodside

Located in the borough of Queens, this street market is open from July to the end of October and offers shoppers a glimpse of the locality's diverse crafts, products and food offered by an international mix of vendors.

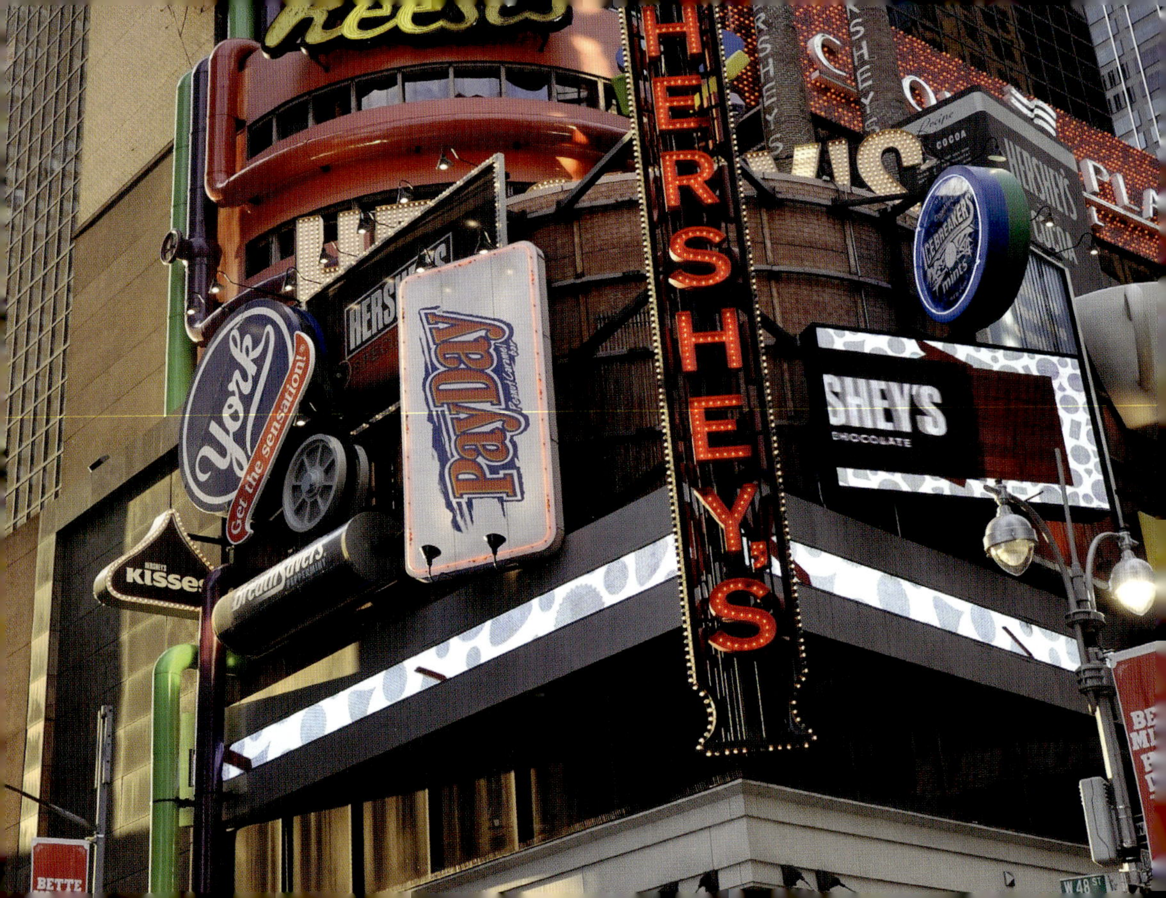
HERSHEY'S
York
Get the sensation!
PayDay
Peanut Caramel Bar
KISSES
SHEY'S
CHOCOLATE
ICE BREAKERS
mints
COCOA
BETTE
W 48 ST

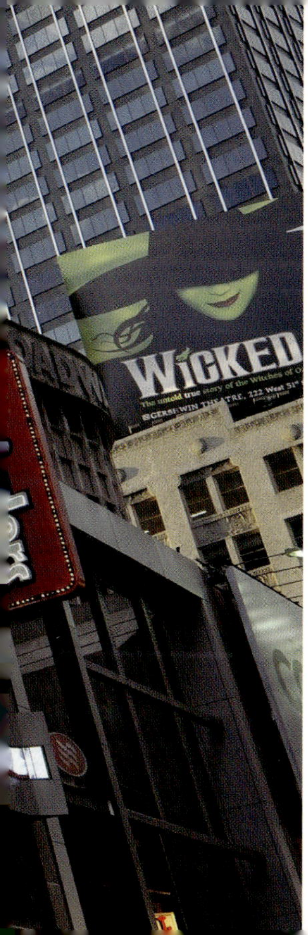

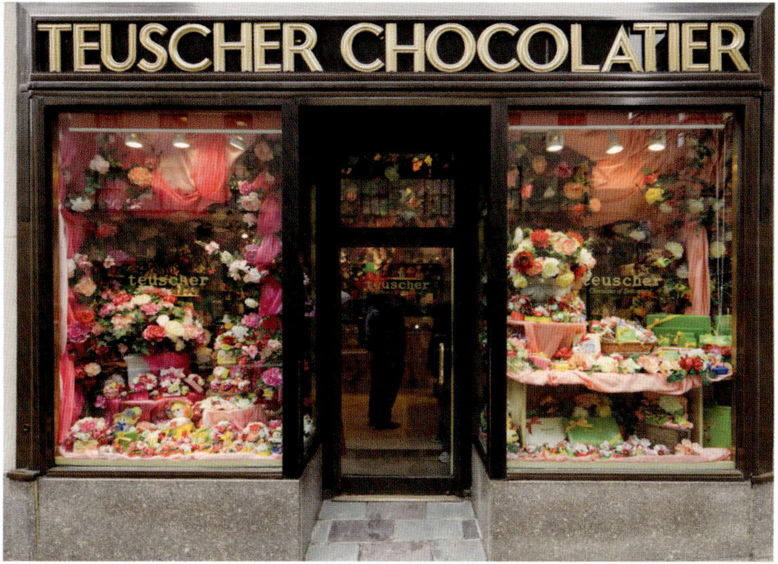

OPPOSITE:
Hershey's Chocolate World
If you're looking for something sweet to eat, this shop will more than help. Located in Times Square, visitors will find more than just their favourite candy as they explore the in-store attractions.

ABOVE:
Teuscher Chocolatier
In operation for over 80 years, this famous Swiss chocolate company has two locations in Manhattan – one on Madison Avenue and the other on Fifth Avenue.

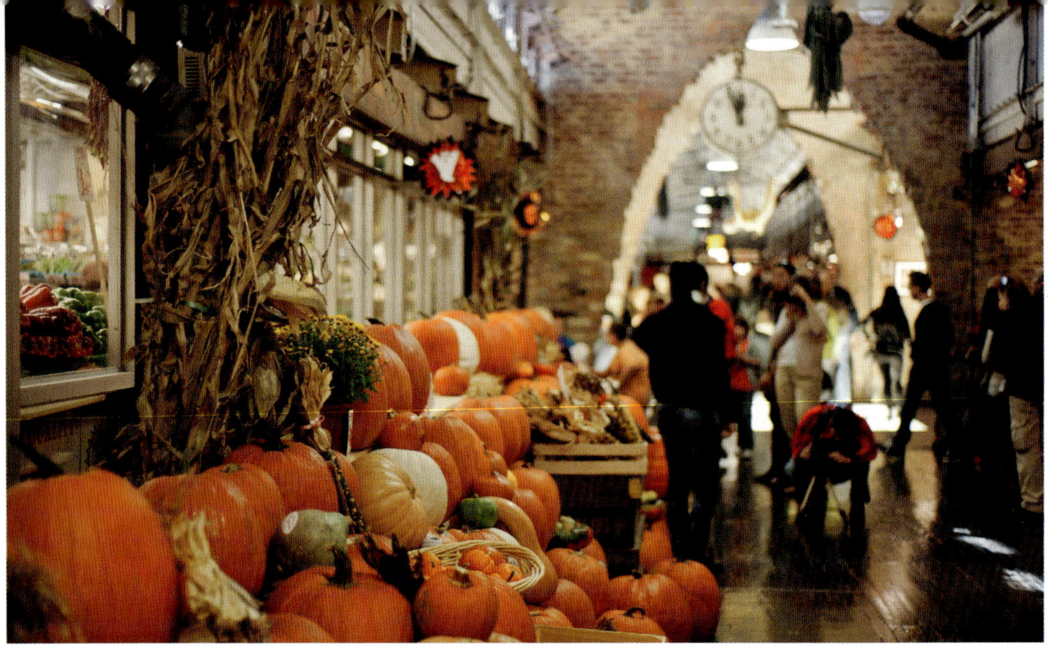

ABOVE:

Halloween pumpkins

Pumpkins are a common sight in the month of October as Halloween approaches. Naturally, pumpkin pie, pumpkin doughnuts, and a hot or cold pumpkin coffee all follow.

OPPOSITE:

Black Friday

Known as the busiest shopping day of the year, this annual sales event offering deep product discounts begins early on the Friday morning following Thanksgiving.

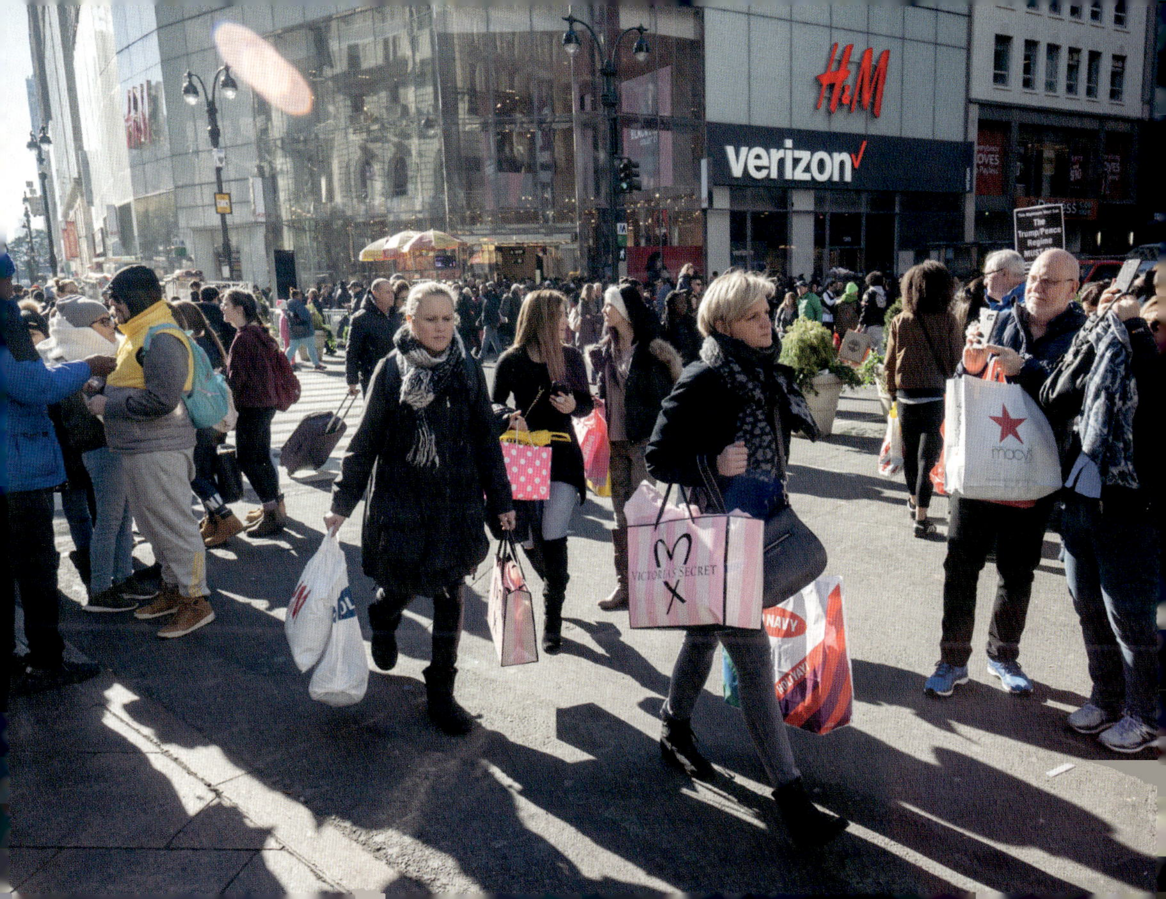
H&M
verizon
VICTORIA'S SECRET
NAVY
macy's

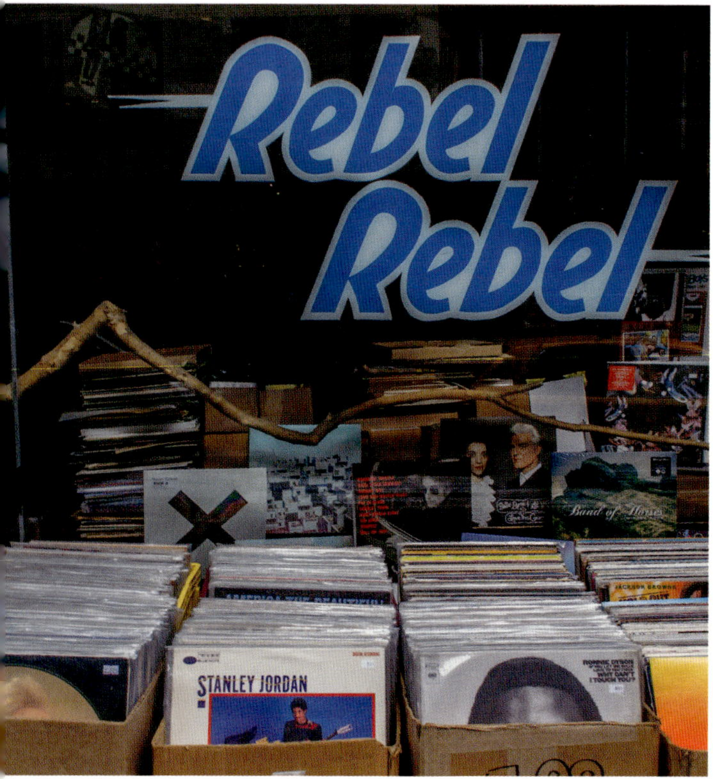
Rebel
Rebel
Band of Horses
STANLEY JORDAN
RONNIE DYSON
WHY CAN'T I TOUCH YOU?
JACKSON BROWNE

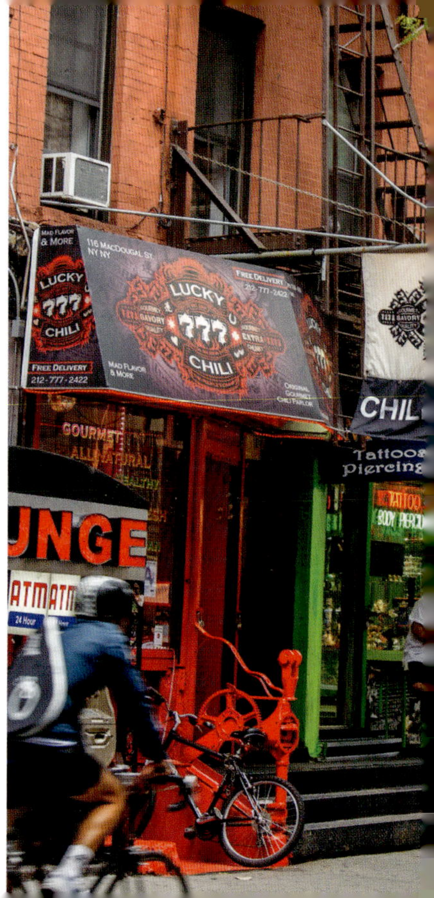
MAD FLAVOR & MORE
116 MacDougal St. NY NY
LUCKY 777 CHILI
FREE DELIVERY
212-777-2422
MAD FLAVOR & MORE
GOURMET
CHIL
Tattoos
Piercing
UNGE
24 Hour

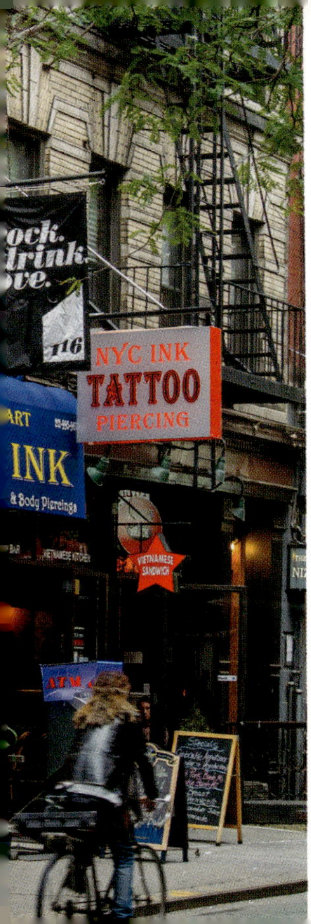

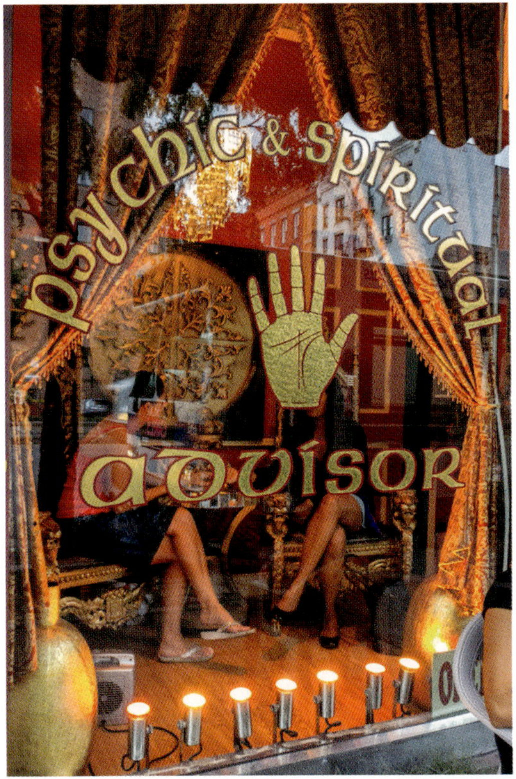

ALL PHOTOGRAPHS:
Greenwich Village
Once known as the epicenter of the New York punk scene, this area of Lower Manhattan still displays the artefacts of its musical past. Today, shoppers can sift through boxes and flip through vinyl albums, buy vintage clothing, shop for a tattoo or piercing, and even have their palms read and futures told by psychics.

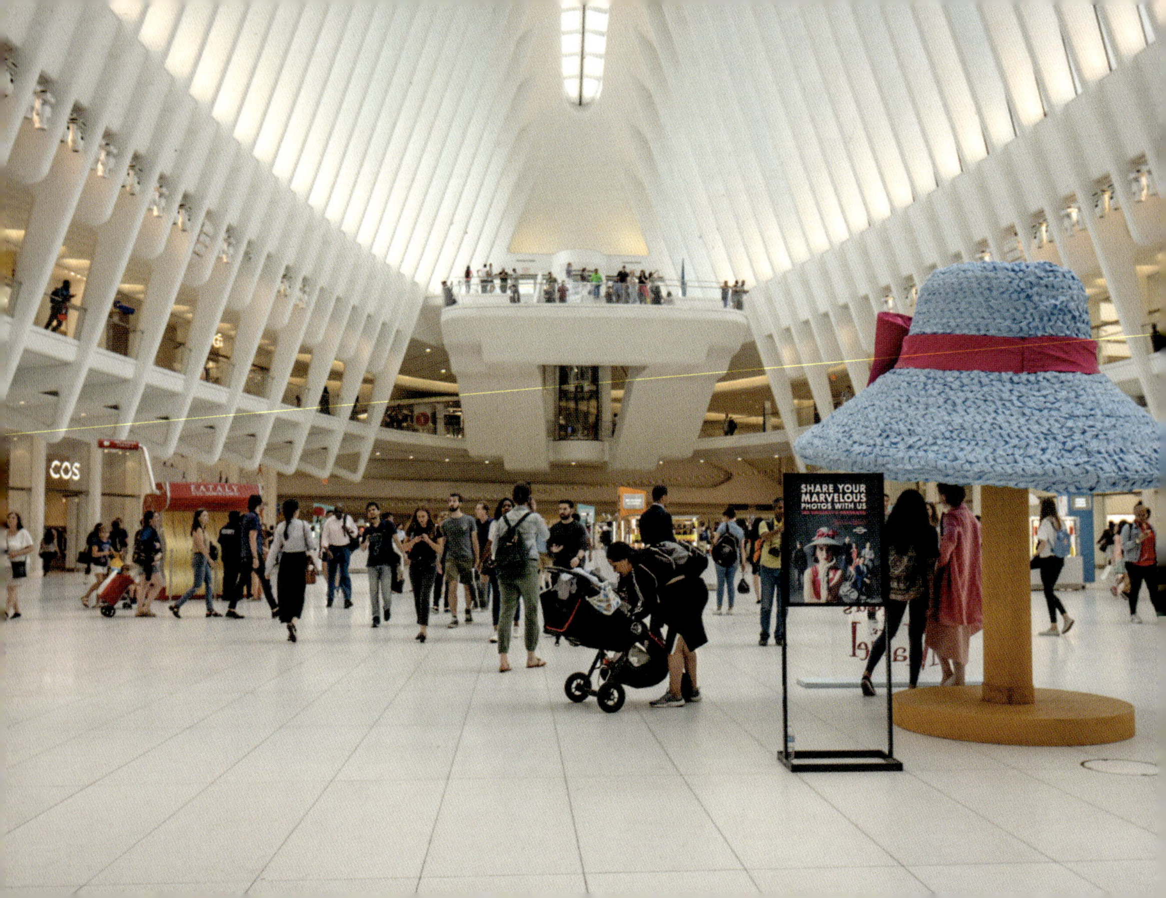
COS
EATALY
SHARE YOUR
MARVELOUS
PHOTOS WITH US

OPPOSITE:

Westfield Shopping Mall

More than 100 stores and restaurants are located in this double-level, downtown shopping mall. Opened in 2016, Westfield is the largest mall in Manhattan and is located indoors and underground at 4 and 5 World Trade Center.

RIGHT:

Juicy Couture

Located in Midtown East in Manhattan, this women's clothing store sells athletic and lifestyle clothing, fragrances, handbags, luggage, shoes and accessories, but is particularly known for its signature velour track suits.

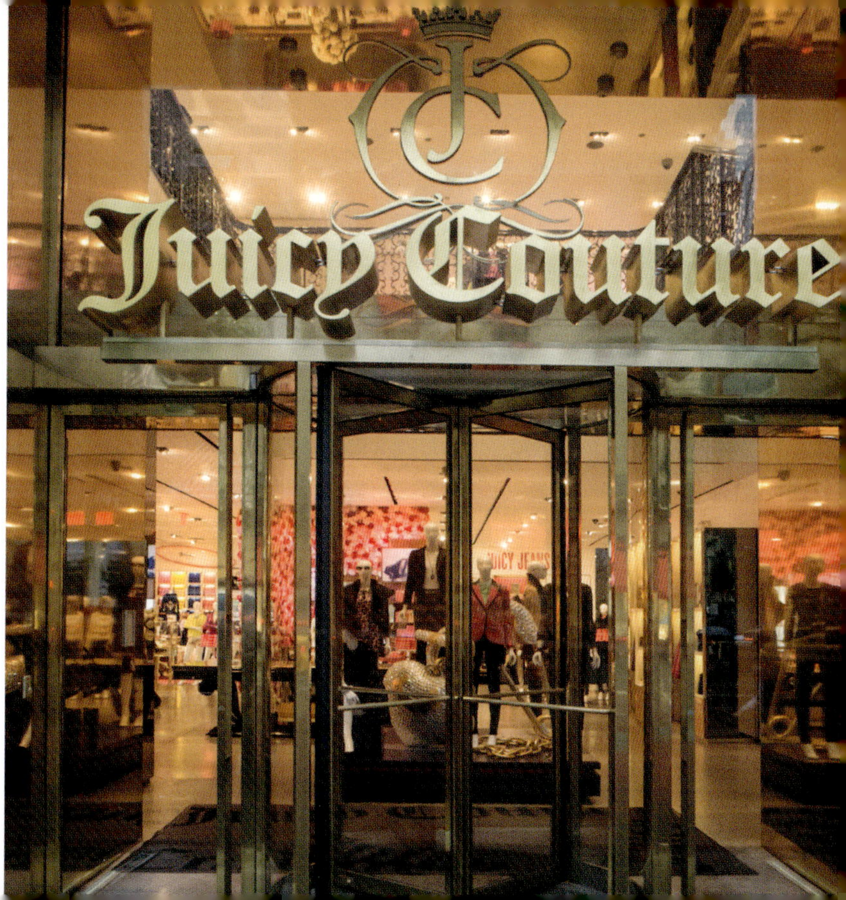

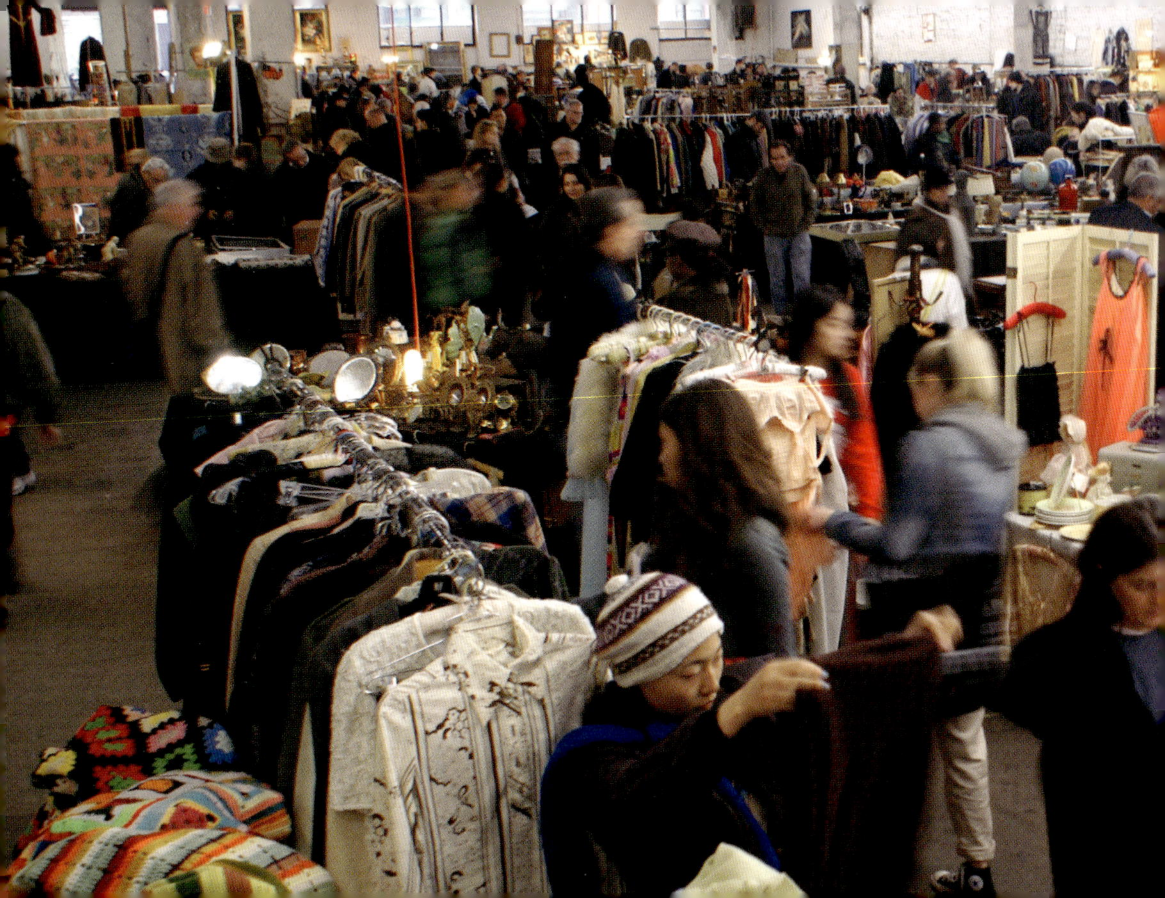

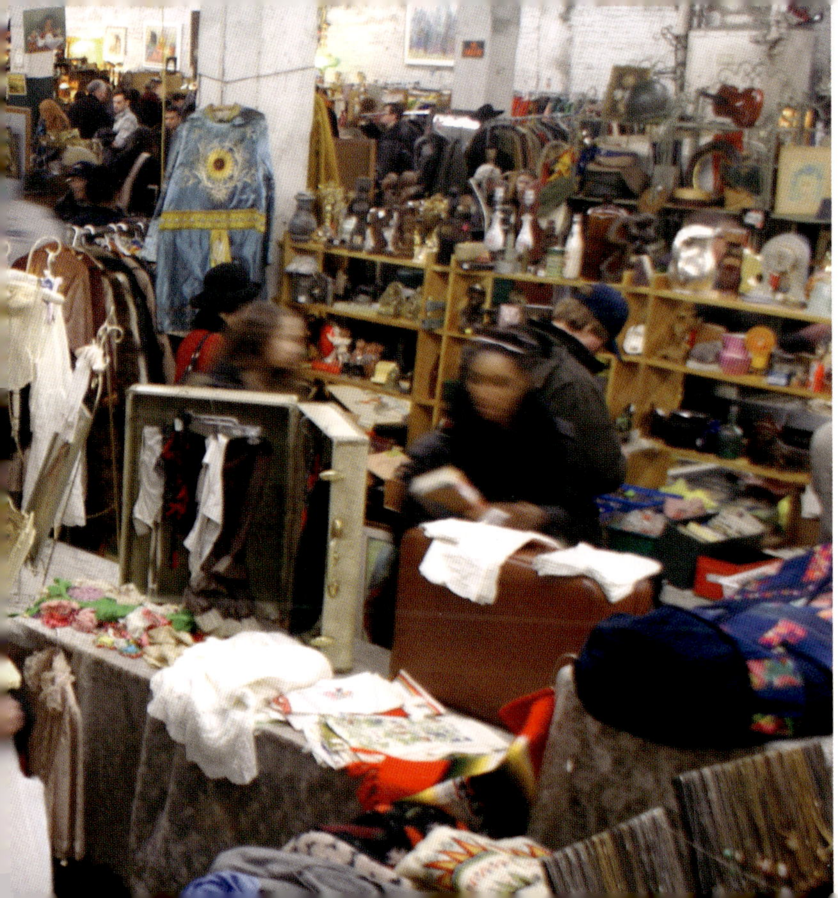

The Antiques Garage Flea Market

Open only on weekends, this Chelsea flea market is housed in a two-floor garage and hosts over 100 traders and vendors selling antiques, fabrics, clothing, rugs, shoes and jewellery, plus every type of collectible imaginable including vintage toys, games, music and books. Around since 1994, this is a popular location for shoppers looking for a one-of-a-kind buy.

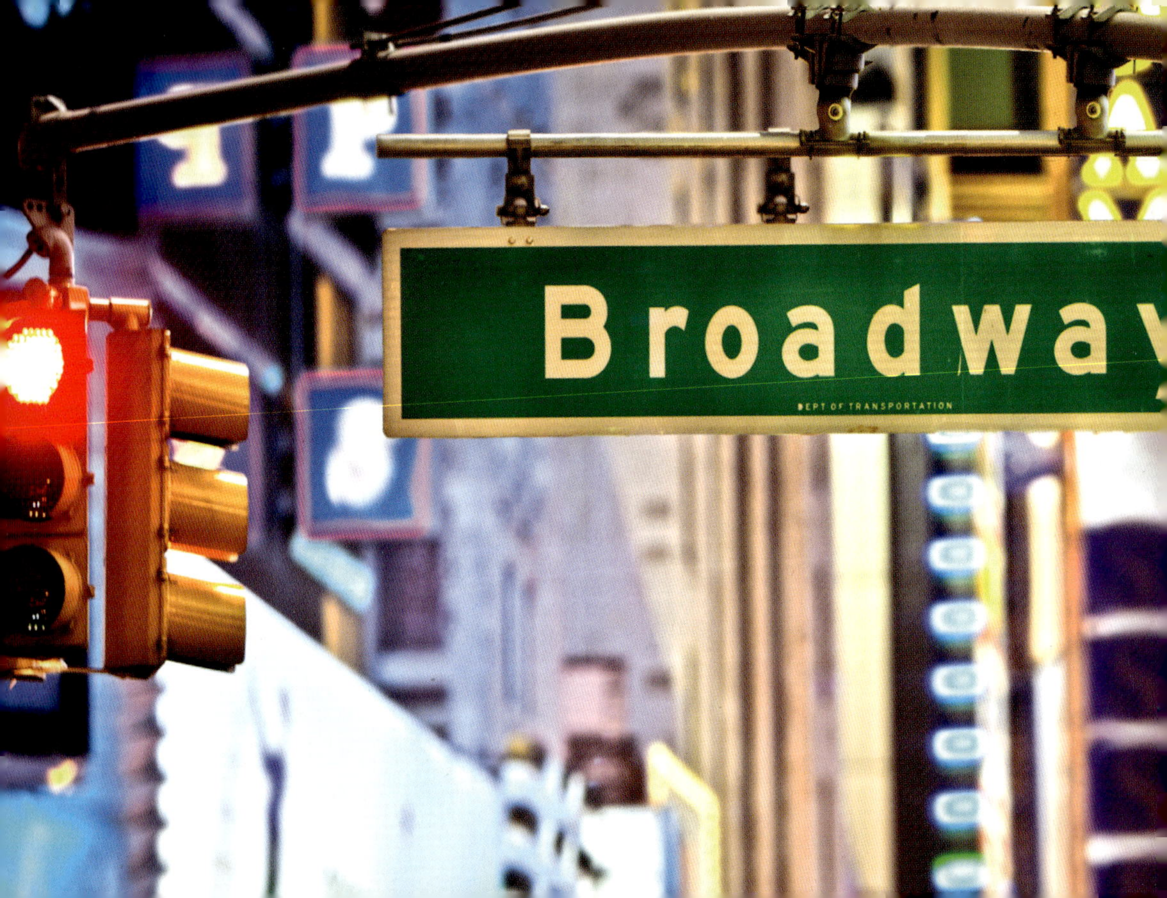
Broadway
DEPT OF TRANSPORTATION

Entertainment

Nothing says New York like the bright lights of Broadway. The Theater District is the epicenter of all the top-grossing musicals and plays, ranging from long-running productions to newly released box-office hits. But if you're looking for more than a Broadway show, then you don't have far to go. After all, there's also Off-Broadway and Off-Off-Broadway, where productions are smaller but just as entertaining.

New York City is a magnet when it comes to attracting people looking to have a good time. There are thousands of restaurants, bars and clubs, as well as venues that combine all three. Whether it's watching the sun set from a rooftop bar or seeing it rise at the end of a long night, New York holds up to its reputation as the 'city that never sleeps'.

The city is also where sports' lovers get to root for their teams. Large sports venues can be found across New York City's boroughs – Yankee Stadium in the Bronx, Citi Field in Queens, Barclay Stadium in Brooklyn, and Madison Square Garden in Manhattan.

The good news is that finding something fun to do or watch does not need to break the bank, though that option is also available! Music flows through the city's streets, through its parks, and underground in subway stations at all hours. It's also in the numerous cultural events that occur across the city and throughout the year.

OPPOSITE:
Broadway
Although now packed with performance venues, Broadway is actually one of the oldest roads in New York, dating back to when the city was called New Amsterdam and this road was named 'Gentleman's Way'.

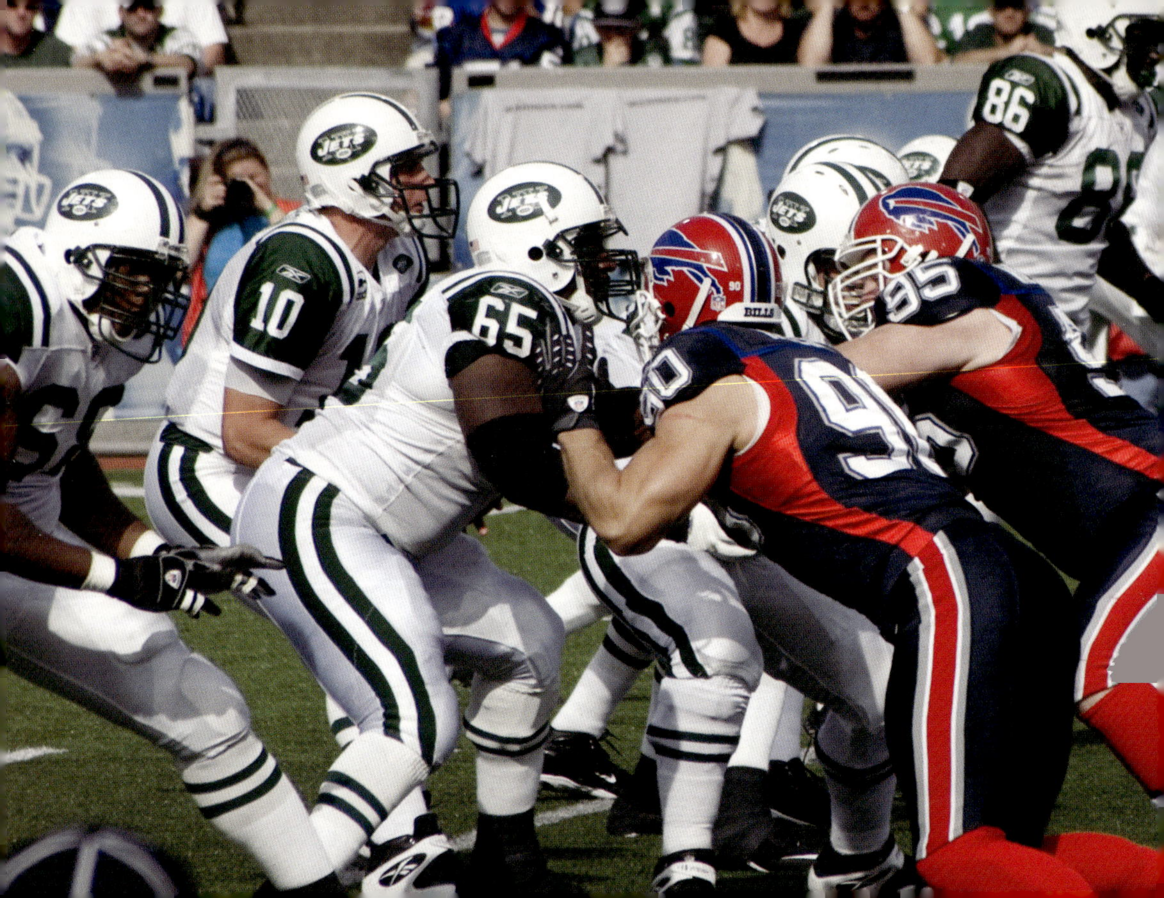
JETS
10
65
86
90
95
BILLS

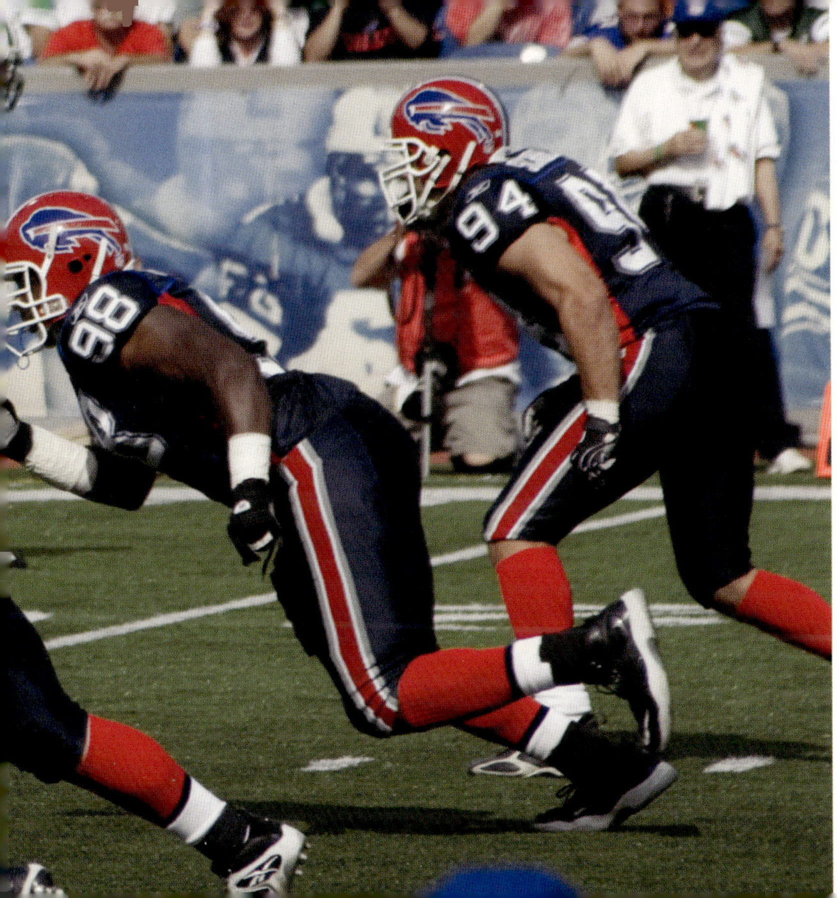

Jets! Jets! Jets!

Originally known as the Titans, the name of this NFL team changed as they went to play near LaGuardia Airport in Queens. Today, the Jets represent one of the two New York Metropolitan football teams (the other being the Giants). Both teams share the MetLife Stadium in Rutherford, New Jersey, 8km (5 miles) west of New York City.

Madison Square Garden
Located in Midtown Manhattan atop Penn Station between Seventh and Eighth Avenue, this indoor arena, referred to by many as 'The Garden' or simply MSG, has been hosting sports and entertainment events since 1968. New Yorkers and visitors from other states and around the world go to the MSG to watch and enjoy professional sports including basketball, hockey, wrestling, concerts and other popular events.

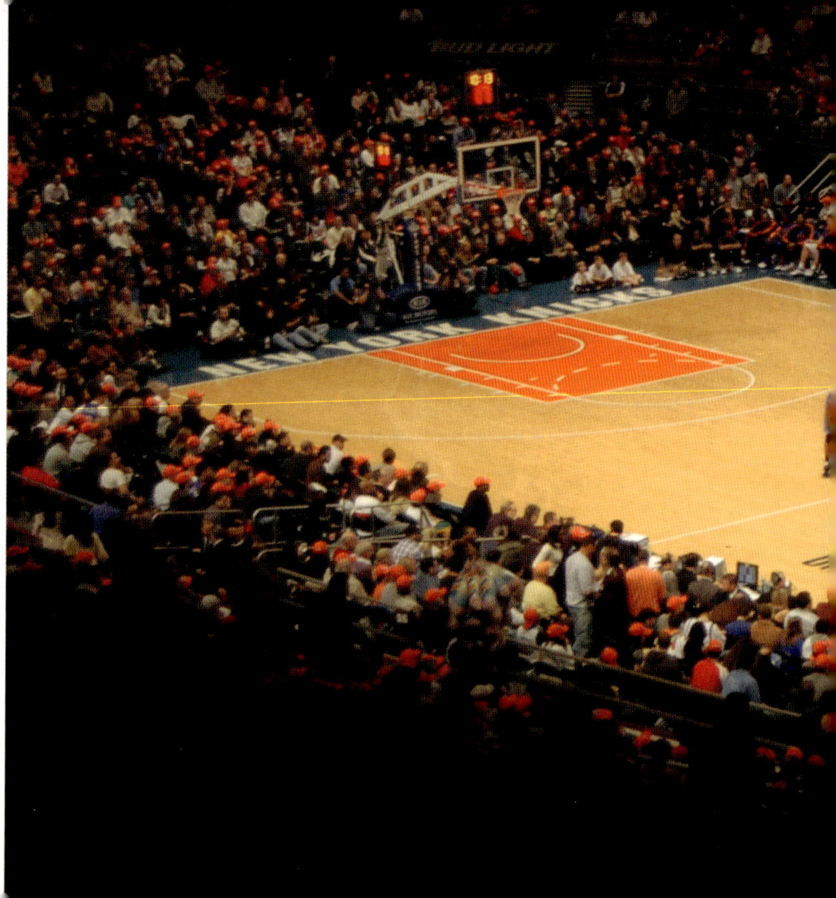

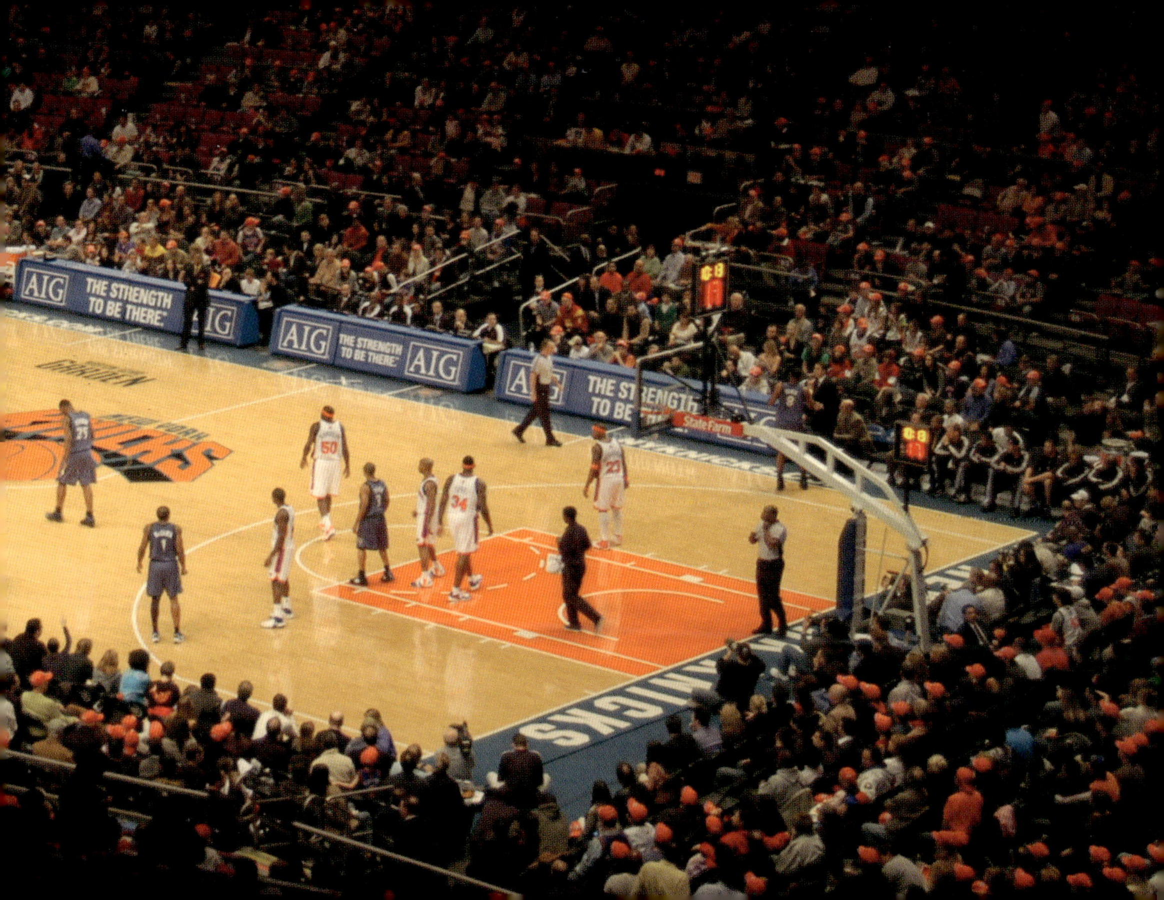
AIG
THE STRENGTH TO BE THERE.
AIG
State Farm
KNICKS

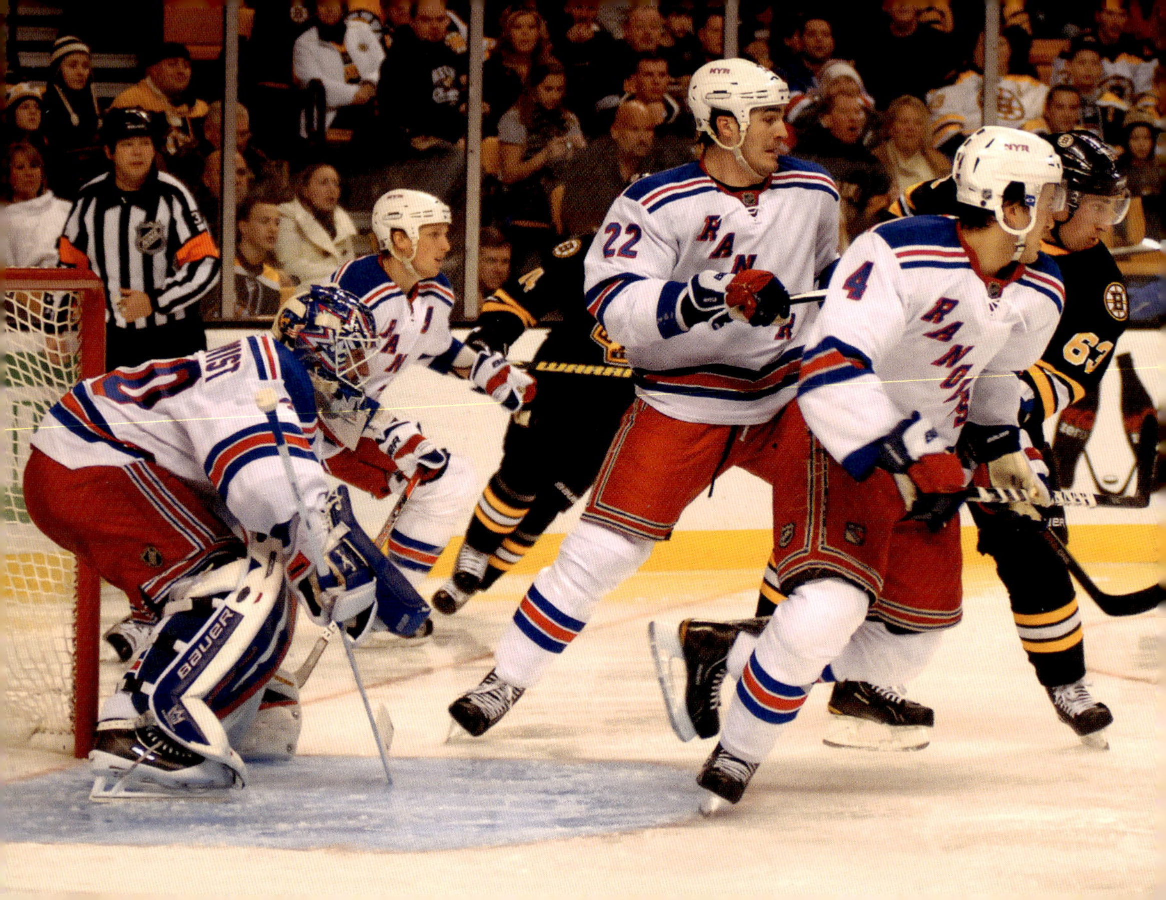
NYR
NYR
22
4
63
BAUER

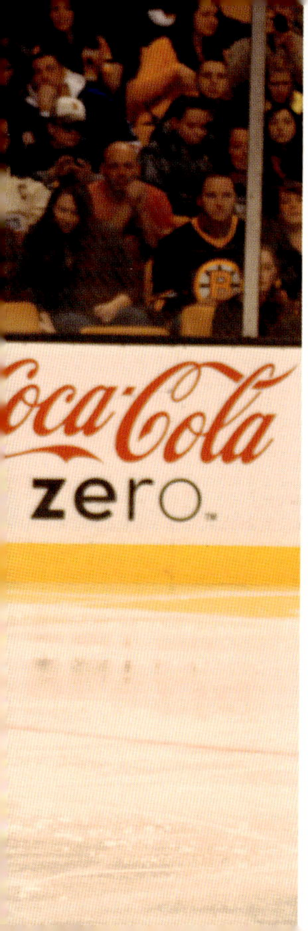

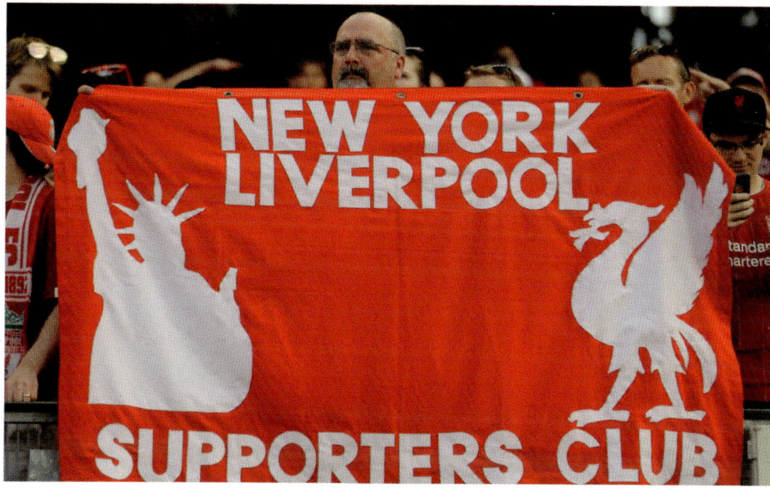

LEFT:
New York Rangers
Over four million people visit Madison Square Garden annually to watch a sporting event or attend a concert. One of the most popular draws is New York's ice hockey team, the Rangers. With close to 60 games played during the season, more than half are home games from MSG.

ABOVE:
MSG–Liverpool FC
Madison Square Garden has a 21,000-seat capacity. Whether it's a concert, sporting event, or even the dog show, the arena holds an average of 320 events each year, including hosting other major sporting institutions from around the world.

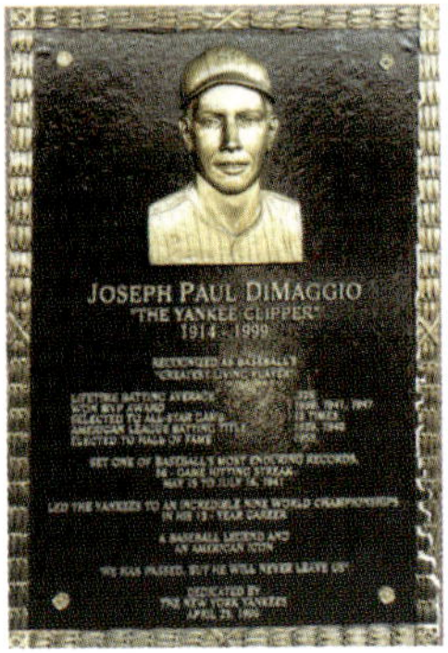

ALL PHOTOGRAPHS:

Let's go Yankees!

The stadium is the home field of one of the most successful baseball franchises in history – the New York Yankees. Famous players who have worn the Yankees uniform over the last 120 years include Mickey Mantle, Babe Ruth, Joe DiMaggio (above) and Lou Gehrig.

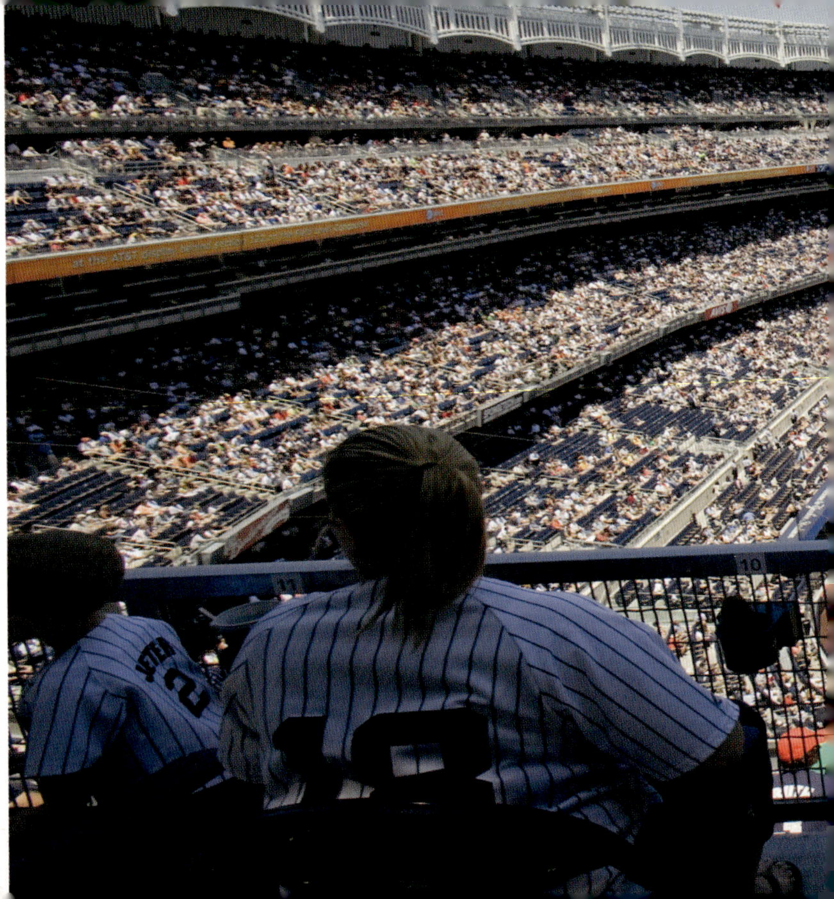

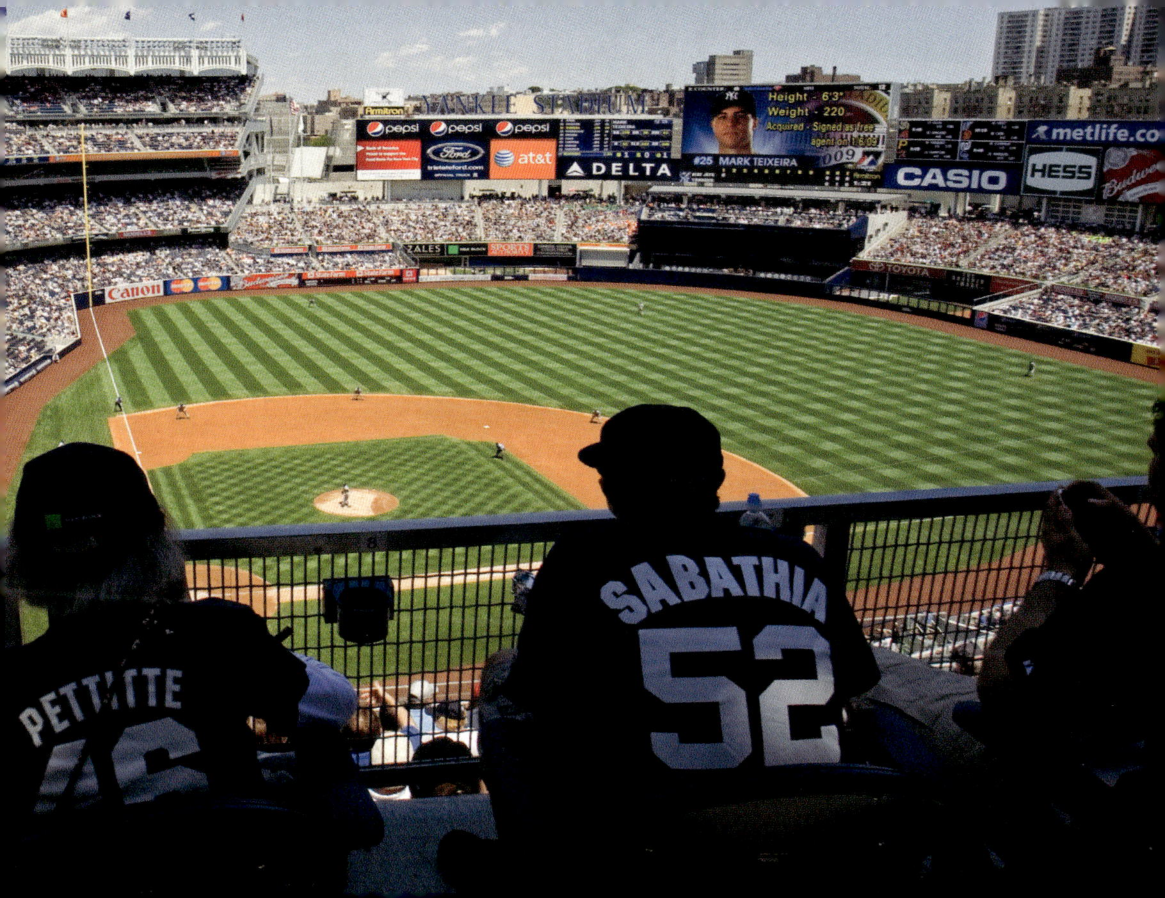
YANKEE STADIUM
Armitron
pepsi
pepsi
pepsi
Ford
tristateford.com
at&t
DELTA
Height - 6'3"
Weight - 220
#25 MARK TEIXEIRA
metlife.co
CASIO
HESS
Canon
ZALES
TOYOTA
SABATHIA
52

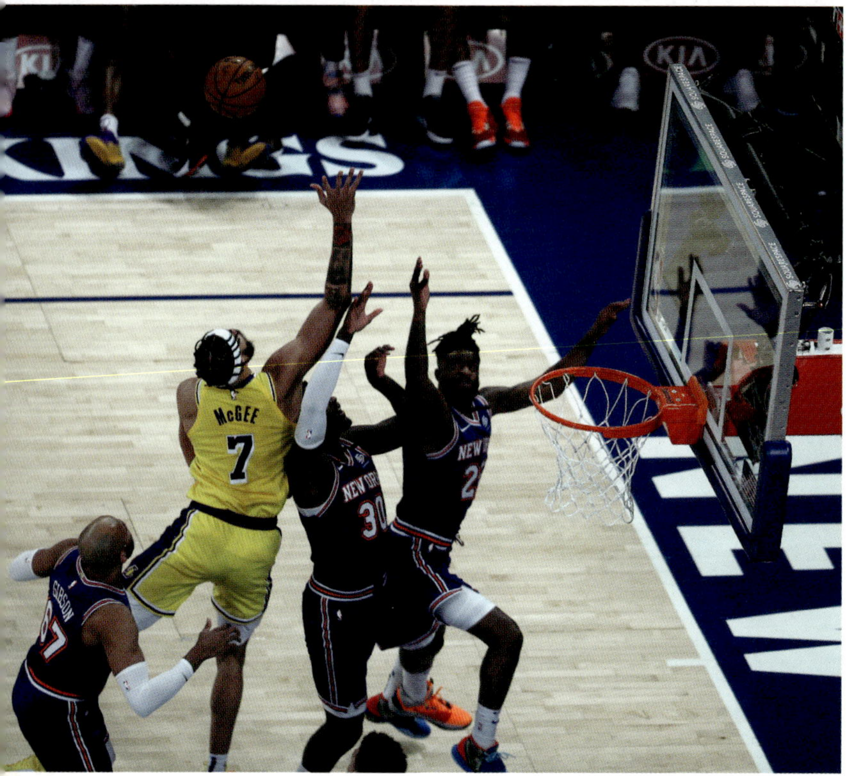

LEFT:

The Knickerbockers

Once known as the New York Knickerbockers, the team name was trimmed down to 'Knicks'. The second NBA team in the city is the Nets, with their home arena, the Barclay Stadium, based in Brooklyn.

OPPOSITE:

Yankee Stadium

Located in the Bronx, the new Yankee Stadium was built in 2009 at a cost of $2.3 billion (about £1.6 billion) and with a seating capacity close to 50,000.

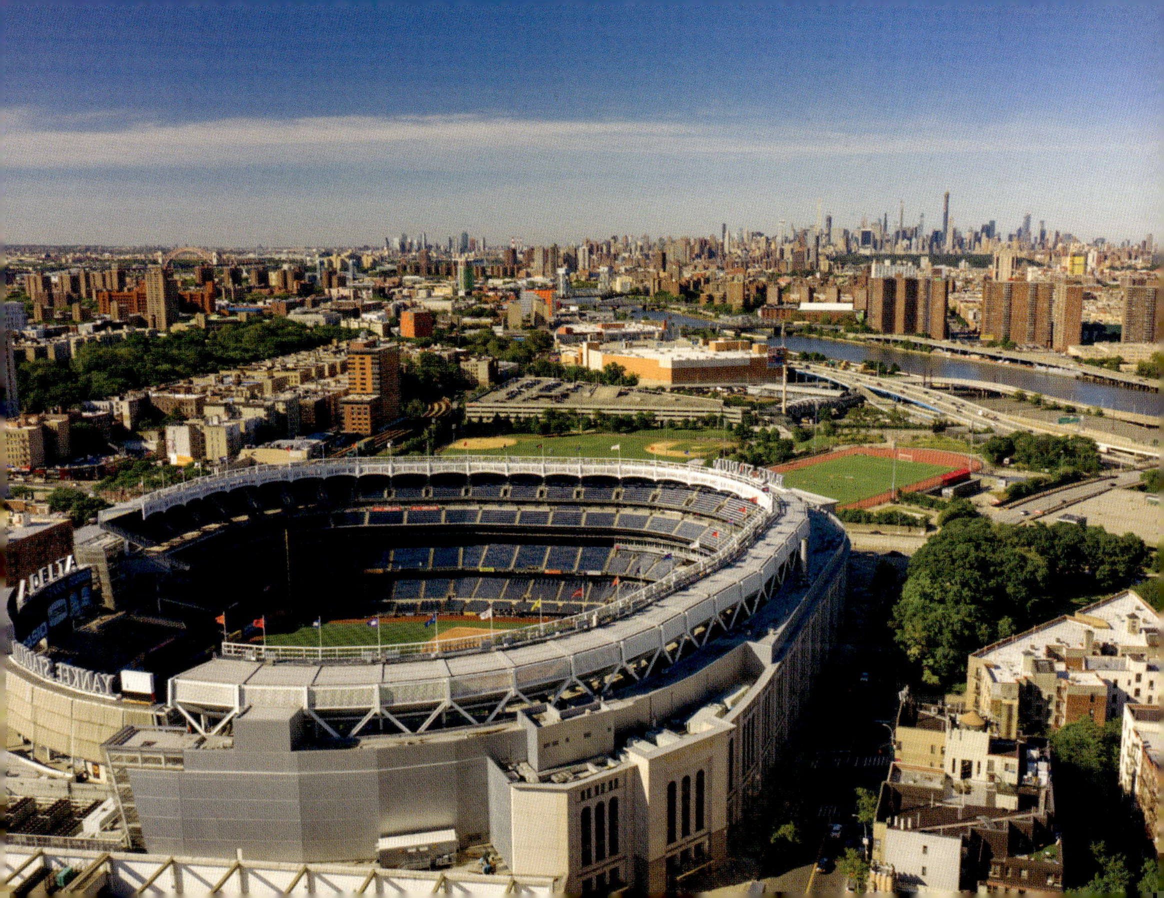
DELTA

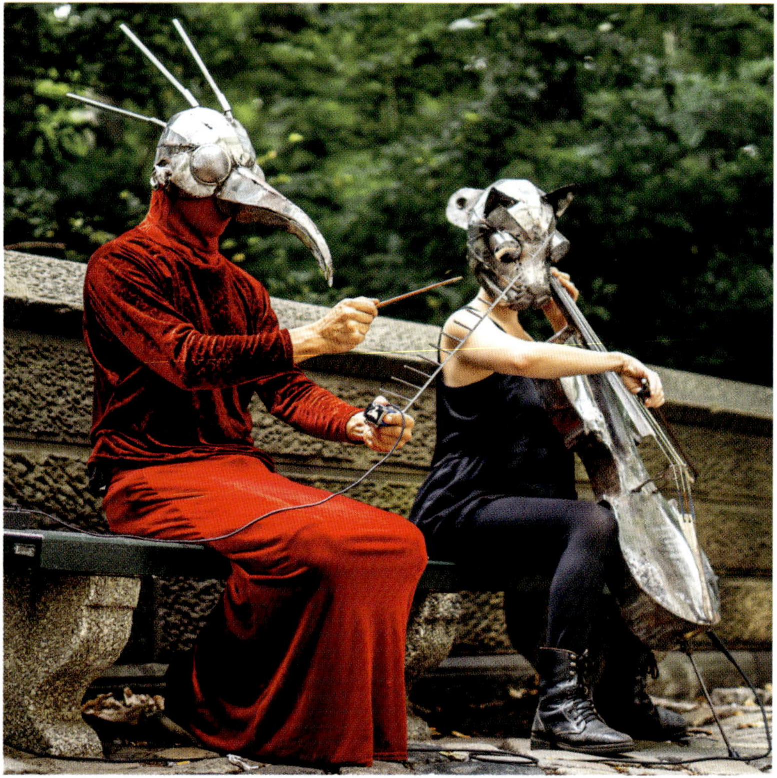

ALL PHOTOGRAPHS:

Street music

Walking down the street, through a park, or waiting for a subway, there's one New York City experience that's hard to miss – finding and listening to a musical performance. Some musicians come with speakers, stands and full drum kits, while others may just sit on a milk crate and play a bucket.

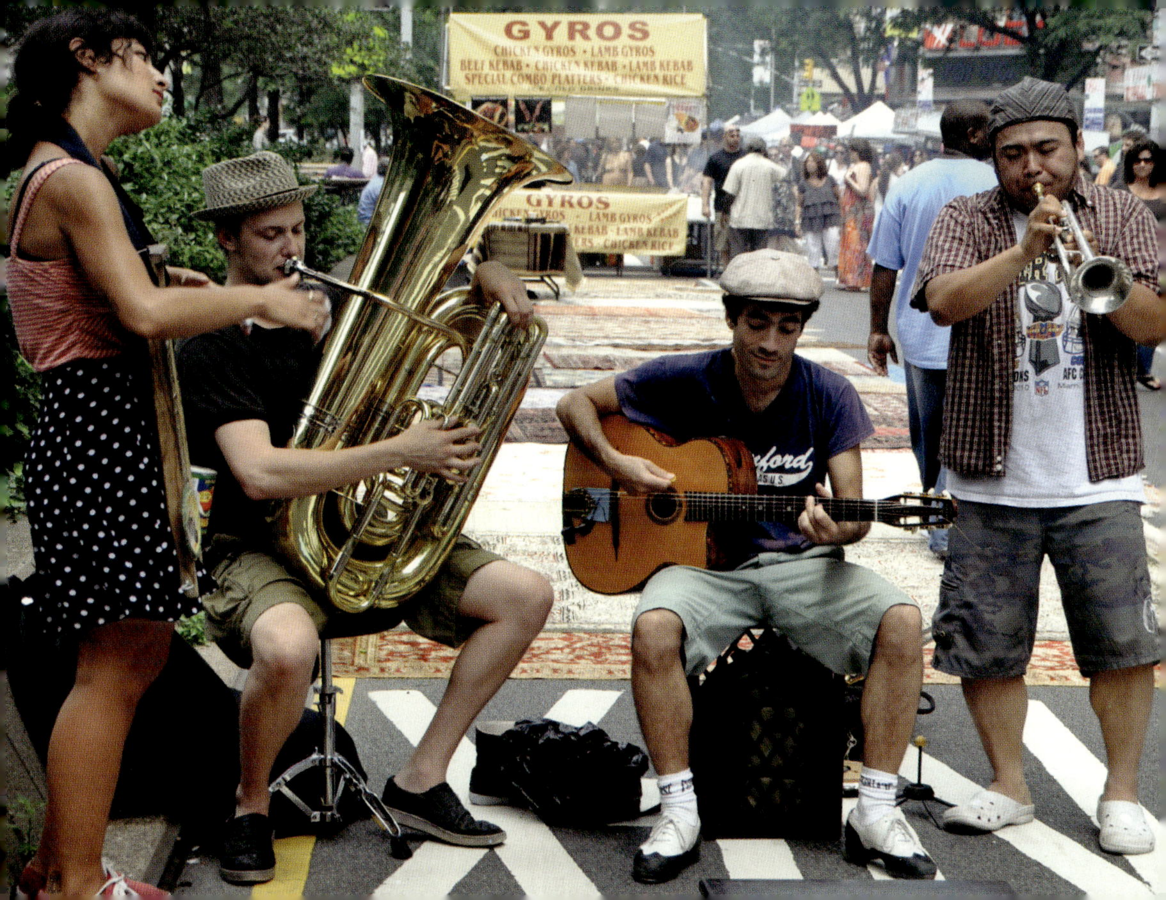
GYROS
CHICKEN GYROS • LAMB GYROS
BEEF KEBAB • CHICKEN KEBAB • LAMB KEBAB
SPECIAL COMBO PLATTERS • CHICKEN RICE
GYROS

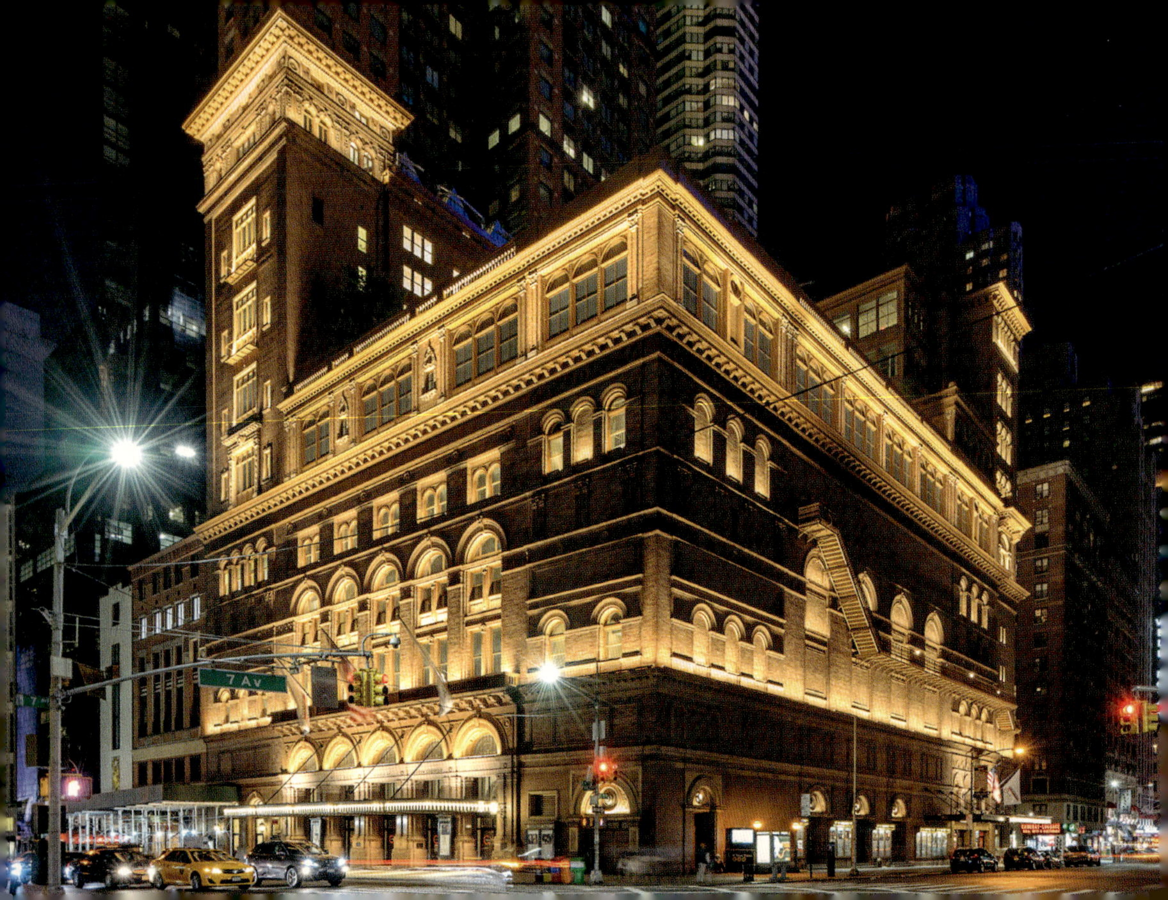
7 Av

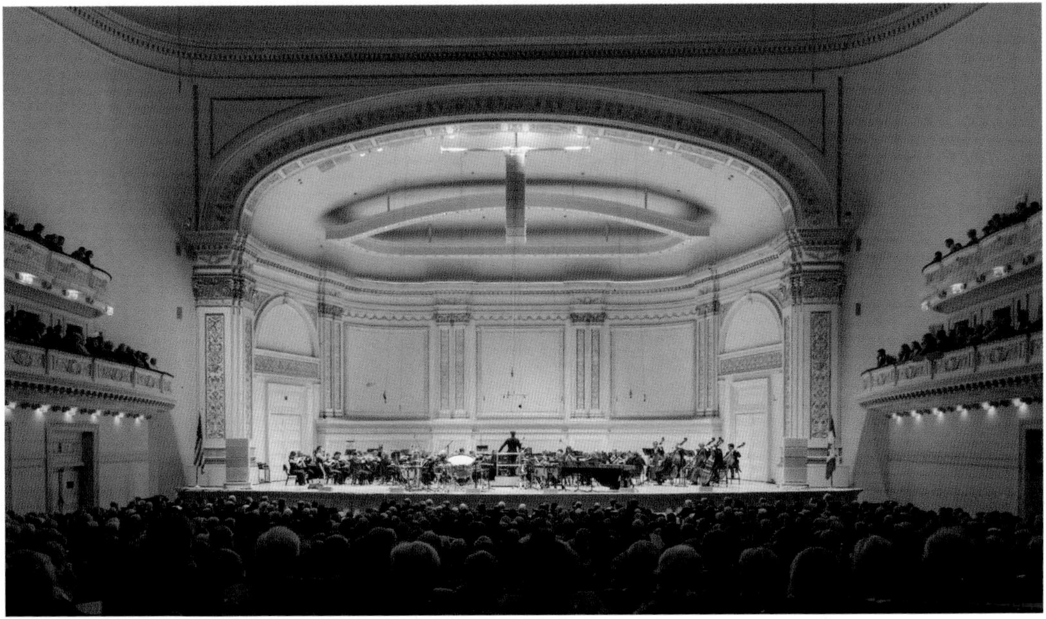

ALL PHOTOGRAPHS:

Carnegie Hall

One of the most famous music halls in the world, Carnegie Hall first opened its doors in 1891. Located in Midtown Manhattan on Seventh Avenue between 56th and 57th Streets, the site is easy to find, especially at night, thanks to its beautiful lit-up facade. The building, featuring Rennaissance-style architecture, is divided into three venues: the Main Hall (above), Zankel Hall and the Weill Recital Hall.

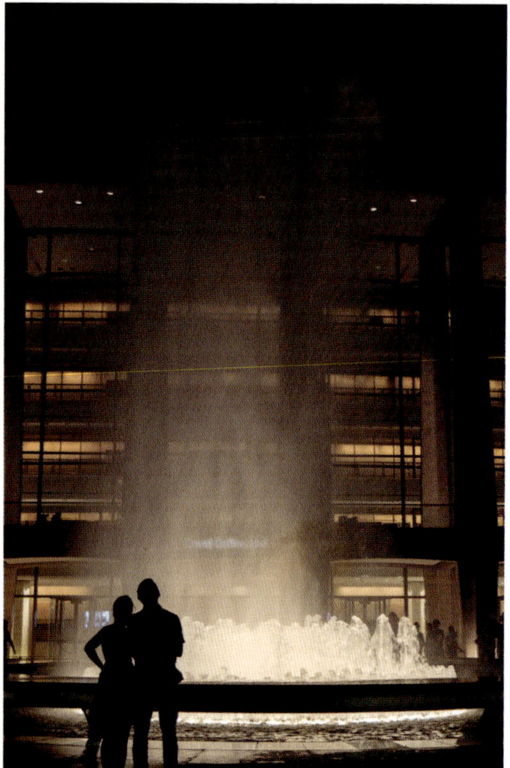

ALL PHOTOGRAPHS:

Lincoln Center

The Lincoln Center of Performing Arts is a multi-building complex in Lincoln Square and is the site of 30 indoor and outdoor facilities. It is home to 12 world-renowned organisations including the Metropolitan Opera, Julliard, and the New York Philharmonic. Each year, five million people visit the building.

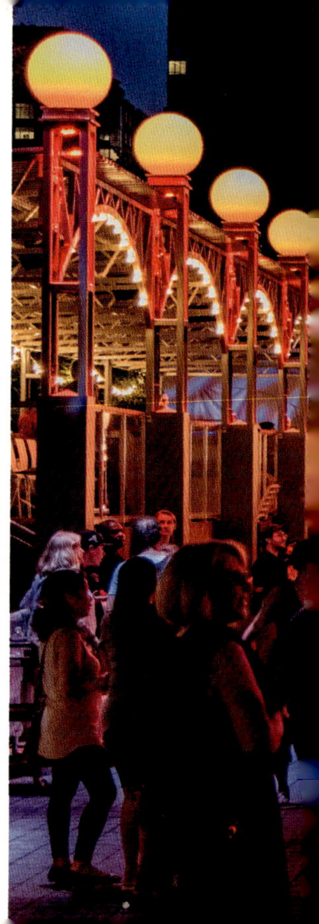

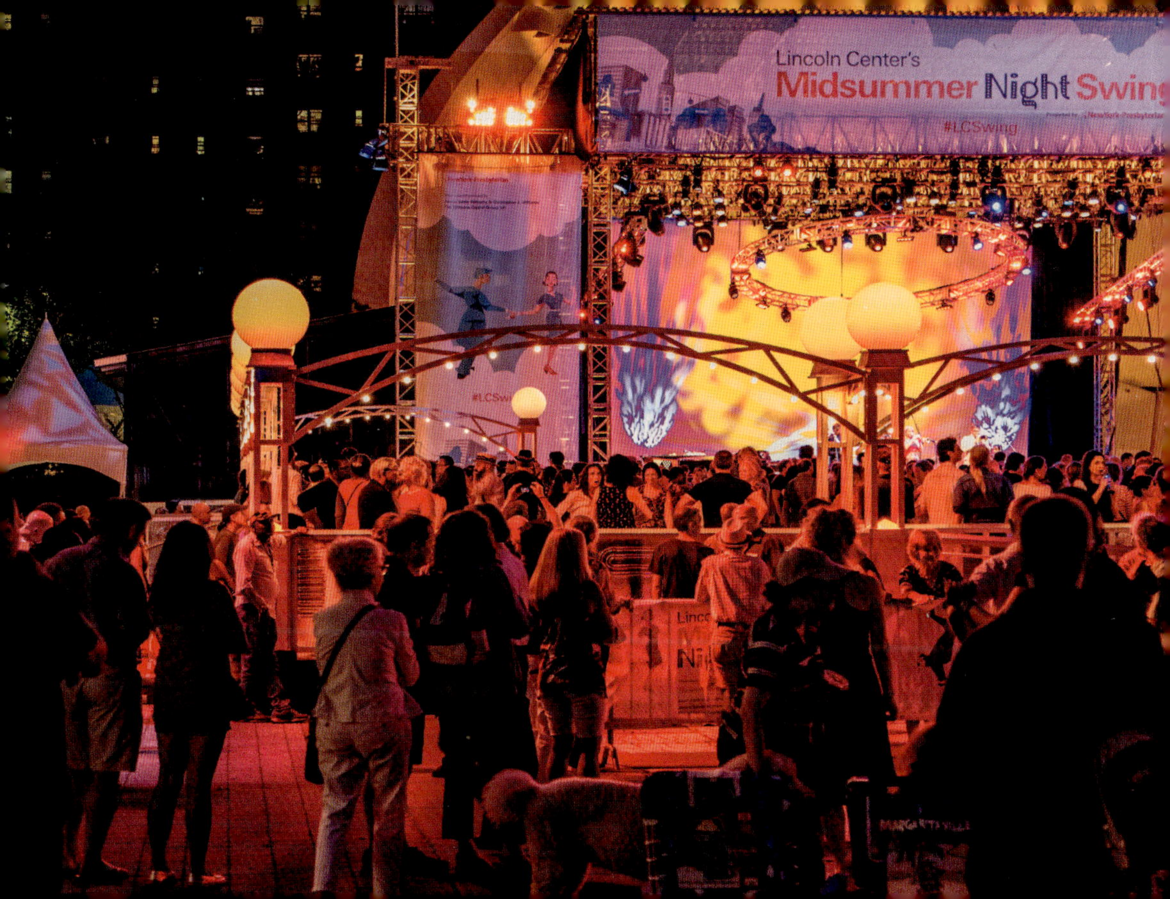
Lincoln Center's
Midsummer Night Swing
#LCSwing

ALL PHOTOGRAPHS:

Broadway lights

One of the top tourist destinations in Manhattan, millions of people go to Broadway shows each year to watch the dozens of musicals and other big spectaculars. Attendances for the 2018–19 season topped 14.7 million tickets, bringing in nearly \$2 billion (about £1.5 billion)!

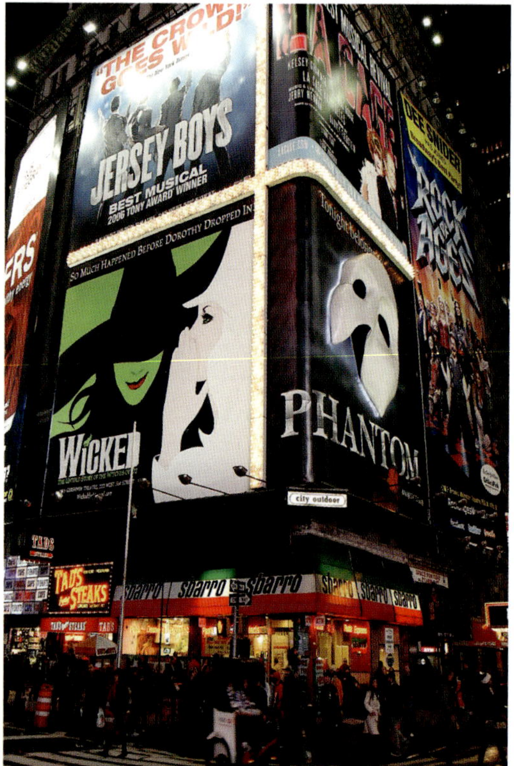

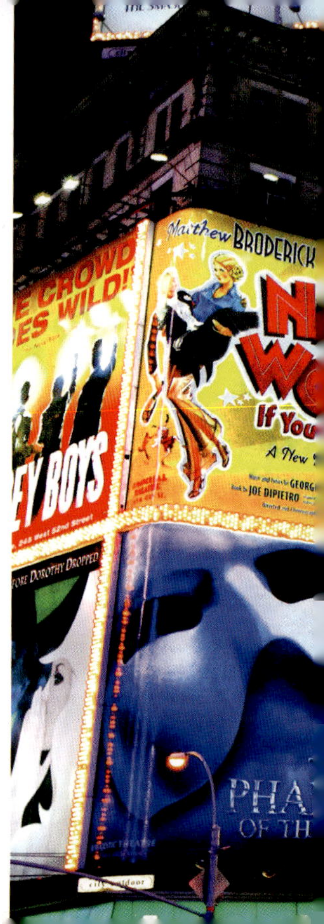

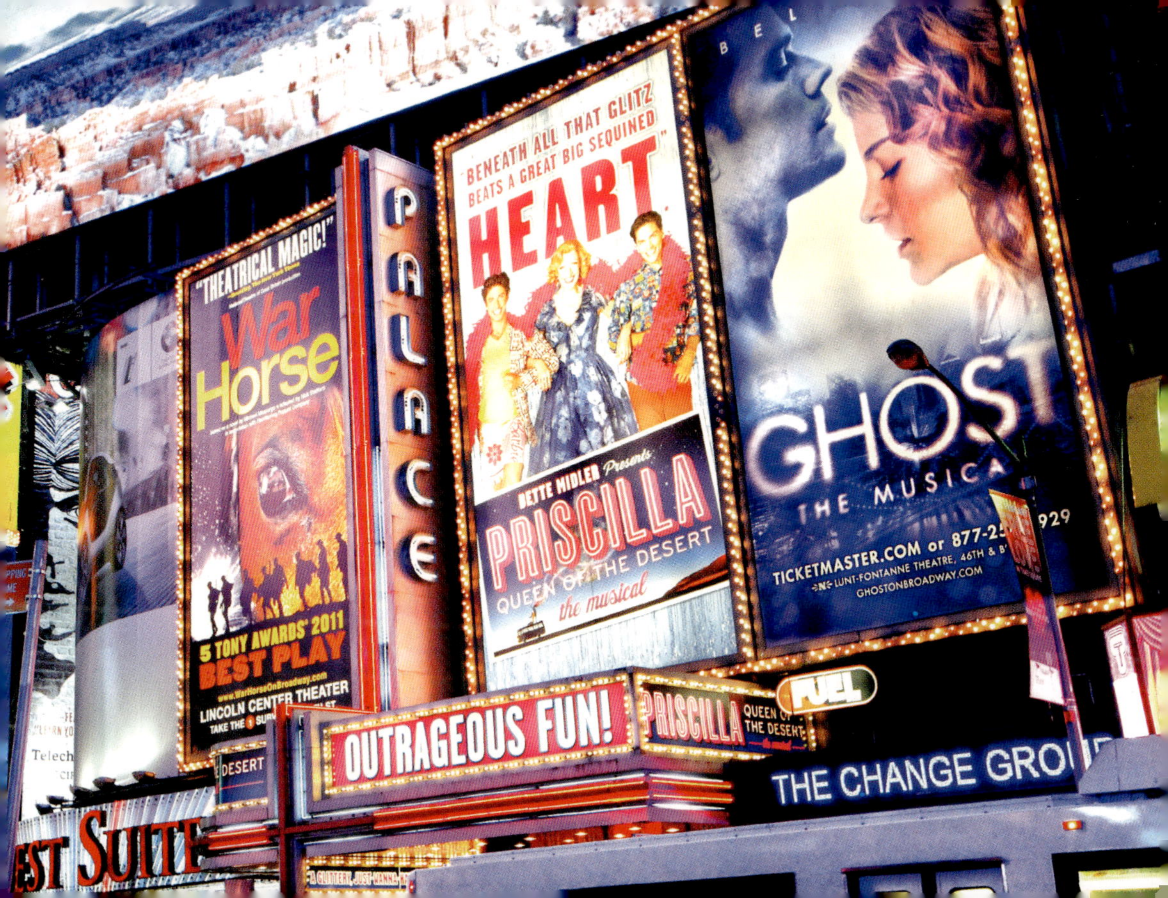
"THEATRICAL MAGIC!"
War Horse
5 TONY AWARDS 2011 BEST PLAY
www.WarHorseOnBroadway.com
LINCOLN CENTER THEATER
PALACE
"BENEATH ALL THAT GLITZ BEATS A GREAT BIG SEQUINED HEART"
BETTE MIDLER Presents
PRISCILLA
QUEEN OF THE DESERT
the musical
GHOST
THE MUSICAL
GHOSTONBROADWAY.COM
OUTRAGEOUS FUN!
PRISCILLA
QUEEN OF THE DESERT
FUEL
DESERT

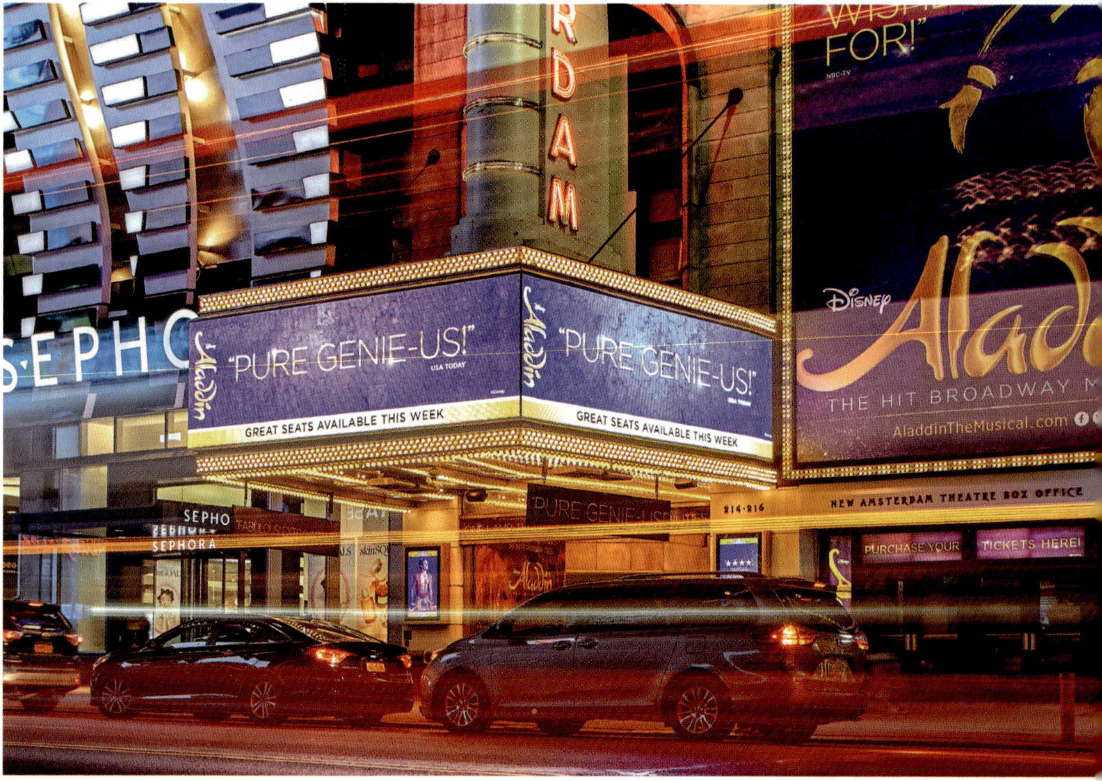
"PURE GENIE-US!"
USA TODAY
Aladdin
GREAT SEATS AVAILABLE THIS WEEK
FOR!"
NBC-TV
Disney
Aladdin
THE HIT BROADWAY M
AladdinTheMusical.com
NEW AMSTERDAM THEATRE BOX OFFICE
214-216
PURCHASE YOUR
TICKETS HERE!
SEPHORA

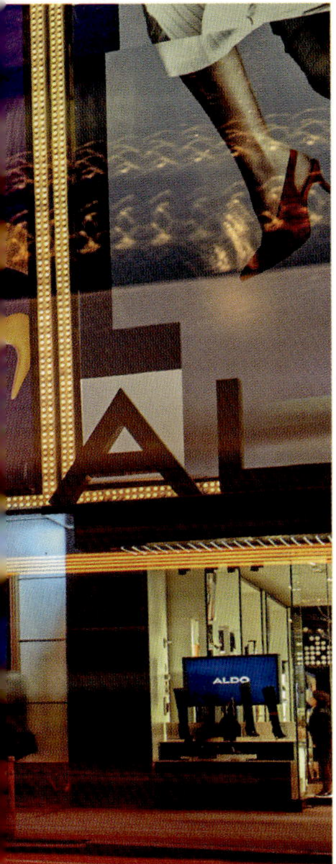

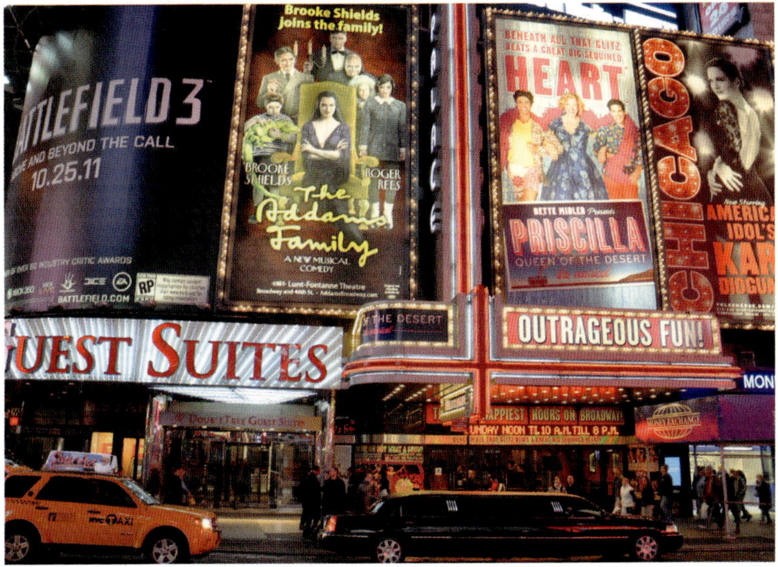

ALL PHOTOGRAPHS:

Theatre District

Commonly referred to simply as Broadway, this part of Midtown Manhattan is home to 41 venues and is one of the most active and visited parts of New York City.

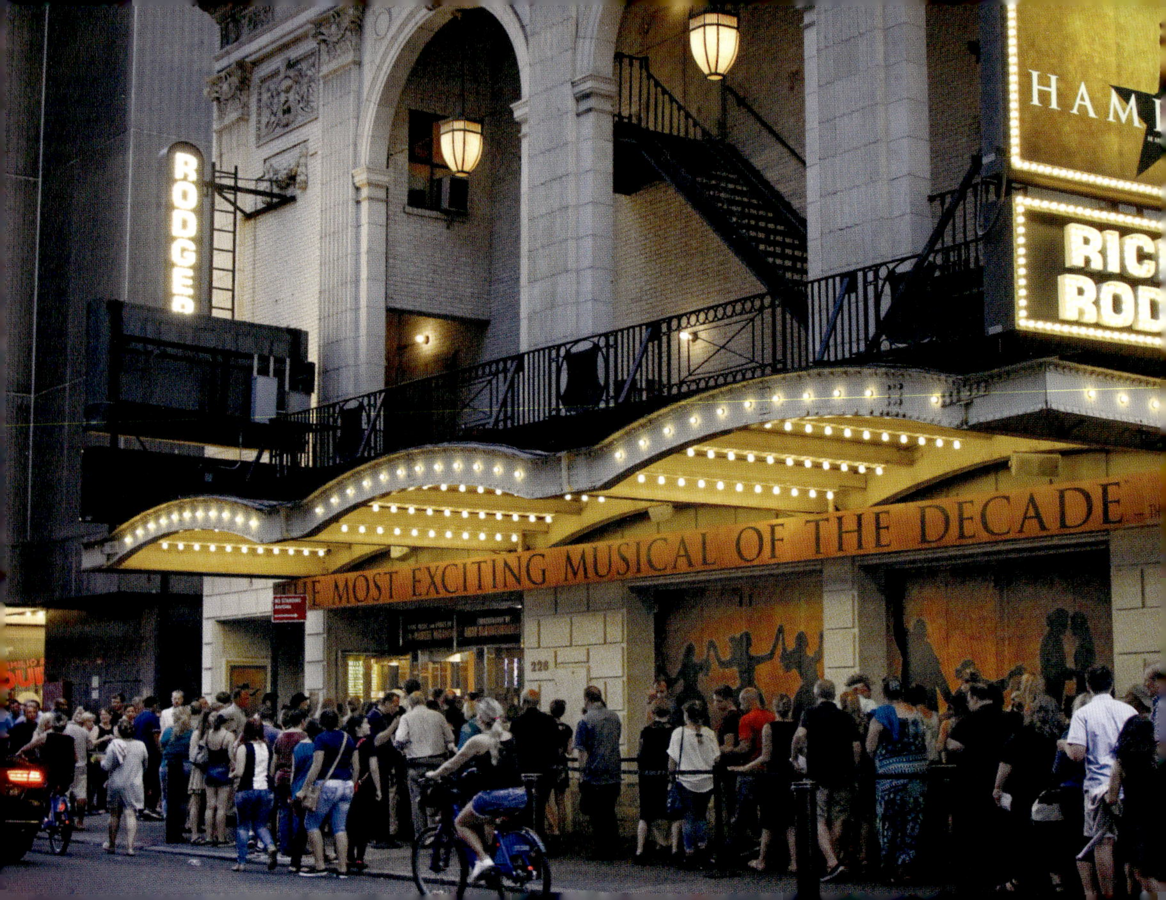
MOST EXCITING MUSICAL OF THE DECADE
228

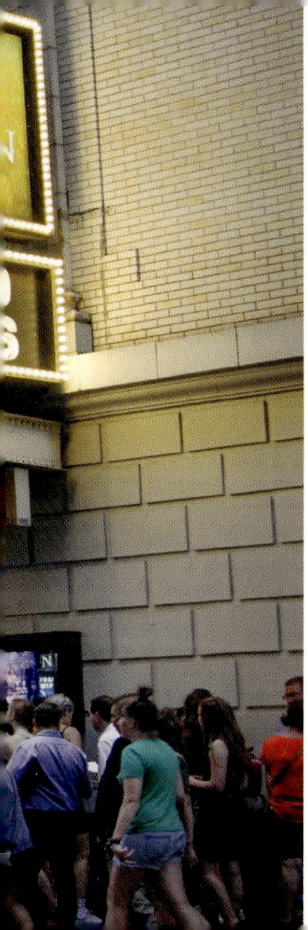

LEFT:

Broadway hits

Broadway is home to some of the longest-running productions, including *The Phantom of the Opera* and *Cats*. One of the most recent Broadway hits is *Hamilton*.

RIGHT:

Apollo Theater

James Brown, Billie Holiday, Sammy Davis Jr and hundreds of other famous musicians, comedians and entertainers got their start in this city landmark, on 125th Street in Harlem. Home to *Showtime at the Apollo*, the variety show was first televised in 1987 and ran for over 20 years, airing 1,094 episodes. An estimated 1.3 million people visit the venue each year.

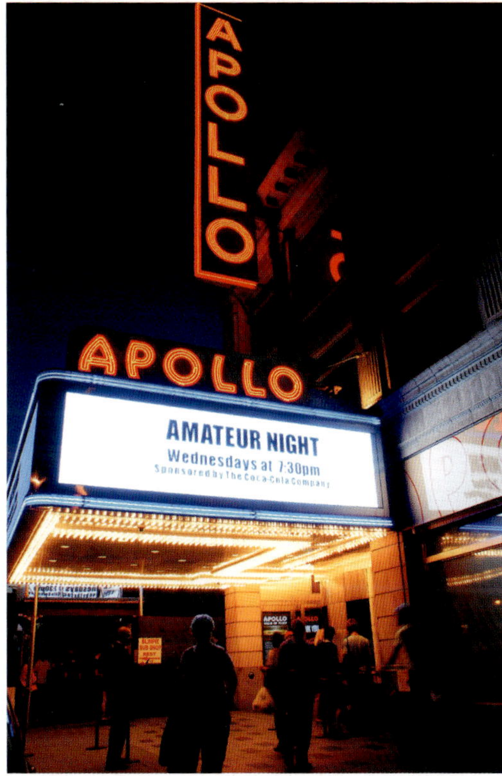

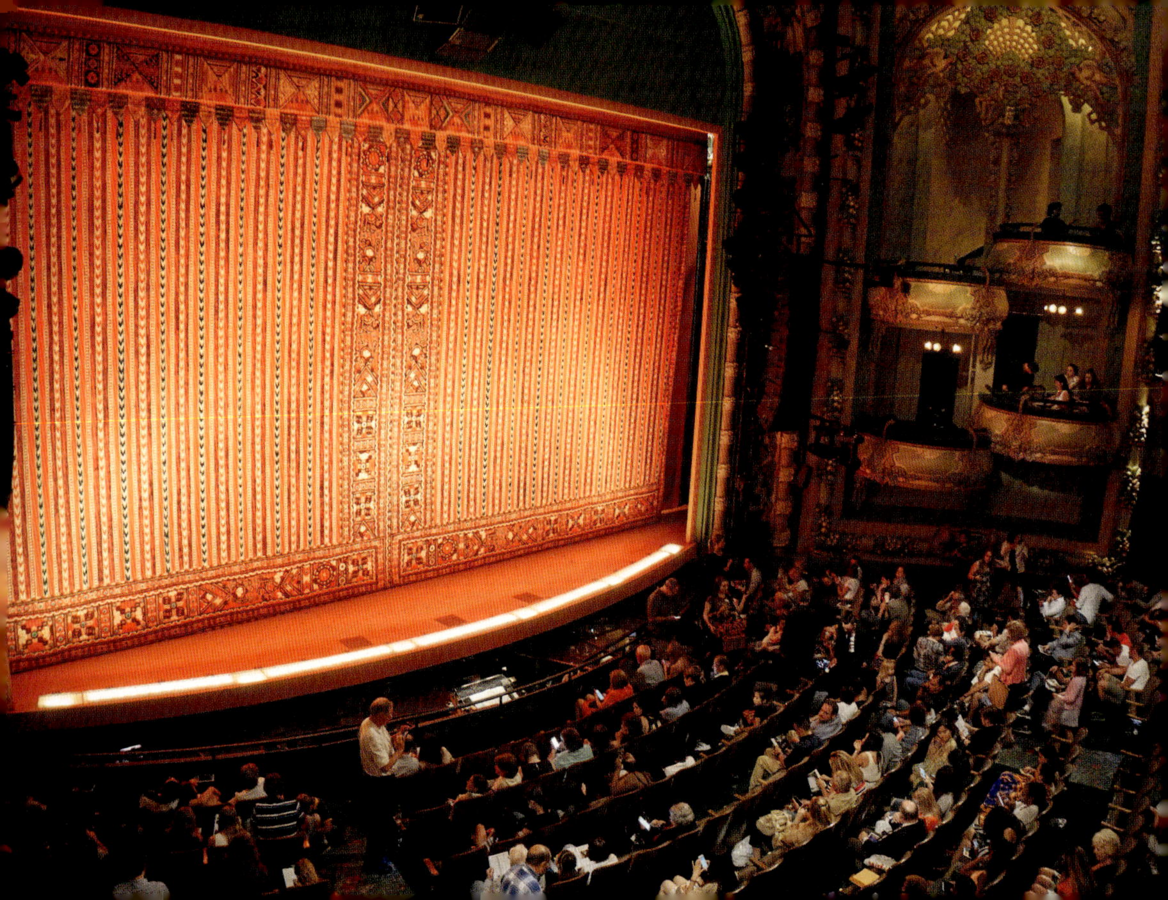

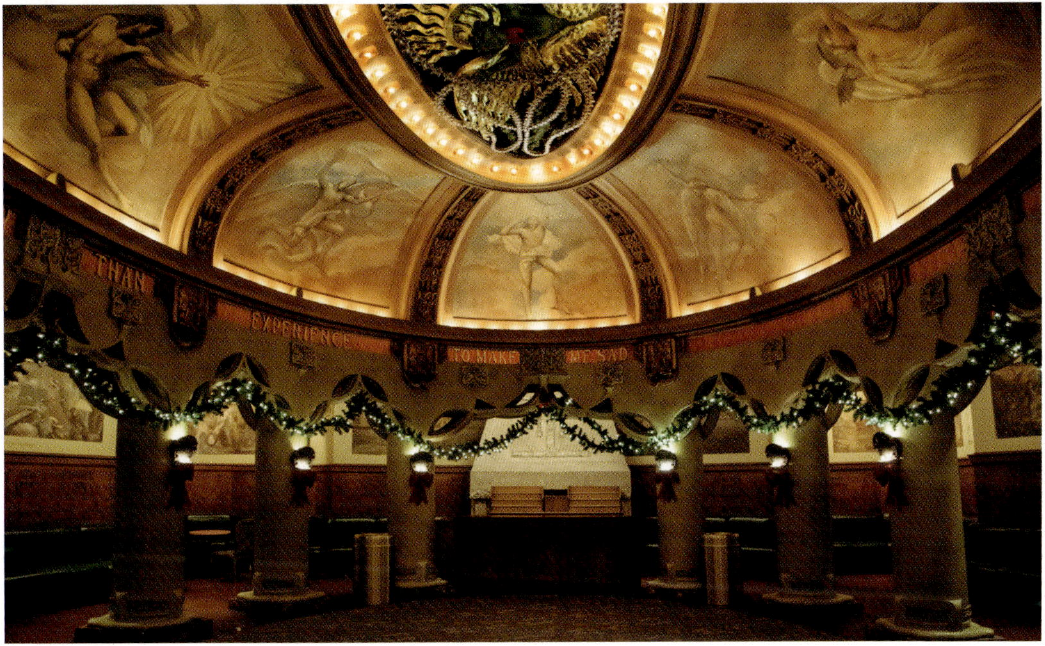

ALL PHOTOGRAPHS:
New Amsterdam Theatre
Built in 1902, this is one of the oldest buildings in Manhattan. Located on 42nd Street in Times Square, the venue has over 1,700 seats and has recently been used for a variety of large-scale Disney productions, including *Mary Poppins*, *The Lion King* and *Aladdin*.

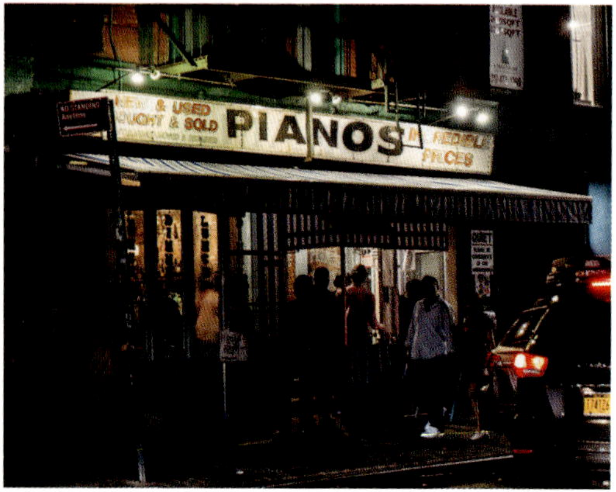

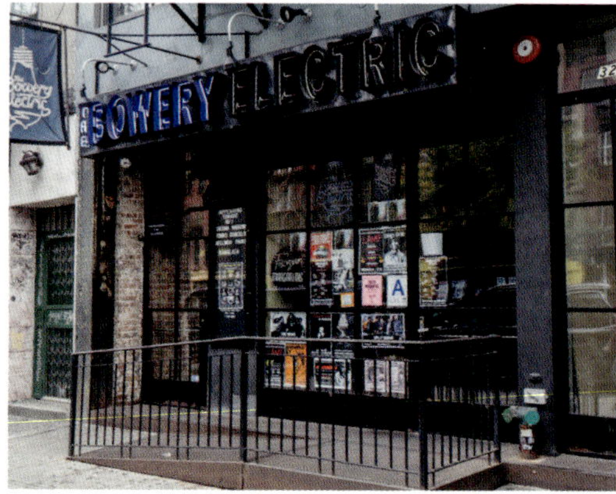

ABOVE:
Pianos
Once a piano store, today the site is a two-level bar and grill, and a live music venue. With its original signage still in place, this popular destination in the Lower East Side is known for its mix of DJs and live bands.

RIGHT TOP AND BOTTOM, AND OPPOSITE:
Live music
Whether it's country, jazz, punk or rock 'n' roll, the music scene in New York City is world-class. Many venues have been fixtures for decades, launching the careers of countless musicians.

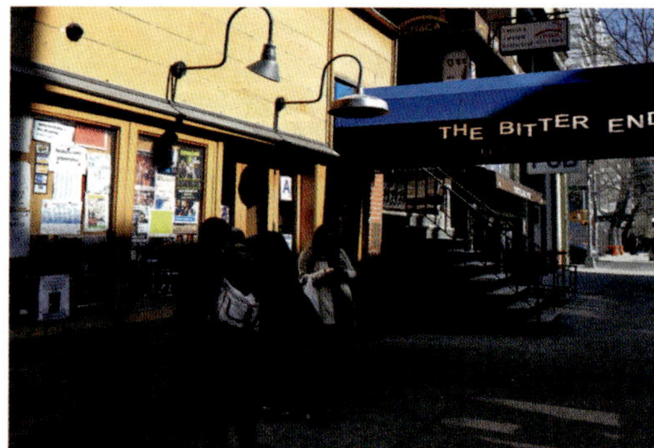

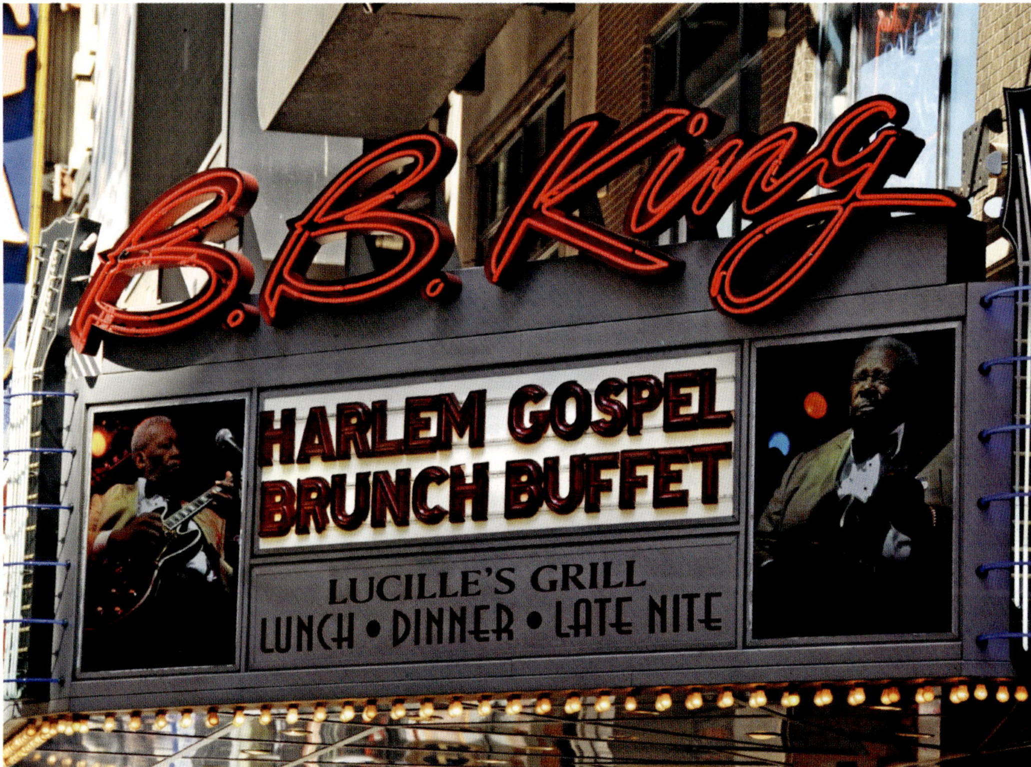
B.B. King
HARLEM GOSPEL
BRUNCH BUFFET
LUCILLE'S GRILL
LUNCH • DINNER • LATE NITE

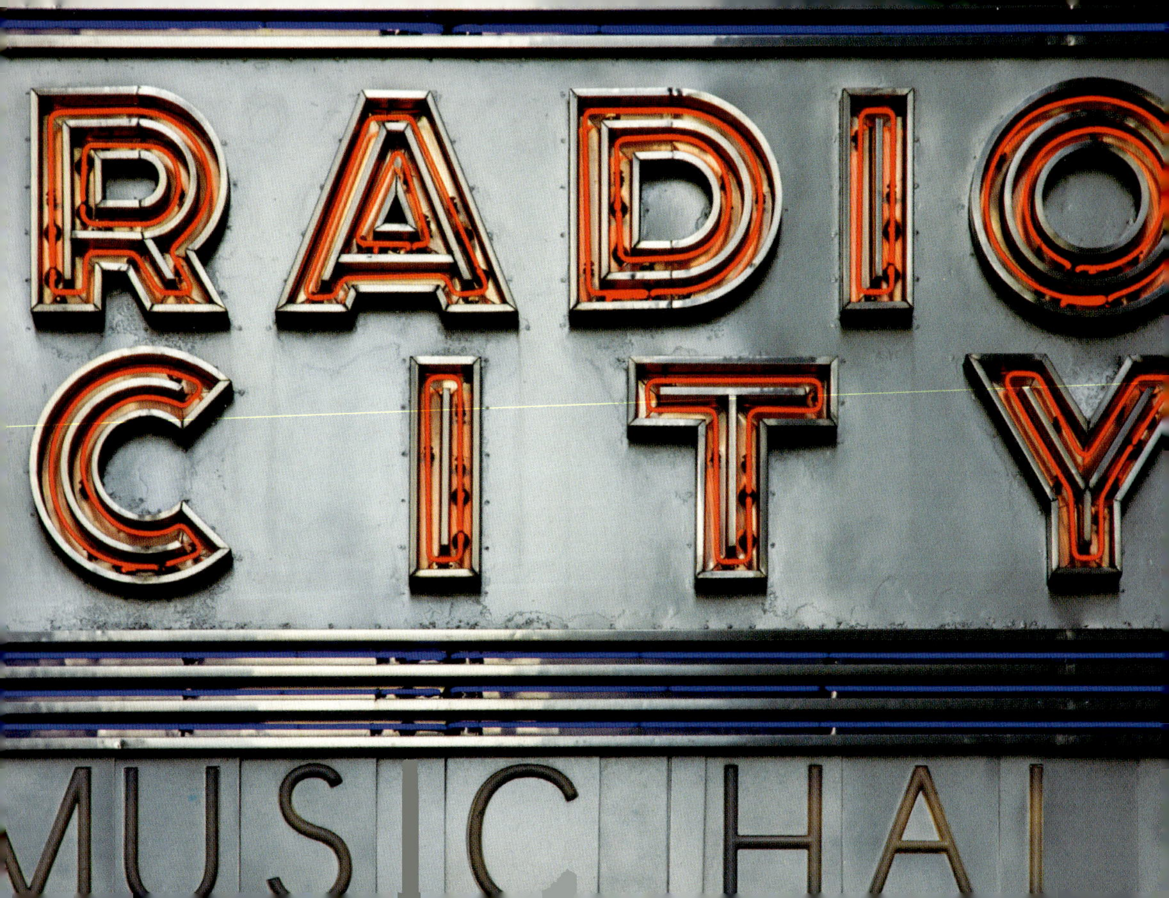
RADIO
CITY

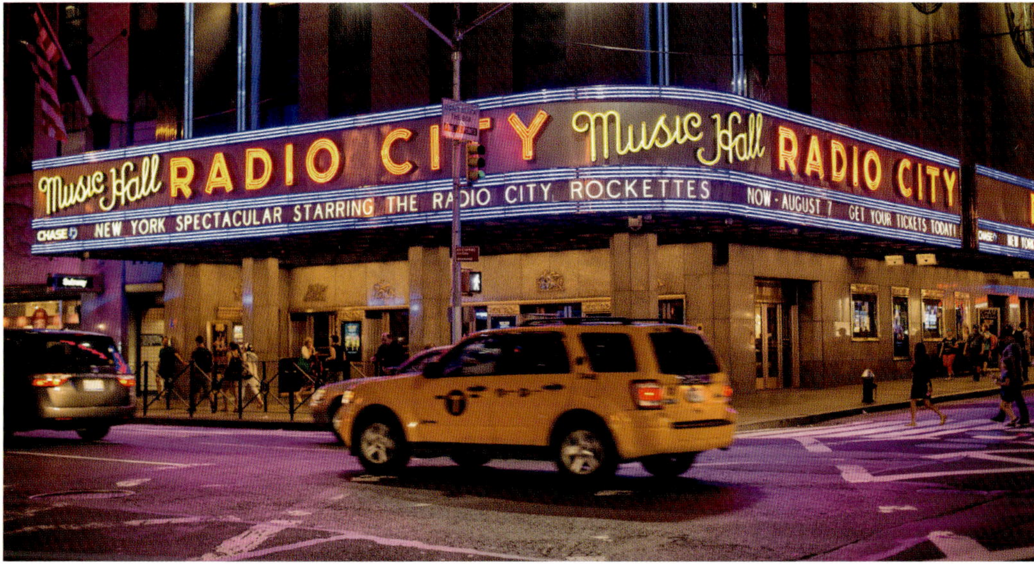

OPPOSITE:
Radio City Music Hall
Located in Midtown Manhattan, this city landmark has been in operation since 1932 and entertains over a million visitors annually. Inside, guests walk through a lavishly decorated lobby, leading them to the orchestra section and three tiered levels of mezzanine seating.

ABOVE:
Christmas spectacular
Radio City Music Hall has hosted the 'Christmas Spectacular starring the Radio City Rockettes' since 1933. The holiday extravaganza runs from mid-November to early January with up to four shows a day.

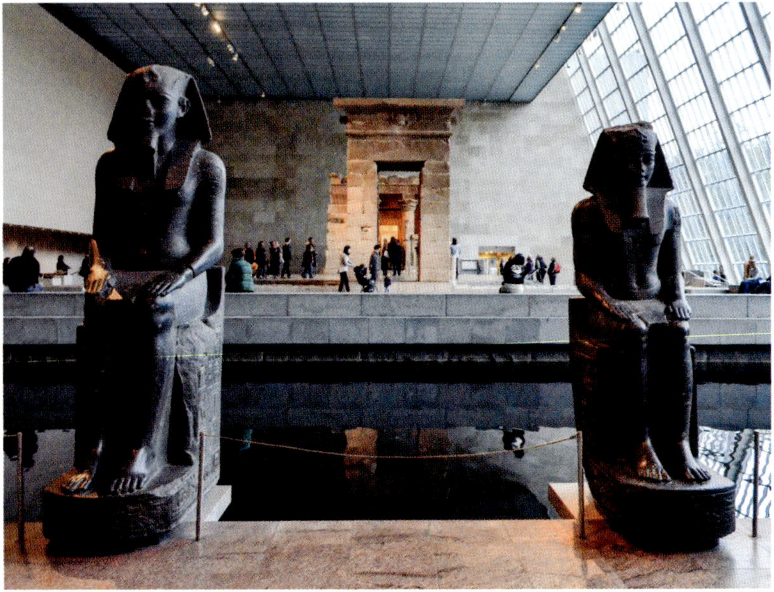

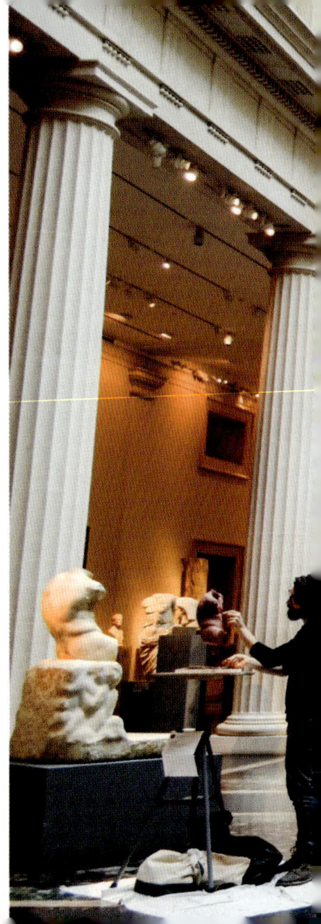

ALL PHOTOGRAPHS:

Metropolitan Museum of Art

Commonly referred to as 'The Met', this art museum is the largest in the United States and is home to two million pieces of art, including works from Van Gogh, Degas, Rembrandt and Pollock. Exhibits from the ancient world include Egyptian artefacts, Greek and Roman sculptures, and over 35,000 pieces of Asian art dating back to 3000 BCE.

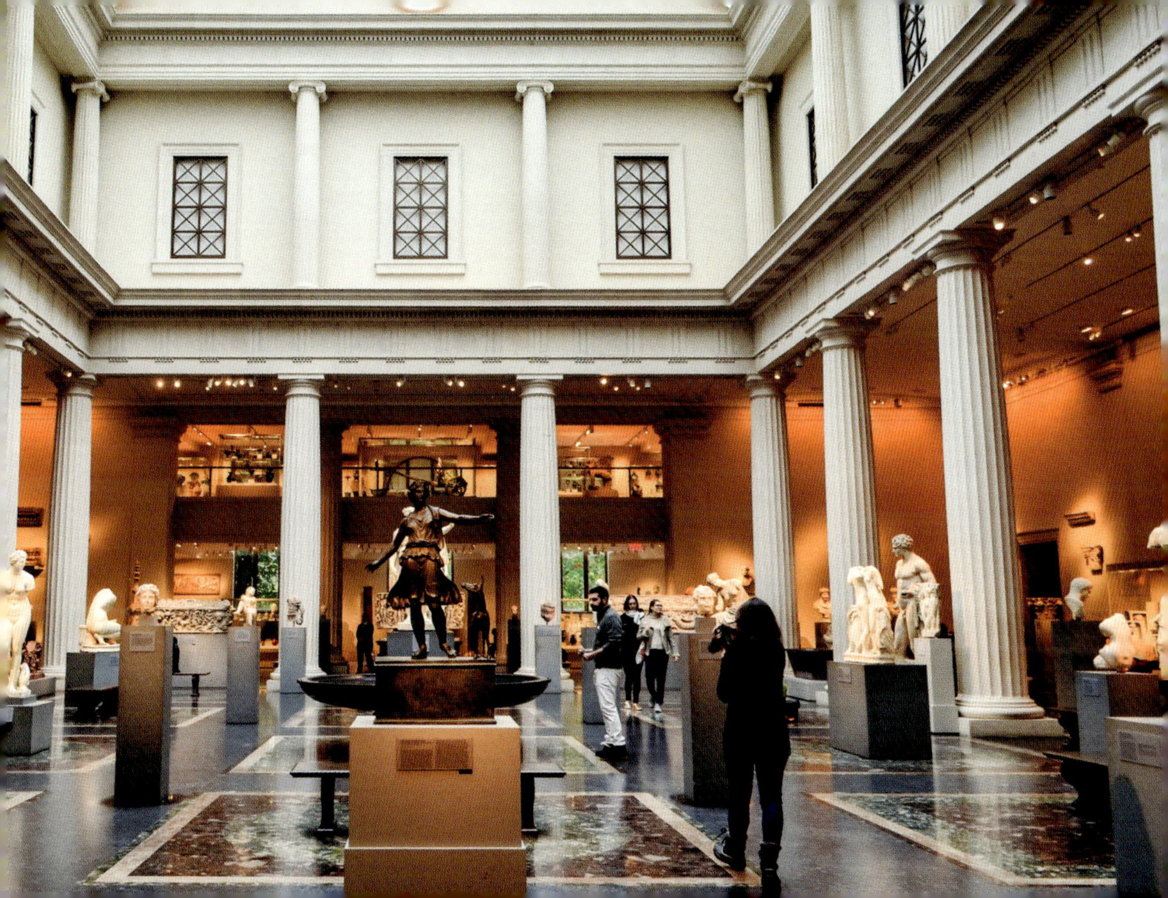

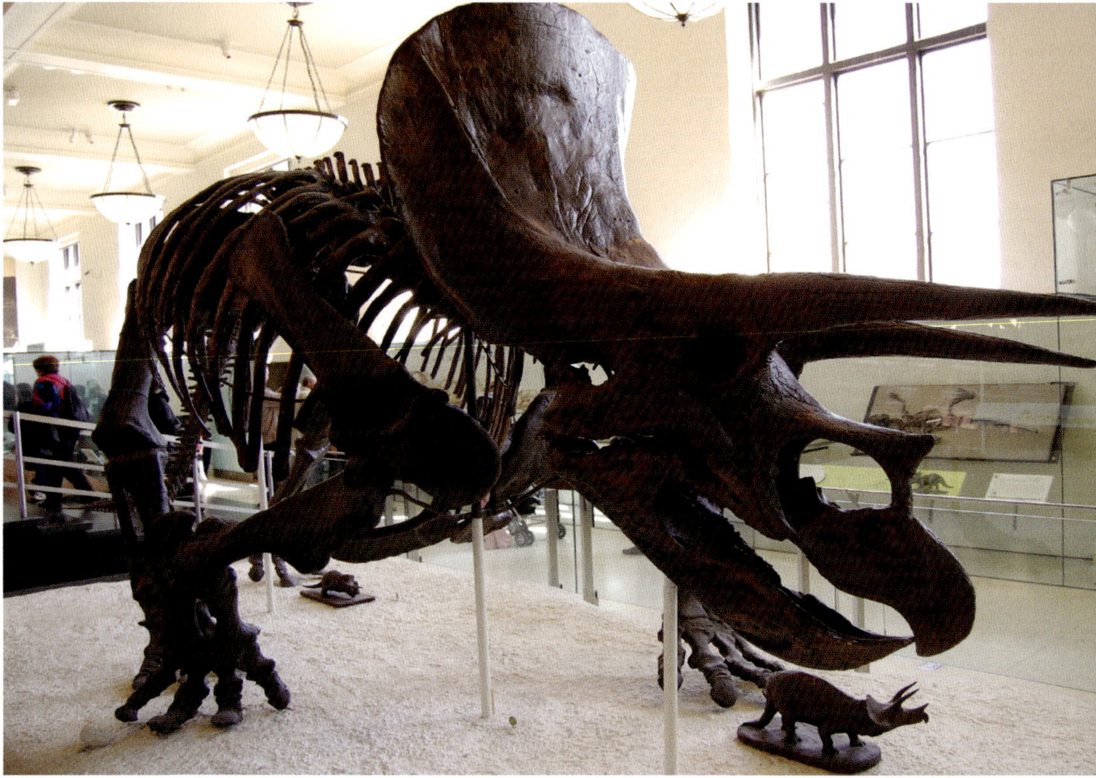

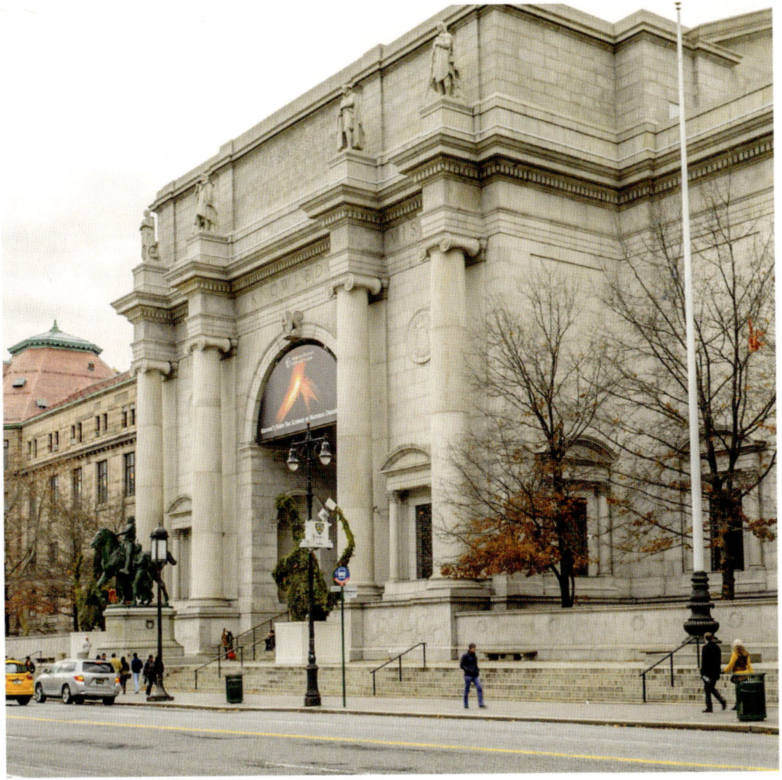

ALL PHOTOGRAPHS:
American Museum of Natural History
Located on the Upper West Side of Manhattan and across the street from Central Park, the museum houses over 33 million specimens and artefacts, including full-sized dinosaurs. Exhibits offer visitors a glimpse of the prehistoric world and extinct wildlife, plus halls that are focused on biodiversity, the environment, human origins and culture.

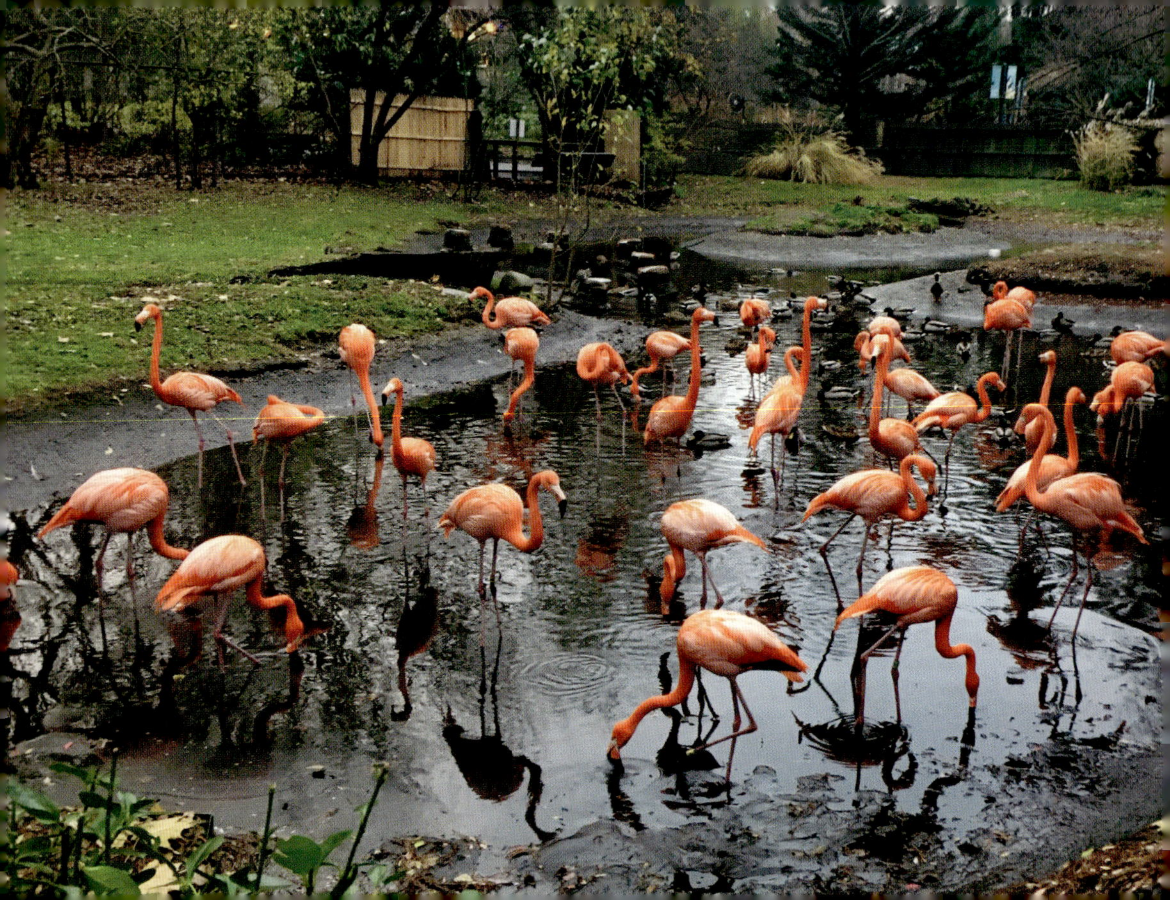

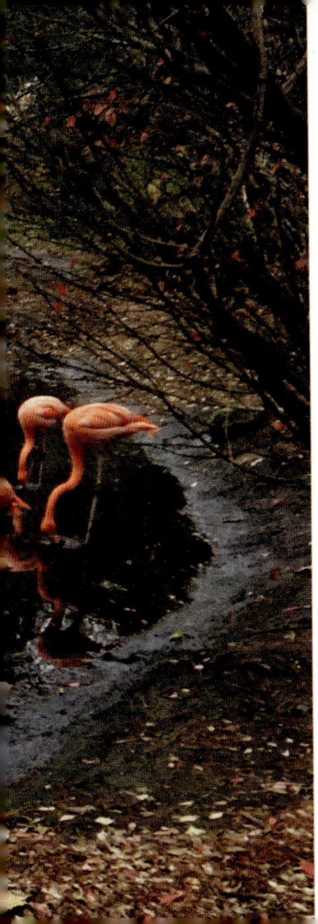

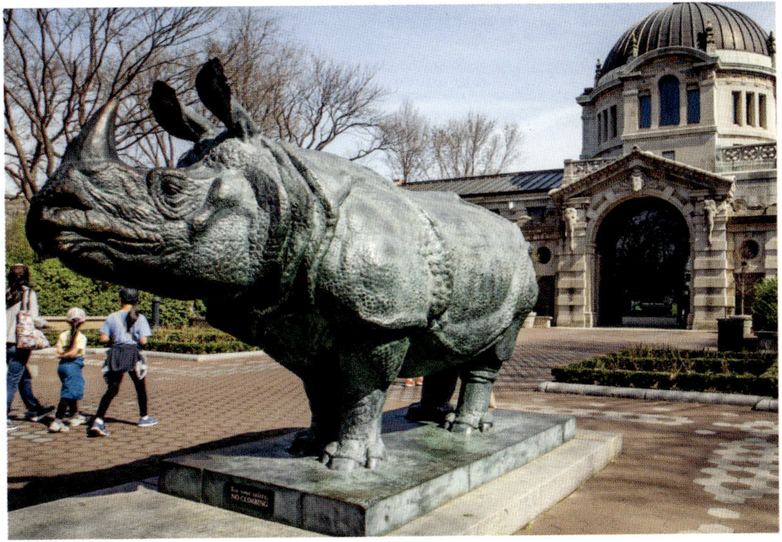

ALL PHOTOGRAPHS:

Bronx Zoo

Situated in the heart of the Bronx, the zoo is the fourth-largest zoo in the United States and the largest urban zoo in the country. Encompassing 107 hectares (265 acres), the location is home to over 6,000 species, from tiny chinchillas and poison dart frogs to massive Asian elephants.

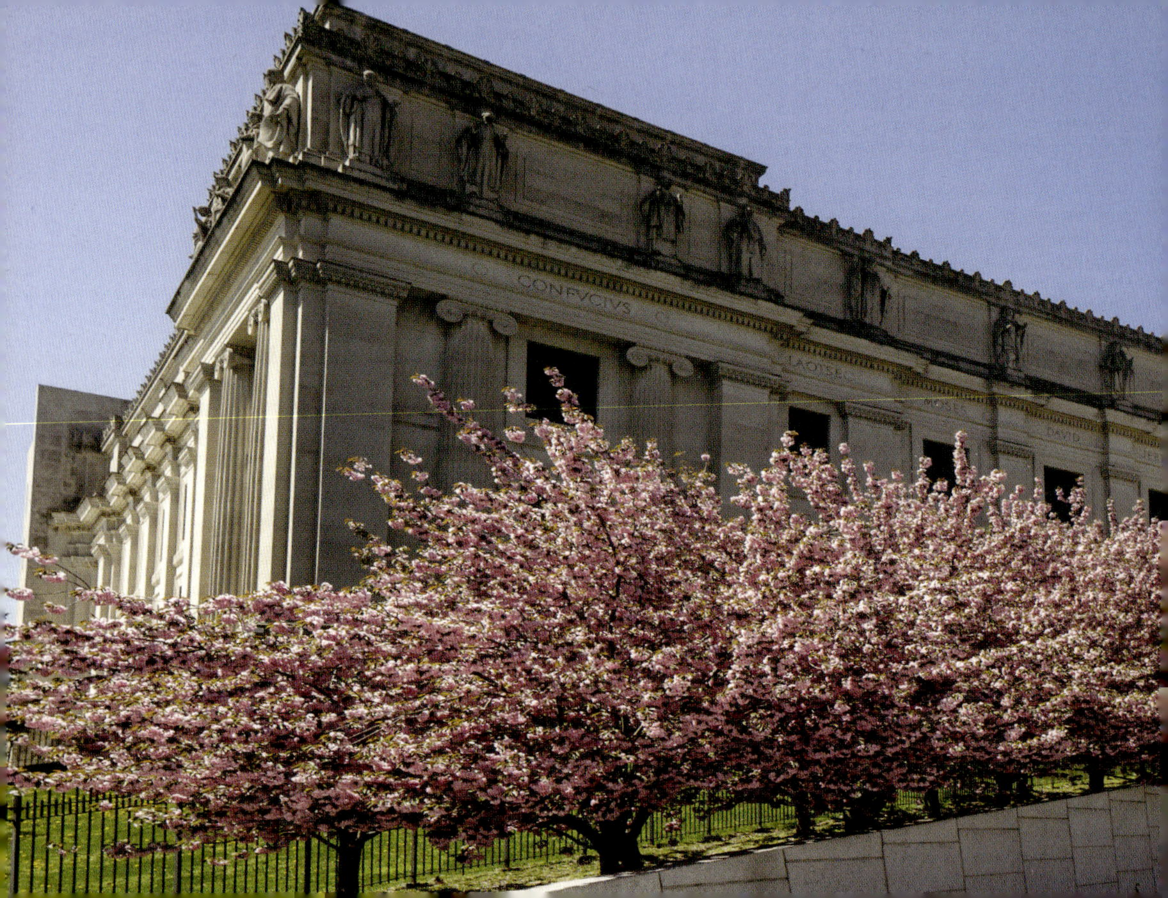
CONFVCIVS

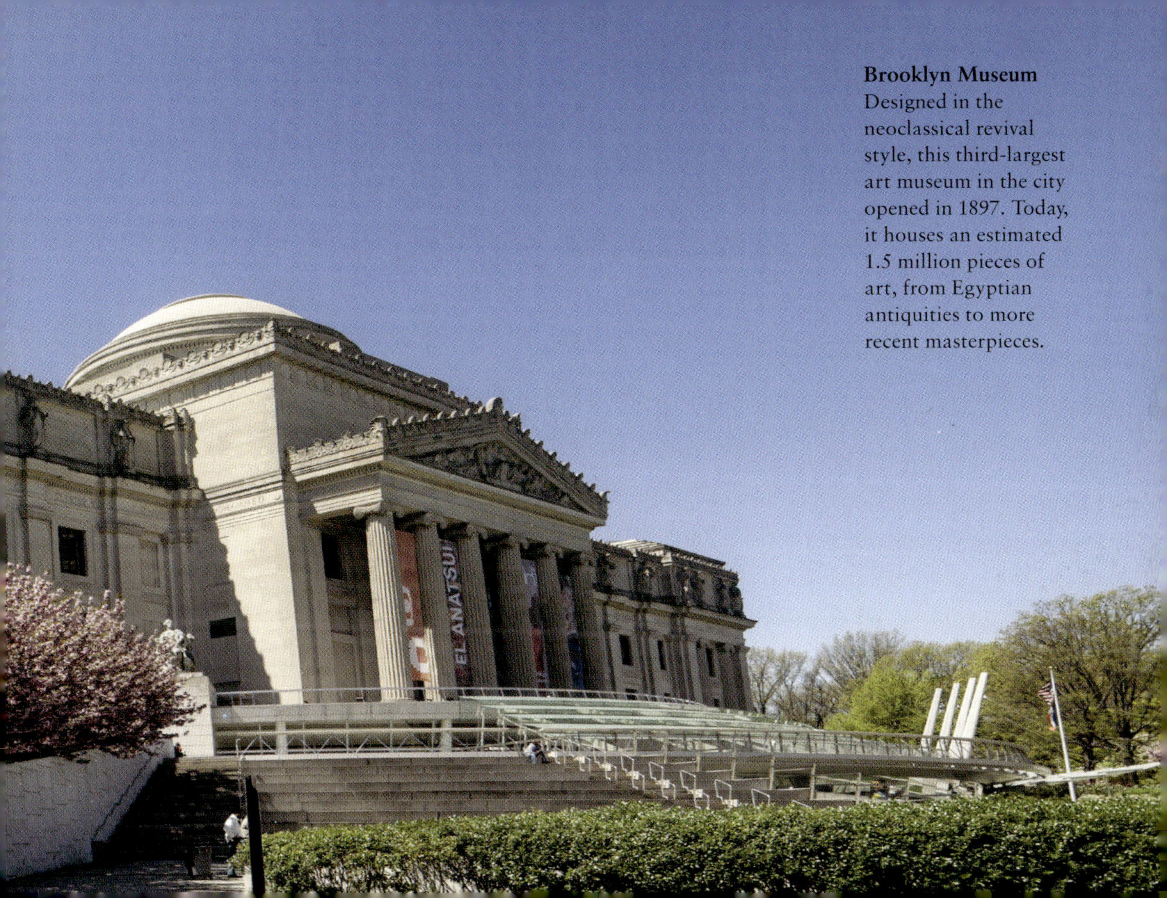

Brooklyn Museum
Designed in the neoclassical revival style, this third-largest art museum in the city opened in 1897. Today, it houses an estimated 1.5 million pieces of art, from Egyptian antiquities to more recent masterpieces.

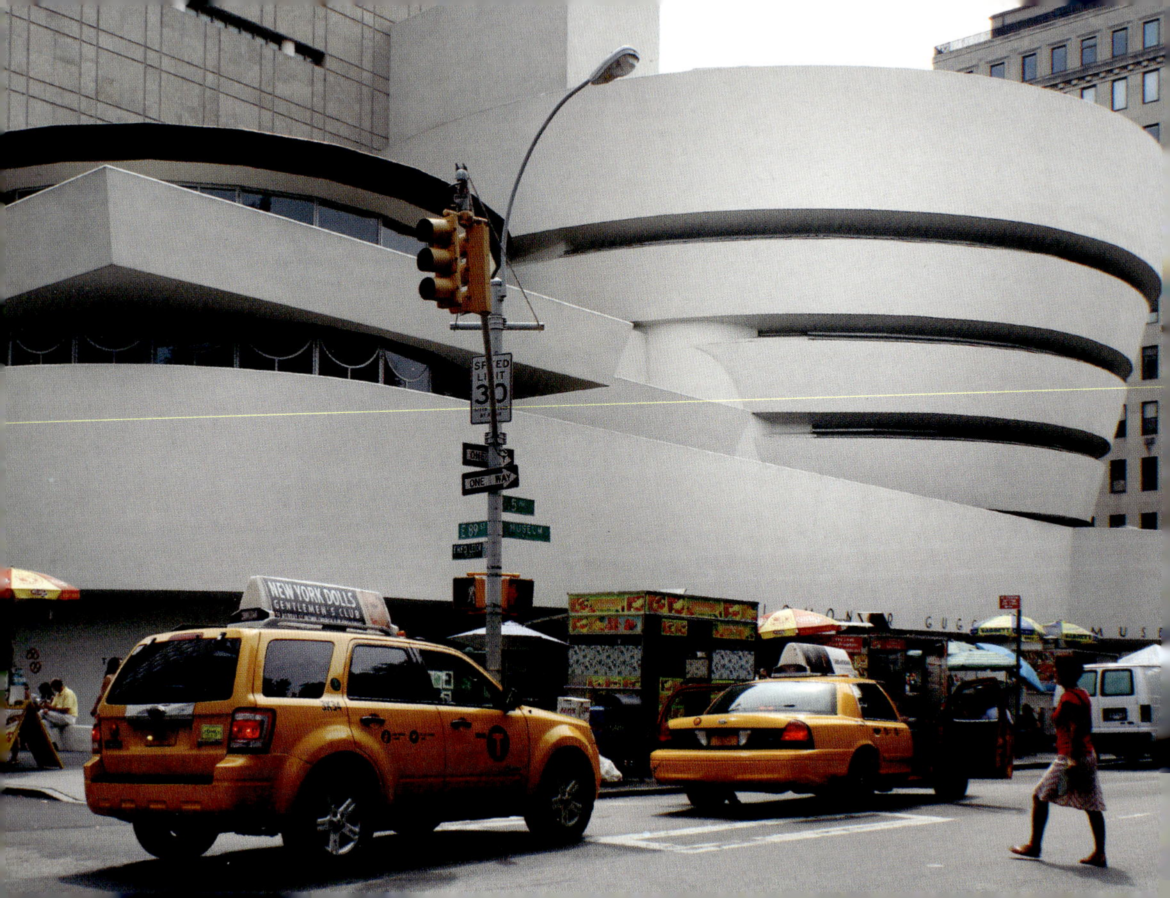
SPEED LIMIT 30
ONE WAY
NEW YORK DOLLS
GENTLEMEN'S CLUB

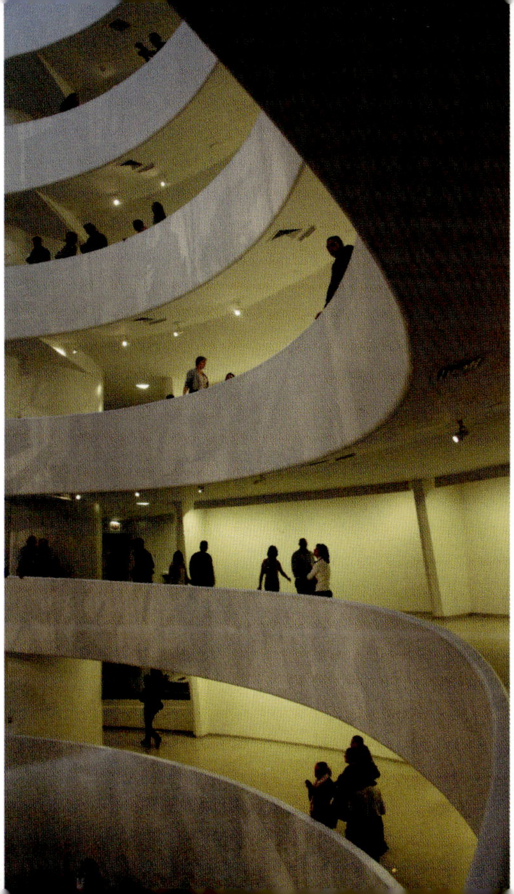

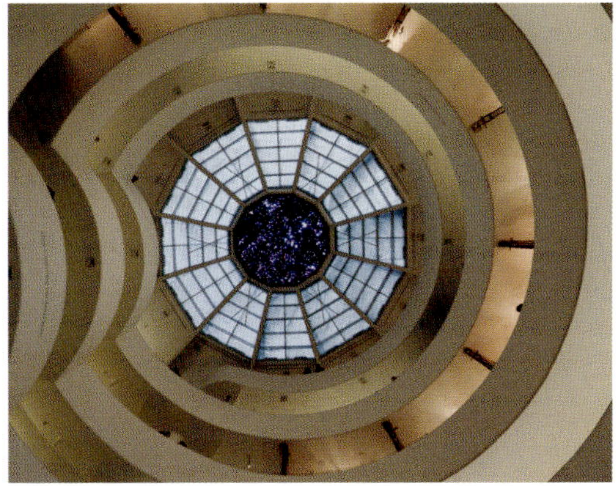

ALL PHOTOGRAPHS:

The Guggenheim Museum

Located in the Upper East Side on Fifth Avenue, and designed in the shape of a sea shell by famous American architect Frank Lloyd Wright, the Guggenheim is a designated city landmark and home to a large collection of early modern and contemporary art, including Impressionist and Post-Impressionist artworks. Inside, winding paths lead visitors to the different exhibits, including permanent and guest works by artists from around the world.

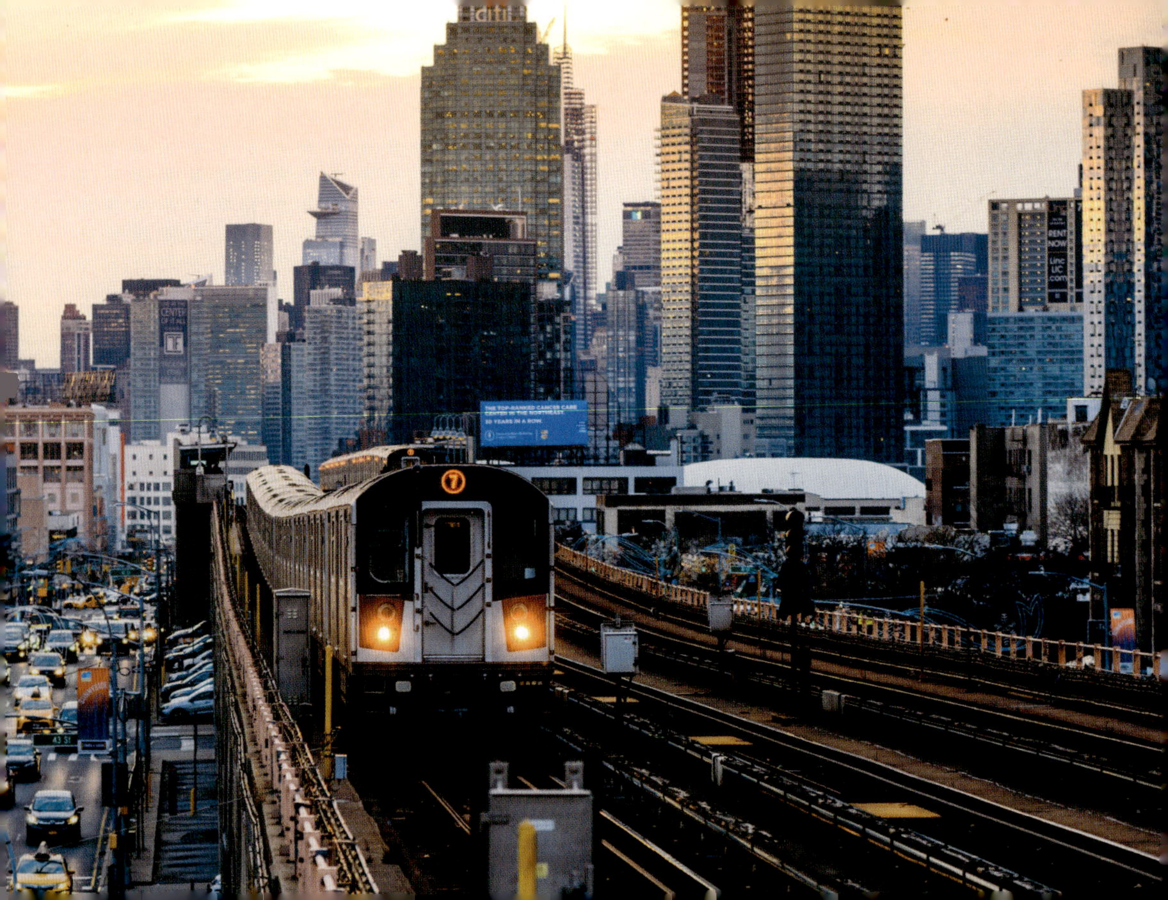
7
THE TOP-RANKED CANCER CARE
30 YEARS IN A ROW.
RENT NOW
Linc LIC .com
43 St

Transport

Hailing a cab in New York City is considered by many to be an art form. It's also an experience that every visitor to the city should have. The fleets of yellow cabs are easy to spot as they drive down streets and avenues, or double-park in front of restaurants, bars and hotels. But taxi rides aren't the only way to get around town. New York has one of the largest subway systems in the world with close to 500 stations and 26 lines ferrying passengers across different parts of the city. And if you prefer making your way above ground, there are over 4,300 city buses travelling thousands of miles each day.

But getting around the city isn't possible without the landmark bridges and tunnels that connect the different boroughs. Or without the iconic train terminals and international airports that make travel to the city so convenient for millions of commuters and visitors each year.

Public transport plays an important role for both native New Yorkers and tourists. This is particularly true because owning a car is not a serious consideration for many people who live in Manhattan and the more crowded parts of the city – it's much easier to walk, grab a cab or take a train than it is to find a parking spot.

OPPOSITE:

Elevated subway lines

The 7 train runs from 34th Street Hudson Yards to Flushing, Main Street, in Queens and has a wonderful urban backdrop.

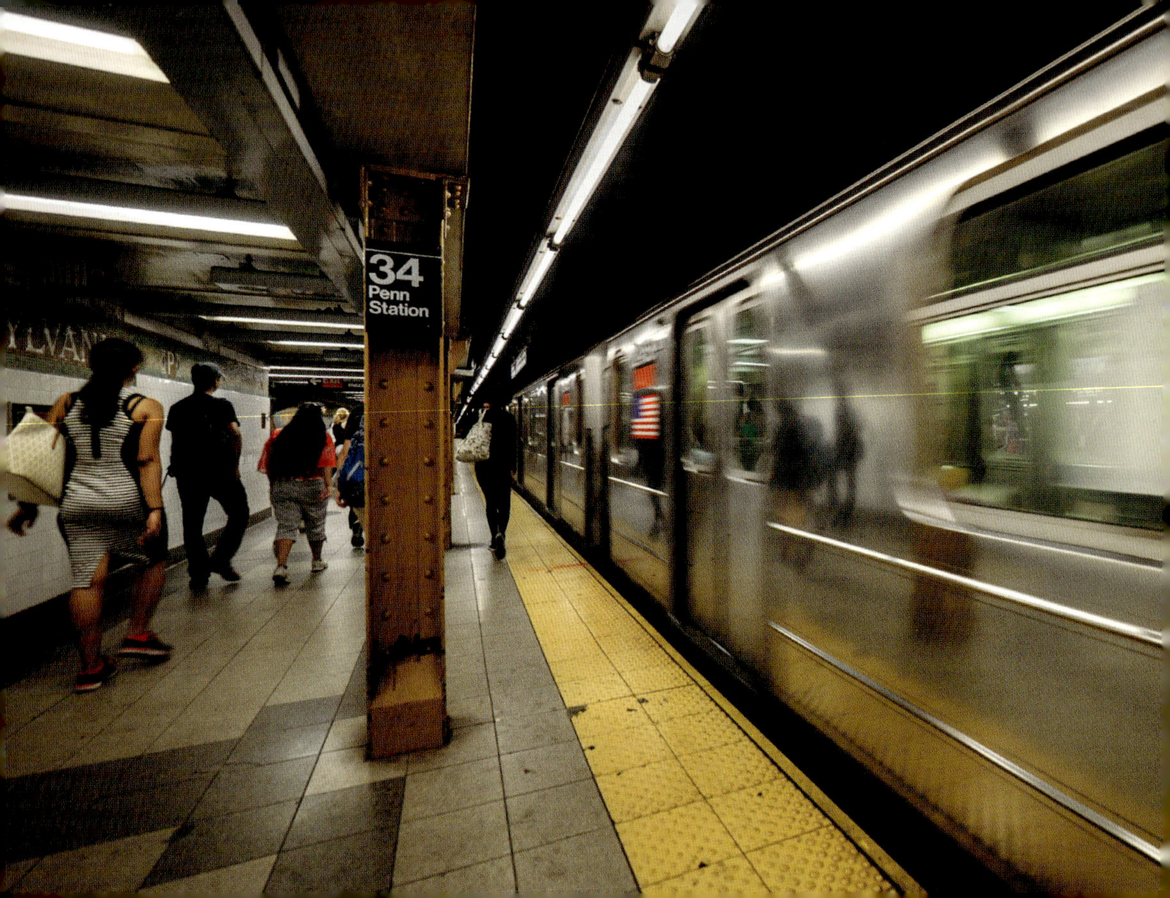
34
Penn
Station

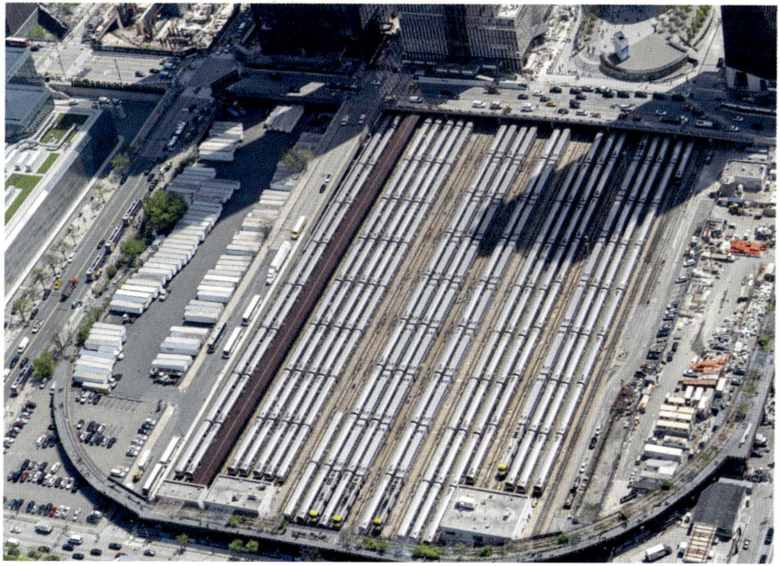

ALL PHOTOGRAPHS:

Pennsylvania Station

Commonly referred to as Penn Station, this is one of the busiest transport hubs in the world. An estimated 650,000 people go through this major Manhattan landmark each day, travelling to and from work, across the city and throughout the country.

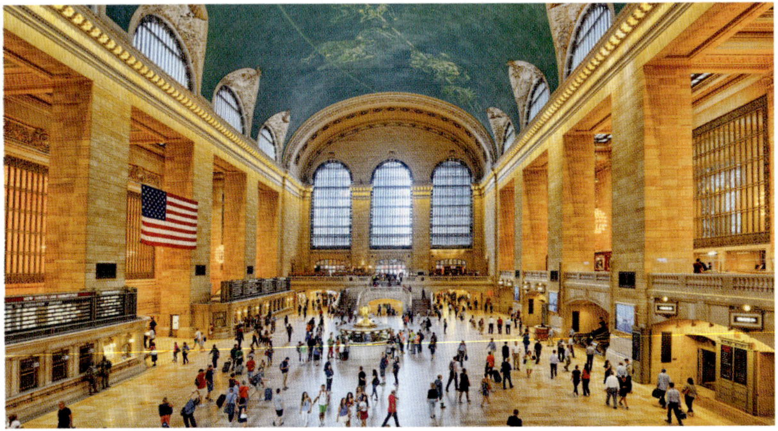

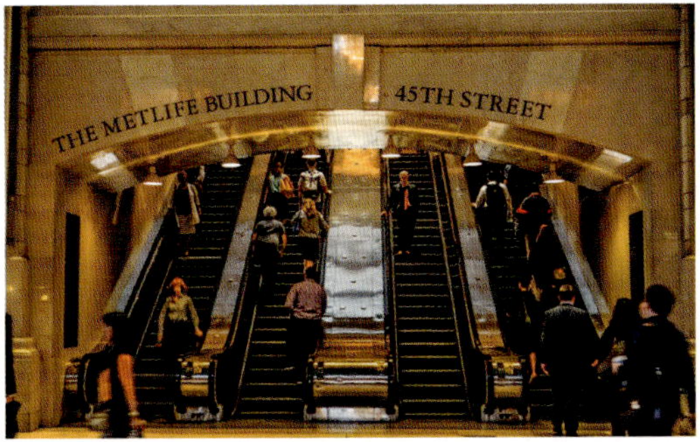

ALL PHOTOGRAPHS:
Grand Central Station
Located on 42nd Street in Midtown Manhattan, Grand Central is the second-busiest train station in North America (after Penn Station). It's the hub of the Metro-North Railroad and a subway station serving several lines.

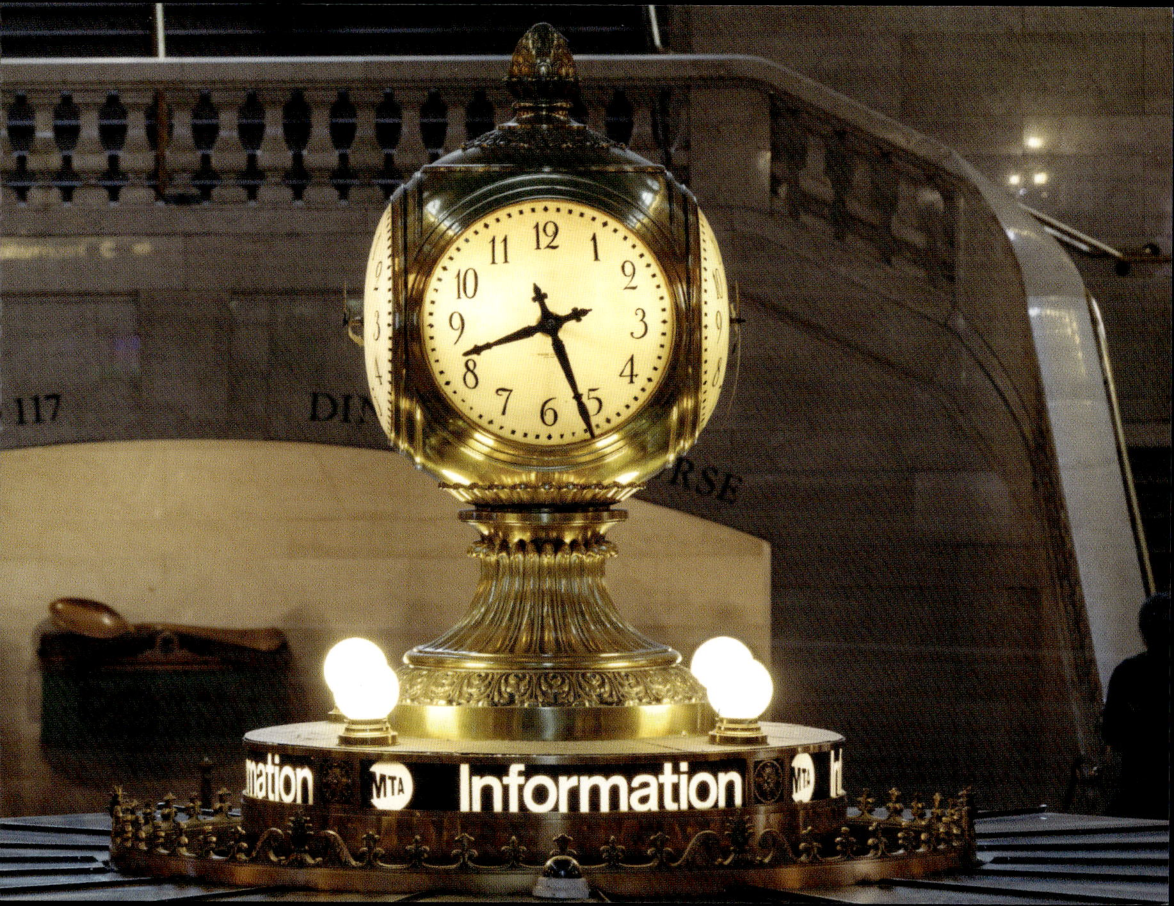
mation
MTA
Information
MTA

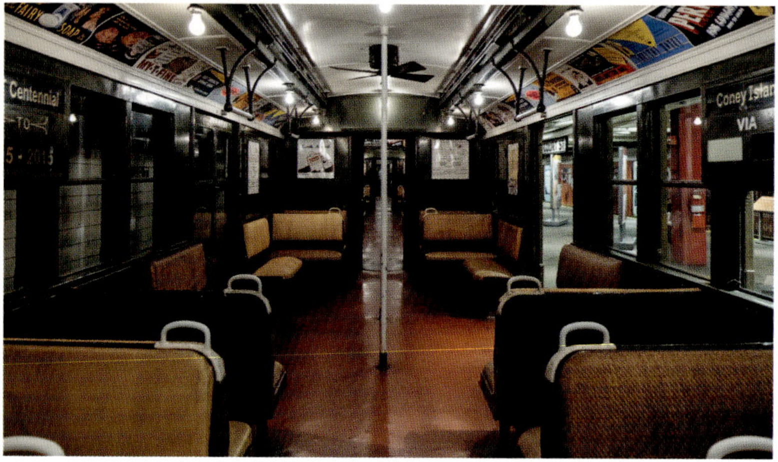

ALL PHOTOGRAPHS:

New York Transit Museum

This decommissioned subway station in Brooklyn takes visitors back in time to the vintage buses and subway cars dating from earlier years of public transport.

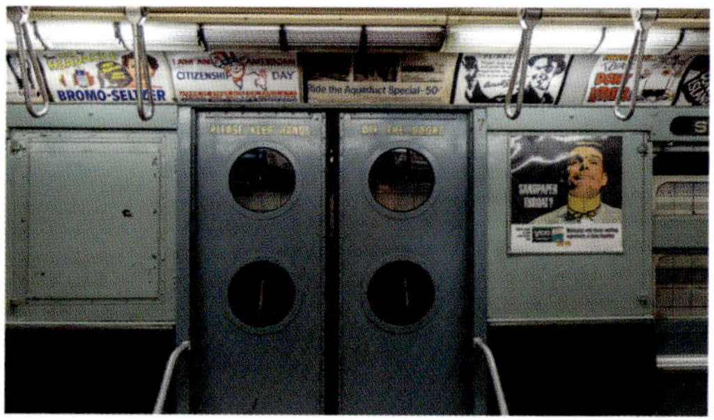

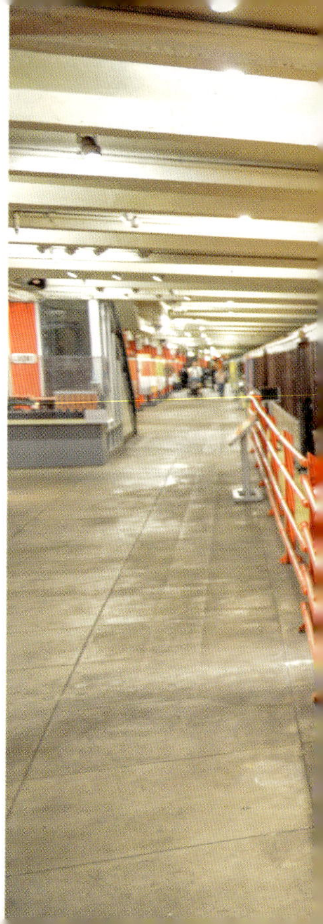

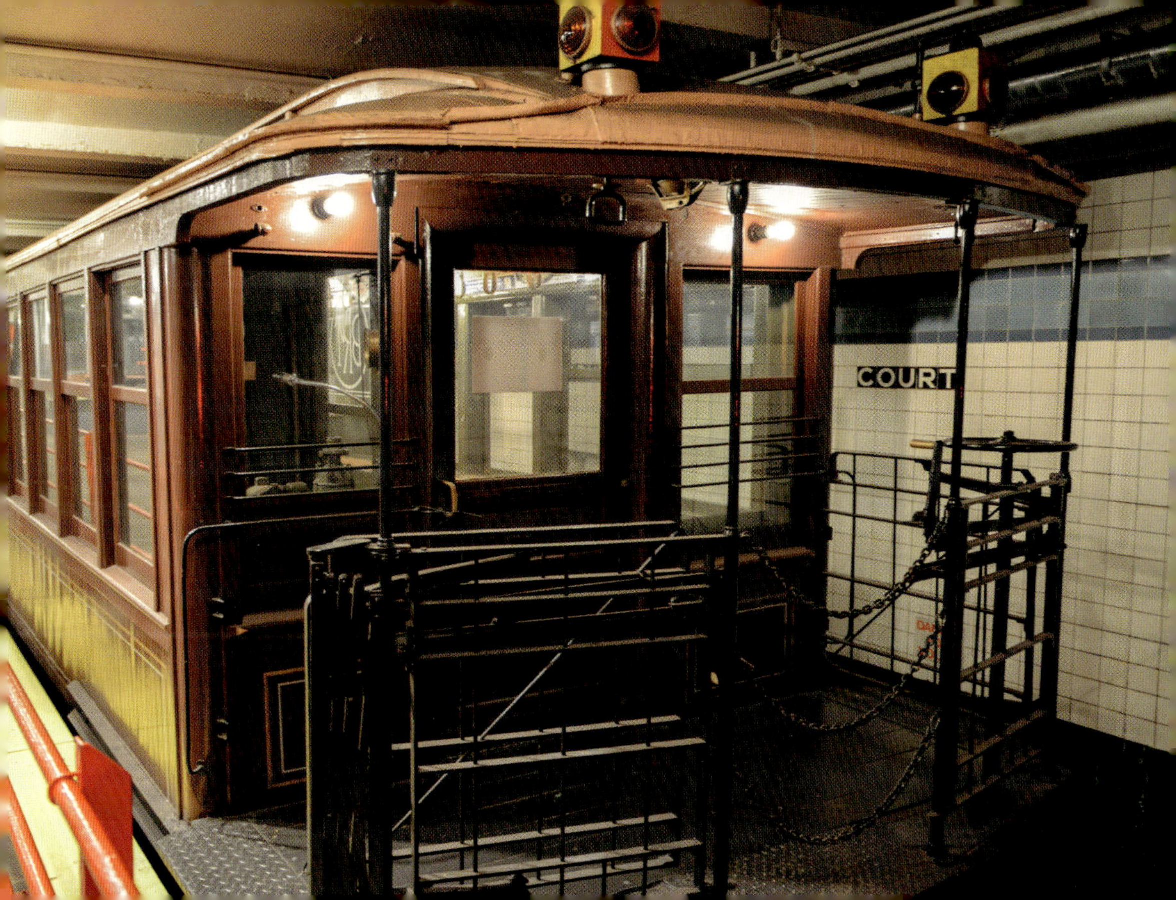
COURT

Park Avenue

Notorious for its bumper-to-bumper traffic jams – especially during morning and afternoon rush hours – a drive down this busy avenue will require patience and a fair amount of self-control to avoid honking the horn.

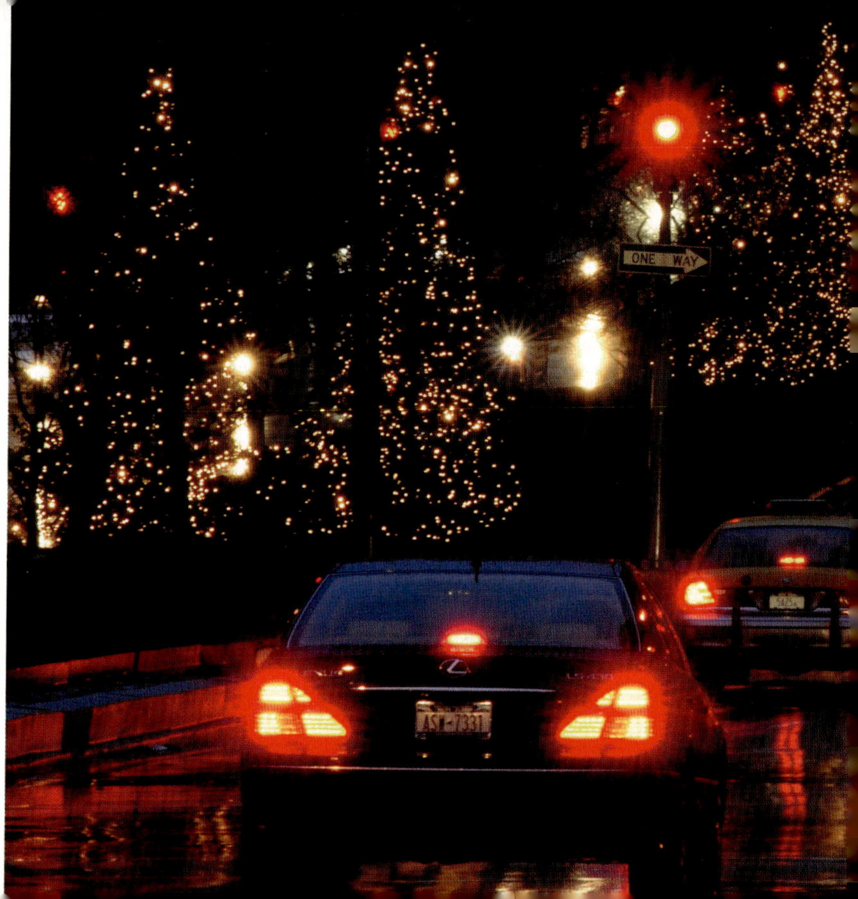

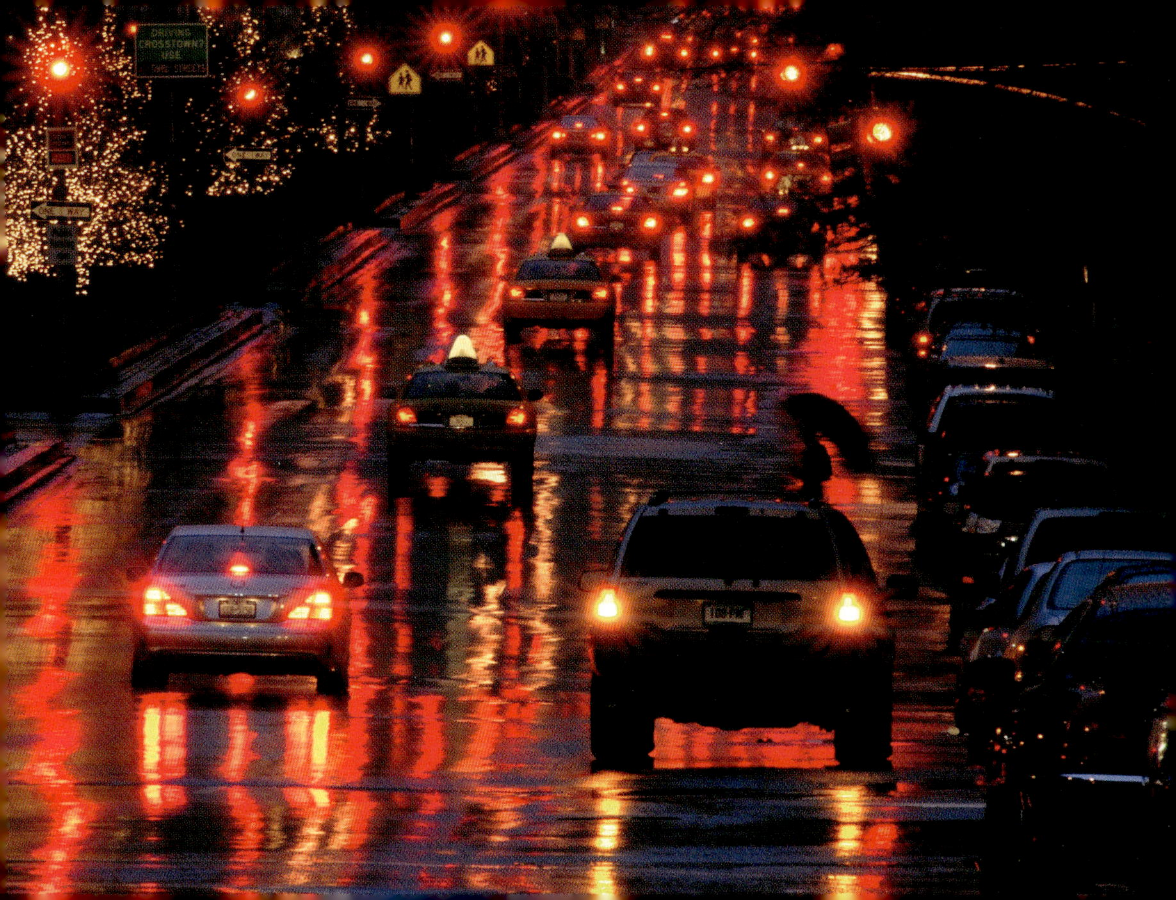
ONE WAY

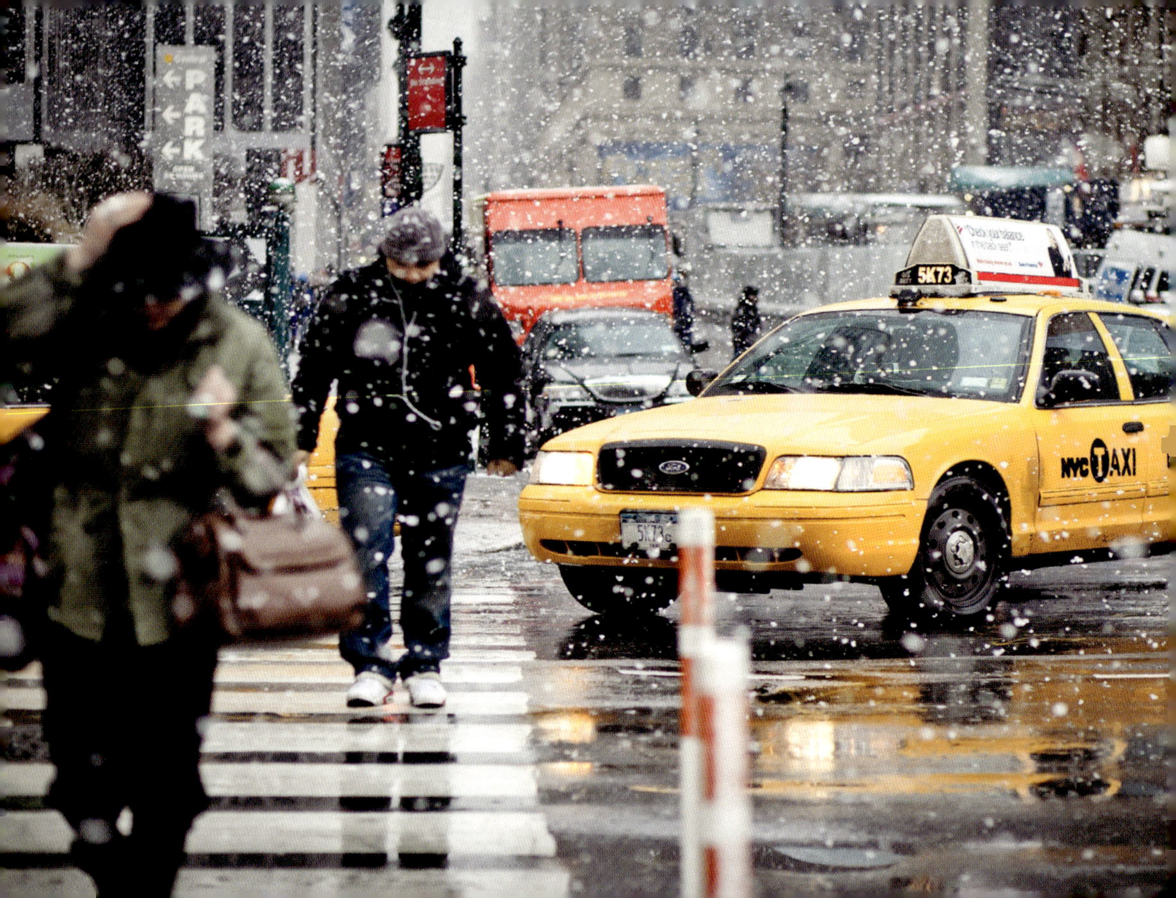
PARK
5K73
NYC TAXI

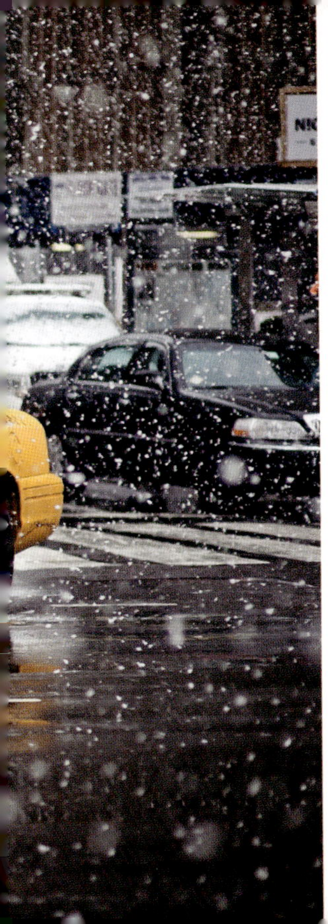

LEFT:

Yellow taxis

New York yellow cabs are an easy-to-spot symbol found throughout the city. There are close to 14,000 taxis in New York City ready to pick up and drop off passengers.

RIGHT:

The city that never sleeps

Regardless of the time of day or weather conditions, there are always people walking the streets or driving down avenues in this busy metropolis.

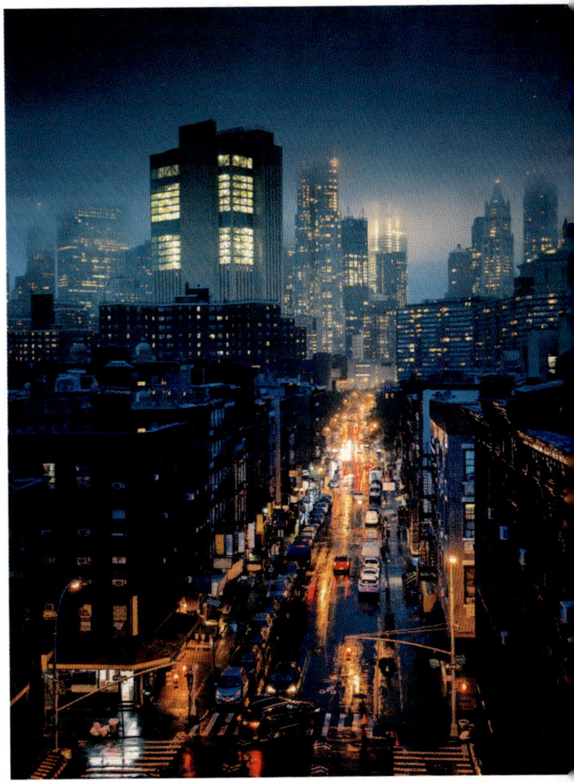

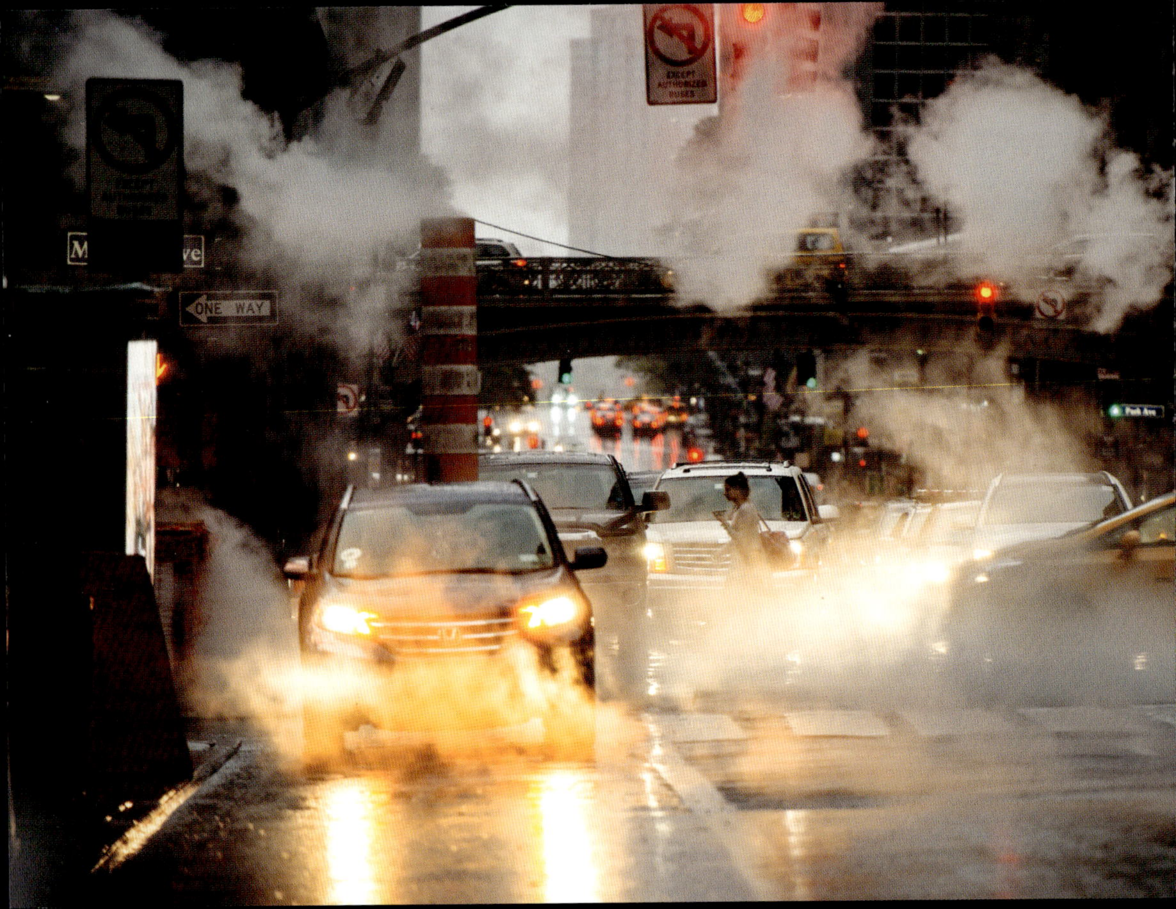
ONE WAY

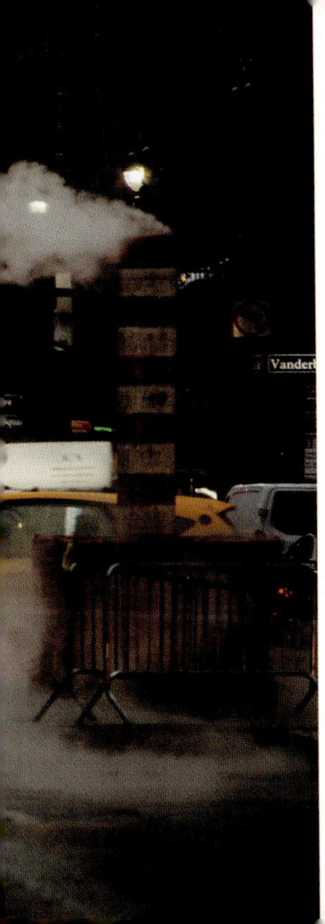

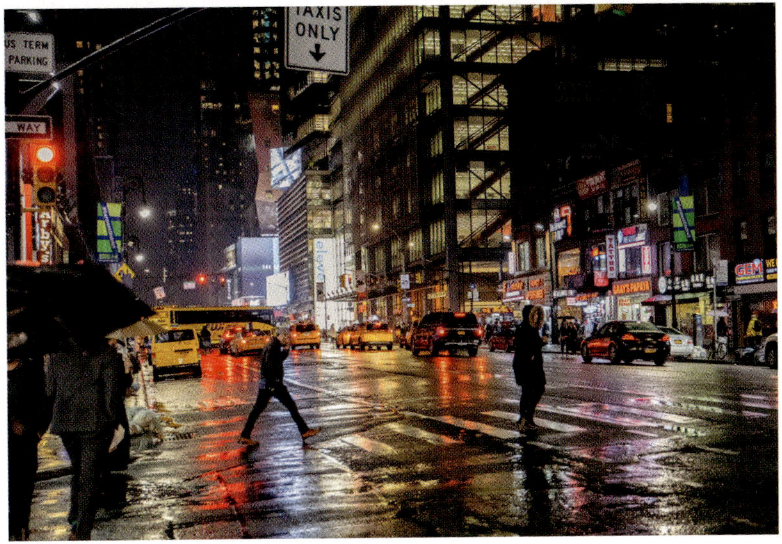

ALL PHOTOGRAPHS:

Cold New York streets

Winters in New York City are cold, with average temperatures ranging between 7°C (45°F) and -4°C (25°F). The coldest day recorded in Manhattan was on 9 February 1934, at -26°C (-15°F) – cold enough for people to skate off the shores of Staten Island and Lower Manhattan!

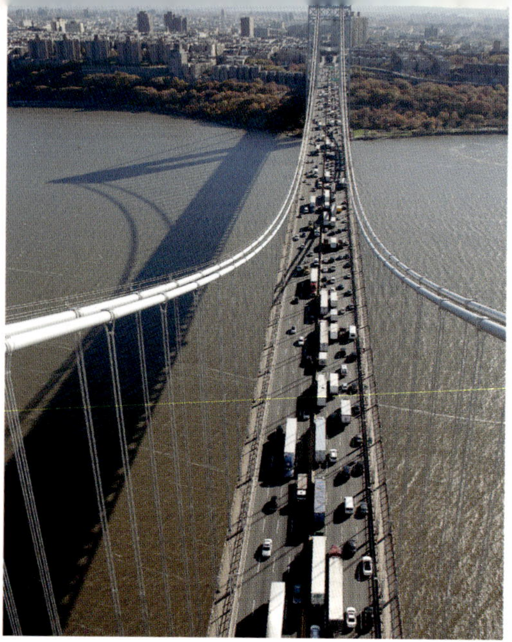

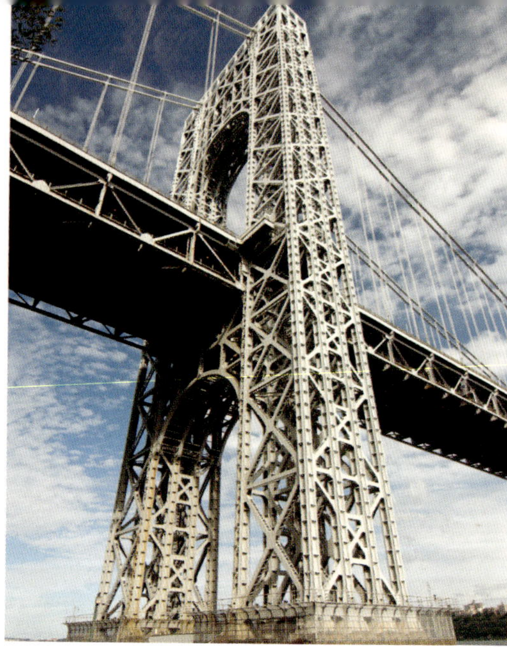

ABOVE AND RIGHT:

George Washington Bridge

Named after the first president of the United States, this double-level suspension bridge spans the Hudson River and connects New York to New Jersey. Over 100 million cars travel across the bridge annually.

OPPOSITE:

Manhattan Bridge

This 2,089m (6,855ft) long suspension bridge connects Lower Manhattan to Downtown Brooklyn. Built in 1909, it was the last of the three bridges built across the East River.

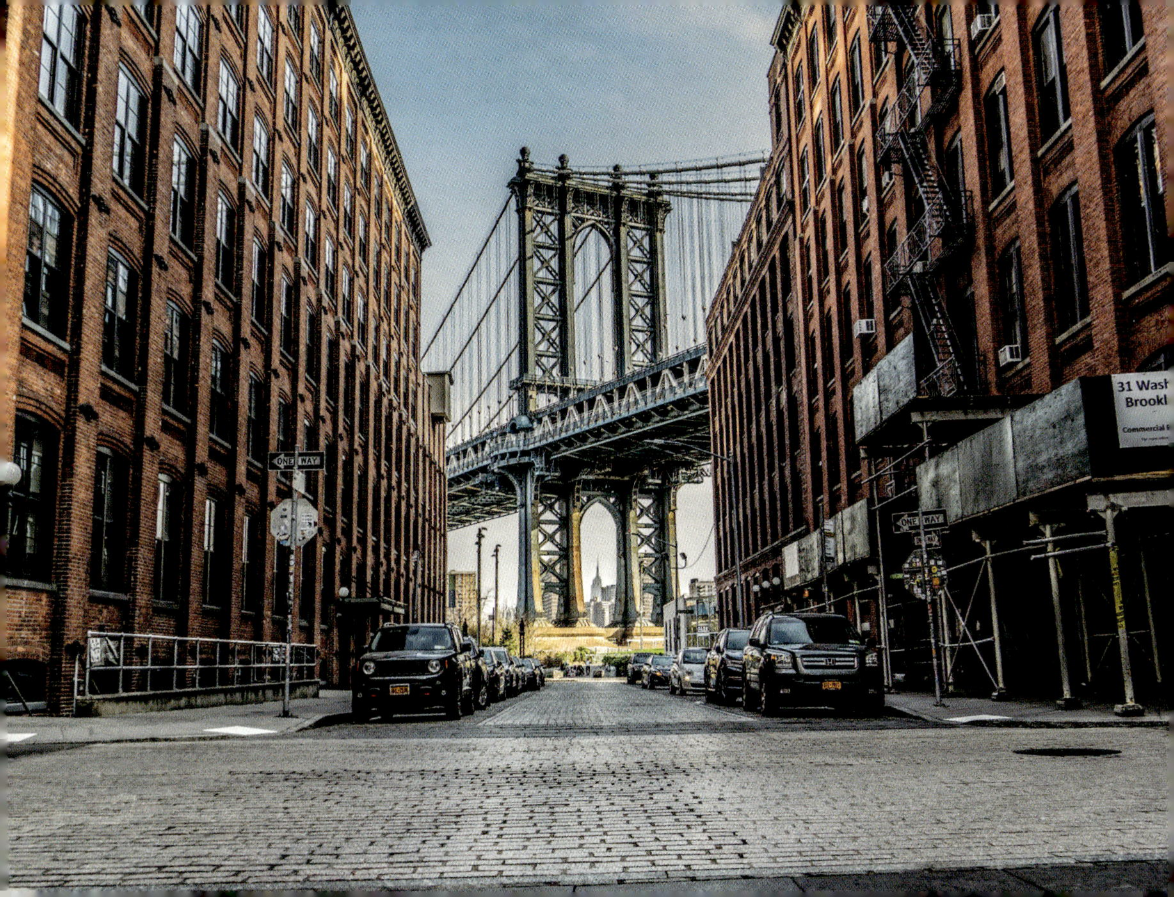
ONE WAY
ONE WAY

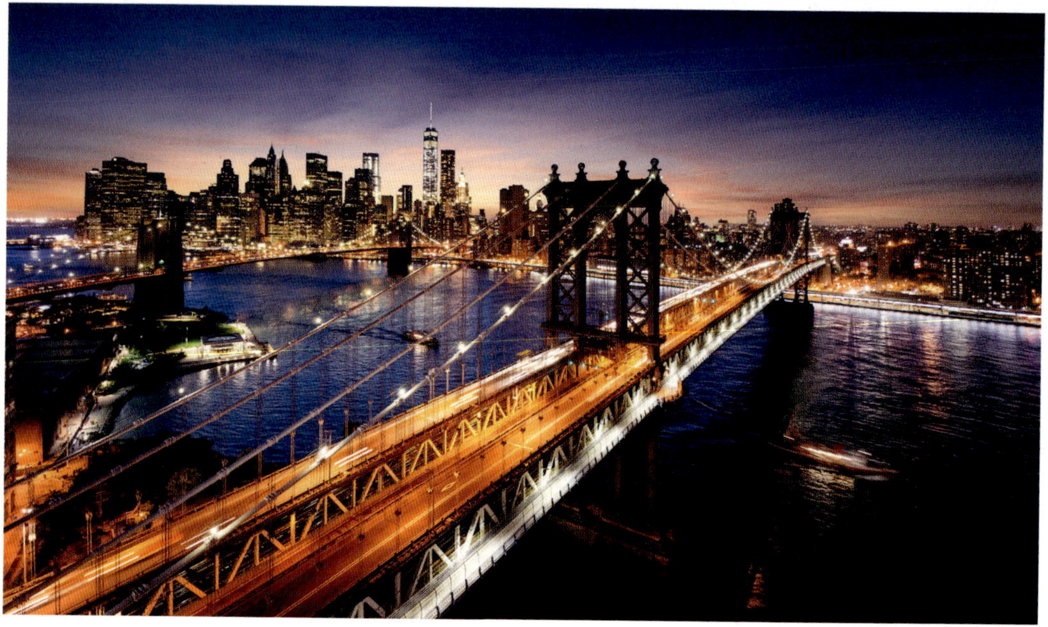

ALL PHOTOGRAPHS:

Brooklyn Bridge

Opened to the public in 1883, Brooklyn Bridge is one of the oldest suspension bridges in the country. One of the four toll-free bridges connecting Manhattan to Brooklyn, it has an estimated daily traffic of over 100,000 vehicles. Pedestrians and cyclists also have access to the bridge on a promenade located above the vehicle lanes.

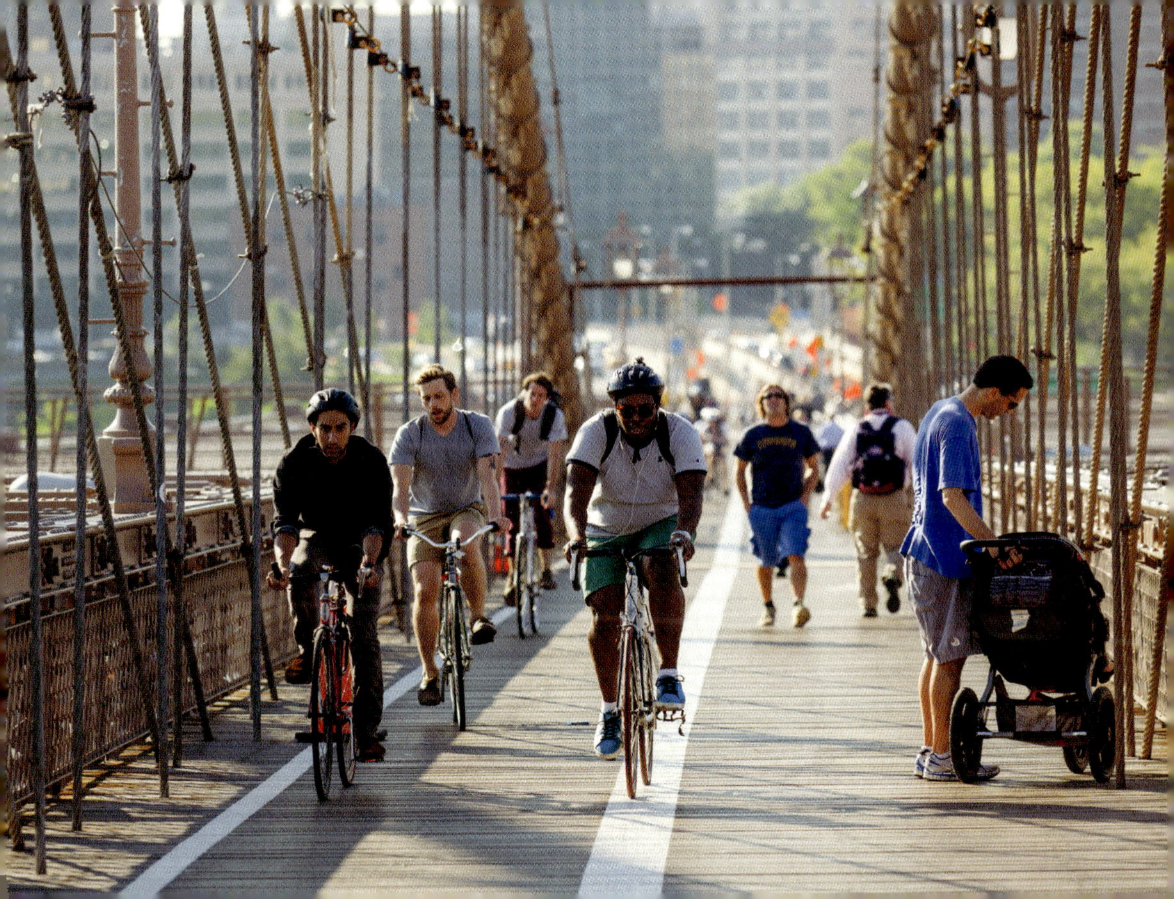

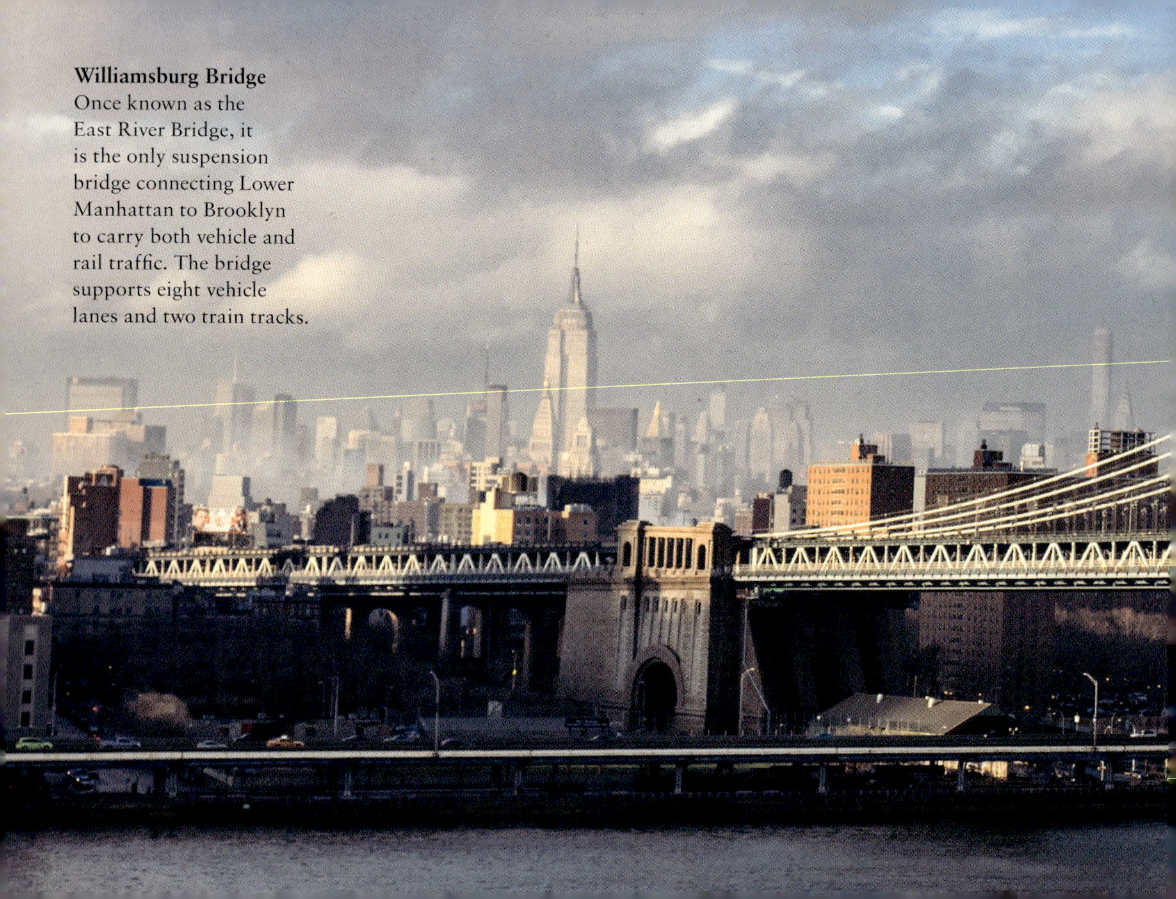

Williamsburg Bridge
Once known as the East River Bridge, it is the only suspension bridge connecting Lower Manhattan to Brooklyn to carry both vehicle and rail traffic. The bridge supports eight vehicle lanes and two train tracks.

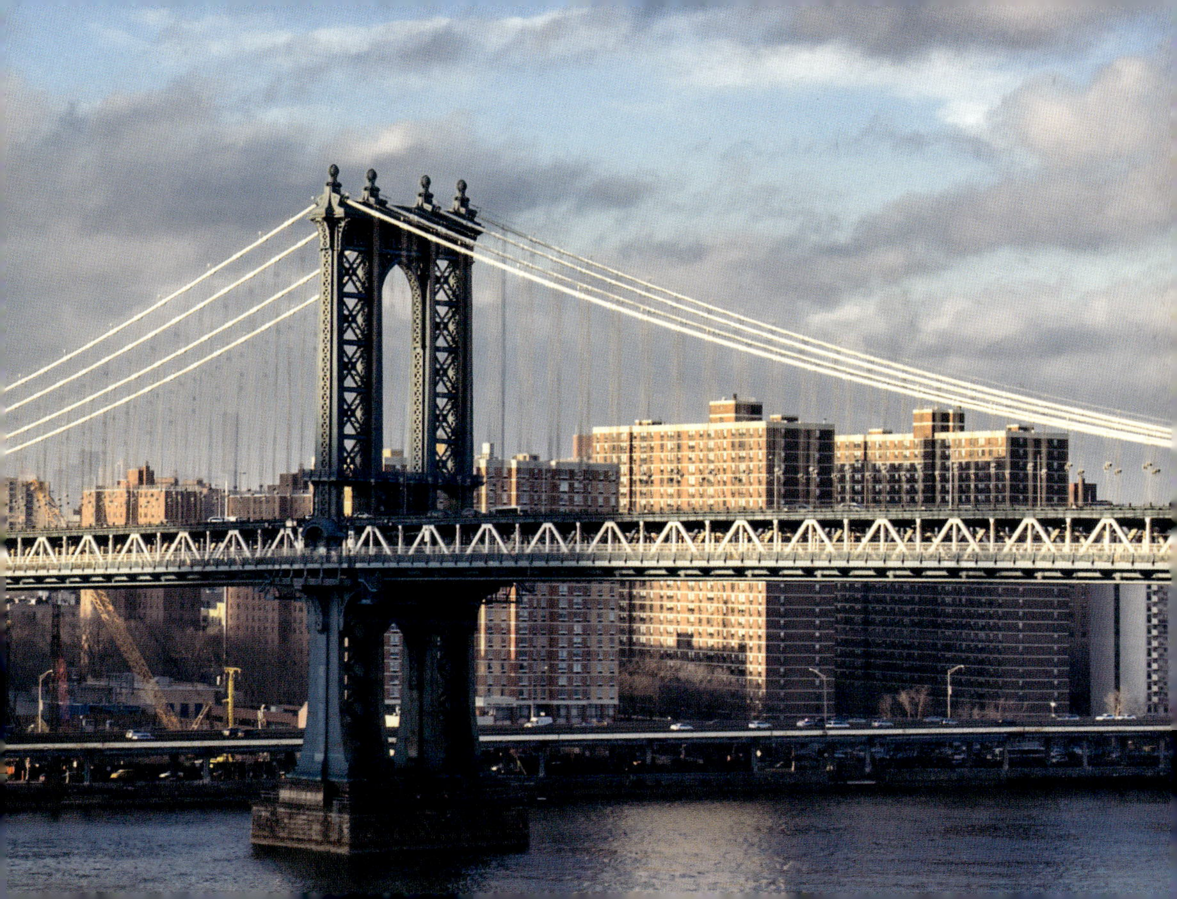

Lincoln Tunnel
Vehicle traffic to and from New York and New Jersey have another option when it comes to crossing the Hudson River, and that's going under it. Located 30m (97ft) below the Hudson, the tunnel was opened in 1937 and is approximately 2.4km (1.5 miles) long.

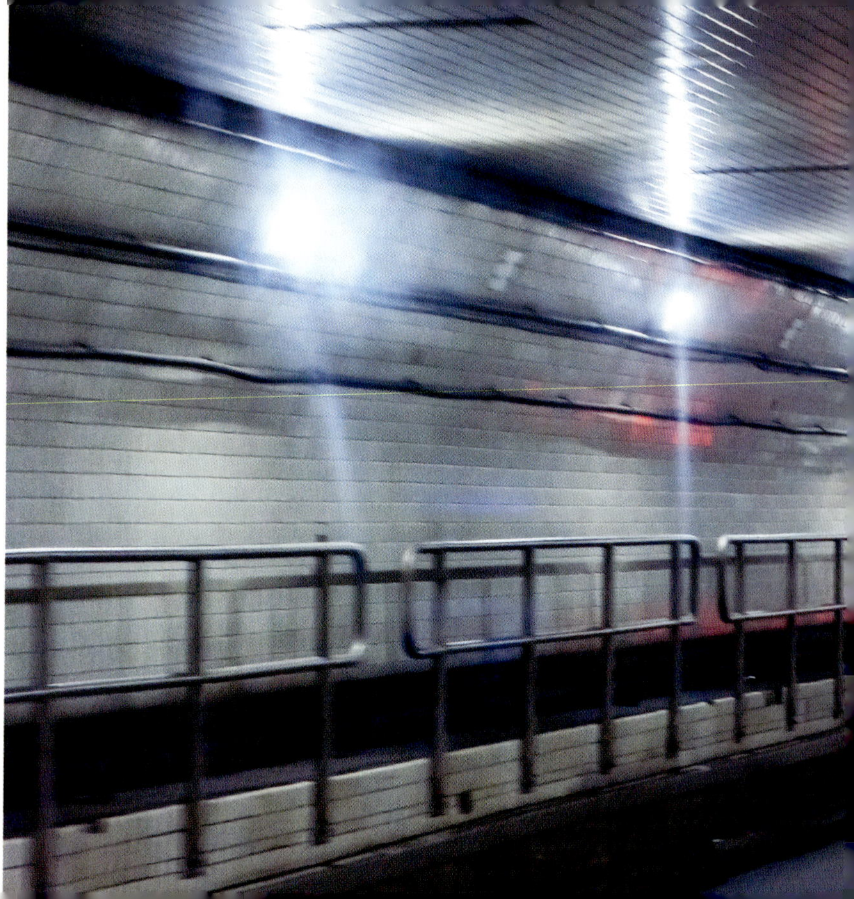

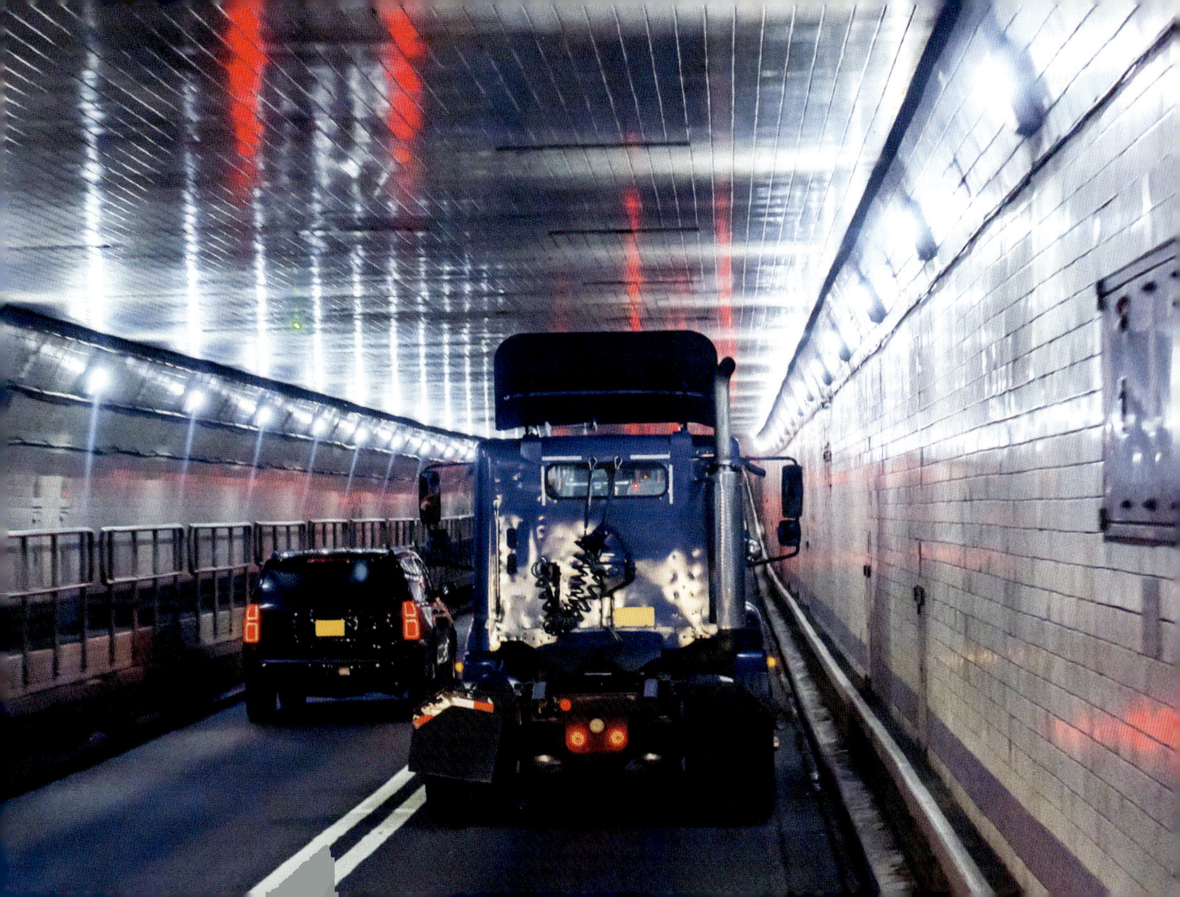

Staten Island Ferry
In operation since 1905, the ferry service runs from Saint George Terminal on Staten Island to White Terminal in Lower Manhattan and carries around 25 million passengers annually. For many commuters, the 25-minute ferry ride helps beat the delays and long travel times caused by heavy vehicle traffic.

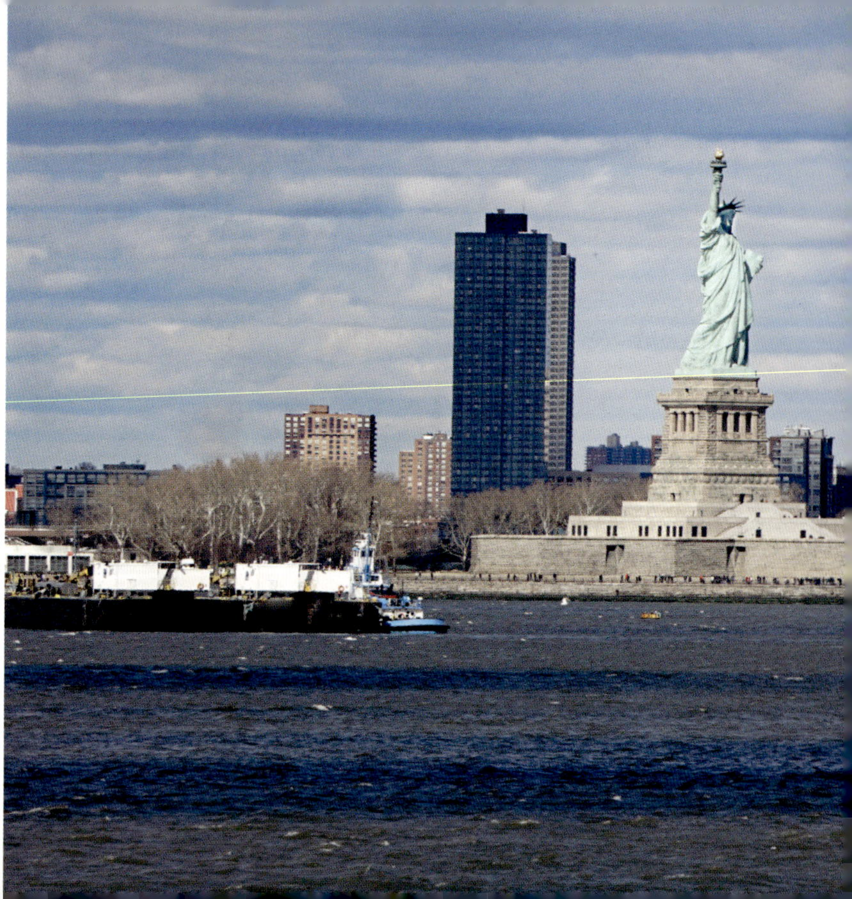

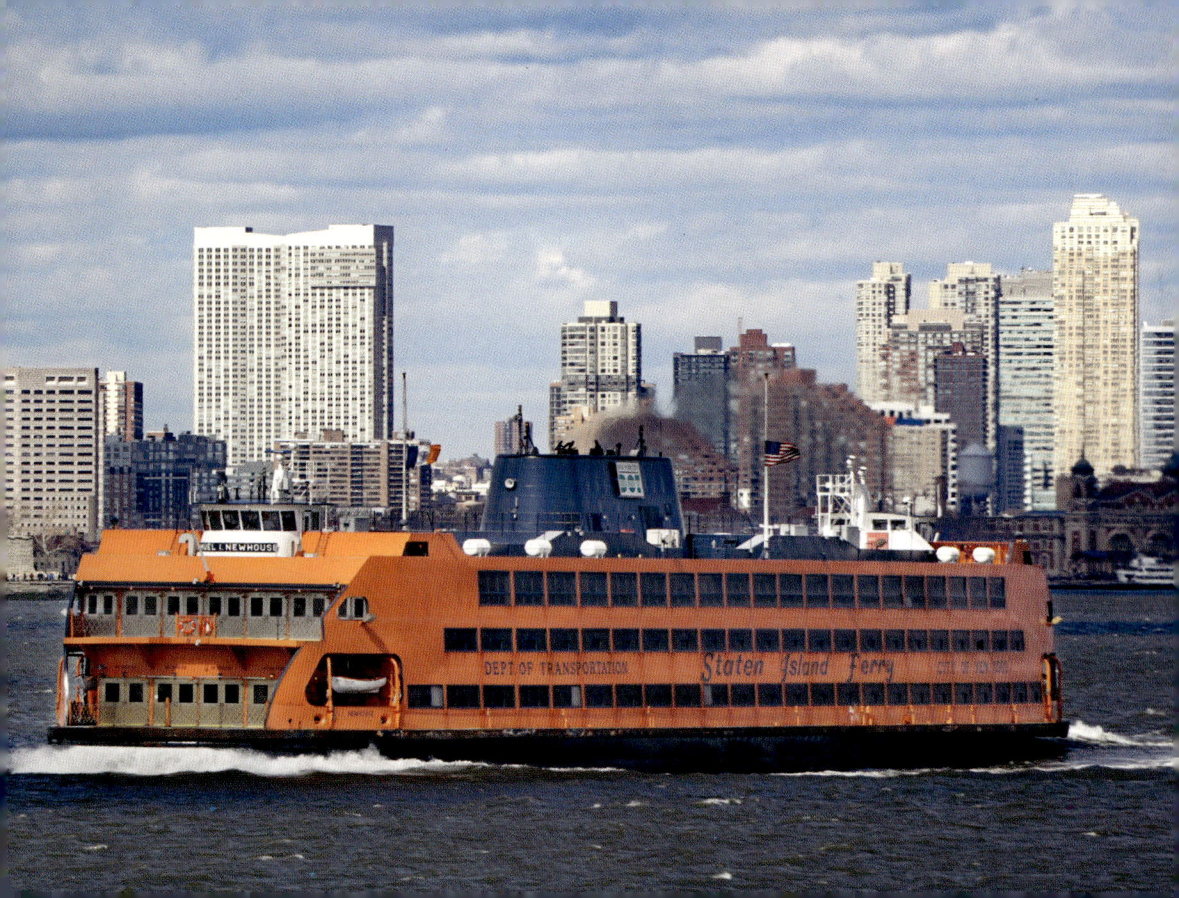
DEPT OF TRANSPORTATION
Staten Island Ferry

Battery Maritime Building
Located on the southeastern tip of Manhattan, this site was once a busy waterfront ferry service hub. Renovated in 2021, the building is now the location of the Casa Cipriani luxury hotel. Not in a rush to let go of the past, three ferry slips on the ground floor of the building still support travel to and from Governors Island.

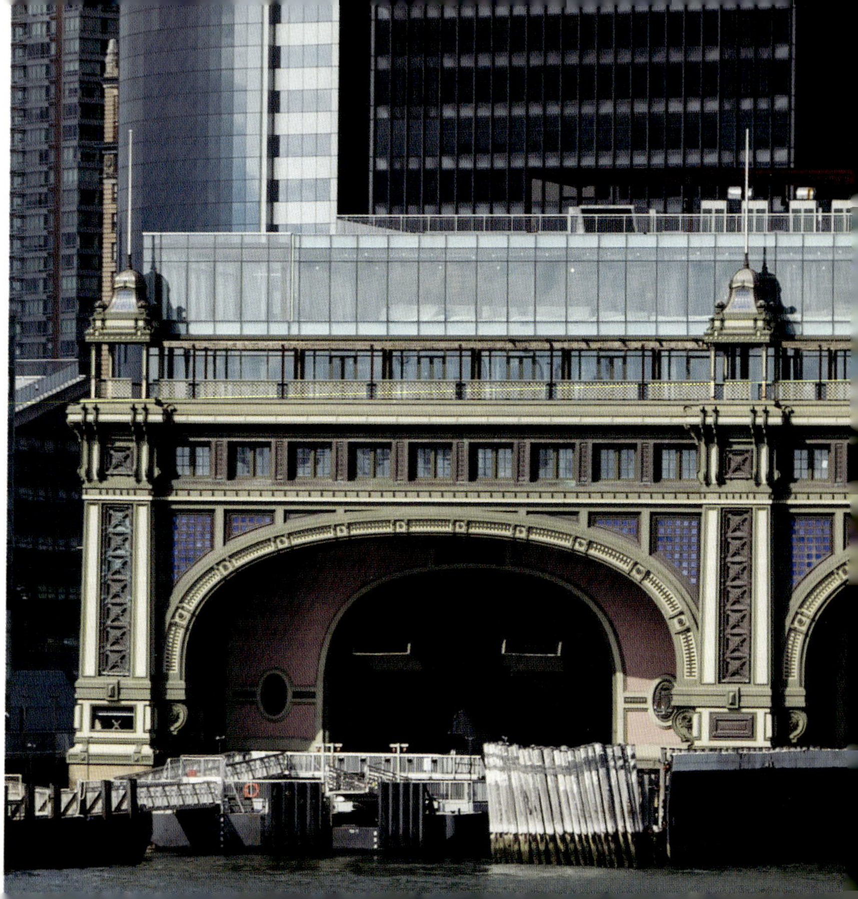

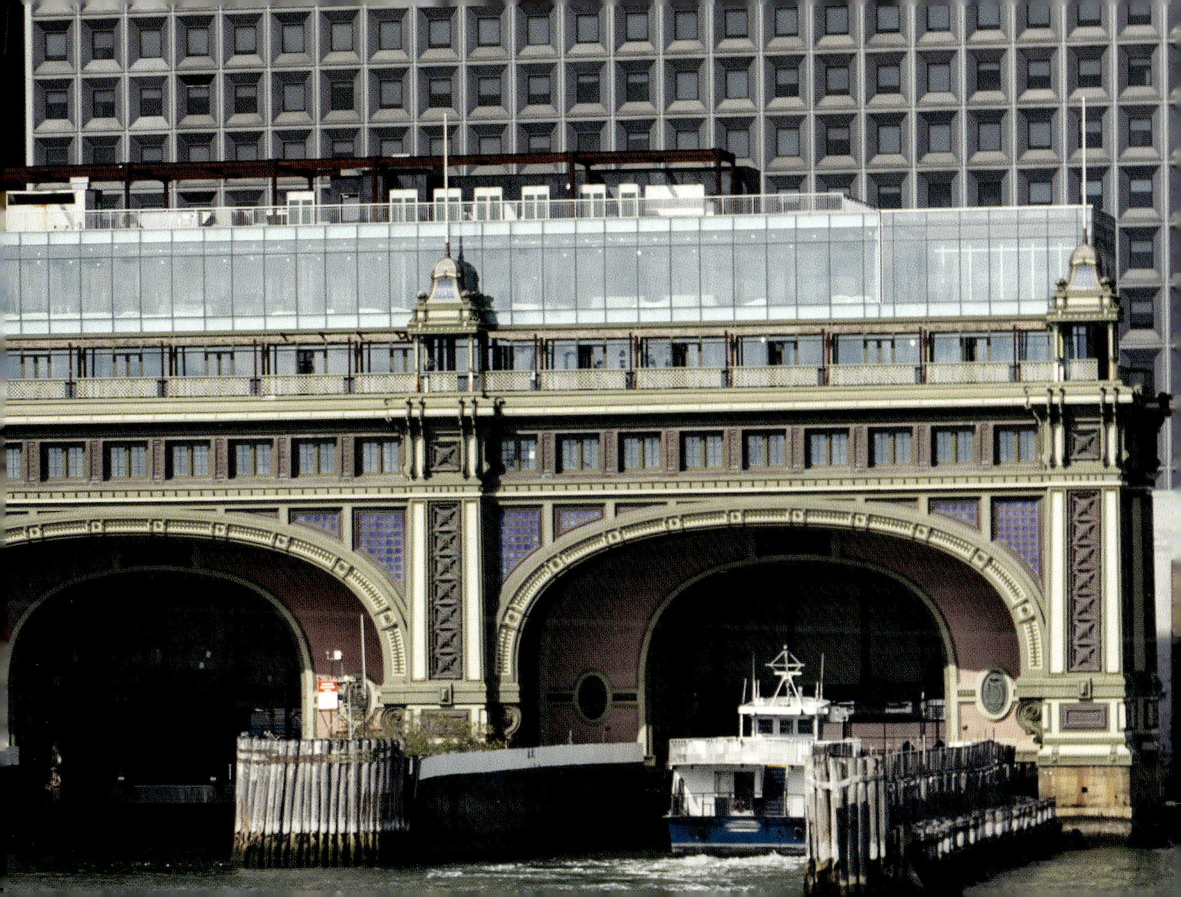

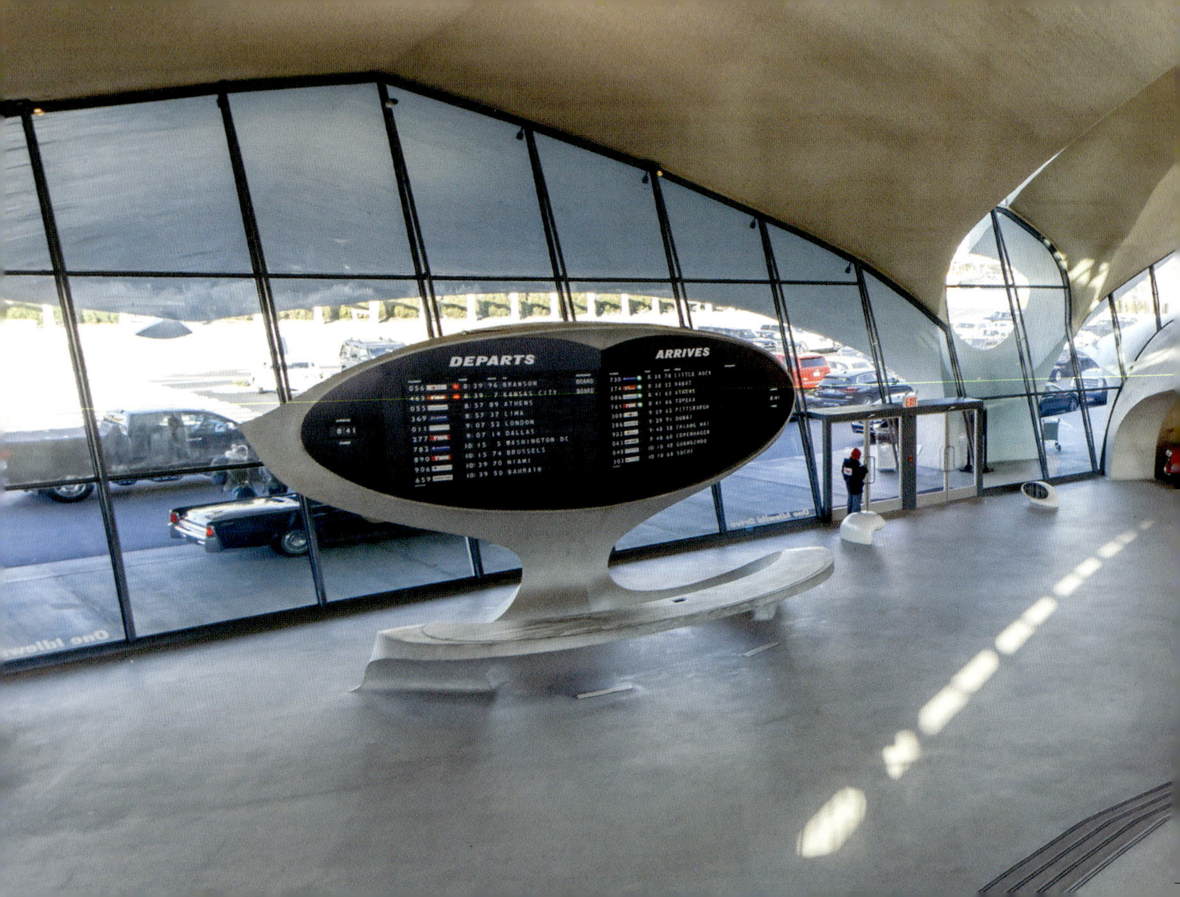
DEPARTS
ARRIVES

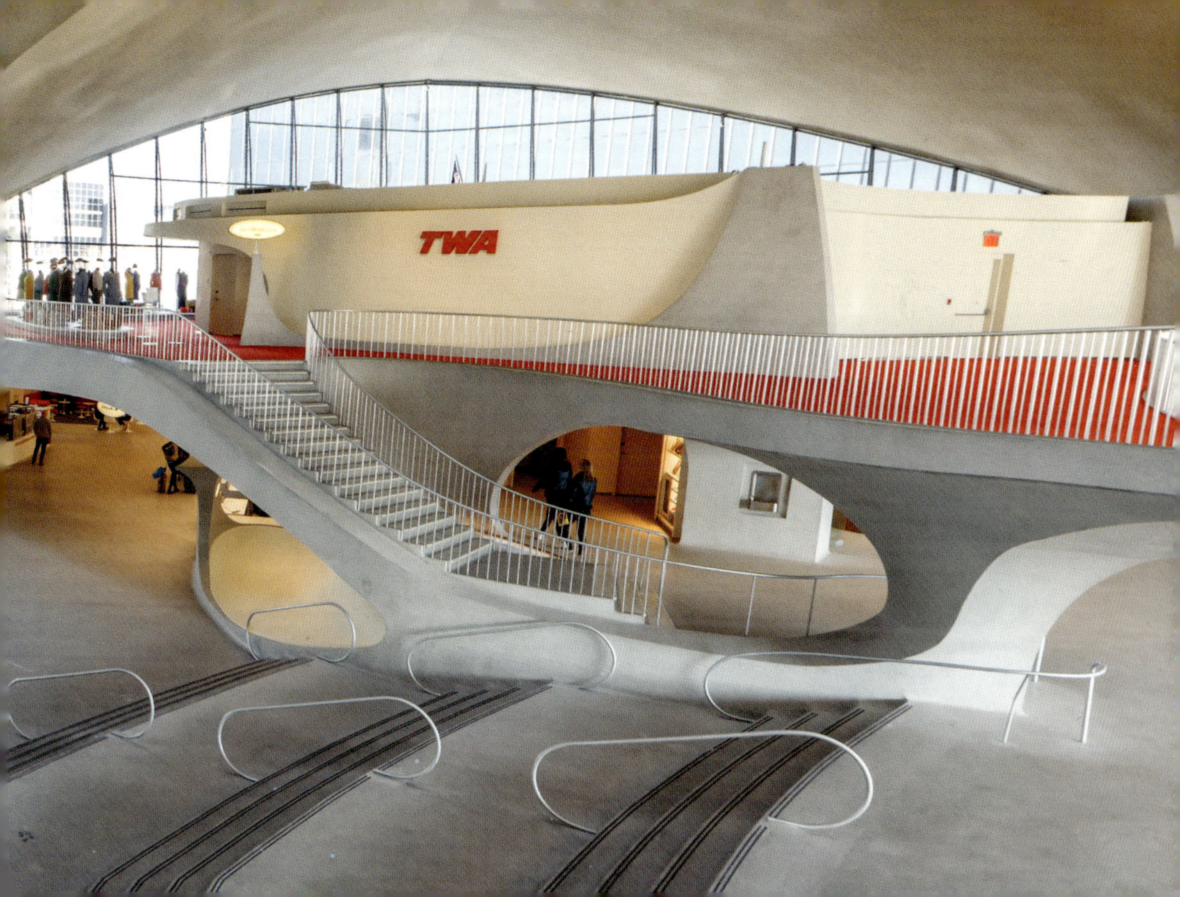
TWA

PREVIOUS PAGES:

JFK Airport

More than 70 airlines operate out of this international airport that is also the biggest gateway to foreign travel to the United States. Based in Jamaica, Queens, JFK services over 60 million passengers each year.

RIGHT:

LaGuardia Airport taxis

An average metered cab ride from LGA to Manhattan may be $40–50 (about £30–37), depending on the time of day and traffic.

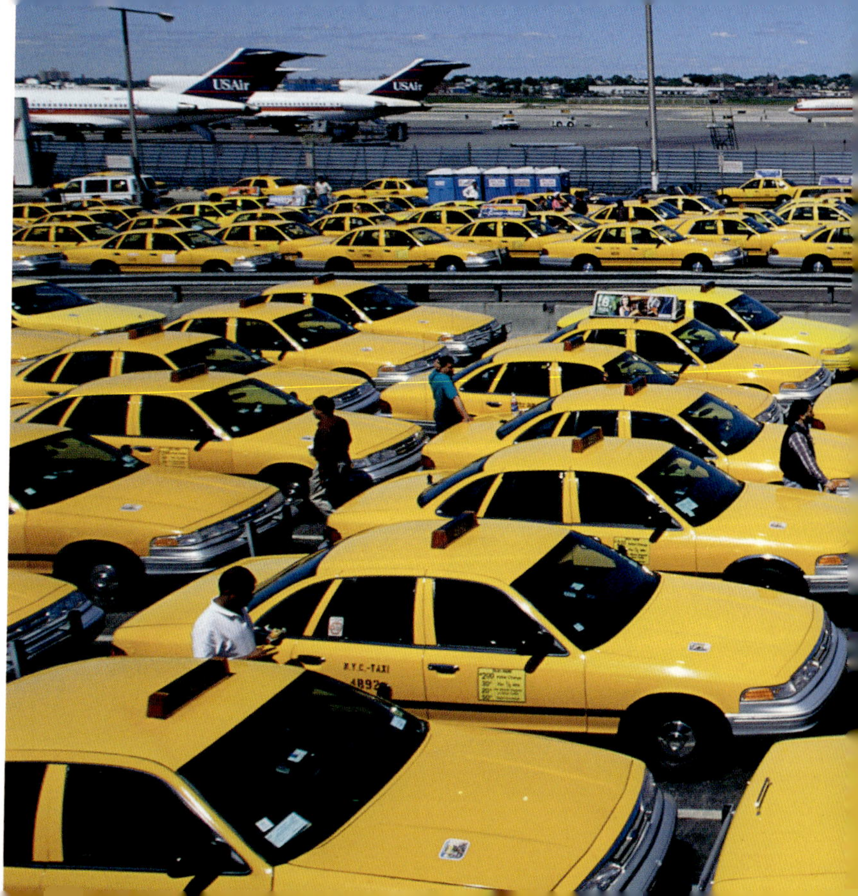

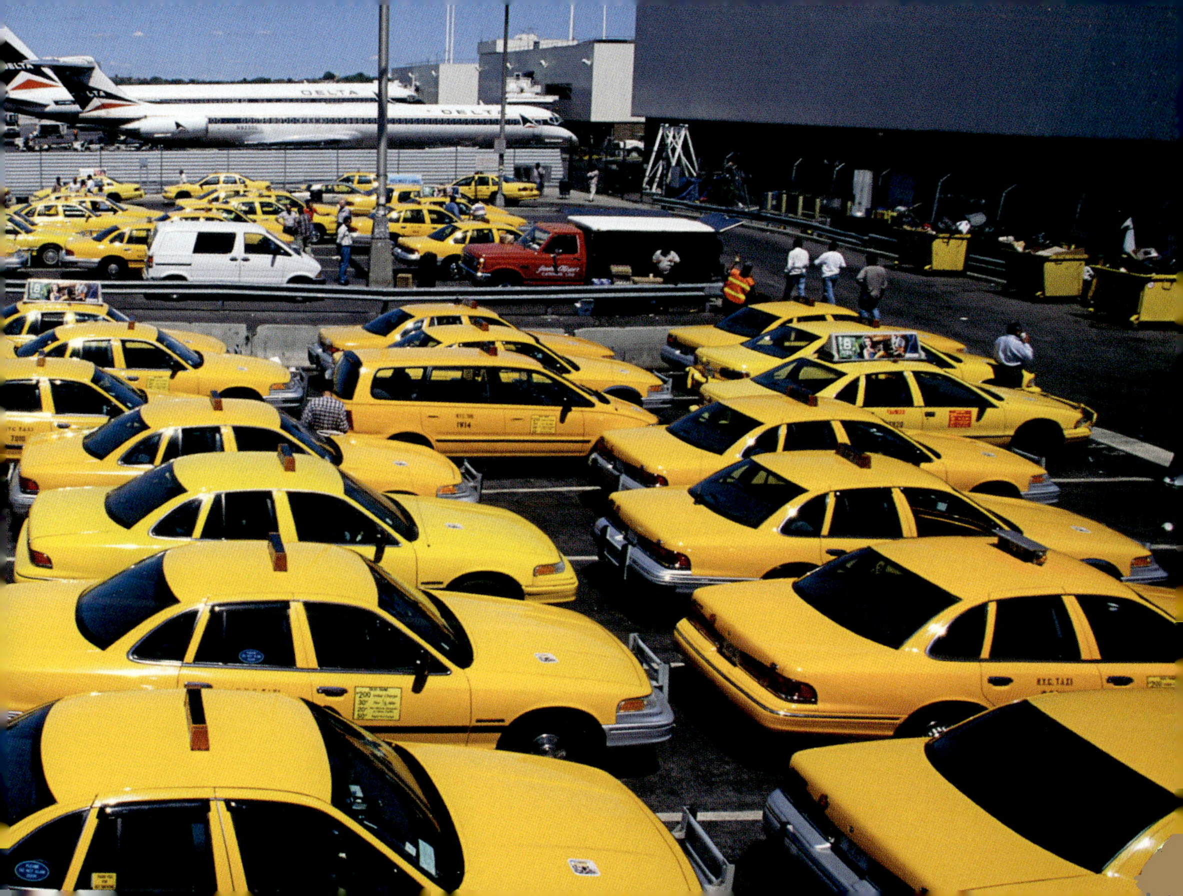
DELTA
N.Y.C. TAXI

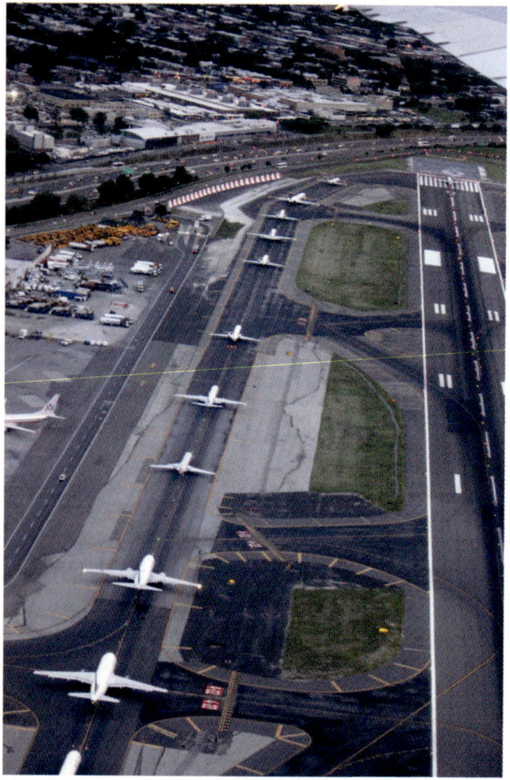

ALL PHOTOGRAPHS:
LaGuardia Airport
Accommodating both domestic and international flights, LaGuardia is the third-busiest airport after JFK and Newark Liberty (New Jersey). It is located along the northeastern coast of Queens between Bowery and Flushing Bay. Inside, the recently renovated airport displays a fluid design with bridges and open walkways connecting to concourses and gates.

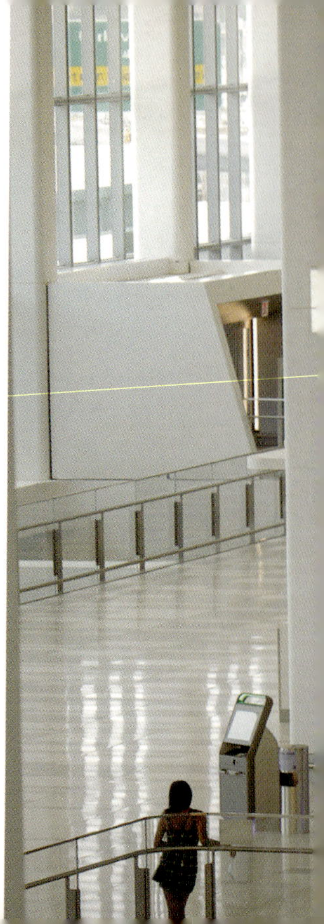

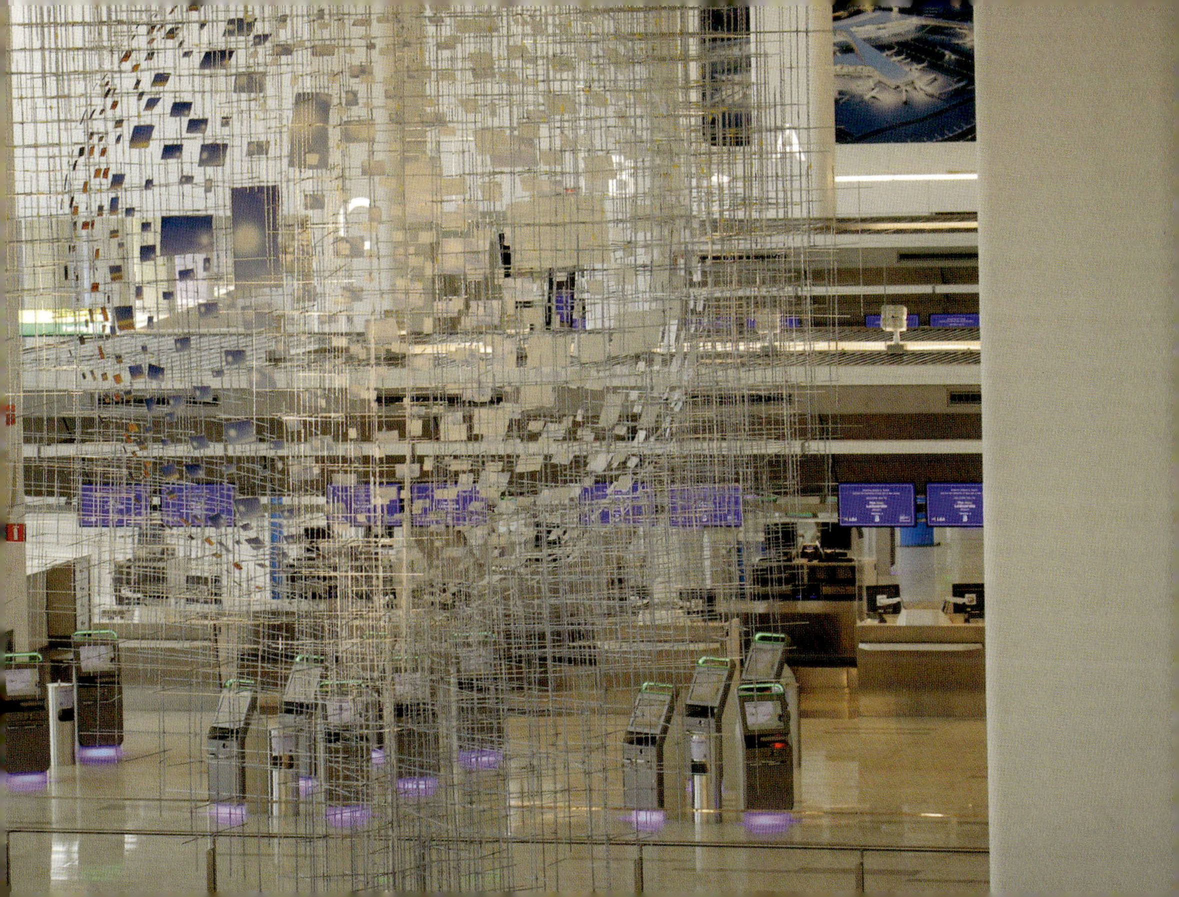

Picture Credits

Alamy: 33 (Sergi Reboredo), 40 (vdbvsl), 44 (Cavan Images), 47 right (Elizabeth Holmes), 54/55 (Nat Chittamai), 72 (Inge Johnsson), 73 (Evan Spiler), 90 (travelstock44), 109 (Ed Rooney), 110 (Edd Westmacott), 111 bottom right (Jeremy Graham), 114 (Juergen Hasenkopf), 116/117 (travelstock44), 118 (Frances Roberts), 120 (Jeffrey Isaac Greenberg 10+), 131 (Paul Kim), 134 (eyetooth/stockimo), 136 (Pictures Colour Library), 140 (Philip Scalia), 141 (directphoto.bz), 143 (Ian Dagnall), 146 & 147 all (New York City), 149 (travelstock44), 161 (Citizen of the planet), 167 (Design Pics Inc), 176 top both (Emma Swann), 176 bottom right (Len Holsborg), 223 (Reuters)

Dreamstime: 10 (Mazuciukas), 11 (Stephen Smith), 12 (John Anderson), 13 (Fabio Formaggio), 14 (Kmirargaya), 15 (Alfredo Garcia Saz), 16/17 (Saletomic), 18 (Rebekah Burgess), 19 (Rorem), 20/21 (Leo Bruce Hempell), 22 bottom (Kit1nyc), 23 (Zoltan Tarlacz), 24 (Maciej Bledowski), 25 top (Madrabothair), 25 bottom (Zhukovsky), 26 top (Giovanni Gagliardi), 26 bottom (David Evison), 27 (Byelikova), 28 (James Andrews), 29 (Arnaud Pierard), 30 (Jose Terrero), 31 (Linda Harms), 32 (Jose Terrero), 34 left (Steven Rivieccio), 34 right (Maurie Hill), 35 (Maria1986nyc), 36 (Carlos Neto), 38 (Makoto Honda), 39 (Tossi66), 41 (Sean Pavone), 43 (Ryan Deberadinis), 46 (Meunierd), 47 left (Songquan Deng), 48 (Andersastphoto), 49 (Dean Riley), 50 (Umerpk), 51 (Shutterbas), 56 (Bartolomiej Holowaty), 57 (Vacclav), 58/59 (Maria Olsen), 60 & 61 (Pilotf18), 64/65 (Bojan Bokic), 66 (Valentin Armianu), 67 (Jon Bilous), 68 (Jesus Carpio), 69 (John Takai), 70 (Kev303), 71 (Palinchak), 74 (Kmiragaya), 75 (Ritu Jethani), 76/77 (Littleny), 78 (Amy Harris), 79 (Ang Wee Heng John), 80/81 (Jakub Zajic), 82/83 (Makoto Honda), 84 (Bernhard Richter), 85 (Steve Heap), 86 (Demerzel21), 92/93 (Eq Roy), 94 (Flavijus), 95 & 96 top (Elultimodeseo), 96 bottom (Salomi1986), 97 (Sergio Torres Baus), 98/99 (Rawf88), 100 both (Zhukovsky), 101 (Olivier Guiberteau), 102/103 (Julia161), 104 (Marysmn), 105 (Littleny), 106/107 (Julie Feinstein), 111 top and bottom left (Maksym Fesenko), 123 (Sandra Foyt), 124 (F11photo), 125 (Sandra Foyt), 126/127 (Erik Lattwein), 128 (Zeynep Ayse Kiyas Aslanturk), 129 (Francoisroux), 132 (Loran Zutic), 133 (Littleny), 137 (22tomtom), 138 (Zhukovsky), 142 (Viocara), 148 (Askoldsb), 150/151 (Freephoton), 152 (Stuart Monk), 154/155 (Darleen Warnes-stry), 156/157 (Andrew Harrison), 158 (Jerry Coli), 159 (Zhukovsky), 160 (Penelope 82), 163 (Felix Mizioznikov), 164 (Pongpol Wathakul), 165 (Lei Xu), 166 (Gordon Bell), 168 & 169 (Stef Ko), 171 (Brett Critchley), 172 (Jerry Coli), 173 (James Kirkikis), 177 (Nigel Spiers), 178 (Fewerton), 179 (Mykyta Starychenko), 180 (Carmenmurillo), 182 & 183 both (Joe Ahead), 184 (Oriol Oliva), 185 (Nikos Avrantinis), 186 (Justin Warner), 187 (Littleny), 188/189 (Colin Young), 190 (Carlos Neto), 191 left (Weopixel1101), 191 right (Alexandre Fagundes De Fagundes), 194 (Vitaliy Pozdeev), 195 (Izanbar), 196 top (Vitalyedush), 196 (Makoto Honda), 197 (Yooran Park), 198 both (Edichenphoto), 199 (Demerze121), 202 (Andrey Bayda), 206 right (Shabbang), 208 (Ilja Masik), 209 (William87), 210/211 (Kasto80), 212/213 (Resul Musulu), 214/215 (Paul Hamilton), 216/217 (David Wood), 218/219 (Boarding1now), 222 (Think Design Manage Services Ltd)

Getty Images: 8 (SOPA Images), 22 top (Timothy A Clary), 37 (Siegfried Laydia), 52 (Bloomberg), 53 (Tim Clayton/Corbis), 97 (Ben Hider), 162 (Anadola Agency), 192 (Marco Bottigelli), 220/221 (Alan Schein Photography)

Shutterstock: 6 (Benoit Daoust), 7 (T photography), 42 (Agnieszka Gaul), 62/63 (Alex Cimbal), 88 & 91 (littlenySTOCK), 108 (Alena Veasey), 112 & 113 both (Leonard Zhukovsky), 115 (poludziber), 121 (Kamira), 122 (Andriy Blokhin), 130 (Lev Rodin), 135 (Inspired By Maps), 139 (DW Labs Incorporated), 144 (Boris-B), 145 (rblfmr), 170 (RightFramePhotoVideo), 174 (Pit Stock), 175 (Conchi Martinez), 181 (Wangkun Jia), 200/201 (T photography), 203 (IM_Photo), 204 (travelwild), 205 (rawf8), 206 left (Jonathan Collins), 207 (Jason Sponseller)